THE TIME OF

The author with his father, Vladimir Antonov-Ovseyenko, then Soviet ambassador to Czechoslovakia, Prague 1926.

Anton Antonov-Ovseyenko

THE TIME OF STALIN
PORTRAIT OF A TYRANNY

Translated from the Russian by
George Saunders
with an Introduction by Stephen F. Cohen

A Cornelia & Michael Bessie Book

HARPER COLOPHON BOOKS
Harper & Row, Publishers
New York, Cambridge, Philadelphia, San Francisco
London, Mexico City, São Paulo, Sydney

A hardcover edition of this book is published by Harper & Row, Publishers, Inc.

This work was first published in the Russian language in the United States by Chekhov Publishing Corporation. Copyright © 1980 by Khronika Press.

THE TIME OF STALIN. English translation copyright © 1981 by Harper & Row, Publishers, Inc. Introduction copyright © 1981 by Stephen F. Cohen. All rights reserved. Printed in the United States of America. No part of this book may be used or reproduced in any manner whatsoever without written permission except in the case of brief quotations embodied in critical articles and reviews. For information address Harper & Row, Publishers, Inc., 10 East 53rd Street, New York, N.Y. 10022. Published simultaneously in Canada by Fitzhenry & Whiteside Limited, Toronto.

First HARPER COLOPHON edition published 1983.

Designer: C. Linda Dingler

Library of Congress Cataloging in Publication Data
Antonov-Ovseyenko, Anton.
    The time of Stalin—portrait of a tyranny.

    Includes index.
    1. Stalin, Joseph, 1879-1953. 2. Heads of state
—Soviet Union—Biography. I. Title.
DK268.S8A6713 1981   947.084'2'0924 [B]   80-8681
ISBN 0-06-039027-1 (pbk.)   AACR2

83 84 85 86 87 10 9 8 7 6 5 4 3 2 1

CONTENTS

Photographs follow page 220

THE SURVIVOR AS HISTORIAN

(Introduction)

Stephen F. Cohen

Professor of Soviet Politics at Princeton University

It would have been better to tell everything.
Murder will always out.
—KHRUSHCHEV REMEMBERS

The reader is opening a book about terrible historical crimes. Its style and contents are not the product of academic dispassion but of personal experience, forbidden research, and anger that these crimes are still covered up by the Soviet government. It is a book written, the author tells us, as "a duty to those who died . . . to those who survived . . . to those who will come after us."

Anton Antonov-Ovseyenko is a sixty-year-old survivor of the Stalin-shchina—or "the time of Stalin." Some Soviet citizens see in the Stalin years only a mountain of national achievements; others see in them a mountain of crimes. The first view can be debated, but the second cannot be denied.

Stalin's policies caused a Soviet holocaust, from his collectivization "pogrom" against the peasantry in 1929–33 through the relentless mass terror that continued until his death in March 1953. Millions of innocent men, women, and children were arbitrarily arrested, tortured, executed, brutally deported, or imprisoned in a murderous system of prisons and concentration camps. No one has yet managed to calculate the exact number of deaths. Among those who have tried, twenty million is a conservative estimate, excluding the twenty to thirty million who died during World War II.

For a brief time after Stalin's death, it seemed possible that the Soviet government would admit and repudiate these crimes, however episodically. Official revelations about the recent past, or de-Stalinization, began with Khrushchev's assault on the Stalin cult at a closed session of the Twentieth Party Congress, in 1956, and reached a crescendo with his public revelations at the Twenty-second Congress, in 1961. But they ended shortly after Khrushchev's overthrow in 1964. Since that time, the Brezhnev leadership has refurbished Stalin's reputation as a great national leader and reimposed official silence about the crimes of his rule.

Uncovering and telling the truth about the past, therefore, has fallen to a small but still growing number of dissident Soviet writers. They work alone for the most part, and often clandestinely. Their writings can be circulated only in *samizdat*—in worn typescripts passed from reader to reader—or published abroad. Uncensored Soviet writing about Stalinism has grown into a valuable body of memoirs, monographic studies, and belles-lettres since the 1960s. But until recently only two major historical accounts of the whole Stalinist era had appeared: Roy Medvedev's *Let History Judge* and Aleksandr Solzhenitsyn's *The Gulag Archipelago*. Now there is a third—Antonov-Ovseyenko's *The Time of Stalin*.

* * *

Almost all of the dissident chroniclers of the Stalinist past who have emerged thus far are themselves survivors of the terror or relatives of its victims.* Like survivors of the Jewish holocaust, they are bitterly determined to tell what happened. Antonov-Ovseyenko is no exception. "Stalin murdered my father. . . . My mother committed suicide in one of Stalin's prisons. I spent my youth in his prisons and camps."

Millions shared the fate of Antonov-Ovseyenko, but he is unique in one important respect. He is the only child of a martyred Soviet founding father to emerge as both a witness and a historian of Stalinism.[1] The author is the son of Vladimir Antonov-Ovseyenko, the famous Bolshevik revolutionary who led the party's seizure of the Winter Palace in October 1917, who served in the first Soviet government, and rose to still greater prominence as a Red Army commander in the civil war and as political chief of the Red Army in 1922–24. The father's political career in Moscow ended in 1925; a member of the defeated Trotskyist opposition, he was banished to diplomatic life. He served the next twelve years as Soviet ambassador to Czechoslovakia, Lithuania, and Poland, and as proconsul to the Spanish Republic in 1936–37.[2]

The reader will learn more about Vladimir Antonov-Ovseyenko later, when the son tries, in several passages, to judge his father's degree of honor and complicity in Soviet political history. Whatever the balance, the father's fate transformed his son's life. Vladimir Antonov-Ovseyenko was recalled from Spain in August 1937, as Stalin's blood purges were destroying the Old Bolshevik Party. After a meeting with Stalin, he was appointed commissar of justice of the Russian Republic. A few weeks later, in October 1937, he was arrested and falsely accused, as were most Old Bolsheviks, of perfidious crimes against the Soviet state.

Kept in Butyrka prison (where his son would also be imprisoned), his health ruined but his spirit unbroken, Vladimir Antonov-Ovseyenko refused to sign any confession. On February 8, 1938, Stalin's high court of

---

*To name a few: Roy and Zhores Medvedev, Solzhenitsyn, Pyotr Yakir, Yevgeny Gnedin, Mikhail Baitalsky, Nadezhda Mandelstam, Evgenia Ginzburg, Lev Kopelev, Suren Gazaryan, Mikhail Yakubovich, Dmitry Vitkovsky, Lydia Chukovskaya, Varlam Shalamov.

terror sentenced him to ten years' imprisonment. Actually, as happened to so many others, he was executed, or tortured to death, later that year.[3] His name remained an anathema in the Soviet Union for the next twenty years, until Anastas Mikoyan, a Politburo member and Khrushchev's ally, publicly exonerated him at the Twentieth Congress.

Ineluctably, children became the secondary victims of Stalin's terror. The author's own fate is told in fragments throughout this book and more fully in his autobiographical foreword to the Russian edition published in New York.[4] He was a seventeen-year-old history student at a Moscow institute and a member of the Young Communist League in 1937. Anton Antonov-Ovseyenko was expelled from both institutions in 1938 for refusing to renounce his father as an "enemy of the people"; but then, on appeal, he was reinstated long enough to receive his diploma in 1939. Even at this late date, a year after his father's execution, he still believed that "Stalin's name was sacred," that the leader was innocent of the injustices of the terror.

The son's reprieve, and his faith, soon ended. Anton Antonov-Ovseyenko was arrested in 1940, released, and rearrested on June 23, 1941, one day after the German invasion. He spent the next twelve years, except for a brief period at liberty in 1943, as a forlorn prisoner in several of the hellish Gulag islands that figure in this book—in Lubyanka, Butyrka, and Lefortovo prisons, and in the Arctic forced-labor camps of Vorkuta. The charges against him, "terrorism" and "anti-Soviet agitation," were unremarkable for the time of Stalin and, of course, entirely false; his only real offense was his father's fate.

Survivors of the Gulag, perhaps seven to eight million people, finally began returning to society in a trickle after Stalin's death in 1953, and then in a mass exodus in 1956. Upon his release from the Arctic camps in late 1953, Antonov-Ovseyenko settled in the warmer regions of Soviet Georgia and the Crimea. Apparently, he sought obscurity, working there quietly in local tourist and cultural organizations.

His father's posthumous exoneration in 1956—Vladimir Antonov-Ovseyenko was among the first of Stalin's prominent victims to be officially rehabilitated under the Khrushchev leadership—and Anton's own judicial exoneration in 1957 brought certain practical benefits. Legally blind, Antonov-Ovseyenko received a disability pension and, in 1960, permission to return to Moscow. There he began to publish historical studies of the revolution, collect materials for a biography of his father, and defend his father's name against neo-Stalinists who wanted to "un-rehabilitate" Stalin's victims.[5]

Apart from signing a 1967 petition circulated by children of Communist Party victims of the terror, which protested Stalin's rehabilitation,[6] Antonov-Ovseyenko seems to have steered clear of the dissident politics of the late 1960s and 1970s. Instead, he produced this book, a work of historical dissent, which remains unpublished, and politically unpublishable, in his own country.

* * *

The Time of Stalin is a book of historical revelations. (Parts II and III are the centerpiece, Part I being mainly a prologue to Stalin's tyranny.) The author cites a variety of published materials, but his main sources are a wealth of personal testimonies, from unpublished memoirs and oral accounts, by people who survived the Stalin era—victims and accomplices, high officials and unknown citizens. Although Medvedev and Solzhenitsyn also used many private sources, Antonov-Ovseyenko's family background evidently gained him the confidence of important witnesses who had not testified previously, or at least so fully, and whose identities he still cannot always divulge. It seems clear, for example, that the author had access to people who conducted Khrushchev's official investigation of the Kirov assassination and its terroristic aftermath—their voluminous report was subsequently suppressed—and to the late Mikoyan.

The result is a horrifying panorama of Stalin's twenty-five-year tyranny, full of new information about important political events, forgotten people, and the despot himself. Above all, we are shown, in vivid detail, the everyday workings of Stalin's police terror, the fates of so many victims, and the complicity of so many others. (The author also gives astonishingly high figures, reputedly from police sources, on the number of arrests in 1935–40 alone.) Certain aspects of the terror are portrayed more fully by Antonov-Ovseyenko than by any other chronicler. He is obsessed, for example, with the plight of the children. (Few readers will easily forget the arrival of "the first mama," Marshal Blyukher's widow, at an orphanage for children of "enemies of the people.") And he is unsparing toward major and minor accomplices of the terror, including police officials who themselves perished, toward petty henchmen who survived to be "hangmen on pension," and even toward Mikoyan.

Western readers may be startled by the author's furious, often sardonic voice, not unlike Solzhenitsyn's in this respect. But as they read Antonov-Ovseyenko's exposé of the murderous despot who was deified in his own lifetime, and whom Soviet leaders and a great many ordinary citizens still praise, they will understand the source of his anger and the purpose of his mockery. Readers may also be baffled by the author's occasional interpretative asides. Was the Stalinist evil the only possible outcome of the Leninist system, as Antonov-Ovseyenko says in some places? Or was Stalinism so monstrous, and so closely linked to Stalin's own character, that there must have been a Soviet alternative, as he implies elsewhere? His inconsistencies, or ambiguities, on these interpretative issues probably derive from his own family heritage and the complexity of the questions.

But Antonov-Ovseyenko is thunderously unambiguous on the great historical question of the nature of Stalin's long rule—a question that still deeply divides Soviet citizens. The thesis of his book is the "criminal essence" of Stalin and Stalinism. (Thus his episodic analogies to the tyranny of hardened criminals over political prisoners in the camps.) He is contemptuous of those Soviet citizens and leaders who still worship the Stalin cult: "The facts are known to everyone who has a spark of humanity left and the desire to know." To those who see both good and bad in Stalin's rule, he is emphatic: "In three decades, the Gensek didn't . . . carry out one good action." And to those who say Stalin was not responsible for the crimes, Antonov-Ovseyenko answers here: "He knew. . . . He did the planning. He gave the orders."

It is the voice of a survivor, a witness, a historian, telling his people, and all of us, that for such historical crimes, there is no statute of limitations.

New York City
October 1980

NOTES

1. Pyotr Yakir, the son of Army Commander Yakir, published a small autobiographical account of his own prison years, *A Childhood in Prison*, New York, 1972.

2. See *Great Soviet Encyclopedia*, Vol. 2, New York, 1973, p. 183; and Georges Haupt and Jean-Jacques Marie, *Makers of the Russian Revolution: Biographies of Bolshevik Leaders*, Ithaca, N.Y., 1974, pp. 325–30.

3. Some Soviet encyclopedias say that Antonov-Ovseyenko died in 1939. Correct information is provided by his son in the foreword to the Russian edition of this book, *Portret tirana*, New York, Khronika Press, 1980, p. 1. For an eyewitness report on Antonov-Ovseyenko in Butyrka prison in February 1938, see *Novy Mir*, No. 11 (November), 1964, p. 212.

4. See "Avtor o sebe," in *Portret tirana*, pp. 1–2. My account of his life is based on this foreword and the autobiographical passages in this book.

5. See, for example, A. V. Antonov-Ovseenko, "Memuary V. A. Antonov-Ovseenko kak istochnik po istorii revoliutsionnykh sobytii 1917 goda," in *Trudy moskovskogo gosudarstvennogo istoriko-arkhivnogo instituta*, Vol. 24, Moscow, 1966, pp. 203–19.

6. See George Saunders (ed.), *Samizdat: Voices of the Soviet Opposition*, New York, 1974, pp. 248–50.

TRANSLATOR'S PREFACE

This is a translation of the Russian-language book *Portret tirana* (New York: Khronika Press, 1980), with some abridgments but also some important additions that reached me during the work of translation. The main addition is the long chapter "Behind the Mask," which does not appear in the Russian edition. Other, smaller additions occur throughout the book. While the work as a whole has been shortened in this translation, the main abridgments are in Part I, where four of the chapters in the Russian edition are compressed into the chapters entitled "Against Lenin" and "Opponents." There were two considerations here. First, the freshest material and the major focus of the book are in Parts II and III and the Epilogue, which deal with Stalin after he became sole dictator. Second, as the author himself explains, the account of Stalin's rise to power in Part I is not intended as a thorough, detailed study ("my modest remarks do not pretend to fullness by any means") but as a kind of prologue to the rest of the book. In shortening Part I, I therefore have compressed the author's discussion of well-known episodes, while preserving his main generalizations, interpretations, and new information about this early phase of Stalin's career.

In regard to the spelling of Russian names and terms: in the text they are transliterated by the more familiar and readable system (e.g., Krupskaya, Mayakovsky, not Krupskaia, Maiakovskii). Bibliographical items in the notes follow the Library of Congress system. Names that appear in both the text and notes are given in the more readable form throughout. Where possible, first names are used rather than initials, but when the first name has not been available, initials appear as in the Russian text. Most first names are not Westernized. The exceptions include some Russian rulers (e.g., Nicholas, Peter, and Catherine, not Nikolai, Pyotr, Yekaterina) and others best known by their Westernized names. Thus, Joseph (not Iosif) Stalin, Leon (not Lev) Trotsky, and Alexander (not Aleksandr) Orlov.

George Saunders

February 1981

AUTHOR'S PREFACE

An entire library could be made up of the books written about Stalin. Yet the fascination with him and what he did is undiminished. Understandably. People feel compelled to peer into the abyss into which they were nearly plunged.

Some Soviet historians concentrate on the history of the two world wars. Some delve into the experience of the revolution. To me there is a more important area of investigation: the history of the counterrevolution. The lessons of the counterrevolution carried out by Stalin are more instructive. This was not Stalin*ism* but Stalin*shchina*—an entire historical epoch during which the vilest and bloodiest kind of evildoing flourished upon this earth. It was gangsterism enthroned. On the moral plane, it operated outside the framework of human values. What attitude should one take toward it: condemn it? pass over it in silence? or perhaps accept and support it? Here is a dividing line between good and evil.

The Stalinshchina, with its genocidal destructiveness, its degradation of the individual, its justification of violence in theory and use of it in practice, had consequences more ruinous than the two world wars. (I have sought to show this statistically in several chapters that follow.) Our age is unhappily renowned for its periodic "crimes of the century"—assassinations, kidnappings, bank robberies. But none of these crimes can compare with those of Stalin. In a historically brief period he managed to rob the peasants of their land, the workers of their factories, the intellectuals of independent creative work, and all the peoples of the multinational Soviet state of their rights, including the right to move about freely. In the process he annihilated millions of people.

Truly the crime of the century.

Stalin ruled a country of many millions for more than a quarter of a century and somehow contrived never to have a dialogue, not once, with his subject population. He did not grant even the possibility of such a dialogue. His was the *monologue* of the unchallengeable sovereign. A monologue to which it was not enough to listen—you had to act on it, carry it out to the letter. No one played up the glories of the "workers' paradise" so shamelessly as Stalin. Yet no one did so much as he to discredit Communism. He dealt the world Communist movement a carefully calculated, crushing blow, from which it has never recovered.

Stalin and the Stalinshchina are subjects that will not go away. Without an understanding of him and his tyranny, the tragedy and shame of the Soviet people cannot be understood. Some who have been granted the right to state part of the truth prefer to speak of the "period of the personality cult." We are willing to grant, they say, that Stalin violated party democracy. He could be pretty rough at times, the Father of the Peoples. But what loving father does not whip his disobedient children for their own good?

For the official ideologists in the USSR Stalin has remained the Great Leader (Velikiy Vozhd), the victor over Hitler, and the builder of "socialism."

"Humanity consists of the living and the dead," Auguste Comte once noted. But the rulers don't read the philosophers; they liquidate them or suppress them. In fact, it can happen that the dead are more dangerous than the living.

In our day, chemicals can be used to make people lose their memories. Rulers have grown proficient in giving entire populations amnesia by other means: the daily blare of propaganda, falsification of history, repression. Soon society renounces its past and its true forebears. Over the course of a generation substantial, often irreversible, shifts take place in the collective memory. Important facts, events, names, entire historical strata disappear. The next generation enters life with built-in amnesia, artificially induced and maintained.

George Orwell left us a vivid description of the mechanics of such falsification by the state. In some places, his book *1984* is greatly feared; you can go to prison for reading Orwell. Quite an honor. That kind of acknowledgment is worth more than any literary prize.

In some countries the young generation grows up without any knowledge of ancient mythology. Children are fed modern myths glorifying the invincible might of their own nation and claiming divine origins and powers for their rulers. Thus extreme nationalism and great-power chauvinism are born. And idol worship. What will grow on such artificial soil, however? Not a generation of free and responsible citizens, but a new batch of cannon fodder.

* * *

The generation of Stalin's victims and of those who followed his orders is still alive. The names of the butchers, the informers, the pogromists must be made known *today, now.* Bring them out of enforced obscurity, the celebrated leaders first of all, but also the ones who were "only following orders." Telling the truth about those who died should not be put off until later. The children and grandchildren do not have the right to turn their backs on the truth, because the fate of those who perished is their own fate. They have an obligation to know who is to blame. And to know it *now.*

Nikita Khrushchev was once advised to carry out a far-reaching investigation into the crimes of Stalin's repressive apparatus and to make known the names of those who were guilty of the deaths of tens of millions of their compatriots (at least that!). Khrushchev answered: "No. That we cannot do. It would mean a repetition of 1937. After all, back then *everybody* was denouncing *everybody.*"

Thus "everybody" is to blame. Stalin's guilt and that of his collaborators is shifted onto the entire population—both living and dead. There is a grain of truth in this, but only a grain. One man was chiefly to blame. He died surrounded by honors and has now been restored to the pantheon —as though the Twentieth and Twenty-second congresses, at which the truth about his crimes was partly revealed, had never really happened.

A great deal has been destroyed in the interim: documents, memoirs, photographs. Many people have perished: revolutionaries and the murderers of revolutionaries, top party bosses and lowly party secretaries. Among those who were granted the luxury of dying in their beds were *knowledgeable* witnesses—and participants. But most of them remained silent to the very end—both old associates of Lenin's and accomplices of Stalin's. They bequeathed their deathly fear to their children and grandchildren.

Some historians have sought to survey and assess Stalin's legacy as a whole. But it does not belong just to history. It persists in the habits, behavior, and thoughts of the living. The ignorance and the silence are also part of his heritage. The open wound cannot be healed by silence. The past must be investigated and publicly condemned. Revelation of the truth about Stalin is an act of simple justice, which must be carried out first of all in his own country.

The literature on Stalin published in the West is generally unavailable to Soviet historians. I have had the good luck to read several basic studies and some of the memoir literature from the West. My primary concern, however, has been to present information that was previously unknown or known only to a limited circle. In the case of first-hand witnesses or participants, I have by no means named *all* my sources, or given the names of all authors of unpublished memoirs. For obvious reasons. Moreover, some information is not accessible to formal documentation or verification: many official archives are sealed, and much evidence has been destroyed or lost.

However, nothing in my book has been made up. I have striven for truthfulness, and not only from a historian's sense of responsibility. There are no fabrications in this book. What would be the need? The truth is horrendous enough.

In my portrait of Stalin I have tried to expose his criminal essence, to reveal the gangster and hoodlum that he was. I may be accused of painting the picture too darkly. But can Stalin and the crimes of his rule really be presented too darkly? Perhaps the book will seem overburdened with bloody scenes from those terrible times. If so, the reader might bear in mind that I felt obliged to leave out many pages, even though they told of crimes that should be known.

Perhaps the author has not sufficiently restrained his personal feelings as a survivor of the terror. I have heard such reproaches from my friends. But it is hard to be brief and "restrained" when you are trying to restore a canvas of criminality on such a scale.

My father, the revolutionary Vladimir Antonov-Ovseyenko, fought against the tsarist regime, took part in the October insurrection, and commanded several battlefronts in the civil war. He did not do this so that a filthy criminal could entrench himself in the Kremlin. Stalin murdered my father, just as he murdered thousands of other revolutionaries. My mother committed suicide in one of Stalin's prisons. I spent my youth in his prisons and camps.

It was late in life, terribly late, that I came to realize Stalin's true place in history, and in the life of our society. Once I learned about it, however, I felt I had to speak out. It is the duty of every honest person to write the truth about Stalin. A duty to those who died at his hands, to those who survived that dark night, to those who will come after us.

I understood that to remain silent about Stalin today is to betray. And I resolved to do my duty as a human being.

Moscow
May 1979

HOW DID HE DO IT?

I

THE FIRST TRY:
The Martov Case

1

On March 31, 1918, the Menshevik leader L. Martov published an impassioned article against the Bolsheviks in his newspaper, *Vperyod* (Forward). In it there was the following noteworthy sentence, which set off a revealing train of events.

"That the Bolsheviks have long attached themselves to all sorts of daring undertakings of an expropriatory nature is well known, at least to Comrade Stalin, who at one time was expelled from the party organization for having had something to do with expropriations."

A serious accusation. As early as 1906 the Fourth Congress of the Russian Social Democratic Labor Party (RSDLP) had passed a resolution condemning "the theft of any funds in the name of or under the auspices of the Social Democratic Party." The congress called on party members to struggle against "expropriators."

What was Stalin to do? Perhaps the wisest thing would be to keep quiet. Every day the revolution brought so many new events that Martov's attack might soon be lost in the whirlpool and forgotten. But no. The commissar of nationalities and Central Committee member reacted instantly. He brought Martov before the revolutionary tribunal for press affairs. Without any formalities, and avoiding a People's Court, Stalin had dealt directly with the presiding officer of the tribunal.

The Menshevik leader tried to protest. The protest was rejected. Martov then asked that witnesses be called and he listed them by name:

1. Isidor Ramishvili, a Social Democrat and well-known public figure. As chairman of a party court in 1908, he had established the fact that Stalin had taken part in the expropriation of the steamship *Nicholas I.*

2. Isidor Gukovsky, the Bolshevik commissar of finance. In that same year, 1908, he had investigated an attempt on the life of a worker named Zharinov who had exposed Stalin's involvement in the expropriations.[1]

3. Stepan Shaumyan, one of the leaders of the Transcaucasian regional committee of the Bolshevik Party.

4. Noi Zhordania, head of the Menshevik government of Georgia and a leader of the Transcaucasian Social Democrats.

These people had known Dzhugashvili-Koba-Stalin for a long time. They knew him as an expropriator who had violated the party resolution, and they knew a few other things about the complicated life the commissar of nationalities had led. Martov named other witnesses as well, includ-

3

ing such Bolsheviks as Voroshilov, Samoilova, Yezhov, Mirov, Panishev, Frolov, and Dzhibladze.

The names of the proposed witnesses appeared on April 6 in the newspapers *Vperyod, Izvestia,* and *Pravda.* Martov was unable to present any documentary evidence. The decision of the underground Transcaucasian regional committee of the RSDLP to expel Stalin from the party had not been preserved. In those years the revolutionaries tried to do without written records.

What move would Stalin make now? The affair was taking a scandalous turn. Something had to be done to retrieve the situation. On Martov's side there were witnesses; on Stalin's the machinery of state.

At the tribunal session Stalin denounced Martov as a vile slanderer. "In order to disarm him," the commissar of nationalities explained, "Martov has to be tried. The case should be heard *right away,* without waiting for witnesses to be called."

Stalin's game was not so primitive as it might seem at first glance. Stalin was afraid of witnesses. That was obvious. But something far more important was hidden behind that energetic phrase "right away." In it could be heard an order for the state apparatus to take measures against Martov. But how to do it, under what pretext? To begin with, Martov, the "vile slanderer," was not just slandering Stalin personally—oh no, that wasn't what upset the commissar of nationalities. He was slandering the party! That was what infuriated Stalin, why he wanted Martov tried right away. The Menshevik leader had spoken only of *Stalin's* expulsion from the party, but Stalin, in an article in *Pravda,* attributed to Martov the charge that the *entire Baku committee* had been expelled.

Only a few days had gone by since March 31. Anyone could have looked at the newspaper *Vperyod* and called Stalin to account for—to put it mildly—twisting his opponent's words. Why was he so obviously trying to distort the public record? Stalin was counting, not without justification, on the government to support him. In exchange, as a kind of guarantee, the government expected at least the appearance of a refutation of the "slanderous" charges.

At the hearing before the tribunal, the Bolshevik journalist Lev Sosnovsky appeared as prosecutor for the plaintiff. Martov was defended by Aleksandrov and Lapinski. The dispute was heated. The arguments on both sides were bitter and drawn out. Stalin again demanded that the "slanderer" be condemned and that no witnesses be called. But Martov's fame as a brilliant polemicist was well founded. He reminded the court of the case of the one-time Bolshevik leader Malinovsky.

In Switzerland in 1914, Martov had voiced suspicions that Malinovsky was an agent of the tsarist secret police, the Okhrana. Martov had then been taken to court and had not been able to present witnesses or evidence. The Bolsheviks had denounced him as a slanderer. A few years later the very same Malinovsky was exposed as an agent provocateur. Now, in 1918, Martov said, he was far from making the same assertion in regard to Stalin. There were many things he did not know. It was important to him to make that clear to the court. In conclusion Martov said:

> If it is physically impossible to hear witnesses, that is my misfortune. But if witnesses are not going to be questioned because Stalin does not want it, that is Stalin's misfortune.

The trial was not held that day. The hearing was postponed for a week so that witnesses could be called.

A victory for Martov? So it would seem. But Stalin had the next move. More exactly, a surprise move was made in his behalf by the government. The revolutionary tribunal for press affairs was dissolved!

Another intermediate but important step followed. On April 10, *Izvestia* ran an article by Mikhail Kakhiani entitled "Fight the Enemy, but Do It Honestly." Simple, no? But exquisite. Peeking out from behind *Izvestia*'s large pages was Stalin's face—the grinning mug of a *kinto*, a hoodlum kid from the streets of Tiflis. He stuck out his tongue at those who had gathered to watch the farce.

A series of similar moves followed. So what if historians and commentators would call them improper later on. For Stalin what counted was results here and now. He was never embarrassed about the means he used.

The plan to subpoena witnesses was dropped, and Martov was invited to appear before the revolutionary tribunal of the city of Moscow for questioning by an investigator in regard to Stalin's complaint. Martov still had his newspaper. He published a protest: "The revolutionary tribunal is intended, according to the decree published by the Bolsheviks, to try crimes against the people. In what way can an insult to Stalin be regarded as a crime against the people? Only if Stalin is considered to be the people."[2]

Stalin took pains to see to it that the witnesses did not appear before the tribunal. For the new show he assumed a fresh role—victim of partisan political warfare. Martov, Stalin explained, wasn't slandering him personally: "Are there many expropriators running around out there? But Martov doesn't care about them. The slander has a well-defined purpose. On the eve of the elections—to discredit me as a member of the Central Committee, as a Bolshevik. To say to the voters: 'See what they're like, your Bolsheviks?' " This was printed in *Pravda* on April 17, 1918, the day after the session of Moscow's revolutionary tribunal, in the sixth month of Soviet rule.

And another item from the public record. The day *before* the hearing, the newspaper of the Smolensk Soviet (also called *Izvestia*) reported that Martov was sentenced to seven days in jail for slander.

Koba was inexhaustible in coming up with such things.

At the April 16 hearing, Martov asked that the case be transferred to a People's Court. The members of the tribunal consulted for more than three hours. The tribunal did not dare violate the procedural norms. It decided to reject Citizen Stalin's complaint, made as part of a civil case, since the matter did not properly come under its jurisdiction.

Stalin had failed to impose his will on the Moscow tribunal.

Unfortunately, Martov was too impulsive. In his March 31 article he had attacked the government with excessive heat. His journalistic sally was deemed criminal. The tribunal found Martov guilty of undermining the authority of the government and publicly reprimanded him for that.

A victory for Stalin? Winning *this* way didn't satisfy Stalin at all. Martov had to be destroyed!

Nikolai Krylenko headed the revolutionary tribunal in the spring of 1918. He was a hard-line Bolshevik, an active participant in the revolution, whose attitude toward the Mensheviks was quite intolerant. Stalin used that to his advantage. Under his never-slackening pressure Krylenko came around and, on April 25, announced at a session of the Central Executive Committee of the Soviets that the decision of the tribunal in the Martov-Stalin case had been wrong and that an appeal should be heard.

Martov could not object. He was denied the floor and removed from the room. Two days later he was stripped of his last means of self-defense —his newspaper was closed down.

It seemed as though Stalin had done everything possible, and impossible as well, but the full victory, in which you see your opponent completely crushed, was still lacking. He had not refuted Martov's charge, or removed the blot from his reputation. Stalin was compromised. He decided the time was favorable to remove himself from Moscow for a while. The civil war was going on, and many Central Committee members were at work in distant provinces and at the front. In late April Stalin went to Kursk to take part in negotiations with the Ukrainian Central Rada. It is no accident that this period is glossed over in his official biographies.

During the summer of 1918, Stalin worked in Tsaritsyn—that is, to the full extent of his powers prevented others from working. In November Stalin turned up as a member of a Ukrainian revolutionary council in charge of a special group of troops in the Kursk area, under the command of Vladimir Antonov-Ovseyenko. Then he was sent to Perm, along with Feliks Dzerzhinsky, to look into the situation in the northern section of the Eastern Front. Another third-rate assignment from Lenin. Not very soon would Stalin recover from Martov's blow.

In 1920 Noi Zhordania published an article in a Paris newspaper in which he told about Stalin's expulsion from the RSDLP because of his suspicious connections with criminal elements and his unauthorized expropriations. But no one in Russia wished to hear what the émigré Zhordania had to say.

Why did Lenin remain silent in the spring of 1918? Why didn't he support Martov's demands? The two men had been linked by party work at the turn of the century and were cofounders of the St. Petersburg League of Struggle for the Emancipation of the Working Class in 1895. Lenin said to Gorky once: "What a shame, what a terrible shame that Martov is not with us. What a splendid comrade he was, what an absolutely pure man. . . . And what a mind. Alas!" Martov was a close friend of Lenin's once. Why did Lenin permit the dissolution of the tribunal for press affairs and the closing of *Vperyod?* Why didn't he stop the baiting of Martov in the press?

The great democrat Lenin, the furious critic of the capitalist system, became intolerant in the years when the proletarian dictatorship was being established—intolerant of criticism of the new system. Strict censorship of the press was introduced in the very first days of Soviet power.

Lenin acted—or, in the Martov-Stalin case, failed to act—for the sake of what he saw as the supreme interests of the party: "The end justifies the means." But his silent complicity with Stalin as a representative of Bolshevism was an irreparable error. He allowed Stalin to compromise the party leadership thoroughly. Martov, by 1921, had lost all hope for a more enlightened Soviet regime. He decided to leave his homeland. Lenin placed no obstacles in his way.

A few years ago the ninety-year-old Aleksandra Ryazanova, who has since died, recalled how sympathetically Lenin inquired about Martov's circumstances as an émigré: "Shouldn't we help him somehow? Is he in good health?" Not long before he lost his powers of speech, Lenin said to his wife: "They say Martov too is dying." Krupskaya remembered his intonation: "There was something especially tender in his voice."[3] A victim of his own dogmas; how inconsistent Vladimir Lenin really was!

His successor made up for that with his ironclad consistency. He succeeded, over time, in destroying almost every witness of his Baku crimes, along with those who so unwisely defended him in 1918—Sosnovsky, Kakhiani, Krylenko. But Martov died before Stalin could get to him. How unfair!

Stalin extracted much that was useful from the Martov case. He uncovered Lenin's weak points as a leader, felt around and found certain convenient pathways within the party and government machinery. And tried his hand at manipulating public opinion, controlling the press, and putting pressure on government institutions. Of course, it didn't come off without overhead costs, but, then, it was only his first try.

THE SECOND TRY:

Tsaritsyn

2

On May 8, 1918, Lenin signed an authorization appointing Andrei Snesarev, a representative of the General Staff, as military commander of the Northern Caucasus military district. Snesarev went to Tsaritsyn. Guerrilla methods, the absence of a unified command, scattered military units, and a supply system in total disarray were what he found. This former tsarist general set to work energetically, organizing the defense of the city and establishing a regular army to replace the scattered guerrilla units. Within a month he had stopped the enemy's offensive.

On May 31 Lenin signed a decree of the Council of People's Commissars appointing Stalin general director of food supplies for the south of Russia.[4] Stalin traveled to Tsaritsyn in a special train guarded by a unit of the Latvian Rifles. He showed up at the headquarters of the Northern Caucasus district while the commander was absent and took over his office. When Snesarev arrived and made the acquaintance of this plenipotentiary from the central organization, Stalin *ordered* that a battle map of the front be brought to him. Snesarev stepped out and came back with the map and, after spreading it out on a table, remarked: "I hope that you will never again get the idea that you are dealing with a child to send on errands. Before this I commanded the Ninth Army Corps and the government has entrusted me with the command of this front."

Stalin was a people's commissar and a member of the Central Committee, but it wasn't his consciousness of his important position in the party and the government that guided him on this occasion.

At a distant camp in the Pechora region, in the remote women's section closed off behind barbed wire, a tough old woman thief sits on a top bunk. In a tone at once haughty and indifferent she tells another thief to bring her some water. She doesn't really want a drink, and when the water is brought she barely wets her lips. She only wants to remind all the women—and to show the guy with the ten-year term that has just walked in—who is boss in that barracks.

* * *

"After having cleared, with a stern hand, the city of White Guard plotters and dispatching substantial supplies of food to the starving capitals, Stalin . . . ruthlessly broke the resistance of the counterrevolutionary military experts appointed and supported by Trotsky and took swift and vigorous measures to reorganize the scattered detachments." That's how the story is told in the *Short Biography* of Stalin.[5]

In reality Stalin demolished everything Snesarev had built up with such care and crushed Snesarev himself. "The military instructor Snesarev in my opinion is very skillfully sabotaging our effort. He doesn't want to wage a real war against the counterrevolution," Stalin telegraphed Lenin, demanding that the saboteur be removed. Stalin, empowered to mobilize food supplies, accused General Snesarev of "defensism" and denounced his plans for the defense of Tsaritsyn as "wrecking activity."[6]

Stalin's deeds were as good as his words. In mid-July he arrested the entire staff of the military district, forced all the commanders onto a barge, and sank it in the Volga River, drowning all the "traitors." After that he arrested Snesarev himself. Stalin wasn't content with the assignment and the powers he had been given. He usurped the status of commander and ordered an offensive, striking out southward from Tsaritsyn. But military tactics are a little different from drowning people on barges. This had become evident by August 4, three days after the beginning of the "offensive." The links between units and sections of the front were disrupted, communications were broken, and the city found itself threatened by encirclement.

Meanwhile, how did things stand with the delivery of food supplies, the purpose for which Stalin had been sent? The experienced expropriator solved this problem in his customary way. Stalin assumed jurisdiction over the Volga steamship lines and seized all the vessels with their cargoes of fish—two million poods [approximately 36,000 tons]. In a short time he accumulated an enormous quantity of food supplies in the warehouses of Tsaritsyn, but he was in no hurry about sending them northward.

A special commission was sent from Moscow to Tsaritsyn headed by Aleksei Okulov, a member of the Revolutionary Military Council of the Republic (RMCR). The first thing Okulov did was to free Snesarev. Later, in 1937, Stalin was to take full revenge by destroying them both —the old general Snesarev and the Old Bolshevik Okulov. But in 1918 Okulov was able to gather a lot of curious information about Tsaritsyn, which he reported to the delegates at a closed session of the Eighth Party Congress. We present some of this information in the following tabular form.

	TENTH ARMY	WHITE ARMY
Number of Soldiers	76,000	26,000
Cannon	256	70
Machine Guns	1,000	100

In Tsaritsyn Stalin was feeding 150,000 freeloaders at the expense of a starving population. One division alone, which had 6,400 soldiers, received rations for 20,000.

Among criminals serving time it's considered a feat of prowess if you manage to get an extra bowl of prisoners' gruel or an extra ration of bread. In the camps there was a special word for success in this kind of finagling —*zakosit* (literally, to mow someone else's field).

* * *

In the summer of 1918, Bolshevik power in Baku was tottering. The city was threatened by Turkish intervention, and the leaders of the Mensheviks (who had a certain influence in the city) took an uncompromising attitude toward the Bolsheviks. Stepan Shaumyan, the head of Baku's Council of People's Commissars and a close associate of Lenin's, sent anxious letters to Moscow asking for help. Cut off from the capital, the Baku Bolsheviks maintained contact with Moscow through the city of Astrakhan or by a more roundabout route, through Kaushku and Tashkent in Central Asia. Baku was the citadel of Bolshevism in Transcausasia. Its oil was an object of desire for the Turks, British, and Germans. In fact, the German government promised to stop the Turkish advance if the Soviets would share their oil.

Lenin followed the course of events with great concern. On June 29 he sent greetings to "Dear Comrade Shaumyan," informed him of Stalin's arrival in Tsaritsyn, and asked that correspondence to Moscow be forwarded through him. In July, when the political crisis in Baku reached its peak, Lenin insisted that Stalin keep in constant contact with Shaumyan.[7]

If only Lenin had known about Koba's past in Baku, his hostility toward Shaumyan, and his rivalry with him for leadership.

The head of the Baku Soviet was asking for help, but Moscow itself was in difficulties. At last, the RMCR gave the order for the Southern Front to send aid to Baku posthaste. When he learned this, Shaumyan said to his closest comrades: "Wait and see. Stalin won't carry out the order. He would never help me, even if he had a surplus of everything."

Shaumyan knew Koba from their work together in the underground in Baku and Tiflis. But let us be objective. Could Stalin have done without a certain number of people and weapons in his area when he had only a three-to-one advantage over the White Guard "bands" of General Krasnov? The same question for food supplies. Although he had a surplus, perhaps he needed to build up several years' reserves. It was probably with that end in mind that Stalin confiscated for his own forces' use a large shipment of grain on its way from the Northern Caucasus to starving Baku.

However, Stalin couldn't bring himself to sabotage Lenin's order openly. He did send a small unit to Baku. These "reinforcements" came rushing in in early August, after Soviet power had already collapsed in Baku. A unit of British troops arrived in Baku at the invitation of the new government, the Dictatorship of the Sailors' Union of the Caspian (the so-called Centro-Caspian). Shaumyan and his comrades were imprisoned. In mid-September Turkish troops entered the city. By then the Bolsheviks had been freed and were on their way to Astrakhan on a steamship; however, the crew docked the vessel in Krasnovodsk and turned the Bolsheviks over to the British.

Along with Lenin, Joseph Stalin, who in the meantime had become a member of the Revolutionary Military Council (RMC) of the Southern Front, would mourn the deaths of the twenty-six Baku commissars.

This RMC of the Southern Front was formed on October 17. Besides Stalin its members were Sergei Minin, president of the Tsaritsyn Soviet, Pavel Sytin, commander of the Southern Front, and Klim Voroshilov, assistant commander.

Stalin wouldn't leave Sytin as commander, however. He proclaimed *himself* chairman of the RMC of the Southern Front and, despite the harm it caused the military effort, transferred the headquarters of the front and the council to Tsaritsyn. Now he had troops, weapons, supplies, and military personnel under his command. And he pursued one intrigue after another, both in the southern command and in Moscow at top party levels. Within ten days after the formation of the Southern Front, he reported to the Revolutionary Military Council of the Republic as follows:

(a) Sytin, "in a very odd way," takes no interest in the situation on the Southern Front as a whole.

(b) We have decided to make preparations for a broad offensive against the Whites without him.

(c) For this purpose, without delay, send cannon, rifles, ammunition, and uniforms—the more the better!

(d) Otherwise, "we will be forced to suspend military operations."[8]

Let us not overlook the style of Stalin's report. It seems that history itself had summoned him to "liquidate the Vendée in the Don region." To fulfill this historic mission Stalin spared no "living forces." He ordered a division that had been hastily put together from untrained new recruits thrown into battle. The entire division was captured by the enemy. When the Cossack cavalry leader Boris Dumenko succeeded in freeing the captured Red Army men, Stalin ordered that the "traitors" be executed.

The central leadership decided at last to establish unity of command and to rein in the southern dictator. The RMCR sent Konstantin Mekhonoshin and Pavel Lazimir to Tsaritsyn to become members of the RMC of the Southern Front. But the special orders of the RMCR assigning these men were not acknowledged. Stalin organized a campaign of denunciation against Sytin and Mekhonoshin with the support of Voroshilov and Minin, whose record had already cast doubt on their competence in commanding the front. "With my own hand I will remove army commanders and commissars," Stalin promised Lenin in regard to those he considered "traitors." "Our hand will not tremble."[9]

This new spate of petty intrigues and personality clashes alarmed the central leadership. A telegram from Sverdlov reminded Stalin that subordination to the commands of the Revolutionary Military Council of the Republic was obligatory for all, including Central Committee members.[10]

When, in early October, the Central Committee discussed the necessity for party officials to carry out the decisions of the central bodies without fail, they had one person in mind above all—Stalin, who had brought the Southern Front to the point of disaster. His fiercely hostile attitude toward military specialists, needless repression, sergeant major's style of discipline within the Red Army divisions, uncoordinated guerrilla methods on the battlefront, petty tyranny on the home front, and intriguing against the commanders and the RMCR—all led to severe losses. Sixty thousand troops paid with their lives for Stalin's adventurism.

With such a reliable ally inside Tsaritsyn, the White Army, numbering only twenty-six thousand, waged a successful offensive, surrounding the city on three sides and coming right up to its walls. Soviet armored cars and armored trains were involved in the battle for days on end. Grigory Kulik, the artillery commander of the Tenth Army, had nearly three hundred artillery emplacements in the streets of the city and on its periphery but was running out of shells. On the morning of October 22, the decisive battle for the city began. On the balcony of the headquarters of

the Tenth Army appeared Voroshilov, Minin, Kulik, and two others—
Yefim Shchadenko and A. I. Selyavkin. The only one absent was Stalin.

Binoculars brought the battlefield into view. It seemed that the regiments of the three White Guard generals, Drozdov, Kornilov, and Mar-
kov, would break into Tsaritsyn at any moment. The Cossacks and the
White Guard commissars were hemming in the defenders of the city more
and more. Suddenly, in the rear of the White regiments and on their
flanks, there appeared row upon row of mounted troops in black Caucasian felt cloaks, which fluttered in the wind like black clouds. Thousands
of spears and sabers flashed in the sunlight. The men on the balcony froze.
These black clouds would sweep over the Red cavalry and all would be
lost. But instead the cloaked cavalrymen slashed their way into the lines
of the White officers. The counterrevolutionary regiments rolled back
from the walls of Tsaritsyn leaving hundreds of dead behind them.

The Tenth Army command knew that Dmitry Zhloba's Steel Division
was on its way from the Northern Caucasus to relieve Tsaritsyn, but communications had been broken and no one was expecting help to arrive that
day. Zhloba, however, came in time.

The encirclement of Tsaritsyn was broken, the enemy driven back
120 kilometers beyond the Don River.

For five days Zhloba's men rested. On the sixth day the division
formed up on the main square of the city. On a wooden platform stood
the members of the Tenth Army command—including Stalin this time.
Where had he been on the day of the final battle? On the other side of the
Volga in his train, protected by the Latvian Rifles. On one occasion, with
this same reliable guard, reinforced by an armored train removed from its
assigned position, Stalin had visited the troops in their outlying trenches.
That's how his one historic visit to the front lines was organized. The rest
of the time he preferred to sit things out on the opposite bank of the river,
showing up in Tsaritsyn only for meetings of the RMC. During the last
week before the battle, Stalin had not shown up at all. Evacuation of the
city had begun, and there was no smell of victory in the air. On the day
of the last battle he had hastened down to the docks to decide a question
of the greatest urgency: which way to flee, upriver or down?

But now things were different. He could step up to the speaker's stand
and, as leader of the revolution in the south of Russia, greet the heroes.

"Dear Comrade Zhloba. Our party and the Soviet government will
never forget your heroic exploit—the saving of Tsaritsyn. Never!"

With these words Stalin handed Zhloba a large gold cigarette case
bearing a triumphal inscription. In those days they didn't yet award orders
and medals, and the commanders with curiosity hefted these unfamiliar,
weighty items on their palms.

That was what really happened. But let us see how these events
are portrayed in the *Short Biography*—or, more accurately, Stalin's autobiography, because the Master personally went over every line in the
book.

"Stalin's iron will and brilliant farsightedness saved Tsaritsyn and prevented the Whites from breaking through to Moscow."[11]

As president of the RMCR, Trotsky more than once demanded the removal of Stalin and Voroshilov as senseless and quarrelsome types who were hurting the cause.[12] Discussing the situation with Lenin, Stalin denied everything and defended Voroshilov as a highly valuable and irreplaceable functionary. Voroshilov repaid him many years later by writing a book about his patron's military "exploits," crediting him as "founder" of the Red Army and organizer of all its victories.[13]

Stalin's correspondence of the civil war years displays the bootlicking that is the natural accompaniment of crafty intriguing. On August 21, 1918, he wrote a letter from Tsaritsyn to "Dear Comrade Lenin" with a request that several minesweepers and submarines be sent at once. The way he signed himself is revealing: "I shake the hand of my dear, beloved Ilyich. Yours, Stalin."[14]

Back in Moscow Stalin found himself somewhat compromised by his activities on the Southern Front. He tried to penetrate the building where the top military authorities were housed. But how could he get around Trotsky? Trotsky had Lenin's full confidence. Stalin was unable to hurl him down at that point. So the thing to do was to be appointed to the RMCR and try to work from within.

Stalin assured Lenin that from now on the RMC of the Southern Front would be a model of military discipline; there would be no more conflicts with the RMCR or the commander in chief of the Red Army. He persuaded Minin and Voroshilov to submit unquestioningly to orders from the central authorities and dropped his attempt to remove Sytin and Mekhonoshin. He even expressed his willingness to collaborate with these two on the RMC of the Southern Front. Stalin dreamed of returning to the Southern Front as a member of the RMCR: that, plus his status as a Central Committee member, would allow him in fact to dominate the council and the front.

Stalin had enjoyed the role of dictator in the south. He had tasted blood. Who can estimate how many thousands of officers and soldiers were killed on his orders at Tsaritsyn? It proved to be a testing ground for his later career in butchery.

In 1918 that perspicacious leader Lenin saw only that Stalin was harsh and hard to get along with, traits easily explainable by his "Caucasian temperament." He asked Trotsky to "make every effort to work smoothly with Stalin."[15] But Trotsky had realized even in 1917 that no fruitful collaboration was possible with Stalin, and he refused the recommendation. Besides, he wasn't going to endanger his creation, the Revolutionary Military Council of the Republic.

Within a year Stalin would take impressive revenge. He would reach a rung on the party's hierarchical ladder alongside Trotsky. Even if we discount the obligingness of *Pravda*'s editors, who placed Stalin's name *fourth* in listing the members of the presiding committee at the Ninth

Party Congress—already *fourth,* after only Lenin, Trotsky, and Bukharin!
—the very fact that he had "caught up" with such recognized party leaders as Kamenev, Rykov, and Tomsky by the third year of the revolution
must be regarded as a major accomplishment for Stalin.

AGAINST LENIN

3

Why did Lenin remain silent when Stalin was hounding Martov in 1918?
Was it only out of reluctance to discredit a member of the Central Committee? Only out of considerations of party prestige?

There are reports of strain between Lenin and Stalin as early as 1920,
indications that Lenin distrusted Stalin, was uncomfortable about his activities, perhaps even feared him.

Margarita Fofanova was very close to Lenin. It was at her apartment
in Petrograd that he hid in September and October of 1917. She was also
a close friend of Nadezhda Krupskaya, his wife. In 1973, not long before
her death, Fofanova told about her visit to Lenin's office in the Kremlin
in 1920, to ask his advice on whether to take a job with the Workers' and
Peasants' Inspectorate (commonly referred to by the Russian acronym
Rabkrin), which was then being reorganized. Fofanova told Lenin she had
heard that Stalin was going to be put in charge of Rabkrin. Lenin had not
been aware of that, apparently, for his face clouded over. He began to pace
up and down his office, then asked her to give him two days to think the
matter over seriously. When she returned to his office, this is what Lenin
had to say:

"Margarita Vasilyevna, I've thought about your problem a lot. I've
even talked it over with Nadezhda. We both agree that you shouldn't
volunteer to work with Stalin. You don't know the man. He doesn't tolerate anyone who will contradict him. But you are an independent-minded
person. You'll get into conflicts if you work with him."

Lenin again began to pace the room with a troubled air. Then he
added: "There's something else you should know. Stalin is a vindictive
person. Who knows unto which generation his vengeance will carry? And
you have children."

* * *

During the last three years of Lenin's life he clashed repeatedly with
Stalin.

In 1921, at the Tenth Party Congress, Stalin participated in the discussion on the national question, fully armed with superficiality and the arrogance of great-power chauvinism. (Lenin had always advocated that the Bolsheviks pay special attention to the grievances of the national minorities, formerly oppressed by the Russian majority in the tsarist empire.) Stalin made no attempt to refute the supporters of Lenin's position with scientific arguments. He let loose instead with an arsenal of swindler's tactics and out-and-out demagogy, vulgarizing and twisting his opponents' views, labeling them as deviations of one kind or another, always seeking to intimidate.

G. I. Safarov had dared to criticize the theses Stalin presented on the national question as commissar of nationalities. Stalin branded Safarov a "Bundist." Back in 1903 the Bundists had advocated national-cultural autonomy, and Safarov was advocating the same thing here at the Tenth Congress. So it all fit. Really? By equating the conditions of tsarist Russia at the turn of the century with the situation in the Soviet federation of states, Stalin was proving only that his main aim was to discredit any audacious critic.

After the congress the commissar of nationalities continued to push his own line on the national question, rather than Lenin's, and his attacks on Safarov developed into full-scale baiting. Lenin supported the "dissident" Safarov, sending Abram Joffe to Turkestan to help him. On December 22, 1921, Lenin wrote to Grigory Sokolnikov, president of the Turkestan bureau of the party's Central Committee:

"I am sending this to you *in secret*. I think that Comrade Safarov is right (at least in part). I urgently request that you investigate objectively, so as not to allow petty intrigues, personal squabbles, and vindictiveness to spoil our work in Turkestan."[16]

Why was the letter sent in secret? Who was Lenin hiding from? Who did he regard as dangerously vindictive? The answers seem obvious. (This letter, incidentally, lay unpublished in the archives for more than thirty years, along with hundreds of other documents that too clearly revealed the face of Stalin.

By 1921 Stalin, with the help of an obedient apparatus, was treating the founder of the party more and more contemptuously. Grigory Shklovsky, an old comrade of Lenin's, asked for an assignment outside the country. (Shklovsky and Lenin had worked together as émigrés in Western Europe before the revolution.) Lenin proposed Shklovsky's candidacy to the State Bank and the Commissariat of Foreign Trade. But the Orgburo* rejected the party leader's recommendation. Stalin, letting other members of the Orgburo speak for him, accused Lenin of favoritism. On June 4, 1921, Lenin answered a letter from Shklovsky as follows:

> You are absolutely right that the accusation of "favoritism" in this case is utterly outrageous and disgusting. I repeat that there is a complicated intrigue here.

*Orgburo: the Organizational Bureau of the Bolshevik Party Central Committee, which by 1921 was already dominated by Stalin.—TRANS.

They are taking advantage of the fact that Sverdlov [Stalin's predecessor as the party's central organization man], Zagorsky, and others have died. You will have to start over "from scratch." There is both prejudice and stubborn opposition and *deep distrust of me* in this question. I am extremely pained by this, but it is a fact. . . . "New people" have come in. They don't know the old ones. You repeat your recommendation—their distrust is redoubled. They get stubborn: "But we don't want it!" !!!

Nothing remains but this: starting over "from scratch," by struggle, to win the new youth to our side.

(To this day Lenin's letter remains unpublished. I quote from a manuscript copy.)[17]

The conflict between Lenin and Stalin over nationalities policy in Georgia in 1922–23 is well known.* In January 1923 Lenin wrote a letter denouncing Stalin and Dzerzhinsky for their "truly Great-Russian nationalist campaign" and concluding that "a fatal role" was played by "Stalin's hastiness and administrative enthusiasm as well as his hostility toward so-called 'social-nationalism.'" Lenin's letter "On the Question of Nationalities Policy, or 'Autonomization'" was meant to be presented at the Twelfth Congress (scheduled for March 1923 but actually convened in April). Conveniently for Stalin, Lenin had a severe stroke on March 10, from which he never recovered. And at the Twelfth Congress the supporters of Lenin's policy did not make an all-out fight to discredit Stalin and remove him from the leadership, as Lenin presumably would have.

Nevertheless, the Twelfth Congress did not go smoothly for Stalin. True, he managed to extricate himself through great effort and trickery, but he was brought to the edge of the abyss and forced to look down. The Gensek† was seized with cold, satanic fury. He decided to take revenge and to stop matters from going any further, despite the fact that the congress had resolved to struggle against Russian "great-power chauvinism." But it was not Stalin's way to oppose Lenin's line openly or try to reverse the decisions of the congress. He used a different technique.

A man by the name of Mirza Sultan-Galiev had worked in the Commissariat of Nationalities. He had been a hard worker who enjoyed Stalin's confidence. But he began publicizing the results of the Twelfth Congress on the national question and the ideas in Lenin's letter. He was too incautious. Stalin struck without warning. On his orders the GPU‡ placed Sul-

---

*The Lenin-Stalin conflict: Detailed accounts and documentation may be found in Moshe Lewin, *Lenin's Last Struggle,* New York, Monthly Review Press, 1978; *Lenin's Fight Against Stalinism,* New York, Pathfinder Press, 1975; and Robert C. Tucker, *Stalin as Revolutionary,* New York, Norton, 1973.—TRANS.

†Gensek: shortened Russian form of "general secretary," the post achieved by Stalin after the Eleventh Party Congress in April 1922, under circumstances discussed in detail in the next chapter. The position of Gensek gave him power over the secretariat of the Bolshevik Party's Central Committee and, thereby, control over much of the central organizational activity of the ruling party.—TRANS.

‡GPU: initials by which the Soviet state-security agency was known in the 1920s and 1930s (also OGPU). From 1917 to 1922 it was known as the Cheka. After 1934 the designation changed several times, to NKVD, MVD, MGB, and is now KGB.—TRANS.

tan-Galiev's activities under special surveillance. He was followed by GPU agents, his phone was tapped, and his mail was read. Thus a member of the government was placed "under the fishbowl" by the agencies of detection and punishment.

The Organs* had been under party control from the very first year of the Soviet regime. Once he became Gensek, Stalin began to bring the Lubyanka† under his own personal control—long before the Great Terror.

Three months after the Twelfth Party Congress, the Central Committee called an expanded conference on the national question, with party activists from the national republics participating. It lasted four days, June 9–12, and throughout this time the participants discussed Sultan-Galiev, criticized Sultan-Galiev, and denounced Sultan-Galiev. He himself was unable to reply. Before the opening of the conference he had been arrested—for counterrevolutionary activity.

The documents of the conference lay waiting to see the light of day for more than half a century. What actually happened at this secret conference? First there was a report from the Central Control Commission by Kuibyshev on the "antiparty and antistate activity of Sultan-Galiev." Not a report from the Politburo or the Central Committee on how to implement the decisions of the party congress on the national question, but the bark of a policeman from the Control Commission.

When he thought up this administrative trick, Stalin foresaw the possibility that members of the Central Committee would object. Therefore Kuibyshev and the man who presided at this conference, Kamenev, and the man who represented the Bolsheviks of the Tatar Republic, Ibragimov, all cited the revolutionary services of the accused and the authority he had earned in his work for the Tatar Soviet Republic. Why, then, was he suddenly being put up against the wall? For the time being it was enough to discredit Comrade Sultan-Galiev, to coin the political epithet "Sultan-Galievshchina," to start talking about "a national deviation passing over into treason," and to mention, incidentally, the expulsion of three hundred "deviationists"—all that was enough to intimidate any recalcitrant representatives of the national minorities. And there was one more aim—to discredit Lenin and his letter.

People were found to do the dirty work. First was Dmitry Manuilsky, a man totally lacking in independent will but fairly well known in the party. He undertook to lecture the delegates from the national minorities on the lesson to be learned from the Sultan-Galiev case—not to give too much thought to great-power chauvinism but to energetically combat local nationalist deviations. That was exactly the anti-Leninist line of the

---

*Organs: a general term for the Soviet security agencies, regardless of the official initials at any time.—TRANS.

†The Lubyanka: headquarters of the Soviet security establishment over the years, located on what was formerly Lubyanka Square in Moscow, with a notorious central prison attached. For the author, "the Lubyanka" is also a symbol of the Soviet secret police and its powers in general.—TRANS.

Gensek. But no, Manuilsky was not opposed to the decisions of the Twelfth Congress; he welcomed them. The only problem was that they had led to the unleashing of an "anarchic, unruly national element" in the local areas. The resolutions of the congress cannot, comrades, be transformed into some sort of "charter of liberties" to be taken by the national minorities.

The Old Bolshevik Manuilsky conscientiously performed his solo part in the Stalin orchestra. The Gensek picked an impressive accompaniment for Manuilsky—Seid-Galiev, a compatriot of the arrested "deviationist." The result was an enjoyable administrative show with an Asiatic cast.

The resolution of the Central Control Commission stated that great-power chauvinism was the cause of undesirable reactions in the national areas.

Seid-Galiev stated, "If it is awkward to remove this passage, then it must be stressed that [local nationalism] is not a reaction, but the result of *intrinsic* nationalism."

As for Lenin's letter to the congress, in the speaker's opinion it had become the object of rumors and "inaccurate interpretations," but in its actual content this letter "represents an awful lot of nothing." (Laughter in the room.)

Why did Stalin put this clown on the stage? He knew from the reports of his agents that there was bitter personal enmity between Seid-Galiev and Sultan-Galiev. When the grain confiscation policy was being followed during the civil war years in the Tatar Republic, Seid-Galiev had permitted glaring inequalities in the amount confiscated, favoring Russians over Tatars. And the rebellion of the discontented he proclaimed a counter-revolutionary insurrection. Seid-Galiev was removed from the Tatar Republic at the insistence of Sultan-Galiev as an incompetent administrator. But now, at this conference, the offended man could get back at Sultan-Galiev without any interference.

This was characteristic. The Stalinist leaders, when they prepared the Central Control Commission resolution, did not bother to analyze the causes of Sultan-Galievshchina. The local situation, the personality of the "deviationist"—all this remained outside the scope of the resolution. But one thing the Gensek did not forget was to use the arrested Communist's personal enemies against him.

No matter how carefully Stalin prepared the staging of this conference, he could not prevent criticism in some of the speeches. Akmal Ikramov reproached the Central Committee for the absence of any real ideological and educational work in the national regions, and for an infatuation with sending out circulars. Mikhail Frunze criticized the Central Control Commission report for shifting the emphasis away from urgent political problems toward "formal and juridicial" matters. He said that a furor was being whipped up over the Sultan-Galiev case to the detriment of the main task—the struggle against great-power chauvinism. Frunze called on the party to take the initiative in promoting the national revival of the backward nationalities.

Nikolai Skrypnik gave battle to the Stalinists in the most uncompro-mising way. He openly declared that some delegates were trying to use the Sultan-Galiev case to change party policy, in opposition to the line established by the Twelfth Congress.

"Absolutely right," Trotsky called out from the floor. But he limited himself to that single outcry, instead of exposing Koba both at the Twelfth Congress and at this conference, along with the other Leninists who spoke up.

A delegate from Turkestan spoke then, Turar Ryskulov. It turned out that not long before Sultan-Galiev was arrested, he had learned that the GPU was watching him. Sultan-Galiev had not been thinking in terms of a secret organization; he simply wanted to speak out along with other comrades at the next congress of Soviets in defense of an intelligent policy in the national border regions. He had written about that to Ryskulov, and Ryskulov presented to the delegates the contents of his letter. But Ryskulov's voice was lost in the chorus of those thirsting for vengeance.

Ibragimov proposed that all "Sultan-Galievites" should be questioned in person and asked "with what sign of the cross they cross themselves," and that those who would not "declare Sultan-Galiev to be a counterrevo-lutionary should be driven out of the party with clubs."

Shamigulov urged that all those involved with Sultan-Galiev be called to account (exactly in what way? one wonders). The meeting hall had the reek of a police station.

Perhaps most indicative was the speech by Ikramov. He said that a great many questions having to do with the party's nationality policy had accumulated in the local areas and that not a single party official felt free to ask Stalin or Kamenev for explanations: "They're afraid. They have the impression that they would be arrested or shot."

Before me I see, through the celebrated whiskers, the dry smile of Stalin. The Gensek could be quite content. He was feared not only in Moscow.

The June 1923 conference helped Stalin to determine more exactly the disposition of forces. Kuibyshev and Manuilsky had handled their roles beautifully. Years later, after he had become the Great Leader, Stalin graciously allowed them to die in their own beds at home. He settled the fate of his critics differently. Frunze was to be the first victim. He was to die in October 1925. Eight years later Skrypnik, hounded mercilessly by Stalin, would shoot himself. Ikramov would be taken care of in 1937.

The Sultan-Galiev case was a political provocation carried out by Stalin with full professional skill, with the participation of the GPU; it was provided with a thick layer of ideological covering by Kamenev and Zino-viev, while Trotsky looked on with demonstrative neutrality.

The records of the June conference were immediately hidden away. Only a limited edition was made available to leading party officials.

At the conference Skrypnik made an astute comment: "I fear that the very approach to the Sultan-Galiev case at this conference will lead to a certain shift in our political line."

The shift had already taken place, and not only in the political line. Such features of party life as lack of sincerity and political wheeling and dealing were already observable by then. Skrypnik spoke openly about it at the conference. In the spring of 1923 it was still possible to retrieve the situation; within a year it was too late.

Lenin had begun to see the truth, but he did not fully detect the gravedigger of the October revolution behind the mask of "Comrade Koba." He wrote with alarm about the bureaucratization of the state apparatus and the party, a process that had already begun *in his time.* He came close to realizing the source of the danger. But the grain of truth still eluded him. Only episodically did he seem aware of the ominous figure of Stalin—for example, in that conversation with Fofanova and in some conversations with his secretaries in late 1922 and early 1923.

Lenin was inclined to idealize his closest associates. He could not imagine that Stalin's vindictiveness and intolerance were only two ugly traits in a nature richly endowed with ugliness. All through 1922 Lenin busied himself with Rabkrin,* deciding finally to replace Stalin with Tsyurupa. At the same time he advised those responsible for the work of reorganizing Rabkrin to consult—with Stalin!

What amazing inconsistency. A man of profound intelligence, a sharp polemicist, and an energetic organizer, Lenin was remarkably conciliatory in the face of Stalin's insolence. He did not understand that Stalin could bring the whole cause to disaster. During the revolution and civil war Lenin showed so much determination, will, and courage. But toward Stalin, such unforgivable tolerance. Despite Lenin's awareness of degeneration in the party and state, despite his concern for the future and the fate of the socialism he had always fought for, he could not see that Stalin was more dangerous than Kerensky, the head of the pre-Bolshevik government in 1917, and the White generals Denikin, Wrangel, and Kolchak put together.

In 1921 and 1922 Lenin more and more frequently gave thought to the problems of improving the work of the central apparatus of the party and deepening its links with the masses. He was also concerned about the condition of the top government bodies. He searched for new and more effective forms of control over the activity of state agencies and presented his thoughts in the form of proposals for the Twelfth Party Congress. On January 13, 1923, he finished the first version of the article "How We Should Reorganize Rabkrin" and submitted it for publication in *Pravda.* Days went by, but the article did not appear in print.

At a Politburo session Bukharin, then the editor of *Pravda,* reported that Lenin was troubled by the delay in publication. In Krupskaya's words, Ilyich was becoming "very fretful." Kuibyshev then proposed that a single copy of *Pravda* be printed with Lenin's article in it to console the ailing leader.[18] Kuibyshev, a secretary of the Central Committee, would hardly

---

*Stalin had indeed been placed in charge of Rabkrin, the Workers' and Peasants' Inspectorate, in 1920.—TRANS.

have dared make such an obscene proposal on his own. We can easily guess who encouraged him from the shadows.

Lenin's article was finally published on January 25. On the same day, however, the Secretariat mailed instructions to all provincial committees not to attribute any practical importance to the article. Here the Gensek left his trail in full view. The instructions were signed by Stalin personally. Lenin was ill, said the instructions, and did not himself realize what he was doing.[19]

In fact, Lenin knew very well what he was writing and why. He recommended that Politburo sessions be conducted in the presence of "a certain number of members of the Central Control Commission" and "that it be seen to that no one's authority, neither *that of the general secretary* nor that of any other member of the Central Committee, be allowed to prevent Central Control Commission members from making inquiries, examining documents, and in general insuring absolutely full information and the strictest and most correct procedure in all functioning."[20]

That was what made Stalin nervous. Incidentally, the passage where Lenin referred to the general secretary had disappeared when the article was published. It is not hard to guess who personally saw to that.

Ten years later, when Lenin's article was being called a work of genius and when Stalin had already turned his Gensek's chair into an autocrat's throne, he ordered his letter of instructions removed from all archives. Two copies have been preserved nevertheless. And several old-time party members, former secretaries of provincial committees who by chance survived, confirmed, during the brief thaw,* that those instructions of Stalin's had indeed been received in their areas.

* * *

Lenin died in January 1924. On May 22, 1924, on the eve of the Thirteenth Congress, a plenum of the Central Committee convened in St. Vladimir's Hall in the Kremlin. A number of organizational questions were to be resolved, a presiding committee for the congress to be designated, as well as various commissions for the congress, and so on.

Krupskaya was the first to take the floor. She presented the letter Lenin wrote that is known to history as his Testament. Lenin had asked that the letter be read aloud to the Twelfth Congress while he was still alive, but this had not been done. Krupskaya demanded that the deceased leader's will be carried out at the first session of the Thirteenth Congress the following day. Nikolai Krylenko made an alternate motion, to publish the Testament immediately. Zinoviev, Kamenev, and Stalin spoke against that.

The plenum adopted Krupskaya's motion, but the Central Committee members wanted to know the contents of the letter in advance.

---

*Thaw: the period under Khrushchev, roughly 1956–64, when Stalin was officially condemned and many public revelations about the mistakes and crimes of his rule were permitted.—TRANS.

Krupskaya began to read. She had a soft voice and her reading could not be heard. Her emotions were also affecting her.

Someone proposed: "Let Yevdokimov read it."

Grigory Yevdokimov, a Central Committee member and representative of the party's Leningrad committee, had a strong voice and clear diction. He read the Testament through to the end. Lenin had given brief characterizations of his possible successors—Trotsky, Zinoviev, Bukharin, and others—and especially warned the party in regard to Stalin. All these men were seated at the presiding committee's table.

Other matters were immediately set aside. The document turned out to be so important that everyone felt it was necessary to read it individually. The plenum assigned the presiding committee to reproduce the text for all Central Committee members and to suspend the proceedings in the meantime.

After a few hours the session resumed, and the text of Lenin's letter was distributed to all present. Someone made a motion that the Testament be read to each party delegation before the congress was opened, in the presence of Central Committee representatives.

A list of those who would serve as Central Committee representatives was drawn up there and then.

All questions concerning the congress agenda were then quickly approved, and the participants went to their homes or, in the case of those from other cities, to hotels. It was quite late and everyone needed rest.

But there was one man who didn't feel like sleeping. The roar of car engines broke the silence of Moscow's night. GPU agents were on their way to all the hotels and apartment buildings housing the Central Committee members. Calling themselves couriers for the Central Committee, they rounded up all copies of the dangerous Testament and asked the bearers to sign a special register.

It's impossible to determine today whether the Gensek took this hasty action himself or coordinated it with other Politburo members. He could have done this in "workmanlike fashion" by polling the members separately. However it may be, someone's firm hand was certainly felt in that nighttime operation.

Lenin's Testament almost knocked Stalin out of the saddle, but cursing Lenin wouldn't have helped matters. The Gensek had begun undermining the authority of the document even while its author was alive. In April 1923, behind the scenes—along the corridors at the Twelfth Congress—his agents spread the word that the postscript to the Testament was written *right after* the incident involving Krupskaya.* Stalin wanted to imply that Lenin, ill and angry, hadn't meant what he had written.

---

*Stalin had rudely insulted Krupskaya over the phone on December 22, 1922. On March 6, 1923, Lenin wrote Stalin a note threatening to break all personal relations with him if he did not apologize to Krupskaya. Lenin regarded this rudeness toward his wife as a direct attack upon himself.—TRANS.

In fact, according to Maria Joffe, Lenin had frequently complained to his comrades about Stalin's rudeness and disloyalty, the same terms he used in the postscript, where he suggested that "the comrades think about a way" to remove Stalin from the Gensek's post.

* * *

For a year or more Stalin had waited impatiently for Lenin to die. Once he was dead the Gensek could allow himself a few liberties. Stalin was present at the reading of the Testament to the Moscow delegation as the representative of the Central Committee and was heard to mutter angrily: "Couldn't die like a *real* leader!" (This ugly remark was reported by Galina Serebryakova; she was told by her first husband, Grigory Sokolnikov.)

The Thirteenth Congress ended, the first one without Lenin. Another Central Committee plenum was about to be held, which would elect a new leadership. What stunt would the Gensek pull this time? After making sure his people were in place, his own Central Committee claque, he assumed a pose of offended innocence.

"If the comrades feel that the Testament is a document that requires the withholding of all political confidence in me, I will resign from the post of general secretary."

Koba already had one foot over the abyss, but Zinoviev saved him. He assured everyone that Stalin had recognized his mistakes and had fully absorbed the criticisms Lenin made of him, that in practice he had shown his willingness to maintain a correct and comradely attitude in dealing with party members.

And so the comrades talked Koba out of resigning. These party ideologues didn't want to assume the burden of administrative work. Stalin had accumulated substantial experience at giving orders and organizing things. Moreover, he couldn't become dictator. The conditions weren't present for that. Fourteen years later Koba would generously repay his saviors—both those who had poured out words to support him and those who had supported him in silence.

Thus, against Lenin's wishes, the Testament was not read to the party congress and was not published. Stalin remained general secretary, and the party expressed confidence in him both at the congress and at the Central Committee plenum. People who had been given supreme power by the party, revolutionaries who had years of underground work and prison behind them and who had faced death—these people lost their heads the year Lenin died. They saw in Stalin a new Leader, a resolute man who knew no doubts.

They were not to realize their mistake right away. Some would only realize it in a torture chamber of the Lubyanka. There some of them would meet face to face with "enemies of the people" who had secretly kept copies of the seditious Testament. For merely referring to Lenin's Testament you could be tried, during the thirties, under Article 58, points

10 and 11, for *anti-Soviet agitation,* and get ten years in the camps. You could also be shot. The death penalty for having Lenin's letter. What more could Stalin want? (Not until 1956, thirty-two years after Lenin's death, was his Testament finally published in the USSR.)

OPPONENTS

4

The Russian philistine, after the years of revolution and civil war, longed for order. Rule by an iron hand was the cure-all for hunger, ruin, and anarchy. A dictator was needed, not necessarily a wise one and not necessarily a good one—but a *dictator.*

> In Russia they worship
> The tsar and the whip.

Those lines by the nineteenth-century poet Polezhayev were true not only in his day.

As long as Lenin was alive, the masochistic instincts of the herd were somehow restrained. Once he was gone, the people couldn't stand it any longer and began fashioning a new tsar, a new little father.

Was Stalin's rise to power accident or necessity? History has already answered that question. Stalin was the man of the hour, in the right place at the right time. In 1922 a Paris newspaper wrote: "Lenin is mortally ill. When he dies that bewhiskered Ingush will come to power and organize a bloodbath for the whole bunch of them."

Amazing foresight. But the "boulevard gutter sheets" of the "White émigré trash" were not read by Trotsky or Zinoviev, still less by the bedridden Lenin. And if they had read such a thing, they would have snorted: What are you saying? Behind the mask of our energetic Gensek, a murderer? Come off it.

Trotsky, with his hypertrophied self-esteem, underestimated Stalin's driving power. Trotsky considered himself so obviously superior to the "gray blur"—Sukhanov's description of Stalin in 1917, which Trotsky often repeated—that he looked down upon the Gensek's political pranks with haughty contempt. Trotsky could have become the number-two man in the government, with full official status, but he stubbornly refused the post of Lenin's deputy. When he finally decided to fight, to appeal to the "party rank and file," the train had already left. Stalin could not have made better use of the blunders of his chief rival.

Zinoviev and Kamenev did not want to dirty their hands with administrative work. Let Koba occupy himself with such matters, they thought. He's uneducated and rude, that's true, but his hand is firm. There's no other way of dealing with our self-willed Bolshevik crowd. Let Koba sit in the Gensek's chair for a while, as we do the theorizing.

All of them—Trotsky, Zinoviev, Kamenev, and Bukharin—looked upon him as a kind of provincial actor making his debut on the big-city stage. His aspirations to be number one seemed to them laughable because he had no real training or talent to back them up. General secretary? Very amusing. But let him play at it if he likes. They didn't take Stalin seriously. And when they realized that this actor had taken over the stage entirely, it was too late.

Kamenev had a special soft spot for Stalin. Fate had thrown them together in exile in the Turukhansk region. A group photograph showing Kamenev and Koba with their arms around each other has survived.

In the spring of 1915, Grigory Petrovsky spoke at a meeting of Bolshevik exiles about the government's trial of the Bolshevik members of the Duma. Stalin was the only member of the Central Committee who refused to criticize Kamenev's behavior at this trial. (Fearing the death penalty, Kamenev had dissociated himself from the Bolshevik opposition to Russia's part in World War I.) The exiles at the meeting charged Stalin and Sverdlov with the task of drawing up a resolution, but Comrade Koba simply left. He went home, giving no explanation.[21]

In the spring of 1917, Kamenev and Stalin together took control of the editorial board of *Pravda* and opposed Lenin's Bolshevik line on the central questions of the time.

October 1917. Lenin from his hiding place lashed out at Zinoviev and Kamenev as "strikebreakers" for opposing the Bolshevik plan to seize power and for making the plan public. Stalin intervened in defense of Kamenev.

For many long years, Koba played Kamenev's disciple. Kamenev never doubted for a moment that things would always be that way. He was one of the acknowledged leaders of the party, and the disparity between his and Stalin's administrative experience, erudition, and culture was too great. One could strengthen one's position in the Politburo with Stalin's support; in fact it was time the party had a secretary who would carry out his, Kamenev's, will.

On April 2, 1922, the last day of the Eleventh Party Congress, the delegates came up to the ballot boxes and dropped in voting slips listing the candidates they favored for membership on the Central Committee. When the members of the elections commission opened the ballot boxes, they looked at each other in disbelief. Many voting slips had this notation: "Stalin—Gensek, Secretaries—Molotov and Kuibyshev."

Nikolai Alekseyevich Skrypnik, chairman of the elections commission, had no problem deciding what to do. He proposed that all such voting slips be annulled, since they were in patent violation of the party rules. The congress had no authority to elect a general secretary.

Skrypnik had no doubt that this attempt to predetermine the results of the voting at the next plenum of the Central Committee came from Kamenev, and with the authorization of the elections commission, he appealed to the presiding committee of the congress. Lenin, however, recommended that the voting slips be left as they were: "We will force Kamenev to speak and disavow this maneuver in front of the congress and at the Central Committee's organizational session after the congress."

Kamenev was obliged to explain to the delegates the motives for his action. The text of his remarks was published in the bulletin of the congress, but no copies have survived, and when the proceedings of the congress were published that text was left out.

The Central Committee's plenum on organizational questions opened on April 3. Kamenev was obliged to speak again. "The plenum is not bound in any way by the names added to the ballots," he stated. After that the plenum passed a special resolution:

"To take note of Comrade Kamenev's explanation that during the elections, with the full approval of the congress, he stated that the notations on some ballots referring to secretarial posts should not put any pressure on the Central Committee plenum in its voting and merely expressed the wish of a certain number of delegates."

Kamenev was to render Stalin valuable service more than once thereafter. And Zinoviev too. The main thing was to block the way for the autocratic Trotsky. Better the thickheaded and rough-mannered Koba.

Thus, Stalin became one of three main secretaries of the Central Committee Secretariat, along with Kuibyshev and Molotov. But the other two did not have his powerful will and ambition. By 1922 Stalin had mastered all the mechanics of party elections, and the technology of administering the central apparatus held no secrets for him. He formally consolidated his leading position in the secretariat by acquiring the title "general secretary." At a Central Committee meeting this right man at the right time introduced the appropriate motion and someone seconded it—Stalin surely knew quite well who—and in no time the "question" was put to a vote and passed. The post of Gensek had been created.

It would be interesting to know which of the Politburo and Central Committee members besides Kamenev proposed Stalin for his various posts—Central Committee secretary, general secretary, people's commissar of nationalities, commissar of Rabkrin, and finally that of supervising Lenin's medical care. They undoubtedly included Molotov, Voroshilov, and Kuibyshev. Who else? Who objected or who was opposed (if anyone)? The authors of the fairy-tale biography of Stalin contend that he was elected general secretary on a motion by Lenin at a Central Committee plenum on April 3, 1922.[22] The book is crammed full of such inventions, which are not even worth refuting.

Stalin held the post of Gensek for more than thirty years, to the very end (with the formal qualification that in October 1952 he had his title changed back to "secretary of the Central Committee"). In early 1922 neither Lenin nor anyone around him considered the post of much importance. The Central Committee was headed by the Politburo. Zinoviev became its chairman in 1922 (when Lenin withdrew on account of illness). A year later Kamenev replaced Zinoviev. The general secretary did not determine the party's political course, nor could he. Or so the party leaders thought.

Kamenev, Zinoviev, and Bukharin handed Koba the key to the Secretariat. They felt sure he would dance to their tune. It soon became apparent, however, that Stalin had his own flute. He breathed some very weighty content into the seemingly harmless bureaucratic formality of his title. Little by little he enlarged the functions of the Gensek's office, gaining more and more influence over the central apparatus and the peripheral bodies of the party. The local leaders in the provinces, districts, and capitals of the national republics gradually gained the impression that Comrade Stalin had great personal power. Circulars, resolutions, decisions, letters of instruction came pouring out into the local regions, bearing his signature. The documents of Central Committee members on official missions were countersigned "J. Stalin." Above all, he assigned party personnel to local areas.

The assignment of higher-level personnel was in the hands of the Orgburo. Stalin laid siege to that agency immediately. As early as 1921, being a member of the Politburo, he was placed on the Orgburo. He soon assumed the stance of unchallengeable decision-maker and began putting his own people everywhere—in the central apparatus, in the national republics, and in the territorial and provincial committees. Boris Bazhanov, at that time one of his secretaries, relates that the Gensek had the habit of pacing up and down in his office, puffing on his pipe, then buzzing for his assistant to issue a curt command: Remove such-and-such a secretary of a provincial committee and send so-and-so to replace him. And the Orgburo, entirely under his control, with uncharacteristic speed and without any bureaucratic red tape would process the removal and appointment of these party officials.

* * *

No one argued with the Orgburo. This suited Stalin quite well. If it hadn't been for the all-powerful Politburo still standing over him, he might have thought the game, begun so well, was already won. And in fact, not many years passed before those who had placed the Gensek in his post learned to step to his tune, and the Politburo was reduced to nothing but dancing attendance on the sovereign. In the early twenties, though, the members of the highest body of the party had no desire to view the world from under the visor of Stalin's cap.

Stalin did not at first control *all* of the Central Committee apparatus, and had not yet placed his own people in all the decisive sectors, devoted people who would do his bidding, who would never dare to look down on him as Trotsky did. Or to look him directly in the eye as Skrypnik or Zatonsky did. People who looked at him from under their brows, and caught every order that dropped carelessly from beneath his whiskers.

There were such people already—Molotov, Kuibyshev, Voroshilov, Andreyev, Yaroslavsky—but not yet enough of them. So Stalin persistently and methodically strengthened his forces in the Orgburo, in the Secretariat, in the Central Committee, on the editorial board of *Pravda,* and in the Council of People's Commissars.

In the years 1921–24 the party bureaucracy was just starting to grow, but Stalin already felt the invincible force the apparatus represented. Any decision of the Central Committee could be buried in the bowels of the apparatus, even a resolution of a party congress. Whoever controlled the apparatus could block the instructions of the Politburo or of a Politburo member. The same person could have his own instructions carried out under the guise of Central Committee directives.

Under Lenin every member of the Central Committee could raise any question in the Secretariat, the Orgburo, or the Politburo, defend his own point of view, and, if necessary, appeal to a plenum of the Central Committee. And a plenum decision, which was binding for all members, could be appealed by a Central Committee member to a party congress.

This Leninist tradition limited the Gensek's operations and stuck in his throat like a bone. He endured it until 1925. At the Fourteenth Congress he allowed the minority to speak for the last time. The party's democratic tradition withered away after that. At the Fifteenth Congress no one argued with the Gensek. Not a single freethinker was even elected as a delegate.

* * *

How did he do it? The old proverb that a fish rots from its head invariably comes to mind in considering the degeneration of the Bolshevik Party. The process began at the top. Stalin assumed the role of catalyst, and under him the process of disintegration of the party leadership went three times faster.

At the very top were the party mandarins. At their service was the Central Committee apparatus, which implemented their directives. Down below was the voiceless rank and file, bound and frozen by total party discipline. This is how relations within the party had taken shape by 1923. Even the dying party leader, Lenin, was powerless to change things.

One attempt to take the central apparatus out of Stalin's tight grasp is known to history. In August 1923 a number of prominent party officials were on vacation at Kislovodsk, including Zinoviev, Bukharin, Grigory Yevdokimov, Voroshilov, Lashevich, and Frunze. They went for a walk one day to the suburbs of the resort town, where they sat down in a cave to discuss the situation in the Central Committee apparatus. They were aware that the Orgburo was removing people, appointing new ones, shuffling personnel around without consulting the Politburo.

A letter was sent to Stalin in the name of this group. The Gensek quickly arrived in Kislovodsk. He soothed the comrades' fears. No one was ignoring the Politburo; no one was breaking the party rules. It's hard to believe, but he actually invited the Politburo members to attend Orgburo sessions regularly.[23] Not the Secretariat: the Orgburo. The comrades took what Koba had said under advisement. But no one except Zinoviev actually showed up at Orgburo meetings. And he only came haphazardly, for a few minutes each time.

None of them detected the full scale of the organizational preparations the Gensek was making with his apparatus. No one knew that even under Lenin, Koba had kept the leader and his comrades under the closest surveillance. Not a single conversation, scribbled note, or sheet of carbon paper that passed through the Secretariat or was handled by the Politburo members' personal secretaries was missed. None escaped the yellow eyes of Joseph Stalin.

A year after Lenin's death the Gensek improved his system of surveillance. Boris Bazhanov, Stalin's one-time assistant, had long been troubled by one question: What did Stalin do for hours at a time? The Boss would sign things, barely looking at them, and he ignored problems requiring serious attention. One day Bazhanov stepped into Stalin's office and saw him at his desk with a telephone to his ear. But what phone was this? All the office phones were in place. The secretary noticed a wire going down into the Boss's desk. At that moment Stalin raised his head and stared at his secretary, while keeping the phone to his ear. Bazhanov left without a word. He told the Gensek's trusted assistant Lev Mekhlis about the episode. Mekhlis remarked curtly that he shouldn't concern himself about that. A Czech specialist had installed the eavesdropping mechanism. The Boss had probably had the Czech taken care of at the Lubyanka afterwards, where they knew how to deal with unnecessary witnesses.[24]

No one expected Lenin to revive, and his associates were now wondering who would replace him. The men at the improvised meeting in Kislovodsk recalled the principle of collective leadership, and they consulted on how to thwart Stalin's aspirations to sole power. The idea was raised that three Politburo members should belong to the Secretariat, since it was acquiring so much power and importance. These would be Trotsky, Stalin, and Zinoviev, though Kamenev or Bukharin could be part of the threesome instead of Zinoviev. Bukharin formulated this proposal and drafted the letter to Stalin along with Zinoviev. Voroshilov spoke against it, but the others agreed with Bukharin. Sergo Ordzhonikidze took the letter to the Gensek in Moscow.

That was the last thing Stalin wanted—other Politburo members in *his* Secretariat. No matter what the composition of the threesome, he, Stalin, would be outvoted. When Stalin reached Kislovodsk he immediately frightened his comrades by offering to resign: "If the comrades insist I am ready to clear out without any fuss, without a discussion either open or secret."[25]

There was more to this theatrical gesture than met the eye. Those who gathered in the Kislovodsk cave in August 1923 had read Lenin's Testament proposing that comrades think about some means of replacing Stalin as general secretary. That recommendation had stung the incipient dictator, and he decided to threaten to resign. His comrades in arms were thrown into confusion. Koba had not understood them. They hadn't suggested *that*.

Nevertheless, the Kislovodsk variant troubled the Gensek. He recalled the incident at the Fourteenth Congress in December 1925, when he made fun of the "cavemen" and referred to the negotiations of that time in an ironic tone, repeating his words about being willing to "clear out."

By then nearly two years had passed since Lenin's death, and his position as Gensek was secure enough for him to joke about it. At that congress Stalin was playing to the public. At the same time he undercut Zinoviev's authority, calling the Kislovodsk proposal a "platform to destroy the Politburo." The Master of Political Intrigue was making his former sponsors dance to his tune.

* * *

How did he do it? One of the keys to Stalin's success was the consistent failure of his opponents to unite against him.

Zinoviev and Trotsky could not unite and did not want to. Each was too ambitious. Each aspired to the role of ideological leader.

In 1925 Krupskaya made an attempt to unite a group of authoritative party leaders with the aim of reining Koba in at last. She believed it was still possible. Lenin's widow joined with Zinoviev, Kamenev, Sokolnikov, and others, and tried to bring Grigory Petrovsky into the opposition as well. Petrovsky was then president of the Central Executive Committee in the Ukraine. She came to see him in Kiev, but Grigory refused to take part in this effort. Thirty years later, after the Twentieth Party Congress, he expressed his belated regrets to his friends, and added: "But in view of what we knew at that time, in 1925, I cannot condemn myself."

In Lenin's immediate circle there was one man who knew that Stalin was flesh of the flesh of the criminal world. That man was Yakov Sverdlov. He avoided all contact with Koba after a certain time during their joint exile in the Turukhansk region and boycotted him throughout 1917. But Sverdlov died early, a year and a half after the victory of the revolution. If he had lived, would he have had the courage and principle to slam the door to the Central Committee and the government in Stalin's face?

In the spring of 1926, not long before his death, Feliks Dzerzhinsky became aware of the danger of a major split in the party and began to sound the alarm. Suddenly Dzerzhinsky was gone. Alarm grew. More and more party members saw where the real danger was coming from.

It was like a scene in a prison cell. The suckers* are hiding under the bunks whispering to one another about their bitter fate, but none of them

---

*Suckers: In the special language of the criminal underworld, the Russian word *frayer* is used for noncriminals, suggesting an innocent, a poor sap, a "greenhorn," an "easy mark." I have translated this by the same term ("sucker") as is used in the English edition of *The Gulag Archipelago* by Aleksandr Solzhenitsyn, which gives a classic description of the hardened criminals' domination over the political prisoners.—TRANS.

dares stand up against one lone filthy bandit. In fact, some of them are ready to do the hoodlum's bidding.

Take Bukharin, for example. At one time in the summer of 1928 he pleaded with Kamenev: "If we don't unite, Koba will cut all our throats." But the "Rights" and Zinoviev-Kamenev did not unite. They talked and talked, then went their separate ways.

In 1934, at a banquet in honor of the Chelyuskin expedition, Bukharin suffered a relapse of blindness, he who had once seen through Stalin so clearly. He came up to the Master and said: "Koba, I'm ready to shit on my own head for having opposed you." Nikolai Ivanovich tried to nuzzle the Master's hand, but the Great One gave "Bukharchik" the brush-off. The time for kissing had passed.[26]

Kamenev, Zinoviev, Trotsky, Bukharin, Rykov, Tomsky, Frunze, Dzerzhinsky, Petrovsky, Skrypnik, Kosior. If these party leaders had united after Lenin's death, they could have barred Stalin's way to one-man rule. But were there any real men among them?

There was another factor contributing to his success. The ladder Stalin used to scramble up to his high throne was none other than the "iron discipline of the party." It bound the will of his potential Communist opponents, who kept trying to return the party to the course of collective leadership. The ladder was placed there for Stalin to use by none other than Lenin.

Many years before, at the Second Party Congress in 1903, Lenin had opposed Martov, who favored the construction of a *mass party*. Instead Lenin argued this way: "Better not to have ten hard-working people as members of the party than to have one blowhard as a member." And he reiterated: "The strength and authority of the Central Committee, the firmness and purity of the party ranks—that is the key."[27]

Stalin seized upon this key and made the best possible use, the most thorough use, of the power of the Central Committee. And he very firmly carried through the line of "purity of the party's ranks." Using Lenin's formula of democratic centralism for his own purposes, Stalin fully justified Lenin's hopes for the creation of an iron dictatorship.

After Lenin's death Stalin felt it was time to take advantage of the ban on factions passed at the Tenth Party Congress. That resolution allowed the Central Committee to expel any member from the party for "factionalism" or violating party discipline, including members of the Central Committee. In Stalin's hands, this resolution became an unfailing instrument for the subordination of the party to the will of a handful of political bosses, and ultimately the caprice of the sole Master.

There was not a single congress at which Stalin failed to call for strict observance of the iron unity of the party. When he attacked oppositionists he always accused them of intending to violate the unity of the party's ranks. The so-called struggle for unity became a means for strengthening Stalin's one-man rule. Any attempt to criticize the Gensek was equated with trying to split the Leninist party.

Lenin's closest associates were the first to rush into battle in behalf of unity and party discipline. At the Twelfth Congress, when Stanislav Kosior called for an end to the ban on factions and groupings, he explained that he didn't mean at all to renounce the idea of unity. It's a shame that such a clever person as Bukharin tried to ridicule him for taking that position. Zinoviev, followed by Bukharin, assured the delegates that the party was now healthier than ever, and that it was the best of all possible parties.[28]

At the Fourteenth Congress, Dzerzhinsky called for unity of the party no matter what: "That should be sacred for us."[29] Two weeks before his death he wrote to Kuibyshev, "Only the party and its unity can decide."[30]

This became the leitmotif of subsequent congresses. The Sixteenth Congress charged the Central Committee with the task of continuing in the future to "ruthlessly reject all attempts to weaken or undermine the steellike party discipline and unity of the Leninist party."[31] Using such powerful levers as party discipline and the dictatorship of the proletariat (which was actually the dictatorship of the party), Stalin hoped to turn the course of history in the direction he personally required.

In order to stop his drive for power, in order to remove him from any position of responsibility, a majority of votes would have been needed. That is why Stalin placed his own people in all key positions with such feverish haste and neutralized those of strong will and honest conviction —that is to say, dangerous people.

The majority is always right; the minority must submit to majority discipline. This Bolshevik Party prejudice was to serve Stalin's purpose countless times.

BATTLE FOR THE THRONE

5

In the fall of 1923 there was trouble in the land. After five years of the people's rule, the economic crisis had not been overcome. The productivity of labor in industry was lower than it had been in 1913. Agriculture was in disarray. The transport system existed in name only. There was a severe shortage of food, housing, and the most essential goods. The value of the currency was shrinking, and discontented workers were going on strike.

The triumvirate of Zinoviev, Kamenev, and Stalin did not know how to cope with these difficulties, and instead of confessing their inability and consulting with party activists, they cracked down harder administratively.

At a plenum of the Central Committee in September 1923, Dzerzhinsky warned the leadership against being dictatorial, abandoning party democracy, forgetting the principle that leaders should be elected, and taking an intolerant attitude toward criticism. The plenum listened seriously to Dzerzhinsky's speech and set up a special commission under his direction.

Trotsky expressed himself in the same spirit, but much more vehemently, in his October 8 letter to the Central Committee. Within a week a group of veteran party members addressed a letter to the Central Committee which has gone down in history as the Letter of the Forty-six. This document, which is full of concern for the fate of the revolution, contains an analysis of the state economy and financial system and the practices of the party leadership.

"The regime established within the party is completely intolerable. It destroys the independence of the party, replacing the party by a recruited bureaucratic apparatus. . . . The situation which has been created is explained by the fact that the regime of dictatorship by a faction within the party, which has in fact emerged since the Tenth Congress, has outlived itself."

The authors of the letter accused the leaders of having lost touch with the party ranks and of pursuing policies that were ruinous for the country. They proposed that an expanded conference of the Central Committee be called without delay. Among the Forty-six was Vladimir Antonov-Ovseyenko, head of the political directorate of the Revolutionary Military Council of the Republic (RMCR). He qualified his endorsement of the letter with the following statement, appended to the letter:

"In essentials I share the views of this appeal. The demand for a direct and sincere approach to all our ills has become so urgent that I entirely support the proposal to call the conference suggested in order to specify practical ways to extricate ourselves from the difficulties that have accumulated."

In the upper echelons the Letter of the Forty-six was perceived as an impudent attack upon the party. A frightened Andrei Bubnov hastened to remove his name, but it was too late. Neither Stalin nor Zinoviev would let such a convenient pretext for political provocation slip by. Stalin and his accomplices were not about to study the letter objectively and engage in an open, comradely discussion. The joint plenum of the Central Committee and Central Control Commission, which was soon convened, branded the authors of the letter factionalists and accused them, along with Trotsky, of "splitting activity." (This was the *kinto* Stalin's favorite tactic: to cry "Stop thief!" as he ran off with the goods.)

There was one especially characteristic touch in this affair. The resolution of the October plenum was not published. The three big party proconsuls refused to make the text of the seditious letter public either.

In the thirties, after he had become sovereign, Stalin killed all the signers of the letter, one after the other. (The letter has not been published in the Soviet Union to this day.) Those who endorsed the unpublished letter were anathematized from all party pulpits as "Trotskyists." However, in late 1923, the Letter of the Forty-six and Trotsky's statements became known to too many party members. The triumvirs had to make a few concessions.

On November 7 Zinoviev publicly agreed, in the pages of *Pravda*, that the present style of leadership was frustrating party democracy. *Pravda* called on all party members to participate actively in a discussion of Zinoviev's article, "The New Tasks of the Party." For three weeks beginning on November 13 *Pravda* published internal party discussion materials. The discussion proved to be so fruitful that by December 5 the Politburo and the Presidium of the Central Control Commission were able to adopt a unanimous resolution at a joint session.

This remarkable document confirmed the principles of collective leadership and freedom of criticism within the party. Known to history as the New Course resolution, it stated, "The leading party bodies must heed the voices of the broad party masses and must not consider every criticism a manifestation of factionalism and thereby cause conscientious and disciplined party members to withdraw into closed circles and fall into factionalism." Calls for "party discipline" in cases where internal party problems were being discussed were acknowledged to be wrong, because that kind of discussion was the inalienable "right and duty of every party member." The Central Committee called for a struggle against "bureaucratic deformations in the party apparatus and in party practices."

There is no need to compare the texts of the Letter of the Forty-six and the Central Committee resolution of December 5, 1923. In spirit and letter they are twins. Isn't that why the text of the resolution was published only once, on December 7 in *Pravda*, and then hidden away for decades? To simplify the task of the throne-room falsifiers of history.

Politburo members themselves were the first to violate this Central Committee resolution. It was one thing to proclaim freedom of criticism but another to tolerate it. The leaders truly abused the confidence of honest revolutionaries. One of the first to fall victim to their deceit was Antonov-Ovseyenko.

Since he was working under Trotsky, chairman of the RMCR, Antonov* was presumably obliged to take the same position as Trotsky. But at a meeting of officials of the army's political directorate, he drafted a resolution in support of the Central Committee and rejected a document presented by opponents of the Central Committee. Antonov felt bound by party discipline and refused to take part in the internal discussion. When he was asked to speak on behalf of the opposition to a meeting at a school of the Central Executive Committee (CEC) of the Soviets, he suggested that Radek or Preobrazhensky be asked instead. When he heard that Zinoviev would speak at the meeting, however, he decided to go argue with the party leader. Antonov went to the meeting along with his aide, a man named Dvorzhets.

*For the sake of brevity the author often reduces the full hyphenated form of the name Antonov-Ovseyenko to "Antonov," as in this passage.—TRANS.

At the meeting Zinoviev behaved like an aristocrat, ridiculed and insulted his opponents, and demanded unconditional obedience to the "line of the Central Committee."

Antonov tried to restrain Dvorzhets, but the young man went ahead and took the floor to blast the arrogant Politburo member. During the intermission Zinoviev sat down next to Dvorzhets. "You spoke like an ensign who graduated under Kerensky." Indeed, Dvorzhets had graduated from a military school and become an ensign under Kerensky, but he had joined the revolution and was later accepted into the party by a direct ruling of the Central Control Commission. He was a registered member of the party committee at the CEC school where the discussion took place that evening.

Soon after that memorable evening, Dvorzhets was called before the Central Control Commission. An adjutant of Antonov's told the head of the political directorate about this and added that Dvorzhets feared arrest.

"Yes, Zinoviev is a cruel and vengeful man," Antonov commented. "He is capable of anything."

Zinoviev decided to destroy the daring debater who had impudently criticized a Politburo member without regard for rank. Dvorzhets was arrested and sent to penal exile for five years. In 1937 he met the fate of millions of others who were no more to Stalin's liking than Zinoviev's. The measures against Dvorzhets in December 1923 were among the first warning signs of the coming terror.

On December 21 Antonov-Ovseyenko submitted a statement to the Central Committee about the discussion at the CEC school, but the Central Committee apparatus was already used to brushing aside such tiresome documents.

On December 27, when Dvorzhets had already been "called to account," Antonov sent a sharply worded letter to the Central Committee defending his subordinate, a party member who had simply exercised his recently proclaimed "right and duty" to discuss internal party matters.

Antonov wrote this letter late at night and in haste.

"We are not courtiers to the throne of party hierarchs!" he hurled in the face of the party brass. Incapable of ruling or leading, they had walled themselves off from the party and were exploiting the prejudice of party discipline—anything to drown out the voices of criticism.

Antonov wrote with anxious alarm that the line of the Central Committee majority and the unending feuds among the leaders were "harmful for the unity of the party and undermine the moral solidity of the army" and the moral authority of the Russian Communist Party within the Comintern.*

"This cannot go on for long. Only one thing remains—to appeal to the

---

*Comintern: the Communist International, worldwide alliance of revolutionary parties founded in 1919, in which the Soviet Communist Party had dominant influence. It was dissolved by Stalin in 1943.—TRANS.

peasant masses who wear the uniforms of Red Army soldiers and call to order the leaders who have gone too far."[32]

Antonov decided to send the letter off at once, but first he read it, early in the morning, to Mikhail Polyak, head of the press department of the political directorate. Polyak tried to deter him, but Antonov decided to do things his way: "I have never acted against my conscience in relation to the party, and I have never been a factionalist," he replied.

It was people like this whom the Stalinists cleared away first of all. Of course it wouldn't do simply to pack Antonov off to a camp right then. Better to limit themselves to the provocation Zinoviev had already organized—accusing Antonov of trying to turn the political directorate into an alleged headquarters for factional struggle against the party.

On January 12, 1924, Antonov was called before a session of the Orgburo. The Gensek hadn't come empty-handed to the meeting. He accused Antonov of factional activity. Stalin's subordinates had prepared special materials "exposing" the head of the political directorate for his attempts to act unilaterally—supposedly he had not informed the Central Committee before calling a conference of party cells in military training institutions. They also charged that the political directorate's circular letter No. 200 had not been cleared with the Central Committee.[33]

These absurd charges could have been refuted only if the hell's kitchen in the Central Committee apparatus had been exposed. The Orgburo passed a resolution, the first point of which repeated these concoctions verbatim. The second point in the resolution was as follows:

"The letter of Comrade Antonov-Ovseyenko to members of the Presidium of the Central Control Commission and the Politburo, dated December 27, 1923, containing a threat directed at the Central Committee to 'call to order the leaders who have gone too far,' is an unheard-of attack that makes it impossible for Comrade Antonov-Ovseyenko to function any longer as head of the political directorate." The resolution of the Orgburo prefigured a similar one by the Politburo, which—we can now see—Stalin already dominated.

A special subcommission of the Central Control Commission (headed by Nikolai Shvernik, one more figure who stood unsinkable for years upon the Kremlin walls) had meanwhile investigated the work of the political directorate and found—nothing criminal! Antonov-Ovseyenko appealed to the next plenum of the Central Committee. At its session on January 15 he analyzed the Orgburo resolution in detail, refuting the charge that he had threatened the Central Committee in writing.

"I consider it the unchallengeable right of a party member to direct the attention of Central Committee members to one or another danger in the party's situation. With my letter I feel that I *fulfilled my duty* as a party member and as head of the political directorate, concerned as I was by the state of affairs in the army and in the party organizations inside the army. Finally, no threat was intended by my letter of December 27 other than to try to modify the *factional moods* among the leaders by bringing to bear the weight of thinking party members through strictly party procedures (such as a conference or a congress)."

At the plenum Antonov-Ovseyenko appealed for elementary justice: "I insist on absolute clarity in the way the question is posed in this case. What is under discussion is the removal of the head of the political directorate, a party member who dared to follow party procedures in speaking against the line of the Central Committee leadership, a line which is harmful for the unity of the party and the moral cohesion of the army.

"I reject with contempt all charges that the political directorate was turned into a factional headquarters by me. No one has demonstrated that, nor could they. Until such time as anything like that is proved, only one thing will be accomplished by removing me, and that is to settle factional accounts before the party congress with a comrade who is too restrained to violate party discipline and is incapable of factional maneuvers."

"I will not be straying from the mark at all," Antonov told the Central Committee members, "to say that a definite tone has been set for this far-reaching campaign by none other than Comrade Stalin."

Antonov was surely not wrong. But he obviously underestimated the strength of those who held the key party positions. Speaking in support of the Orgburo resolution were Molotov, Shvernik, Shkiryatov, and Yaroslavsky. Behind the backs of these servants so anxious to please (they would do their Master many a bloody service in the future) the chief stage director could have remained seated in silence. But Stalin was disturbed by some of the telling points Antonov made in defending himself. So he dropped a few weighty words upon the scale. He repeated the totally unsubstantiated charges about Antonov's refusal to coordinate his work with the Central Committee.

The Antonov-Ovseyenko case moved along smoothly down the conveyor belt. From the Gensek's secretariat to the Politburo, to the Central Control Commission, to the Orgburo, and then to the Central Committee plenum. And the party hierarchs had their way.

The only one who spoke in defense of Antonov was Karl Radek. "A point should be added to the resolution on internal party democracy that would exclude party personnel in the political directorate of the army from participation in the discussion. If Antonov-Ovseyenko had used the apparatus of the political directorate for factional purposes, that would be something else. He should be reprimanded along party lines for the inadmissible tone of his letter. But these are three separate issues and should not be lumped together. Until the investigation into the functioning of the political directorate has been completed it is not correct to remove Antonov-Ovseyenko."

Lashevich spoke several times, viciously "unmasking" Antonov. Bukharin, Tomsky, Dzerzhinsky, and Petrovsky held their tongues. What were they thinking about?

Antonov rushed headlong into battle in the name of party unity. Stalin removed him from his post in the name of the same unity. But that was for public consumption. In fact Stalin could not forgive Antonov for that audacious letter promising to "call to order the leaders who had gone too far." The Gensek quoted these words at the Thirteenth Party Congress a few months later and repeated the crude inventions about Antonov's failure to coordinate with the Central Committee.[34]

Humiliated and slandered, Antonov was sent off on a diplomatic mission to China a couple of months later. "Anton's off to Canton," he said with a bitter smile to close friends who had known him in the underground years by his party name, "Anton." Then they sent him as ambassador to Prague, Kaunas, and Warsaw. In those naïve years troublesome party members were punished simply by "diplomatic exile." There, at their leisure outside the country, they would find time to think things over and decide in their own minds whether the regime of dictatorship by a faction had outlived itself or not.

The conflict between Antonov-Ovseyenko and the leadership group around Stalin and Zinoviev was not a local conflict. It was a cautionary tale revealing the Gensek's destructive and divisive strategy. Stalin played on the Leninist doctrine of party unity. He twisted all the screws of party discipline tighter than ever and drowned out any attempt to criticize the triumvirate. A standard recipe was used to "settle" the conflict. Such recipes from the Master's kitchen would be used for many years by first-class cooks like Molotov, Kaganovich, Shkiryatov, Shvernik, and Yaroslavsky.

During the days of heated political battles (in the fall of 1923 and the spring of 1924) the Gensek was asked a question by Olga Pilatskaya, the widow of Vladimir Zagorsky (killed in a bomb explosion at the Moscow party committee building on September 25, 1919):

"Listen, Koba, explain it to me. What's going on?"

"You want to know, huh? You can't see it for yourself? It's a battle for the throne—that's what."

People like Antonov-Ovseyenko did not wish to participate in that kind of fight. They had not entered into mortal battle against the tsar and the bourgeois Provisional Government for that purpose. They had not made the revolution for the sake of a new monarchy. Antonov saw both the taciturn Stalin and his talkative Politburo colleagues as dangerous usurpers, and he could not remain passive in face of that. (Incidentally, Trotsky in the role of dictator boded no good either. When it came to dictatorial bearing, arrogance, and belief in their own infallibility, Trotsky and Stalin ran neck and neck.)

* * *

In the light of the decades that have passed, one thing can be said for certain: No one has ever thought up anything worse than Stalin's rule, the Stalinshchina. Therefore, regardless of what happened to the other leaders, Stalin should unquestionably have been removed from the leadership, as Lenin suggested in his Testament.

In May 1934, harking back to the events of the previous decade,

Antonov-Ovseyenko wrote: "In the opposition of 1923–1927 I was a conciliator, not an active factionalist. I sought to reconcile Trotsky and Stalin (tried to 'reason' with them). I defended Trotsky because I feared a split in the party (and sought support for my position in what was called Lenin's Testament)."[35]

Why didn't Lenin's comrades carry out his last request?

TACTICS

6

How did he do it? Many volumes have been written on this subject and many more will be. My modest remarks do not pretend to fullness by any means. However, some general conclusions can be drawn about the tactics Stalin used in his struggle for power.

In the Sultan-Galiev case, in the discussion on the national question, and in discussions on the organizational structure of the Central Committee he used intimidation (tacking labels on people, expelling them from the party, having them arrested); he employed stalking horses, took advantage of personal enmities, manipulated Marxist dogmas, and dragged towers of demagogic nonsense rattling around on pseudo-Leninist wheels. And through it all he maintained his insolent self-assurance. An enviable trait.

Another tactic—"filing a countersuit," making countercharges—was one he employed successfully in all stages of his political career.

Stalin had a unique ability to start arguments and inflame debates. For Lenin and his circle, party disputes were a means of arriving at the truth. That was the last thing Stalin was interested in. What interested him in a discussion were any heated outbursts that he could note down and use at a later time as a club or a label to discredit someone.

The Gensek took constant reprisals against oppositionists on the middle and lower levels, criticizing them, dismissing them from their posts, expelling or dispersing them. Thus he isolated the leaders, depriving them of support from the ranks. But for the time being, he did not touch the leaders, especially if they brought grist to his mill. For example, Zinoviev and he agreed on adopting this reassuring formula: "Any criticism of the party line, even so-called left criticism, is at present an objectively Menshevik criticism."[36] A leader like that was of the highest possible value. Stalin could afford to play games, and enter into temporary alliance, with one like that.

But his primary concern was to inflame the feuds and disputes among the leaders. At the Twelfth Party Congress Stalin formed a triumvirate with Kamenev and Zinoviev against Trotsky.

Divide and conquer.

Stalin knew better than anyone how to encourage his rivals to bang their heads together, while himself standing aside—in fact, standing over them.

Sometimes, if the argument assumed special importance, the Gensek would take someone's side, pretending sympathy and thus recruiting one more supporter.

Such demonstrations of concern alternated with his "high principles" act. He would juggle flowery quotations. When necessary he would be smitten with Russian patriotism. Or he would launch a noisy campaign for purity in the party ranks. Crude threats would alternate with subtly calculated insinuations.

Stalin's tactical palette had a rich range of colors. He used them with skill, blending the pigments inventively to suit the occasion.

When he decided to turn against his partners, Zinoviev and Kamenev, he first secured himself the support of Rykov and Bukharin. When the question arose of Lenin's successor as premier, the Gensek persuaded the Politburo that the Russian peasants would not accept a Jew in that post. And so the Russian Rykov became premier. Later in 1924 Stalin made certain cautious moves against Kamenev and Zinoviev, clumsily trying to discredit some of their theoretical pronouncements. They decided to strike back. A special conference of important party officials, with the Politburo and Central Committee in attendance, condemned Stalin's maneuvers, but he once again offered to resign. And once again his offer was not accepted.

In 1925 Zinoviev was in Leningrad, and Kamenev could no longer effectively support him. Stalin managed to recruit the head of the Moscow party committee, Nikolai Uglanov, to his group. Meanwhile, he kept harassing Zinoviev's supporters in Leningrad and provoking them into premature confrontations in an attempt to weaken Zinoviev's position. Stalin carefully prepared the split in the triumvirate.

Divide and conquer.

Suddenly he made a 180-degree turn. Just before the Fourteenth Party Congress he proposed a truce to Zinoviev and Kamenev. But at the congress? His all-out attack is well known.

At that congress the plan for the reorganization of the Secretariat proposed at Kislovodsk came up. The initiator of the plan was said to have been Bukharin. But at that point the Gensek wanted to use Bukharin against Zinoviev, so everyone was denounced for having been a leader of the antiparty Kislovodsk grouping—Zinoviev, Kamenev, Lashevich, Sokolnikov—everyone but Bukharin. Stalin energetically defended Bukharin against Zinoviev.

Divide and conquer.

Another example of Stalin's indefatigable virtuosity in the use of tactics in political infighting came at the Fifteenth Congress. Molotov was giving the report on agriculture—not very coherently, it must be understood—when suddenly, to everyone's surprise, including Molotov's, Stalin took the floor and criticized the report. Stagecraft? Of course. But the Gensek had not warned Molotov, and poor Vyacheslav was thrown into confusion. Meanwhile, Stalin achieved his aims: to test Molotov's loyalty and obedience once again, and to muddy the waters on the question of the party's rural policy in order to see what new differences he might stir up. Molotov went home completely distraught and complained to his wife, Polina Zhemchuzhina, who quotes him as saying at that time: "Stalin will not abide by our mutual decisions. He always messes everything up, and we have a terrible time trying to straighten it all out afterwards. We had gone over everything and agreed to it beforehand. Then he had to get up and attack me."

To organize a provocation and then withdraw into the shadows, to dump the blame on others, to present himself as an "unbending Leninist," this was Stalin's typical pattern in the first decade after the October revolution. And with a few variations (such as having people shot) he stuck to that pattern to the very end.

Throughout his struggle for supreme power in the party he revealed one valuable quality as a political tactician. Even in the most critical situations he saw several steps further ahead in the various possible lines of play than did his rivals.

Through these demagogic and organizational devices, Stalin won the support of "the party swamp," the inert majority at the congresses. He mastered the difficult science of maneuvering among the other party leaders. Gradually, without their noticing it, the hotheaded and none-too-bright Comrade Koba had turned into a tough old wolf.

At the Twelfth Party Congress, in April 1923, Stalin openly threatened Valerian Osinsky, a prominent party member and an associate of Lenin's. Twenty years later, when preparing the fifth volume of his works for publication, Stalin deleted the sentence "Comrade Osinsky should have mercy on himself." By then, of course, Osinsky was gone, a victim of Stalin's terror.

Stalin did not only threaten people. As far back as the twenties, he successfully engaged in political murder. For example, his peculiar insistence in 1925 that Mikhail Frunze, the new commissar of war, have an unnecessary operation. During the operation the patient died. Frunze's personal physician, Pyotr Mandryka, had tried to save his patient. He pleaded that if the operation was performed, they should at least *not* use a general anesthetic—under no circumstances was a general anesthetic called for. Stalin removed the doctor from the case.

On October 31, 1925, Frunze died on the operating table, of heart failure. He had been given a double dose of chloroform. The autopsy showed that the ulcer, which supposedly required surgery, had scarred over. When Frunze's wife realized he had been murdered, she committed suicide. At Frunze's burial in Red Square on November 4, Joseph Stalin spoke of his "boundless grief." "Perhaps this is exactly the way, so easily and simply, that all the old comrades should go to their graves."[37]

Five years later the surgeon Sergei Fyodorov was talking with Yevgeny Ivanovsky, assistant head of the Kremlin medical services.

"The Frunze operation, you know—that wasn't necessary. I was categorically opposed to it. All the indications were against an operation for the commissar. But they went ahead and did him in."

There was quite a lot of talk like that. Enough to point to a definite conclusion. People close to top party circles had no doubt that Frunze's death was a political act to get him out of the way. A brave (or foolhardy?) writer, Boris Pilnyak, wrote an account of the commissar's death, in which Frunze was called an army commander and Stalin figured as "the most important of the three" top leaders of the party. On the orders of the "most important" leader, the army commander was placed on the operating table and died from an overdose of chloroform.

Who suggested the details of the plot for Boris Pilnyak's *Story of the Unextinguished Moon?* Pilnyak was an acquaintance of Yakov Agranov, a member of the collegium of the GPU. In 1938 Stalin was to have them both killed—the writer and the GPU man. Under interrogation Pilnyak admitted that Agranov had told him about the murder of Frunze, and confirmation of this was found in Agranov's dossier. What did they do with them? How they must have tortured them!

The fact is that Pilnyak had other sources as well. An old party member whom we shall call G——ov was distressed by Pilnyak's story, and he asked the writer, "How could it happen that you would write such a slanderous thing?"

"I was first told about Frunze's death by Aleksandr Konstantinovich Voronsky. The details were given me by Karl Radek."

The next time G——ov saw Radek he reproached him: "Karlusha, what did you do that for?"

"Well, you know, everything's fair when you're in a war."

In later years medical murder became a favorite tactical weapon of the Gensek's, but during the twenties he was obliged for the most part to use less direct means.

* * *

There are all kinds of claques—concert-hall claques, theater claques, opera claques. Stalin organized a party claque. He had already surrounded himself with one in the early twenties. It served him at Central Committee plenums, party conferences, and congresses. These obliging fellows could disrupt the speech of any party leader, be it Trotsky himself. And Leon Davidovich certainly knew that.

In 1925 Stalin promulgated his theory about building socialism in one country. This coincided with debates about the New Economic Policy (NEP) and the organizational policies of the Central Committee at the Fourteenth Congress, in December.

Krupskaya took the floor. She had a thing or two to say about the Gensek's escapades. Krupskaya spoke with great concern about the situation in the party and touched on, among other things, the "theory" that the majority is invariably correct. Stalin's claque made it impossible for Lenin's widow to continue. Someone venomously congratulated Trotsky from the floor on his new ally, Nadezhda Konstantinovna Krupskaya. She lost track of what she was trying to say.[38]

Kamenev proved to be sturdier. "Let's agree on something," he said to the wild-eyed hecklers. "If you have orders to interrupt me, why don't you just say so? . . . You aren't going to make me stop talking no matter how loudly a handful of comrades keep shouting."

In conclusion Kamenev, who had spoken out clearly against the Leader's new theory, courageously repeated his main point:

"Stalin cannot perform the function of uniting the Bolshevik general staff. . . . We are against the theory of one-man rule. We are against creating a sole Leader."[39]

A hush momentarily fell over the meeting hall, the way it does when an audience has been moved by the speaker's remarks and is about to burst into an ovation. But it was for oratorical flights like this that the Gensek had carefully prepared his claque.

"Nonsense! Not true!"

"Stalin, Stalin!"

"Long live the Russian Communist Party. Hurrah!"

"The party comes first."

"Long live Comrade Stalin!"

And the claque brought the audience to its feet.

"The delegates rise and salute Comrade Stalin," was how the stenographer recorded it.[40]

A triumph for the art of the claque, no?

Here is another example. At the joint plenum of the Central Committee and the Central Control Commission in July-August 1927, Stalin ridiculed Kamenev and then advanced some foolish arguments against an article by Zinoviev. The Gensek was not afraid to clown. The claque would laugh at the right places, and it would not forget, when the author paused at the appropriate point, to yell "Right!" or "Shame!"

Stalin likened Trotsky to Clemenceau, at which point individual soloists in the chorus emitted dutiful howls: "A comic-opera Clemenceau."

Now the Gensek begs forgiveness. He is obliged, you see, to "say a few words about Zinoviev's attacks against Stalin."

"Please do!" the voices ring out.

The claque knows its job.

Then Stalin comes to the place where he says the opposition is pursuing the policy of an open split in the Comintern.

"Right!" the chorus responds.

The Gensek quotes from the resolution of the Tenth Congress written by Lenin which provides for measures against factionalists, up to and including expulsion from the party.

"Implement it right here and now," shouts the claque.

"Wait, comrades, don't be hasty," Stalin interjects.[41]

Quite a show, isn't it?

As time passed a smoothly functioning system of claques for base-level party meetings, bureau meetings, committee meetings, conferences, plenums, and any other party gathering was organized. The claque could do everything—propose or reject a candidate, approve or block a proposal, build someone up to the skies, or drop him into the pit. With, of course, the approval of the higher-ups. Directing the claque became an art, in fact a science. (Why do the court historians conceal the name of the founder of that science?)

In addition to hired hecklers, the Gensek had speakers ready at hand to oppose his rivals at any congress. He was always able to find monkeys to pull his chestnuts out of the hottest fire. And in the corridors, during breaks in sessions, Central Committee personnel strolled up and down. Courteous and attentive, they would show elderly delegates the way to the lunchroom or any other place and eavesdrop on their conversations. Maintaining Stalin's ever-vigilant watch. The electronic age had not yet arrived.

The technology for preparing and conducting a congress, and all the technical and tactical devices, were worked out in the bureaucratic offices over a period of years and subsequently perfected in field tests under the supervision of the Master himself. Those were some of the ways he managed to do it.

LAST RUNGS OF THE LADDER

7

"I will not permit a coup!" declared Feliks Dzerzhinsky at the joint plenum of the Central Committee and Central Control Commission in July 1926, in reference to the feuding within the party. The dispute at that time involved the newly formed United Opposition, which brought Trotsky's supporters from the 1923–24 period together with what Stalin called the New Opposition, or Leningrad Opposition, headed by Zinoviev and Kamenev, which had surfaced in late 1925. The United Opposition, led by the three Politburo members Trotsky, Zinoviev, and Kamenev, confronted a Politburo majority consisting of Stalin, Bukharin, Rykov, and Tomsky.

Within a few hours of his speech Dzerzhinsky was dead. Was it just a heart attack? No one had time to tell him, "Alas, Comrade Feliks, the coup has already taken place." Long ago, the young Dzerzhinsky, future chairman of the Cheka, had taken a vow to fight against evil. Yet few others did so much to help the triumph of evil as dear "iron-hard Feliks."

In 1927 Stalin began the organizational consolidation of his coup. At the Fifteenth Congress in December the Gensek removed seventy-five active oppositionists from leading party bodies and expelled many of them from the party. Altogether he purged the party of about two thousand members at that time. After the expulsion of the leaders of the so-called United Opposition, Stalin put on a little show at the Central Committee plenum immediately following the congress.

"I think that until the recent period there were conditions that placed the party in the situation of needing me in this post as a person who was fairly rough in his dealings, to constitute a certain antidote to the opposition. Now the opposition has not only been smashed; it has been expelled from the party. And still we have the recommendation of Lenin, which in my opinion ought to be put into effect. Therefore I ask the plenum to relieve me of the post of general secretary. I assure you, comrades, that from this the party only stands to gain."[42]

What an actor. And what a deep mind.

The plenum of course re-elected him unanimously as Gensek. Do you think any of them were tired of living?

That year was the turning point in Stalin's career. He was so confident of his carefully pruned Central Committee that he indulged himself with a reference to Lenin's Testament as a kind of anachronism. This stage-show plenum, performed according to Stalin's script with totally dependable actors, extras, and prompters, opened new horizons for the Gensek. He was not yet the Master, but he was already the Leader.

By then Stalin had fully matured as a party demagogue, with all the skills of an experienced side-show barker and double-talker. He had learned how to fool the ranks on his own, without assistance, and to oppose his rivals successfully, confronting such accomplished speakers as Trotsky and Zinoviev. His favorite oratorical device, which he learned in the seminary, was the question-and-answer method, the stereotyped question followed by a stereotyped answer. This served him reliably in giving his "own" speeches and during debates, when he had to rebut critical assaults by his opponents "off the cuff." His demagogic oratory had a narrowly pragmatic purpose. It helped him up the rungs of power. The great utilitarian attached demagogy to his wagon along with everything else. Stalin showed himself to be the Master of Abrupt Turns and Unexpected Maneuvers. Something he had made ironic fun of yesterday would become his hobby-horse today, his chief propaganda slogan. But whatever his main slogan of the day, he always used it as a whip against his opponents. Expertly wielding the whip-slogan, the Gensek would drive his comrades of yesterday out of the mansions of party power, to the howling and baying of his superbly trained claque.

Let us look at another one of his traits. He taught the party never to rest on its laurels, never to be satisfied with what had been accomplished. If he had dealt a successful blow today, he immediately began to prepare the next blow for the morrow. He had set the proper moral atmosphere leading up to and at the Fifteenth Congress, in December 1927, and so in early 1928 he ventured to take open administrative and repressive measures against his chief rivals. Trotsky and his family were exiled to Alma-Ata. Approximately thirty leading "Trotskyists" were banished from Moscow. Zinoviev and Kamenev were sent to Kaluga.

Such measures were unheard of in the party. They should be seen in historical perspective as a rough, early rehearsal for the mass repressions of the future. As a test, Stalin tossed this stone in the pond and watched from the shore to see what disturbances would result. There: the waves had reached the shore, and zero, absolutely nothing, had happened. It had worked! So it was possible to get rid of rivals by this method too.

In the summer of 1928 Bukharin at last realized that Stalin was leading the party up a blind alley, that he was planning to exterminate Lenin's comrades in arms, starting with the Politburo members he found most obnoxious. Bukharin at that point sought an understanding with Kamenev. His life too was in danger. Allies had to be found and a campaign worked out against the cruel usurper. But things never went beyond words and good intentions. Their bloc was never forged. They didn't have the necessary character.

Meanwhile, word of Bukharin's conversations with Kamenev reached the hairy ears of the Gensek. After all, his eavesdropping system had been in operation for years. At critical moments in Stalin's career action always preceded words. He chose the Moscow party committee, headed by Uglanov, and the Comintern, headed by Bukharin, as the objects of attack. When Bukharin, as chairman of the Comintern Executive Committee, presented his theses to the Sixth Comintern Congress in July 1928, certain figures arose to "amend" those theses, following Stalin's bidding. Someone started circulating rumors about the "Bukharinist deviation." In whispers at first, then louder.

After loading Bukharin down with Comintern work, Stalin relieved him of the tasks of editing *Pravda* and the magazine *Bolshevik*. That is, he deprived him of another source of support within the country. Now any failures of the international Communist movement he could attribute to "Bukharchik" and thus reduce his authority in the party to less than nothing. After the Sixth Comintern Congress all the forces of the party were mobilized to "expose the hostile essence of Bukharin's counterrevolutionary pseudo-scientific theories." That was the name of the latest witch-hunt campaign. The previous head of the Comintern, Grigory Zinoviev, had experienced the same kind of thing.

However, Bukharin—either because he was used to it or because his inherently buoyant nature saved him—continued to work on theoretical questions. On September 30, 1928, he published his "Notes of an Economist," in which he emphasized the great importance of the peasantry for the country's economy. But Stalin continued to weave the web of intrigue around Bukharin and his comrades.

Another leader of the so-called Rights was Mikhail Tomsky, who then headed the All-Union Central Council of Trade Unions. Stalin started a campaign against Tomsky, using all his power as Gensek at the head of the party apparatus, and all the methods he had tested out in years of political infighting. One after another, he removed some of Tomsky's trusted aides, reassigned others, and sent still others to the provinces. Then he began to undermine him theoretically. For starters, he accused Tomsky of "undemocratic methods of administration" and other imaginary sins.

Stalin opened up a decisive battle against Tomsky at the Eighth All-Union Congress of Trade Unions. He had his own people controlling the congress and elected his own people to the presiding committee of the trade-union council. Tomsky was also re-elected to the presiding committee, but not to the post of chairman.

As he dealt with Bukharin and Tomsky separately, Stalin took care to camouflage his actions. No one must think that the Gensek wanted to do away with rivals. Oh no, he was conducting a principled struggle against "Right-Wing Communists" in the Moscow committee. He prompted Uglanov's subordinates to protest the "dictatorship" of Uglanov as first secretary of the Moscow committee. Stalin, it turned out, favored control over party leaders from below, and "self-criticism." Once again he cried "Stop thief!" as he ran off with the stolen goods. And what he stole was power, while he hid behind the broad backs, the hundred silent and obedient backs, of the Central Committee he called "Leninist."

Who could have guessed in 1928 what was behind Stalin's noisy campaign against the "Rights"? That label was pasted on Bukharin, Rykov, and Tomsky for good. It stuck so well that thirty years later Grigory Petrovsky had to cry shame to his comrades: "Drop all this talk about the 'Right Opposition.' All it was, was some fellows who, unlike us old fools, understood that they were dealing with an *Ethiope.*"

* * *

Stalin devoted the fall of 1928 to the struggle against Uglanov. In mid-October, at a session of the Moscow committee, a report by Uglanov was for the first time not approved by the comrades. On October 19 Stalin led a round of denunciations against the Rights at a plenum of the Moscow committee. A month later he lambasted the "Right deviation" at a plenum of the Central Committee. But he didn't take sharp organizational measures against the deviationists. An "ideological struggle" had to be waged against them. On the other hand, "district activists do have the right to remove their secretaries."[43] See what the Gensek was driving at?

When the campaign against the Rights reached its culmination, Tomsky, Rykov, and Bukharin decided to submit their resignations. Stalin could not foresee everything, but he knew how to maneuver, when to retreat in time, and when to seize the moment for a counterblow. He persuaded the Right leaders not to leave their posts. This was a unique situation in which they could have united their forces and come out against Stalin, exposing him as the demagogue and factionalist he was. Instead, the Rights signed a joint declaration with Stalin on the unity of the Politburo. Tomsky, Rykov, and Bukharin chose the tactic of doomed rabbits and remained true to that tactic to the end, showing the world their unique capacity for compromise with their Strangler.

Stalin could now draw up the balance sheet. Bukharin and Tomsky had been exposed, their authority undermined, their supporters in Moscow crushed. Now the "errant" comrades could be forgiven.

You can accuse Stalin of whatever you like, but not of insufficient perfidy. Sometimes it seems that the web of intrigue he wove was too complex and sticky. Wouldn't two or three well-aimed blows have been enough to crush the gullible, orthodox Leninists he had to deal with? Instead, Stalin dealt dozens of short jabs, alternating with "conciliatory" acts. For years, slowly, savoring every moment, he gradually reduced all his opponents on the ladder of power.

In 1927 Stalin visited Leningrad. After the so-called crushing of the so-called New Opposition a change was being made in the Leningrad leadership. In December 1925, Sergei Kirov was put in charge of the Leningrad provincial committee, having arrived at the Fourteenth Congress as first secretary of the Communist Party of Azerbaidzhan. Now, two years later, the Gensek was inspecting the work of his local appointee. The active party membership was convened for Stalin's arrival. The Moscow leader was greeted coldly: he had never enjoyed much popularity in Leningrad.

Late in the evening they had supper at Kirov's apartment. Pyotr Chagin, an old friend of Kirov's and former editor of *Bakinsky Rabochy* (Baku Worker), was also there. He was then working in Leningrad. They ate Caucasus-style. Stalin stuck bits of fish on a skewer and roasted this fish shashlik over the hearth. They drank dry wine.

After supper Stalin lit his pipe. The conversation turned to the difficulties in the party and the situation of the party in general. They reminisced about Lenin. "Lenin's death was a terrible loss to the party," Kirov commented sadly. "We have to close ranks and try to replace collectively what we lost in Ilyich."

Stalin kept walking around the room, as was his habit, listening in silence.

"Yes, of course, the Central Committee, the collective. That's all very well. But the Russian muzhik is tsarist. He wants only one." With these words he raised his index finger. Silence followed. His interlocutors were stunned.[44]

"Is it possible to seize power in a party of one million, full of revolutionary traditions?" Stalin asked this rhetorical question in polemicizing against Trotsky at a session of the Comintern Executive Committee on September 27, 1927. He answered his own question. Not in words but in deeds.

He alone, Stalin, could assume the burdensome mission of giving the "Russian muzhik" what he wanted. All around him were such untalented and spineless intellectuals. But with Comrade Stalin there, the Russian muzhik was obviously in luck. Stalin responded to the imperious command of the times first by usurping power in the party and then, in the last years of the decade, by seizing power in the country as a whole. Using methods of resourceful intrigue, bulldog stubbornness, and unrelenting extortion, he had reached the seat of the general secretary. Then, with the same methods, he turned the Gensek's chair into the most important post in the Central Committee apparatus. All he had to do after that was turn the Gensek's chair into the autocrat's throne—in the name of fulfilling the muzhik's longing.

The man who carried out Thermidor in Russia referred to Trotsky's charges of Thermidorian degeneration as "nonsensical agitation." Those were the very words the Gensek used in August 1927.[45] He himself did not engage in stupid agitation. With the candor of a sovereign, he referred to the arrest of "Trotskyist cadres" in November 1928 as a measure that could be carried out easily and simply. A measure that was on the order of the day.[46] Thermidor had begun.

* * *

When you review Stalin's ten-year progress toward sole power, you come to the conclusion that history was working in his favor. The truly massive people's revolutions in France, Germany, England, Italy, and Spain unavoidably drowned under a powerful wave of counterrevolution. The same thing happened to the Russian revolution. On the crest of the muddy wave rode Stalin. But someone else could have come to the surface just as well.

Lenin's doctrine of the dictatorship of the proletariat contributed to the usurpation of power by a dictator more than anything else. At the Twelfth Congress the Gensek pointed to the possibility of cracks appearing in the proletarian dictatorship. In fact the dictatorship was born with an organic defect. Over the ensuing years Stalin simply worked on that defect, enlarged the crack, until he could slip through and seize the throne he so longed for.

Lenin's milieu proved to be favorable soil for the growth of thistles. Among the heroes of the revolution no one could be found capable of transgressing party prejudices and uniting the trusty comrades against the usurper. As for the careerists, who only played at politics, Stalin was quite content with them. Some of them hoped to use the situation for their own personal "tsarist" ambitions. Together—the "pure ones" and those who were not so pure—they constituted an uncoordinated force. They all preferred grand projects for the future, discussions, and exhortations. Words, words, words.

Lenin suffered from the same shortcomings. He saw that his personal creation, the party, was drowning in careerist scum and foam, but he took no action, trusting in the cleansing power of the "working-class layer" and the veterans of the revolution. What was this, the myopia of the intellectual? Or something else? He feared Stalin, hid from him, wrote Shklovsky a tale of woe (there was nothing he could do), whispered with his trusted comrades, and in his Testament referred to the Gensek's rudeness and disloyalty. Words, words, words.

As party leader Lenin was fairly often unscrupulous about the means he chose. But in relation to Stalin he showed a strange permissiveness and delicacy. The objective reasons that gave rise to the Stalinshchina follow a logical order. But what about the subjective reasons?

THE KREMLIN BIRDMAN

8

Stalin became *Stalin* not only because of historical circumstances. He was an exceptional individual. Pugnacious, crude, intrinsically anti-intellectual, he seemed inferior not only to Trotsky, Kamenev, Zinoviev, and Bukharin but to hundreds of other outstanding figures in the party as well. They had substantial advantages over him: education, oratorical skill, culture. But he surpassed them all in strength of character and fixed striving for a single goal. Stalin possessed a unique complex of the most aggressive qualities.

There was animal cunning and craftiness. Overpowering insolence. And cynicism, absolute cynicism. Also contempt for the individual and for the human race. And refined cruelty. Without these qualities he would never have succeeded in becoming sole ruler.

Still, we have not exhausted the wealth of Stalin's nature.

* * *

"Look at the first puddle you come to, and in it you'll find a vermin which surpasses and eclipses all the other vermin in its venomousness." This observation by the nineteenth-century Russian satirist Saltykov-Shchedrin found unexpected confirmation in research by the American biologist Rose. He made an interesting discovery. Take a group of tadpoles inhabiting a pool. If at a certain point one proves to be larger than the others, it *alone* will grow and put on weight. The rest will stop growing and eventually die off. The naturalist tried replacing one-third of the water in the pool every day with fresh water, but nothing changed. The larger specimen was plainly oppressing the rest through some secretion, some hidden substance it gave off.

* * *

Butyrka prison's transfer unit was in a church building on the prison grounds. In our cell there were 150 prisoners waiting to be sent to the destruction camps, most of them political prisoners—"spies," "wreckers," or "traitors." Only a handful of actual criminals. Repeaters. In the prison they were boss. Under the patronage of the authorities.

Late one night a group of bandits (robbery, murder) was brought in from death row. They had been pardoned by the Supreme Soviet. That kind it was all right to pardon.

The top man in the gang was still young, but he was already a potent ruler of the herd. All it took was a few swift, purposeful strides and an imperious look from his narrowed eyes for the suckers immediately to vacate the bunks in the corner by the window, taking places on the floor.

Out in the world it was 1944, winter, but I didn't see it. Behind me was a long and exhausting investigation, the Lubyanka, and solitary at Lefortovo prison. Soon we would be transported by stages to the camps.

In the center of the large cell was a board table; along the wall, a solid row of bunks. Everyone was lying down, talking in half whispers. Soon they'd be bringing lunch, a ladleful of warm, grayish swill for each of us. Several prisoners didn't feel like lying down. I too was walking around the table, wondering which camp I'd end up in. In front of me the criminal leader was measuring his steps. He had been circling the table since around daybreak, with his head lowered and his hands irritably clasped behind him. Suddenly he turned and came right at me. I didn't have time to avoid him. He looked me straight in the eye and came down hard on my foot. Instantly the space around the table emptied. And now the bandit walked there by himself, in proud solitude, circling the opposite way from the one we had been going.

And it all happened without a word.

* * *

Joseph Dzhugashvili got his start in his homeland, Transcaucasia, but neither in Tiflis, Baku, nor Batum was he able to get along. The local Bolsheviks very quickly saw through this intriguer and careerist with criminal leanings. They steered clear of him.

So Koba placed his bets on Lenin.

The "marvelous Georgian" found a way into the party leader's heart. Shaumyan, Bogdan Knunyants, Orakhelashvili, Makharadze—none of them warned Lenin. The party would pay dearly for their excessive delicacy.

Here were two leaders aiming at different goals: Lenin, working to make a revolution; Koba, out for himself. For him, revolution meant the chance to avenge himself on society for treating him as a pariah. And a way to slake his thirst for power.

Their methods also differed. Stalin used intrigue, provocation, and theft. He stepped on all who stood in his way on the road to power and crushed them—both enemies and those "on his side."

Just like that bandit in Butyrka.

Among the professional revolutionaries, a professional criminal muscled his way in.

* * *

The endless, wordy disputes with which party life was filled in the twenties had no effect on the Gensek. The Russian Social Democrats and orthodox Leninists were incorrigible arguers. In the early twenties debates thundered at every party meeting, plenum, conference, or congress. It was the same in the Central Committee. Lenin himself was an inexhaustible debater. In general it's hard to imagine a more talkative party. In this respect the Bolsheviks left such lovers of verbal wrangling as the French far behind.

Against such a background Stalin's ability to *keep quiet* seems fantastic. The taciturnity which Stalin worked on for decades became a telling weapon. It helped him win more than one political battle.

For Trotsky, Stalin was just the biggest wheel in the bureaucratic machine. But this is a one-sided assessment, merely a quantitative one, so to speak. After Lenin's death, only Stalin knew what to do and how to do it. And he knew it long before the leader's demise. His animal instinct told him: the Kremlin had the smell of *power*.

Nevertheless this amazing monster grew up under Lenin's protective wing—a monster programmed to seize power. And Stalin unswervingly followed this program, devoting all his colossal energy and refined adaptability to it.

Stalin was a genius, if that word is applicable to political brigandage. A genius at behind-the-scenes maneuvers, a man of satanic cunning. No "gray blur" or blockhead could have woven the complex webs of his Kremlin intrigues. Nor just a paranoiac.

One historian has aptly noted that honest zealots, heroes inspired by ideas, make revolutions. But the fruits of their victories are gathered by slick operators. In Russia the supreme operator was Stalin.

No one stopped him; no one seriously tried. Like nightingales they spouted forth, the golden-tongued orators at congresses and conferences. But one branch won't hold more than one singing nightingale. Suddenly so many of them were sent flying. Where had all the nightingales gone? They didn't know that the one who broke off their lyrical trilling would later pluck their feathers as well. And, later still, would set them out in little cage-cells and crush the life out of them one by one. And he would do that, the Kremlin birdman, while his pitiless palace guard kept up a steady drumroll. No one would hear those naïve trillings any more.

JOSEPH THE BUILDER

II

THE PEASANT FIGHTER

1

Ten years had passed since the October revolution, and Russia still lagged noticeably behind the advanced capitalist countries. It had become awkward simply to cite the wartime ruin and dislocation of 1914–20. Something had to be built. But what and how? The New Economic Policy had saved the country from starvation and revived economic life. In Lenin's conception, the NEP was supposed to hasten the development of heavy industry and a socialized agriculture. Stalin, however, was not interested in a scientific search for a solution. In early 1928 he saw that the better-off peasants, whom from then on he called kulaks, had become a force to contend with; they were the main suppliers of agricultural goods. In late 1927 a severe grain shortage had made itself felt. The peasants were in no hurry to sell their surplus grain, hoping for high prices in the spring. The so-called oppositionists, back in the summer of 1927, had proposed that the grain be taken by force. But the Politburo had not agreed to that measure. At the Fifteenth Party Congress, in December 1927, the Gensek himself had spoken in favor of a moderate agrarian policy.

But no sooner had the congress ended and the party purged itself of the Trotskyist-Zinovievist opposition than Stalin sent orders to the local areas: fulfill the grain procurement plan in the shortest possible time by any means necessary. The recommendations of the "oppositionists" came in handy after all. Stalin's directives untied the hands of the local party functionaries. To preserve their power, they now could—in fact, had to—take exceptional measures. In issuing this order on January 6, 1928, Stalin was already acting as the Supreme Leader (Vozhd), ranking higher than the Central Committee itself and having the power to change party policy drastically by his own unilateral decision.

Stalin's historic trip to the provinces dates from this time. But no, he didn't visit a single village or meet with a single peasant. He went to Novosibirsk, Barnaul, and Omsk, gave the party secretaries the word to get going, and warned them in advance, just in case, that liberalism would be punished. With that he left. It was truly a historic visit. No second appearance of the Supreme Leader among the people is known to history.

A wave of violence and confiscation swept the villages. But it soon became clear that terror would not bring in more grain or win the peasants' confidence. It only worsened the agricultural crisis. By summer Stalin sounded the retreat. He announced that administrative pressure, "violations of revolutionary legality" (read: expropriations), and repression were undesirable and harmful. The Gensek promised the peasants that indus-

55

trial goods would be brought to them and procurement prices for grain would be increased in expectation of a good harvest. A resolution to that effect was passed at the Central Committee plenum held in July.

A new zigzag. And you can't tell at first which hypostasis of the Gensek is being manifested now—the bully? or the huckster? All this, of course, had happened before, under another tsar. Then it had been called the policy of "the spice cake and the whip," i.e., carrot and stick.

Winter came again; only a meager flow of grain was registered; and they returned to the policy of the whip. The Central Committee fired off a series of ominous directives. By this time many kulaks had sold off their property, and the rest had cut back on the amount of land under crops. And so the second round of expropriations did not produce much grain either. In the spring, things came to a complete standstill. There was no grain, no food. Ration cards appeared in the cities, harbingers of famine.

The setbacks didn't sober Stalin up. He cast about and came up with a solution, so he thought—total and immediate collectivization.

In 1927 the Fifteenth Party Congress recommended that collective farms not be introduced hastily, but that individual farming by poor and middle peasants be aided by all possible means. All subsequent party decisions confirmed this approach, until the spring of 1929. The Gensek himself had spoken quite clearly on this point. On the eve of the celebration of the tenth anniversary of the revolution, on November 5, 1927, Stalin had assured a foreign workers' delegation that collectivization of agriculture would be carried out gradually by measures of an economic, financial, cultural, and political nature.[47]

Now it was, Pick up the whip and flog the balky old plow horse. The original five-year plan for collectivization, which was modest and thus realistic, was discarded as a useless scrap of paper. March on, with never a backward look, on to total collectivization!

Analyzing the financial and economic situation in the country, Moshe Frumkin, the deputy commissar of finance, informed a Politburo meeting that the policy of all-out collectivization and forced confiscation of grain had already reduced the area under cultivation. This policy was working against our interests; it was undermining the New Economic Policy, which Lenin had intended for a prolonged period.

Stalin came down furiously on Frumkin: "Get that crybaby out of that job!" Rykov, Bukharin, and Tomsky left the meeting in protest of Stalin's administrative caprice. Nevertheless, they signed a statement affirming the unity of the Politburo.

Stalin continued to ram through his line, no matter what.

In a classic case of wishful thinking, the Gensek proclaimed the crisis-filled year of 1929 "the Year of the Great Change." If we set this noisy proclamation against the actual statistics—7.6 percent of peasant households collectivized, representing 3.6 percent of the cultivated area—the only thing left of the "Great Change" is a great fanfare.

But the mad dash for collectivization had begun. If one province vowed to complete its collectivization by the autumn of 1930, the neighboring one would promise the Central Committee to carry out the party's orders by the summer of 1930. Many provincial chiefs and even the heads of the republics reached the finish line by spring 1930, informing Stalin immediately of their feat.

The late Boris Norilsky, author of the short novel *Black and White*, has given a description (based on documentary evidence) of the techniques, plain as porridge, that were used to accomplish total collectivization. Here is how Comrade Myakishev, deputy chairman of the local GPU, instructs Mikhail Sedoi in these techniques. Sedoi is the party official empowered to collectivize the village of Belyaevka.

"You're carrying out collectivization; I'm putting in the passport system. With Belyaevka we've decided things this way: anyone who doesn't show up on your list shows up on mine, and let them weep for their passports. So don't go busting a gut; just give me a whisper and zap!—they're mine. A hundred percent for you and a hundred percent for me. One hundred plus one hundred makes two hundred. Got it?"

For the peasants the highly touted "victory" of the collective farm system proved to be a terrible misfortune—it brought ruin, degradation, and millions of deaths. It was one of the sharpest political about-faces ever. Orders were to "implant" not only collective farms and state farms but even communes everywhere. Implant—that was precisely the term Stalin used in December 1929.[48]

The peasants began to hide their grain and slaughter their cattle and poultry.

One great groan engulfed the villages.

And there was less and less bread to eat in the country.

Another war-ravaged winter was approaching, and Stalin was forced again to retreat. The new zigzag—I've lost count of the number—was called "Dizzy with Success." That was the title of an article the Gensek published in *Pravda* in March 1930. Some comrades, it seemed, had misunderstood the Central Committee's instructions and had improperly tried to force the pace of collectivization, disregarding the necessary voluntary principle.

Stalin's article was just a theatrical gesture. Personally he had no regrets, especially since local leaders were blamed for the "excesses." The Gensek was not about to change his bloodthirsty policies, not one bit. Ten years would pass and Stalin would carry out the same kind of pillaging raid on the peasants of the Baltic region, western Byelorussia, and the western Ukraine after they "voluntarily" swore allegiance to his crown.* And he gave the usual name to that campaign of extermination—"collectivization."

*After the Hitler-Stalin pact and Germany's invasion of Poland in September 1939, the Soviet Union annexed the Polish-held territories of western Byelorussia and the western Ukraine, as well as the Baltic states of Estonia, Lithuania, and Latvia.—TRANS.

Similarly, after the great war of 1941–45, which to his own surprise Stalin was to win, he would sweep through the neighboring lands with the relentless broom of wholesale collectivization. And sweep those countries clean of abundant harvests, along with their freedom.

In the new society, after all, who needs *that?*

Meanwhile, back in 1930, in order to give force and effect to his article "Dizzy with Success," Stalin decreed that local officials should be tried for "ultraleft deviations."

The same old trick. "Stop thief!" as he runs off with the goods.

Many an enthusiastic young tough ransacked other people's households as part of the "liquidation of the kulaks as a class," after being issued a leather jacket, tight breeches, and his heart's desire, a Nagant revolver, for the first time in his life. A Nagant meant power over others. Including over your betters.

In organizing his pogrom of the villages Stalin relied on an army of power-hungry careerists—so-called party activists.

> Bread is got by the sweat of your brow.
> Also by throwing your weight around.

That saying was born in the countryside during collectivization. It was to have a long life.

* * *

The following incident occurred in Bolshaya Korova county, near Moscow.

The secretary of the county committee of the party—let's call him Petukhov—calls up the local district committee of the party: "I have a revolt on my hands. You've got to send troops."

The secretary of the military district—we'll call him Myasoyed—answers that the party will not allow panic. He gives these orders: "Stay in your office. I'll be right over."

Arriving on the scene, Comrade Myasoyed suggests that he and the county committee secretary go together to the most recalcitrant village in the heart of the rebel area. Petukhov picks up his Nagant, snaps his holster to his belt, and is all set to go. "No guns," the older man objects. But Petukhov absolutely refuses to go to the village without his Nagant. They have a long argument. Finally Myasoyed agrees that Petukhov can take his revolver if he keeps it in his pocket and under no circumstances puts it to use.

They arrive in the village and assemble the collective farmers. About a hundred of them fill a crowded peasant hut. They know about Stalin's article in *Pravda* and with a single voice demand, "Dissolve the collective farm!"

"Why the whole thing?" the secretary of the military district committee asks. "People who want to, can submit a statement of withdrawal on their own."

"Oh no," comes the answer from the crowd. "First you dissolve it, then whoever wants to can start a new one."

Till four in the morning they shout back and forth this way. The tobacco smoke's so thick you can't see anyone's face. The crowd presses the two secretaries back against the wall so they're about to suffocate or be squashed.

"We won't let you go till you abolish the collective farm."

Petukhov goes for his gun but the older man stops his hand. There's nothing they can do. They have to give in. As soon as they announce the dissolution of the collective farm, the peasants demand the return of their seed grain.

"That's out of our hands," Comrade Myasoyed has the quick wit to say. "Let the executive committee of the county Soviet decide about the seed." But the peasants stick to their position. "You don't leave till we get our seed back."

Some volunteers go after the keeper of the seed-grain storage facility, but he's made himself scarce. Morning comes. Everyone is exhausted, even the most militant. Registration for a new collective farm is announced. About seven people sign up, poor peasants only. Finally they let the party secretaries go.

The executive committee of the county Soviet of course doesn't give back the seed. Not only that. How in hell are you going to plow and sow when the bosses have turned under all the boundary lines and all the horses have been destroyed?

The peasants are left with nothing.

Meanwhile Petukhov submits a statement to the Moscow committee accusing Comrade Myasoyed of dissolving the collective farm. But Petukhov is arrested that same month as an "enemy of the people." Myasoyed is saved.

An ending true to the spirit of the times.

* * *

Then came another zigzag—the Central Committee decree "On the Struggle Against Distortions of the Party Line in the Collective Farm Movement." The Great Humorist thought this one up. How could you distort a line so crooked to begin with? The Great Ignoramus also had the bright idea of letting the forcibly organized collective farms be dissolved precisely in the spring of the year, when the sowing season began. Who can estimate the new losses? Who can tell the number of districts where nothing was left of collectivization but boarded-up huts? That's how his monstrous political slalom ended.

In some places the party bosses, with their shrewd political instincts, took the Big Chief's article "Dizzy with Success" as a propaganda maneuver and prevented the local post offices from delivering the issue of *Pravda* containing it. Only after all the boundary lines were plowed under, so that the forcibly collectivized sons of the soil could not re-establish the boundaries of their plots, did the authorities allow the local population to see "Dizzy with Success." That's how things were in the Terek region in the Northern Caucasus.

One of the district leaders of that time later ended up in a labor camp,

where he spent seventeen years, but to the end of his days he bragged
about his great skill in fooling the peasants in 1929.

An amazing product of those incredible times.

But there were party officials in the Central Committee and in the
district committees who took Stalin's "Dizzy" article seriously and relaxed
the pressure on the villages. Woe unto the simple-minded. They were
expelled from the party for "conciliationist policies"—in fact, for failing to
grasp the full genius of the Big Chief's most recent maneuver. In the late
1930s, branded as "Right deviationists," they took the road to the death
camps.

It was possible, however, to salvage something even under those
monstrous conditions. In March 1930 many members of the Central Committee, even Politburo members, traveled to the provinces to look things
over and to push the newly straightened, crooked party line. In early April
Sergo Ordzhonikidze arrived in the Ukraine. He visited Zinoviev province, among others. (Earlier, its capital had been Elisavetgrad, in honor of
Empress Elizabeth. After the Kirov assassination it became Kirovograd.)

Stanislav Kosior, first secretary of the Central Committee of the Communist Party of the Ukraine, accompanied Ordzhonikidze. The fury of the
Oprichniks* had not been so great in this region; expropriations and
forced collectivization had not affected the bulk of the peasants. Fairly
efficient party leaders had been selected—they were only somewhat loud-
mouthed and not too cruel. The peasants lucked out. Perhaps for that
reason the collective farms in this province had not collapsed immediately
after the amnesty proclaimed in March. The spring sowing was just being
completed. That is what surprised Ordzhonikidze most of all.

"How could you have begun the spring sowing without orders and
without asking anyone?" he inquired of a local official. "Be sure you tell
me straight," Sergo warned.

"What else could I do? What kind of weather did you have in Moscow
on March twenty-fifth? Freezing, right? But here, where I was, steam was
rising from the steppes. We had to start the sowing right away."

"And what about the voluntary policy?" Sergo wouldn't drop the
subject. "Didn't any of your people leave the collective farms?"

"A lot of them wanted to. About fifteen hundred applications came
in. But there are two hundred thousand households in the province. We
decided to allow all those who wanted to, to leave. But we knew they'd
have to be supplied with seed grain and have plots of land assigned to
them. Fights would start over that, and people could easily have ended up
killing each other. Meanwhile planting time couldn't wait. All the secretaries of the party district committees got together, talked it over, and
decided to hold general meetings in all the collective farms before the

---

*Oprichniks: members of Tsar Ivan the Terrible's special force, the Oprichnina, which
he used to terrorize and crush opponents. The author uses the term for those who did
analogous work for Stalin.—TRANS.

spring sowing. Committees were to be set up everywhere to be sure the voluntary principle was observed when people joined the collective farms and also to check on the state of the winter crops and the shoeing of the horses. Altogether there were sixteen committees. The secretary of the party's provincial committee personally attended one collective-farm meeting, and, with the farmers taking part, general instructions were drawn up for the whole province."

Sergo listened very closely, then repeated the same question:

"But what did you do with the ones who wanted to leave the collective farms?"

"Very simple. We decided to do the planting first and then have a second round of meetings with reports from the committees. When the planting was finished all over the province and the peasants had invested their labor in the soil and had been convinced that no one was really going to force them, eleven hundred of them took back their statements of withdrawal from the collective farms. The rest of them we allowed to leave."

Sergo cursed, then commented: "If only things had gone that smoothly everywhere."

"They didn't go smoothly here. Who told you that? One village refused outright to do the spring planting. Old Believers, they were. I called the director of the machinery-and-tractor station and ordered him to send five tractors out there early in the morning and do all the planting on the Old Believers' fields. That's what they did."

It was obvious from all this, Sergo realized, that local leaders could not be turned into mindless executors of the Supreme Will, and that in agriculture, as in any field of endeavor, political initiative had to be encouraged, not choked off. It was possible to speak candidly with Ordzhonikidze, to "tell him straight," as he put it. (There were not many like Sergo, but I shall not idealize him either. He had quite a few evil deeds upon his conscience too.)

All in all, the most savage aspect of the savage agrarian policy of the Stalin clique was the so-called liquidation of the kulaks as a class. If we turn to the speeches where policy guidelines were laid down, we will see that not only Lenin was opposed to the expropriation of the kulaks; his "great successor" was too. In December 1927, at the Fifteenth Party Congress, Stalin declared, "We must approach the kulak with measures of an economic kind and on the basis of Soviet legality."[49]

That was the only way genuine Marxists could argue, unlike all of your Trotskyists and Zinovievists, who were calling for the expropriation of the village rich. But suddenly this very same Stalin, on December 27, 1929, at the conference for Marxist students of the agrarian question, fired off this slogan: Liquidate the kulaks as a class.

This new zigzag might be explained by the Gensek's forgetfulness. The man forgot the resolutions of party congresses. He forgot there was a Central Committee and a Politburo. He forgot that special commissions had been established. He simply forgot. The whole country, "the entire planet," had just observed his fiftieth birthday. How they praised him! That he remembered. And with all his power, the power and authority of the Father of the Peoples, he issued the command. It was time to get down to the business so dear to his heart.

A month or two later, on Stalin's orders, notice was sent to the local areas: The Central Committee recommends that not every last kulak be expropriated and liquidated, nor all at the same time. The government instructions spoke vaguely about making certain distinctions. A pitiful attempt to rein in the terror.

Officially there were an estimated one million kulak farms. According to the instructions, only one-fifth of the kulaks were subject to deportation, and relatively severe repressive measures were envisaged for "only 600,-000." As far as the real kulaks were concerned—that is, active counter-revolutionary elements—the bulk of them had fought in the White Army, retreated with the Whites when they were defeated, and then emigrated. The real kulaks would not have waited around for representatives of the "poor peasants" to rob them and put them up against the wall. The real kulaks had long ago sold off their holdings and gone with their sons to join the city proletariat. As for their daughters, usually they tried to marry GPU men and become fine ladies. So the main blow of the expropriators and punitive expeditions fell not on the kulak but on the middle peasant.

Within one year as many as three million "kulaks" and their families were deported to harsh northern regions. Some were shot, and hundreds of thousands were sent to their deaths in the camps. After them came the so-called kulak sympathizers. Every hard-working farmer who had built up an economically solid enterprise by his own labor and the labor of his sons fell into this category. Also any poor peasant who had accidentally said anything favorable about a "kulak" or expressed dissatisfaction with Stalin's policy in any other way. And anyone else, whether a middle peasant or an agricultural laborer, against whom a neighbor had a grudge. Thus, additional millions of rural toilers were dragged off to prisons, camps, and exile colonies.

Many who "implemented the party's will" were also sucked into the whirlpool. Behind barbed wire they met again—dekulakizers and dekulakized. That for which Stalin appeared on this earth had begun.

Neighbor robbed neighbor. Everything was taken—wagons, axes, vases, mirrors, fur coats, boots, hogs, chickens, geese, samovars, quilts, shawls. Neighbor robbed neighbor.

Stalin urged the have-nots on against the haves and unleashed a new civil war.

Divide and conquer.

Where did you draw the line between kulak and middle peasant, between middle peasant and poor peasant? That wasn't known even in the Kremlin; how were they supposed to know in the village? At first they robbed the rich, then the more industrious, the fairly well off, then everyone without distinction. Everything that was stolen—shame-faced historians were later to call this the "expropriated property"—invariably ended up in Stalin's bins and warehouses. Units of the Red Army and NKVD, mobilized workers, Young Communist League members, and local officials—an entire army was engaged in this work.

* * *

The time of the robber had come.

A robber, however, with an insatiable political ambition. It was thanks to him, and him only, to his genius and farsightedness, that the enemy class of kulaks was liquidated in time. He carried out his pogrom in the villages, hiding behind the red banner. Over the years the servile ideologists have churned out ethereal programs concerning "reliance on the poor peasant, alliance with the middle peasant, and liquidation of the kulak." They have debated differing versions of this abstract formula and frenziedly quoted and quoted—Marx, Lenin, Stalin. To this day they quote and argue. They agree only on one thing: "The world-historical victory of the collective farm system" was won under the wise leadership of the great Stalin.

The aim of all the noisy propaganda in the ill-fated year of collectivization was to divide the village. But that was not enough for Stalin. He provoked the peasants to fight among themselves, but he also tried to split the traditionally strong peasant family, to use children and adolescents in the struggle against "kulaks and their henchmen."

In one remote village a youngster denounced his kulak father to the authorities. The lad's name was Pavel Morozov.

The child's great deed was immortalized in marble. A son betrayed his father, and a monument went up to him. A son betrayed his father, and songs were composed in honor of the youthful traitor. New generations of Young Pioneers* were trained with Pavel Morozov as their model.

A terrible fate lay in store for the children of "kulaks" who had been shot or deported. If you were branded a kulak's son or kulak's daughter there was no point in your even thinking about going to school in the land of universal education. Disenfranchised person—that was a new term produced by those inhuman times. Millions of dekulakized peasants and millions of peasant children were deprived of everything, their homes, their daily bread, their freedom and civil rights.

When party functionaries or civil servants of peasant origin had to give biographical data about themselves—and Russia's population was mainly rural—they invariably tried to show that their parents had been poor peasants. It was a matter of pride if you could write on a questionnaire, "Born to a horseless peasant family." This was a sure thing, the way noble lineage had been in the old days.

If you referred to your father as a middle peasant, your background

---

*Young Pioneers: Soviet organization to which nearly all school children ages nine to fifteen belong and which promotes official values. It is directed by the Young Communist League.—TRANS.

would be checked into immediately. If you were from a kulak family, you needn't bother filling out a questionnaire at all.

The young people who served in party and government agencies or in the army and security police, these youthful witnesses to the pogrom Stalin carried out in the villages, thoroughly absorbed one lesson: from now on anything was permitted. They had been morally prepared for the Great Terror.

One year the authorities expropriated; another year they liquidated; other times they simply killed, deported, and jailed peasants. Nevertheless, grain deliveries grew smaller and smaller. In the Northern Caucasus entire peasant villages and Cossack towns were deported. But these draconic measures didn't help. The government purchasing price for grain, meat, and vegetables could have been raised on a trial basis; those prices were dozens of times lower than the retail prices anyhow. But what did the Builder of Socialism care about giving the workers and peasants a material interest in socialism? Stalin encouraged the practice of totally depleting food supplies, with no allowance for a bad harvest or consideration of existing reserves. Many collective farms were left without seed grain. After the searches, the peasant huts were stripped clean as a whistle. There might be a jug left, and a cup and a pan with a spoon to go with each.

The Peasant Fighter (Osip Mandelstam paid with his life for that phrase) brought all the power of the state down on the villages, and the sons of the soil didn't stand a chance. All they could do to keep from dying of hunger was to flee. But where? And what do you think the troops were for? You couldn't even steal the food you had earned by the sweat of your brow. You know what you get for stealing socialist property.

In this whole crisis, all Stalin saw was "sabotage of grain deliveries"; that's all he wanted to see. And against sabotage there was only one recourse—terror.

The villages emptied out. The surviving peasants went into hiding. Famine set in. It affected all of the Ukraine, Kuban, the whole Black Earth region, and Central Asia—a good half of the grain-producing regions of the country. Can I cite statistics and provide witnesses or evidence? The facts are known to everyone who has a spark of humanity left and the desire to know. Entire villages perished, including children and old people. The peasant men were the first to die. Those that still had the strength to move headed for the railroad stations and the towns, paving the roads with their corpses. But there were military units and roadblocks all around, as in wartime. And no hope of salvation.

Ten years earlier the people had managed to survive a famine that came in the wake of war and economic dislocation. Seventeen provinces had suffered then, and twenty million peasants were on the verge of starvation.

The famine of 1932 was worse. Not only in its extent. It was the only artificially produced famine in history. A unique achievement.

In 1921 the whole country came to the aid of the Volga region. Twelve million poods of seed and more than thirty million of grain were distributed to the starving villages from government reserves. The Soviet government readily accepted aid from foreign workers and bourgeois governments. Railroad cars with food from the United States, the gift of the American Relief Administration, arrived in the Volga region.

In 1932 the areas hit by famine did not receive a single kilogram of grain from the government. Stalin did not have on his conscience a single child saved from death by starvation. Not one.

It wasn't enough, however, to organize a famine. The gains had to be consolidated. Stalin began to *export* grain. In 1929, 13 million centners; in 1930, 48.3 million; in 1931, 51 million. And in the year when famine was everywhere, grain exports were still 28 million. Not a huge amount. But the very fact . . .[50]

In 1928 some leaders suggested that grain be purchased abroad. These "capitulators, capitalist restorationists, and kulak agents within the party" Stalin accused of "Right deviation." Then the big-time Kremlin merchant began selling grain to Western Europe—taken from the mouths of starving peasants. Call him what you want after that—Left deviationist or Left extremist—a cannibal remains a cannibal.

Millions of deaths by starvation lie at his door. Different sources give different figures—from three to six million dead. Altogether the campaign for forced collectivization, liquidation of the kulaks, and the Stalin-organized famine cost the growers of grain twenty-two million lives. Experienced Soviet statisticians arrived at this figure. We thank these honest specialists and place the figure against the Big Chief's account. We have yet to draw the final balance.

It is not hard to prove that this figure reflects the real situation. An important monograph was published in 1969, *The Population of the USSR* by A. Gozulov and M. Grigoryan. The authors give summary data for the Ukraine. The population declined from 31.2 million in 1926 to 28.1 million in 1939. Three million disappeared. But what about the natural increase? Let's call it 2 percent (which is rather low for an average yearly increase). This would give 600,000 a year, or about 9 million over 14 years. Adding the initial figure of 3 million, we get a total of 12 million. Where did those 12 million Ukrainians go? And remember, the famine that accompanied forced collectivization reaped its harvest among the populations of the Northern Caucasus, the Volga region, and Central Asia as well.

Today, historians, economists, and demographers are pooling their resources in an effort to rehabilitate the Great Collectivizer. Certain publications have appeared that fall outside the sphere of genuine scholarship. For example, not so long ago the magazine *Problems of CPSU History* took up the question of the liquidation of the kulaks as a class. It reported that in 1930, 115,200 kulak families were deported from the villages, and in 1931, 265,800. A total of 381,000 for the two years.[51]

If the average family had five members, we get a figure of about two million. For only two years. Statistics for the other years went unmentioned by the magazine. It did not tell how many "kulaks," with their children and elders, perished or how many ended up in prison or labor camps. Nor what sufferings the children and grandchildren of the deported and arrested people underwent—children and grandchildren stripped of all civil rights. Nor did it say one word about the secret decision of the Politburo to "resettle" five million people in remote areas. Five million.

* * *

No one has dared to speak about the victims of collectivization or of the famine under Stalin. The newspapers and orators have remained silent. How was it that Lenin was not afraid of publicity in 1921?

All the newspapers in Russia wrote about the famine in the Volga region, and reports on it were given at sessions of the League of Nations. Famine relief committees were organized in many provinces and by the All-Russia Central Executive Committee of the Soviets. Vladimir Antonov-Ovseyenko headed the provincial relief committee in Samara, the center of the famine. At Lenin's request, he published several books about the relief effort. The title of one of them was *Hurry to the Rescue of the Starving.* There were daily reports in the newspapers, articles in all the magazines, stories and novels by writers, and speeches at the Ninth All-Russia Congress of Soviets.

After a meeting with nonparty peasants who were delegates to the congress, Lenin called Antonov-Ovseyenko into his office.

"Your Samara peasant Burmatnov spoke well. But look here, Antonov, he said that in the Stavropol region there were instances of people eating human flesh."

"That's not exactly so, Vladimir Ilyich. There have been instances in that region and elsewhere of people eating corpses."

"Eating corpses?" Lenin repeated. He jotted something down in his notebook and said with an expression of pain and anger:

"The foreign interventionists will answer for this."[52]

* * *

If you give it some thought, you realize that it was not only the foreign intervention that was to blame for the disaster. But that is a different question. The question now is, Who will answer for the deaths of millions of grain growers during collectivization?

In February 1933 Stalin convened the first All-Russia Congress of Collective Farm Shock Workers. What didn't the Great Collectivizer talk about? First he did a bit of clowning. He hadn't expected to speak, he said. "But as you insist, and the power is in your hands, I must submit." Then he told the assembled farmers some fairy tales—about twenty million poor peasants who had become virtually well-to-do, about the happy socialist existence that awaited them tomorrow—and a parable on the virtues of patience. It seemed that during the civil war the workers of Moscow and

Petrograd were given an eighth of a pound of grain daily, half of it in the form of oil cake. For two whole years the workers had endured this, without any bellyaching. And so "your present difficulties, comrade collective farmers, seem like child's play."[53]

The kindly wizard went on with his stories, the obedient children listened, played at sloganizing, and praised the outstanding successes. The organizer of this performance talked about anything he wanted, even gave his recollections of an old peasant woman who had lifted her skirts at a meeting—anything and everything except the torments of starvation suffered by tens of millions of those delegates' brothers.

In the middle of this operetta Stalin launched a new slogan, "To make the collective farms Bolshevik and the collective farmers wealthy." He wanted to insult the memories of his victims.

Let us take note of this aspect of his character as well.

All through the winter the famine continued to cut down and sweep away those who fed the country. Fiercely, relentlessly, hundreds of thousands were mowed down. Not a word about that at the Congress of Collective Farm Shock Workers.

Stalin took the land from the peasants. Then he took their very lives, or mercifully deported the less obstreperous ones to the ends of the earth. But even those who remained failed to understand the genius of his intentions. And ever since, there hasn't been enough to eat in Russia.

No matter how many official historians play magic with the figures, thinking up various combinations and clever ways of approaching the statistics, there's no getting around the simple truth: 1928 was the highest point reached in agricultural production for many long years, until the war itself.

Here is a typical example of a rural scene from the 1930s. A railroad station. Next to the tracks, wheat from the new harvest is piled in a high cone. There are no railroad cars and no granary. The grain is rotting under the open skies. And no one dares take any; on top of the cone stands a Red Army man with a rifle.

No shamanistic invocations by the Central Committee about the "further advance of agriculture" could help. Stalin had turned the peasants' hearts against the land. And the land became a curse to the growers of grain.

Stalin disrupted the alliance between the workers and peasants, one of the central principles of the revolution and a cornerstone of the Soviet system. Under his wise leadership an important victory was won for the counterrevolution in its war against its own people. The military merits of the inspirer and organizer of the pogrom against the villages were acknowledged in 1930, when he was awarded the Order of the Red Banner. That good and kind chairman of the Central Executive Committee, Mikhail Kalinin, pinned this second military medal on the chest of our brave warrior.

It is certainly true that Stalin bears the historical responsibility. But that does not free his subordinates from guilt. Molotov, Kaganovich, and the clever Anastas Mikoyan. No one opposed the tyrant. They all lent a hand in the destruction of the peasants.

Before collectivization, only the top brass of the party feared Stalin. After it, the masses acquired the same fear of the man. And that fear stayed with them until the death of the Beloved Father.

And how does official Soviet history evaluate this tragedy?

"The poor peasants gained a secure existence." "A tremendous, world-historical victory of the working class and peasantry" was achieved. "The victory of socialism in agriculture was accomplished." And all of this was "thanks to the daring, wise, revolutionary policy of the party and government." All that is from the *Short Course.* [54]

Later there came a time—one brief, shining moment—when some nuggets of truth found their way into the publications of the Central Committee. For example, a 1962 textbook on CPSU history criticized the errors of collectivization as follows:

"The underestimation by Stalin of the strength of the peasants' attachment to their own farms . . . [and] the lack of desire to listen to the intelligent suggestions of local officials . . . proved to be the source of many errors. Although the instigation of the collectivization drive came from Stalin, his article 'Dizzy with Success' heaped all the blame on local officials." [55]

In later editions you no longer find this passage. To make up for it, there are lengthy quotations from Lenin.

Some find it pleasant to trumpet once again the great victory of the collective-farm system under the wise leadership of Comrade Stalin. Others, who have consciences, like to call the pogrom of the villages an "unsuccessful experiment." But Stalin, when he decided to give the peasants a working over, hardly thought of it as an experiment. An experiment implies a test without guaranteed results. But Stalin knew in advance that he was going to wipe out the peasants, to crush the growers of grain. Unarmed and defenseless, what could they do against the might of the dictatorship?

It was not only and not so much that Stalin needed grain. He wanted to have a political impact, and he achieved the desired effect totally. The Avars have a saying: "To get a chicken he'll sacrifice a sheep." That saying is about Him. About Him, our Benefactor.

Joseph the Builder set about the building of a new society. His first victims were the villages. The cities were to climb Golgotha by another route.

THE INDUSTRIALIZER

2

Was it long ago that the Gensek had encouraged private initiative, placing his hopes in peasant agriculture and the revitalizing energy of the NEP's private entrepreneurs? At the April 1926 Central Committee plenum Stalin had not yet groped his way onto the road of industrialization. At that time he said that to undertake construction of a major dam, the Dneprostroi project, would be the same as if a "muzhik saved a few kopecks and then, instead of repairing his plow and renewing his stock, went out and bought a gramophone.[56]

The theoreticians had not yet worked out a program of economic development, and the available resources—raw materials, technology, labor power, financial reserves—left no room for the planning of a great leap forward. Even Stalin saw that. But 1927 brought an unexpected zigzag. Stalin became the bearer of tidings: an all-out industrial revolution. He announced a nationwide campaign for socialist industrialization and urged on his propagandists impatiently.

By the end of 1927 the party already reported substantial gains in industrialization. The economists scraped together the necessary meager figures for industrial production and agriculture, added the data for fishing and lumbering, and placed a triumphant report on the Gensek's desk: as of the tenth anniversary of Soviet power the country had at least caught up with the tsarist era, that is, had reached the level of 1913. The annual increase of the gross product over 1926 was 18 percent!

Well, if you buy a gramophone with money meant for repairing the plow and renewing the stock, it ought to make some sort of noise.

What I don't understand, though, is why the year 1920 was not included in these statistical games. Then the annual increase would have been 1,800 percent. (The truth is, incidentally, that the Soviet Union achieved the 1913 level in such decisive sectors as the smelting of iron and steel only in 1929.)

Stalin was incapable of independently analyzing the domestic and international situation or assessing the country's real economic possibilities on the eve of his Great Leap Forward and therefore could not project a scientifically based strategy for the future. It was his fate throughout his life to rush from one bank of the river to the other without ever seeing where the river came from or where it went.

At first the Gensek went along with the economic recommendations of Bukharin, Rykov, and Tomsky, the future Right oppositionists. In 1927 he shifted toward the earlier proposals of Trotsky and Zinoviev, giving absolute priority to industry over agriculture. In a word, he put into practice the dictatorship of industry for which Trotsky had called five years earlier.

But the leaders of the so-called New Opposition had proposed that foreign capital be used widely in trying to industrialize the country. The machinery and equipment necessary to build a modern industry did not exist in Russia, nor did the financial reserves and trained specialists that would be needed. Roads and transport were in disrepair. And in the background was a severe agricultural crisis, intensified after 1929 by forced collectivization. Under these conditions the proposal to grant certain factories, mills, and plants as concessions to foreigners and to begin building industrial plants with the aid of the advanced Western powers was an intelligent proposal. At any rate, it was worth thinking about.

But Stalin was organically incapable of thinking in depth or on a broad scale. The practical proposals of the opposition leaders were denounced as "capitulationist" and were soon used as a basis for physical reprisals against them. What did he really care anyhow about strengthening the economy? Strengthening his own authority and power—that's what was worth thinking about. It was worth a lot of thought, constant thought. As for the economy, what he could do there was use force. That had never failed him yet.

The State Planning Commission proposed two variants of a five-year plan to run from autumn 1928 to autumn 1933: an initial or minimal plan; and an optimal one, whose targets would be 20 percent higher. Stalin, with the majority of the Central Committee going along, insisted on the second variant (at the Sixteenth Party Conference in April 1929). To say that that was officially adopted is to put it too mildly. Stalin *forced* the Central Committee to approve his arbitrary maximization of the plan.

By 1929 Stalin felt secure enough in the Gensek's seat to give free rein to his true character. He was burning with impatience to "catch up to and surpass" the advanced capitalist countries. Behind his low forehead, great-power ambitions nestled alongside absolute contempt for the "masses"— or, as they were seen from this angle, the "human resources." In prisoners' uniforms or soldiers' greatcoats (or, in the case of free women, with red kerchiefs on their heads), a million more here or five million fewer there were all a matter of detail that could be disregarded in pursuit of his grand goal.

In 1926, the Gensek had scolded the planners: "There are people among us who sometimes love to draw up fantastic industrial plans without taking our resources into account." But a few years later his message was: "We are fifty or a hundred years behind the advanced countries. We must make good this distance in ten years. Either we do it, or we shall be crushed."[57]

Russia's finest expert on the base and the superstructure patched together his own paper tiger—the bourgeois West—and implanted a dread of the West that lasted for decades. The propaganda apparatus picked up this theme and blared it out. (A gramophone isn't such a bad thing after all.)

The unsoundness of the Gensek's decision was felt right away. The world economic crisis caused a substantial decline in prices for raw materials. And what else did Russia have to offer its Western trading partners at that time? The Soviet plans for exporting industrial raw materials and purchasing foreign technology went awry. The hope for extensive financing by the leading capitalist countries proved unfounded. And there was one other internal problem—the crisis in the villages was accompanied by a substantial decline in agricultural production.

The first year showed that not one of the planning targets could be met within the allotted time. The plans had to be revised quickly. And Stalin revised them. He proposed to the Council of People's Commissars that the targets, which had already been increased, should be doubled.

On the local level, the response was to adopt new plans that exceeded even the ones that had been doubled and redoubled. The loud blare of the campaign for socialist competition and "shock work" drowned out the sober proposal that the material basis for the proposed Great Leap Forward be created and the technical resources prepared before starting in.

As he increased the figures for the five-year plans arbitrarily, Stalin did not forget to urge on the totally emaciated nag of peasant agriculture.

M. S. Iks was the head of the Zaporozhe provincial committee of the party in 1932. When he received the latest planning goals for grain deliveries from the top brass, he reported to the Politburo that the targets were obviously excessive and simply could not be met. Molotov, as secretary of the Central Committee, brought before the Politburo the question of this recalcitrant party leader. Two other Ukrainian officials were summoned to the meeting. Iks was cheerful. When a surprised friend asked him the reason for his good humor, Iks answered: "I'm appearing today in the role of the rooster. Whether I crow or not, the sun will come up."

The decision was to transfer this subversive element, a Communist since 1905, to the Far East, with a reduction in rank to second secretary. (At the same time a man was sent from Georgia to be the first secretary of the party's Far Eastern territorial committee. He was Lavrenty Kartvelishvili, who had not been able "to get along" with Stalin's protégé and favorite in Georgia at that time, Lavrenty Beria.)

At the Politburo session Stalin remained silent and listened to the discussion with a show of indifference. When everything had been decided, the Gensek asked the name of the guilty party. They told him.

"Iks? Listen here, you think you can go to the Far East with a name like that? What will they say in China? What's your first name and patronymic? Mikhail Samoilovich? OK, so you'll be Samoilov."

Didn't the nobility in old Russia assign names to their serfs in the same airy manner?

Off went Comrade Samoilov, the former Iks, to Khabarovsk. We should note, incidentally, that the Far Eastern territorial committee became for the Gensek a standard way station for people on the road to the other world. The secretaries of that committee were swallowed up one after the other by the Lubyanka. When Iks-Samoilov's turn came, he blessed the world with these last words: "Better a horrible end than unending horror."

Responsible officials like Iks who tried to demonstrate the unreality of Stalin's brilliant designs were swept from the scene.

Down with crybabies and pessimists.

It was with this cheerful battle cry that the youth stormed the fortress of Magnitogorsk and the banks of the Dnieper, built tractor factories on the Volga and the Don and in the Urals, and constructed roads and canals.

The Baltic-White Sea canal took some 300,000 martyrs. A few hundred accidentally survived. The canal was declared navigable only on paper, a publicity project that became one vast human grave. One of the first monuments of the early Stalin period.

The same deadly wheelbarrows and spades could be seen in the hands of the "free" women and Young Communists at the "shock work" (top-priority) construction projects of the first five-year plan. Barracks, manual labor, deprivation—the same as at the White Sea canal, only without barbed wire or guard dogs or guard troops.

At the end of World War I, General Ivashchenko built some factories not far from Samara to make artillery shells and poisonous chemicals— yperite (mustard gas), lewisite, and chlorine gas. In the Soviet period the settlement of Ivashchenkov became the town of Trotsk and later was renamed Chapaevsk. The entire surrounding area was yellow from the gases produced there. Everything was yellow: the bare soil, where nothing could sprout; the workers' barracks; the people's faces. The humble geraniums in the window boxes curled up and died.

During the first five-year plan, production at Chapaevsk expanded. The number of workers reached twenty thousand. The pay was good there, and the hungry, ill-clothed peasants came pouring in from the surrounding villages in enthusiastic waves. The enthusiasts signed statements that they would not present any claims against the administration on grounds of health. Breathing masks and rubberized canvas suits were given out in the most dangerous production areas. These didn't prevent poisoning. In a four-hour shift a worker received a poison dose that meant certain doom. After three years of such useful work, the enthusiast became a total invalid and soon died.

Women worked in these plants too. They were assured that if the proper safety practices were observed, there would be no threat to their health. But within a year a woman ceased to be a woman. And the end soon followed.

Some big shot from Moscow came there once and recommended that green areas be established around the factory grounds. But of course nothing would grow in this zone of yellow death.

* * *

The country experienced extreme shortages of food, clothing, and housing. Real wages declined, to reach the 1928 level again only in 1940.

A very strict internal passport system, limiting freedom of movement, was introduced. And a law against absenteeism. And strict limits on the sale of food and manufactured goods. Ration coupons were required for meat, bread, trousers, or shoes. A way of life dominated by the ration coupon began, which was to last more than just one decade.

Joseph the Builder drew his own conclusions from what he had accomplished. Millions came to recognize that in His Russia, forced labor was "a thing of honor and glory, of heroism and valor." Stalin constructed a reliable system of government with a multiple-backup security system. It wasn't everyone that could detect the slaves' manacles beneath the demagogic glitter. Still, if it hadn't been for the enthusiasm of the masses, multiplied by the starvation in the villages and mass unemployment, the construction projects would have been left without a work force.

As if all that weren't enough, Stalin required not simple factories but giants of industry. (Look what we have!) The Potemkin villages of the first two five-year plans were truly astounding in their dimensions. But at what a cost they were built! If the director of a new branch of industry proposed that, to start with, two factories should be built, based on the available resources, materials, and technical possibilities, the Gensek immediately increased the figure three, four, or five times over. The result was the diffusion of scarce resources, the tying up of capital investments, and the prolongation of construction time.

Joseph the Builder expended all of his extraordinary energy in helping to foul up the industrialization of the country. Stalin's leadership created unbelievable extra difficulties which the workers had to heroically overcome. And in the chain of command between the Leader and the masses there were plenty of intermediate adventurers and promoters of impossible projects.

The Magnitogorsk complex required a great deal of water for its construction. The Water Canal Project Institute projected a dam on the Ural River. Women in red kerchiefs piled up a huge bank of dirt with their wheelbarrows, but when the lake made by these human hands filled up, the water flowed around the dam on both sides. A new dam had to be built farther downstream, following the plans and under the technical supervision of American specialists. The second dam is still doing yeoman's service today. The first one, our homemade one, was submerged. Which is a shame, because such monuments to our industrialization should be preserved. And shown to our descendants.

What the Soviet people were able to build in the first five-year plan was the accomplishment exclusively of the people themselves. The only favorable effect Stalin had on the course of industrialization—if a whip can be taken as a positive factor—was the constant goading of the totally exhausted workhorse.

And what stylish slogans Joseph the Builder dreamed up.

The Five-Year Plan in Four Years! Five in Four!

Technology in the Period of Reconstruction Decides Everything!

Cadres Decide Everything!

He drew up his famous *six conditions* for improving production (or they were drawn up for him, and he broadcast them to the masses)—a set of elementary work rules known to every junior apprentice.

Five in Four. This super slogan was repeated around the clock like a ritual prayer, by all the newspapers, posters, radios, and movies. It was declaimed at rallies, assemblies, and conferences. Lecturers and children shouted it, as did leaders of every rank and actors of every degree.

Five in Four—the slogan blasted its way through into the educational system, penetrating the universities.

The theoretical foundations of this new adventure were as persuasive and refined as the jimmy a burglar uses by night.

"The lesson that follows from the Shakhty case is that the pace of education must be accelerated. A new technical intelligentsia must be created from the working class, people devoted to the cause of socialism and technically capable of managing our socialist industry."[58] That's how Stalin preached in 1928.

Five in Four!

Five in Three.

Five in Two. And before you knew it an entire army of engineers, scientists, agronomists, physicians, and philosophers produced by the rapid-action proletarian method came pouring into economic and scientific work.

After deciding that he had to have his own "commanders of industry" in a hurry, Joseph the Builder started in like a house afire. And the hastily produced "engineers" who graduated from 1930 to 1932, untrammeled by any great knowledge but convinced of their class superiority over the rest of the population, took up the task of management and administration with the inexhaustible energy of youth. Very few of them were to become real engineers. But an army of aggressive "blind men" had been created. The majority of them subsequently shared the fate of the bourgeois specialists.* Of those who survived many became professional manager-bureaucrats.

The universities as pressure cookers. What prevented Stalin from patenting that social invention? His inherent modesty, no doubt.

As for slogans, he would continue to bestow them upon the people for a good quarter of a century and insist they be taken seriously.

You can judge how the unenlightened workers looked at Stalin's six conditions from this humorous ditty patterned after an old refrain.

> A tisket a tasket.
> Stalin's six conditions.
> Four conditions of Rykov's.
> Two of Peter the Great.

---

*There is an untranslatable play on words here. The "blind men" are *sleptsy*, who shared the fate of the *spetsy*, the "bourgeois specialists."—TRANS.

Or take the slogan "Technology in the Period of Reconstruction Decides Everything." This slogan wasn't supposed to be regarded humorously, but its similarity to the other slogan, "Cadres Decide Everything," created problems. The people were a little slow; they couldn't figure out exactly which did "decide everything." Apparently that was why Stalin got nowhere with either technology or cadres.

The time came for the first balance sheet to be drawn. And Stalin showed the world a model of unbounded optimism. What of it if not one of the targets of the five-year plan had been reached? In January 1933 he announced that industry had more than doubled in the three preceding years alone, and that the five-year plan as a whole had been fulfilled in four years.

The former seminarian's familiarity with mathematics went no further than arithmetic. Of that elementary branch of mathematics, however, he had full command. Let people insist that two times two equals four. Stalin would creatively expand that postulate, announcing that two times two equals—the five-year plan. (Let us again pay tribute to the Leader's modesty. He could have announced the completion of the five-year plan a year earlier, but he refrained.)

Stalin had carried out an industrial revolution, and with leisurely indulgence he now accepted congratulations. The people were allowed to celebrate on the occasion of this "historic victory." And they did celebrate. In total ignorance of the sad truth.

It's hard to imagine the scale of this industrial sleight of hand without specific examples. The target for smelting iron in the last year of the five-year plan was ten million tons. Stalin increased it to seventeen million tons. But the mills actually produced slightly more than six million. Stalin tripled the plan for tractor production, raising it to 170,000. But they only managed to produce forty-nine thousand in 1932, the original target having been fifty-five thousand.

The ceiling in the Gensek's office was high: the figures he picked off that ceiling did not become reality until a quarter of a century later. But when was it ever necessary for his brilliant conceptions to take into account that sorry Cinderella, the real world?

Stalin needed the pounding of triumphal kettledrums in the year of catastrophic famine and relentless impoverishment of the workers. The most important thing in such feverish undertakings is not to let people stop and think, or cool off. And to keep prodding them, constantly prodding them. Stalin put his people in the same position as Sysiphus, forcing them to roll the heavy wagon of the five-year plan uphill. Behold, the people have achieved the goal, the five-year plan has been fulfilled. And there's the next wagon ready to go, and the people are harnessed up again. And once again the Leader promises every blessing.

However, it wasn't possible to cover up all the defects with the blaring of the gramophone. The discontent of the hungry and half-naked had to be taken into account. Stalin didn't have to think for long. The time had come to sacrifice the technical specialists. His personal prestige, he figured, was worth it. Joseph the Builder began his campaign against the "bourgeois" specialists in the very first year of the five-year plan, with the so-called Shakhty trial. The first frame-up trial. The first use of torture. The first executions.

Poor planning, administrative pressure tactics, and incompetent leadership, the lack of trained technical staffs and skilled workers—all of this was attributed to "sabotage" by hostile elements from the former possessing classes which had not yet been crushed completely. Inclined to hasty political generalizations (when they corresponded to his own personal, monarchical interests), Stalin diverted the discontent of the masses by turning it on the specialists who had been serving the country loyally. Stalin did not launch the slogan "Beat the *spetsy,* and save Russia."* He simply issued the directive, at the April plenum of the Central Committee in 1929, to track down the "Shakhty types" everywhere, "in all branches of our industry."

For four years the country was shaken by thunderous campaigns exposing wreckers in industry (the Shakhty trial, and the trials of the so-called Industrial Party and Union Bureau of the Menshevik Central Committee), in agriculture (the case of the so-called Working Peasants' Party) and in the supply sector (the alleged organization of Professor A. V. Ryazantsev and the former general E. S. Karatygin). The defendants in the Shakhty trial and the members of the mythical Industrial Party had allegedly blown up mines and factories, engaged in espionage, and made preparations for intervention against the Soviet Union in collaboration with the "sharks of world imperialism." The Mensheviks had helped draw up industrial development plans with maliciously low targets. The wrecking activities of the Working Peasants' Party in the countryside had consisted in organizing hundreds of thousands (!) of counterrevolutionaries. The wreckers in the supply sector had organized famine in the country, increased food prices, and sold poisoned canned goods to the population —for which they were shot, all forty-six of them. Invariably another charge was added, like a persistent refrain in a bad song: "They were helping prepare an armed attack upon the land of October; they wished to sell their own people into foreign slavery."

Stalin proved to be a first-rate specialist in the planning of these political provocations. Here both experience and native talent made themselves felt.

It was no great disaster that not everything in the investigations held together, that the most serious charges were not backed up by facts, objective witnesses, or authentic documents. The "candid confessions" of the defendants made up for that. The lively young muse of Stalinist justice was easily satisfied.

And what was the upshot? Hundreds of thousands deported to remote

---

*"Beat the *Jews,* and save Russia" was the slogan of a fascist-type movement in Russia, the Black Hundreds.—TRANS.

areas, thousands shot. Stalin had to create the impression of dazzling victories at any price. Even at the price of people's lives. Not his own though, of course.

Only a few years were to pass before the heads of those who organized the first construction projects and the heads of the industrial enterprises themselves would fly. There was a short list of names known to the whole country, radiant with awards and honors and well-deserved fame. All of them fell victim to Stalin's terror.*

Not until 1935 did Stalin begin his devastation of industry in Leningrad. At the Putilov works alone, 140 people were arrested—for alleged loyalty to the tsarist regime. Then another seven hundred were shot as enemies of the people, Trotskyists and Zinovievists. A new wave of repression washed over the Putilov works in 1937–38. The director, his deputies, the secretary of the party organization, and all chiefs of production shops were dragged off. Among those who perished were the director Ter-Asaturov and P. F. Antiukhin, head of Len-Energo. Leningrad's powerful industry was left denuded, and the state plan for increased production was thoroughly disrupted.

What were economic plans to Stalin, though? He had his own overall plan for bringing Russia to its knees.

He also struck at local leaders who had played a role in organizing Soviet industry—secretaries of the party's provincial committees and territorial committees. Stalin left none of them alive. They had been guided, in their time, by such prominent figures on the economic front as Pyatakov, Ordzhonikidze, Rudzutak, Kirov, Chubar, Kabakov, Dzerzhinsky, and Kuibyshev.

Killing as a means of "constructing." Why not? After all, it's well known that "cadres decide everything."

THE VICTOR

3

Once Stalin felt sure that people were taking seriously his announcement that the five-year plan was completed ahead of schedule—and he waited until late 1933 to be sure—he authorized his throne-room propagandists to proclaim the "world-historical victory" of the party's general line on all battle fronts. It was in those very terms that the delegates to the Seven-

*Omitted from the English edition at this point is a list, compiled by the author, of prominent industrial engineers and managers killed in the terror of the thirties. Interested specialists will find it in the Khronika Press Russian edition, pp. 110–111.—TRANS.

teenth Congress extolled the elusive gains of his rule up to that point.

The so-called Congress of Victors convened in January 1934. Stalin literally basked in the rays of his own glory. Three and a half years had passed since the Sixteenth Congress, when the Gensek had proclaimed "the all-out offensive of socialism on every front." In the intervening period, Stalin declared in his report to the Seventeenth Congress, the Soviet Union had been "radically transformed," had "cast off the integument of backwardness and medievalism." The reporter for the Central Committee went on with his cock-and-bull story, the delegates applauded in all the right places, and the chief actor-dissembler continued his monologue. In the "period under review" the USSR had been transformed from an agrarian country into an industrial power with a thriving mechanized agriculture and a flourishing culture. As usual he mentioned or quoted Lenin at appropriate points—a staging technique that had long been a standard in the Kremlin repertoire.

The production billed as the Seventeenth Congress followed the classic rules of the battle between good and evil. The sun of goodness already shone with overpowering brightness. There weren't enough of the evil antagonists; a more frightening dragon was needed. Stalin decided to piece one together out of the remnants of the "shattered anti-Leninist groups" and "antiparty deviationists." This dragon only *looked* dangerous, however. It did not dare to raise its paper head, blinded by the brilliant lighting effects of "the party's victories." The leaders of the opposition—the *ex*-opposition, that is—took turns recanting. Among the first were Bukharin and Tomsky.

Stalin forced others as well to participate in this sickening display. One was Lenin's close collaborator and one-time deputy as premier of the Soviet government, Aleksei Rykov. A gentle and kindly man, Rykov sat in one of the last rows of the meeting hall and trembled at the thought of what he would have to do on stage. His wife, a doctor working for the Central Committee apparatus at the time, stayed with him all day, giving him tranquilizers.

Two other participants in the orgy of self-flagellation were Zinoviev and Kamenev, later to be lumped together with the "Bukharinists" in the "two-faced Trotskyist gang." Stalin's hired claque howled and bayed in chorus, praising the Glorious Leader with well-remunerated zeal. A few isolated voices timidly recalled the tradition of Bolshevik modesty, but they were lost in the mighty roar of the victorious orchestra.

For example, the Uzbek Communist leader Akmal Ikramov remarked that it was wrong to boast of one's own successes and that praise in moderation was also a good thing. Stalin rudely interrupted this "miserable whiner" and "skeptic." No wonder Ikramov regressed so soon and fell into the camp of "enemies of the people." In 1937 he tried to protest the murder of loyal Communists, and was arrested and destroyed on Stalin's personal orders.[59]

Keeping up a deafening roar about the victories achieved under his leadership was only half of Stalin's job. He also had to stun the people, the whole world in fact, with his grandiose conception: the second five-year plan. For this purpose Molotov and Kuibyshev used a reliable old trick in their reports—taking 1913 as the reference point. Thus, by comparison with the prewar level, industrial output would increase 800 percent by 1937.

This nearly took some listeners' breath away. The general mood was expressed perhaps most picturesquely, in the most colorful officialese, by that inspired "tribune of the party," Sergei Kirov:

"Now you know damn well, to put it in human terms, this is the way people want to live, and keep on living; as a matter of fact, just look at what's been accomplished. And that's a fact!"

Speeches like this were all the rage back then. Intellectuals were avoided, thinking people isolated. Nevertheless, Kirov impressed everybody with his sincerity, his enthusiastic perception of things, and his energy.

There had been talk for a long time about the desirability of transferring Stalin from the post of general secretary to a purely governmental job —in the Presidium of the Central Executive Committee or the Council of People's Commissars. Hide the Testament of the deceased leader as he might, the document was still known to all leading party members. At the Seventeenth Congress, after blitz-collectivization and famine had taken millions of lives, after the experiments at planning and building giant industry had failed—and there were quite a few well-informed comrades among the delegates—and after the highly irregular trials of so-called spies and wreckers had taken place, there were heated discussions (in the corridors, of course) of the following possible variant: Kirov as general secretary; Stalin as premier (chairman of the Council of People's Commissars).

In Paris in 1936, Bukharin told Boris Nikolaevsky that some Bolsheviks had centered their hopes for a change in Stalin's harsh policies on the name of Kirov. For many party officials, both in the central government and in the local areas, Stalin's dictatorial rule had become intolerable. His rude administrative methods and the arbitrary ways of his supporters in the Central Committee weighed too heavily on them.

Did the Great Leader know about these unwholesome moods? No question. As early as January 1933 a joint plenum, at Stalin's insistence, had condemned A. Smirnov, Vladimir Tolmachev, and Nikolai Eismont. These three Old Bolsheviks' only "crime" was to have discussed privately, among themselves—and what were Stalin's agents for?—the possibility of some other leader's replacing Stalin as general secretary. For this subversive desire they paid with their lives.

Similarly, Joseph Pinkerton-Stalin got wind of a conversation held at Sergo Ordzhonikidze's apartment on the evening before the Central Committee elections at the Seventeenth Congress. Gathered at Sergo's place were Grigory Petrovsky, Stanislav Kosior, Boris Sheboldaev, Robert Eikhe, and Mamiya Orakhelashvili. They tried to convince Kirov of the necessity that Stalin step down. In the post of general secretary they wanted Kirov himself. But he, "the leader's best disciple," refused. Replace Stalin? Come off it. You think that's in the power of a mere mortal?

There he stands at the rostrum, the illustrious genius-secretary, his hairy paw outstretched for his ardent companions in arms to kiss. The delegates hasten to press their mouths to it. Who does not long to? They line up in a row. Among the first is Kirov. This is a scene I've only imagined. But it was entirely possible. Wasn't it Kirov, after all, who proposed that Stalin's report for the Central Committee be regarded as a resolution of the congress? Wasn't that motion carried unanimously, with the greatest enthusiasm?

Then came the final and surely the most important day of the congress. At this point we must proceed with the care and accuracy of a verifier of legal documents. An elections commission of forty-one delegates was chosen to conduct the secret balloting for a new Central Committee. Three persons were assigned to each of the thirteen ballot boxes. Incidentally, at the previous congress only two ballot boxes had been used; at congresses before that, only one. Another fact worth noting is that a specific number of voters was assigned to each ballot box, according to voting lists—for example, those with delegate cards numbered one to one hundred. Under this arrangement, of course, the votes of each group of delegates could be determined from the records for each ballot box. How could this be called a secret ballot?

Under Lenin the person regularly elected to preside over the elections commission was Nikolai Skrypnik, a revolutionary of exceptional courage. He could be a real stickler for detail when it came to internal party matters, and this quality was especially valued with regard to his duties on the elections commission. Under Stalin, the person usually put in charge of the elections commission was Vladimir Zatonsky. Zatonsky's deputy was Vasily Verkhovykh, an ex-soldier and a party member of long standing.

The voting process at the Seventeenth Congress took no more than two hours. Each vote-counting group of three delegates opened its ballot box, counted the ballots, filled out a form reporting the number of votes, and handed the results to Zatonsky or Verkhovykh. What's that? Two hundred ninety-two votes against Comrade Stalin? One-fourth of the congress delegates no longer wished to see the Source of Our Triumphs as a member of the Leninist-Stalinist Central Committee?!

The stunned commissioners decided to consult with Molotov and Kaganovich, members of the Politburo and secretaries of the Central Committee. Lazar Kaganovich understood that the end of Stalin's career would be the end of his. A man of action, he ordered 289 of those seditious ballots burned. For the sake of appearances, he let three of them remain. All thirteen voting forms and the summary report had to be changed accordingly. The results were announced to the delegates: all the candidates on the slate had been elected to the Central Committee.

Once, long ago, the Athenian statesman Aristides the Just was ostracized. The voting was done by dropping potsherds into an urn. A vote for ostracism was registered by writing on one's potsherd the name of the man to be ousted. When an illiterate peasant asked Aristides to write his name on the peasant's shard, Aristides did it without a moment's hesitation.

But why bring up Aristides the Just? The living example of Lenin was there before everyone. He always voted against his own candidacy in elections for the Central Committee. And at the Eighth Party Congress, when there were fifty votes against electing Lenin's comrade in arms Trotsky to the Central Committee, no one made a big thing of it.

But times had changed and the ways of the party with them. Now the slate of nominees corresponded exactly to the number of Central Committee members. There was no way a nominee could fail to be elected.

By this time the Gensek alone exercised supreme power in the land. He had the "president," Mikhail Kalinin, in one pocket and the "premier," Molotov, in the other. But 292 votes against—that had never happened in the history of the party.

The record of Stalin's foreign and domestic policies was an unbroken string of disasters. It has been rightly said that even a few of Stalin's catastrophic blunders would have been enough to destroy all confidence in a statesman in the West. But Stalin wouldn't resign. And that was not because the Soviet propaganda machine made each new disaster out to be a "historic triumph." It was the ancient tradition of the Asiatic despot, to whom retirement is an unknown word. Death is the only resignation he knows.

The records of the elections commission of the Seventeenth Congress were kept in the Central Party Archives under top security. Even Central Committee officials were denied access to them. These materials were not examined until 1957, after the Twentieth Congress. A special commission established by the Politburo came to the archives. One of its members was the personal assistant of Nikolai Shvernik, chairman of the Party Control Commission. The ballots and voting forms were kept in a special container closed with wax seals. The summary report was taken out first. It indicated three votes each against Stalin and Kirov. According to the credentials committee at the congress, there had been 1,225 voting delegates in attendance. The summary report listed only 936 voting delegates. The number of ballots was counted. There proved to be exactly 936—that is, 289 votes were missing.

What could have caused the disparity? The voting for the new Central Committee was held at the last evening session, after a break. Could almost three hundred people have met untimely deaths during that interval? Surely there was a more likely explanation. Verkhovykh provided information to that effect.

Verkhovykh was invited to the offices of the Central Committee and asked to give his recollections of that January evening in 1934. For the time being, no mention was made of what had been found in the archives. Verkhovykh gave this account to the investigating commission:

After finding 292 votes against Stalin, elections commission Chairman Zatonsky decided to consult with Kaganovich. Kaganovich asked him to wait a few minutes and left the room. When he returned, he asked how many votes Kirov had lost.

"Three," answered Zatonsky.

"Leave the same number against Comrade Stalin," Central Committee Secretary Kaganovich ordered. "Destroy the rest. This misunderstanding must be eliminated immediately." And so they did.

With whom did the wise and clever Lazar consult? An obvious purpose was served in leaving the same number of negative votes for the Gensek as for Kirov. It served Stalin.

The Politburo's investigating commission asked that Verkhovykh compose an official memorandum and submit it to the Party Control Commission. The next day the investigating commission left for Leningrad. A week later a call reached the commission from Moscow. The head of Shvernik's secretariat, Pavel Bogoyavlensky (remember that name), reported that Verkhovykh had not submitted anything.

"Well, remind him."

"I called him at home, but *your* Verkhovykh gave me the brush-off," Bogoyavlensky replied, with a certain grim satisfaction.

Later, when the commission returned to Moscow, Verkhovykh entrusted his recollections to someone he considered appropriate.

"Why didn't you give this affidavit to Bogoyavlensky or his assistants?" he was asked.

"I don't trust them. A bunch of scoundrels."

Besides Verkhovykh, one other member of the Seventeenth Congress elections commission survived Stalin's prisons and camps. Napoleon Andreasyan was his name. He took a somewhat different line: "Don't know anything and don't remember anything." For two hours they pleaded with him, entreated, appealed to his sense of courage and duty. If Stalin's name had been crossed out on 292 ballots, they reasoned, there must have been such ballots in every one of the thirteen boxes. At last Andreasyan "remembered" that two or three such ballots had shown up in his box. Then he "recalled" that there may have been twice as many. But when it came to making a written statement, Andreasyan clammed up again. New agonizing entreaties met with continuing cowardly refusal. At last he picked up his pen and began to write:

"At the insistence of representatives of the Party Control Commission I hereby state that in the counting of the votes for new members of the Central Committee at the Seventeenth Congress, in the ballot box to which my group was assigned four ballots were found with the name of Joseph Vissarionovich Stalin crossed out. I consider this entire investigation harmful, as tending to undermine the authority of Comrade Stalin."

Andreasyan was friendly with Anastas Mikoyan; they had studied at the same seminary. When he heard of Napoleon's behavior, Anastas was surprised and appealed to his friend's conscience. But Napoleon was more farsighted than Anastas. Eight years went by and Andreasyan came to see him at the Party Control Commission.

"There! See how things have turned around? He's back in the saddle again."

Whenever I think about the degeneration of the Old Bolsheviks, I recall that party veteran Andreasyan. And I think of those nearly three hundred delegates at the Congress of Victors who dared to cast a secret vote against the universal object of worship. What truly courageous people they were.

Mussolini, the idol of the Italian philistines, Stalin's contemporary, was arrested immediately after the Grand Fascist Council passed a vote of no confidence against him on July 25, 1943. Within a year Il Duce had been hanged. A logical step and a worthy end. The logic of history passed Stalin by—or, more accurately, he constantly managed to evade it.

The Seventeenth Congress was Stalin's first warning signal. If it hadn't been for Kaganovich, Molotov, and his other servants, that warning could have been his last. Scared to death, the Gensek decided to draw up an enemies' list. But how to get the names of the 292 who had dared prefer the upstart Kirov over the Leader?

In the breaks between sessions of the congress, Stalin's agents strolled purposefully through the corridors, listening to delegates' conversations. Stalin knew whom he had to put away first of all. But wouldn't it be better to destroy *all* the delegates, leaving only a hundred or so that were known to be loyal and devoted? Preventive medicine is a great thing. And that's how he finally proceeded. Not right away, of course. Knowing how to wait was not the least of his assets in the struggle for power. By 1938 he would be rid of them all. The elections commission would be arrested almost entirely, Zatonsky one of the first.

February 1938. Zatonsky sits in a cell in Butyrka prison, waiting to be called for "trial." The Military Collegium of the Supreme Court, headed by the Stalinist executioner Vasily Ulrikh, would hear his case. In this court everything was decided far in advance, but the three-minute ritual of "hearing the case" was invariably observed. The bolt in the door of Zatonsky's cell clanked. They had come for him. Zatonsky took off his jacket, his trousers, his shoes, and gave them to his cellmates. Then he handed out what tobacco and sugar cubes he had.

"Take them, take them, comrades. I was chairman of the elections commission at the Seventeenth Congress. I know what's in store for me. I couldn't tell the interrogator everything, but I'm going to tell the court. And I won't be back, ever. They won't just shoot me either."

We must assume that Vladimir Zatonsky, a hero of the underground and the civil war, conducted himself heroically before that kangaroo court. Who was it he told about the vote tampering at the Seventeenth Congress? Ulrikh, that uniformed toad with watery eyes.

Having safely cleared the critical obstacle of the Seventeenth Congress, Stalin could look back with satisfaction. He had succeeded in packing the Central Committee with an entire cartridge clip of *his own people:* Genrikh Yagoda, Nikolai Yezhov, Lavrenty Beria, Vsevolod Balitsky, Yefim Yevdokimov, Nikita Khrushchev, Dzhafar Bagirov, Lev Mekhlis, Aleksandr Poskrebyshev.

What a constellation of experts in taking heads off at the shoulder! In addition to Kaganovich, Molotov, Voroshilov, Zhdanov, Andreyev, Mikoyan, and Shkiryatov (Vyshinsky and Malenkov would be added later). These men would constitute the nucleus of Stalin's Black Hundred, which would drown the country in blood.

We see that Vyacheslav Menzhinsky, chairman of the OGPU and a distinguished Old Bolshevik, was dropped from the new Central Committee. He didn't stack up. On the other hand, Stalin added three NKVD functionaries as candidate members—Terenty Deribas, Ivan Pavlunovsky, and Georgy Blagonravov. Nearly a dozen representatives of the security agencies were now on the Central Committee. Likewise, the Gensek reinforced the Party Control Commission with *his people*—Pyotr Pospelov and Matvei Shkiryatov. They served him well to the very end.

Many Old Bolsheviks, collaborators of Lenin, found themselves off the Central Committee, with the mark of "oppositionist" on their foreheads. The Great Victor demoted Bukharin, Tomsky, and Rykov from full to candidate members. The Gensek was getting ready for Act III.

The proletarians of Moscow marched out onto Red Square to greet the delegates to the Congress of Victors. A skillfully organized "spontaneous" demonstration of the workers. Who should welcome this demonstration?

"Kirov!" the meeting hall breathed out unanimously.

"Now you know damn well, to put it in human terms, this is the way people want to live, and keep on living; as a matter of fact, just look at what's been accomplished. And that's a fact!"

THE ASSASSIN OF KIROV

4

After the congress, Stalin called Kirov into his office. The Gensek already knew everything—that they had tried to persuade "Mironych"* to accept

---

*"Mironych": Kirov's full name was Sergei *Mironovich* Kirov. The patronymic ending *-ovich* in Russian names, meaning "son of" (in this case, "son of Miron"), is often shortened to *-ych* to create an affectionate nickname. Similarly, Vladimir Ilyich ("son of Ilya") Lenin was familiarly called "Ilyich."—Trans.

the top party post and that Kirov had answered this way: "If I was appointed general secretary, that would call into question the policies of the party—collectivization, industrialization, nationalities policy, our building of socialism in general. No, that's something I wouldn't agree to. You can't change horses in midstream."

Stalin very much wanted to hear this first-hand from his rival—from his own lips. With anxious heart, beneath a mask of majestic calm, the Gensek peered into the candid, open face of "the favorite of the whole party." Kirov didn't deny anything. He had rejected the proposal the comrades had made, because Stalin was the real chief, in whom the party had confidence. The entire Soviet people looked to him for leadership.

"But," Kirov added, "you yourself are to blame for what happened. After all, we told you things couldn't be done in such a drastic way."

They were on familiar terms, the general secretary and the Leningrad provincial secretary. Stalin demonstrated his friendship for Kirov on every appropriate occasion. He had given Kirov an autographed copy of his book *Problems of Leninism*, with the demonstrative inscription "To a brother and a friend."

* * *

The newly elected Central Committee gathered for a plenary session on organizational matters. Stalin proposed Kirov as a candidate member of the Central Committee's secretariat, but "Mironych" opposed the idea. He was backed by Ordzhonikidze: "We have plenty of people here in Moscow, but there's no one else like Kirov in Leningrad."

Stalin didn't back off so easily. "I think," the Gensek began, "that the two posts can be combined. Let Sergei Mironovich be both secretary of the Leningrad provincial committee and a secretary of the Central Committee." The choice was confirmed. But Kirov's Moscow office remained empty the whole year; he didn't set foot in it even once.

As he left the Central Committee building the evening of that memorable day, Kirov knew that he wouldn't escape the executioner's block. Over dinner at his Moscow apartment on Sadovo-Kudrinskaya Street, he said as much to Filipp Medved, head of the Leningrad NKVD. Medved had been working in Leningrad for four years. Before that he had headed the Cheka in Tula, then in Moscow, and from 1926 to 1930 had worked in the Soviet Far East.

In the NKVD central apparatus, it was immediately clear what kind of situation had developed in the top leadership. Kirov's doom was assured —that was the openly expressed opinion of the agents who stayed at the NKVD hotel (the Select) on Sretenka Street. Kirov had no options. He couldn't overthrow Stalin: his rigid party supersititions and deep-seated infantilism prevented that. The only thing left was to wait passively for his own destruction.

After his return to Leningrad, Kirov took a vacation at the nearby resort of Sestroretsk. He invited his old friend Aleksei ("Alyosha") Sevostyanov, an industrial worker, to go with him. Talking with his friend in Sestroretsk, Kirov let these words slip out: "Alyosha, my head is on the block. They're going to kill me."

In 1956 Sevostyanov was working in the Ministry of Ferrous Metallurgy. At Khrushchev's request he briefly recounted his conversation with Kirov during that memorable spring of 1934 and promised to describe his meetings with Sergei Mironovich in full detail.

Sevostyanov returned home, rang the bell, and, when his wife opened the door, fell dead on the threshold. He was a large, powerfully built man. For men of that type heart attacks are not uncommon.

Sevostyanov was not the only witness who miraculously survived the Stalin years. Kirov also expressed fear for his life in the presence of S. M. Sobolev, secretary of the Leningrad provincial committee of the Young Communist League, and Sobolev's wife.

In 1911, the tsarist premier Pyotr Stolypin said in confidence, a few months before his death at the hands of an assassin, to the minister of finance Vladimir Kokovtsov, "My own secret police are going to kill me." In Kirov's case too it was not that he was tortured by premonitions. He was *certain* he would soon be killed; he expected his own execution.

Sophia Lvovna, older sister of Kirov's wife, Maria, had been a party member since 1911 and within the party was considered the "godmother" of Sergei Mironovich. Twenty-two years after the assassination she would state that from February 1934 on, Kirov lived in daily expectation of death. Every morning her sister Maria's anxious eyes would follow her husband to his car. This went on for ten full months, until the fateful day, December 1. The constant fear for her husband's life deprived her of her reason. During the war Sophia Lvovna removed her stricken sister from Leningrad, under blockade at the time.

Sophia Lvovna died suddenly in 1961, in her bed, as she was listening to the radio reports on the Twenty-second Party Congress. (One more echo of the Kirov murder—and not the last.) She left her memoirs in manuscript form, containing passages on the relations between Kirov and Stalin.

About a month after the Seventeenth Congress, the Gensek began to summon Kirov to Moscow repeatedly. Even before, Stalin had criticized Kirov sharply and frequently for various oversights. But now, each time, he gave Kirov a royal dressing-down. At Politburo meetings Stalin flaunted his power. If someone tried to oppose him, the Master would leave the room. They would have to send Kaganovich or Kirov after him, and it would be a long time before he'd return.

Usually the Gensek would quarrel with Kirov and reject all his proposals. Stalin demanded that the "enemies of the people," of whom there were thousands in Leningrad because of the "gullibility" of the provincial committee, be exposed and destroyed. Kirov flatly refused to take part in any slaughter of party cadres. Nevertheless, from the platforms of party meetings he did pound away with all his lavish intellectual gifts at the followers of Zinoviev. But Stalin was untiring in his reproaches: "You're using the campaign against the opposition just to strengthen your personal power."

After each of these Politburo sessions Kirov would return to Leningrad terribly depressed, and it was a long time before he'd be himself again. On one occasion Kaganovich reported to a Politburo session in his usual devoted way, keeping his "inner anxieties" to himself, that the Moscow organization had shown that it knew how to appreciate Stalin and to pay tribute to his genius. But unfortunately, the same could not be said of the Leningrad comrades. Kirov was forced to summon all the Leningrad district committee secretaries and ask them to reorganize their work. "We must decisively raise the authority of the general secretary in the eyes of the masses," he commanded.

In the Politburo Kirov represented the moderate wing of the Central Committee. In 1932 he was among those who spoke against the execution of Ryutin.* He also spoke in favor of a moderate policy in the famine-stricken villages. He suggested that the party line not be dictated to writers and artists, and that an atmosphere of trust be established between the creative intelligentsia and the authorities. Kirov also had differences with Stalin on the international Communist movement.

But we should not exaggerate their differences. Like all the other Stalinists, Kirov called for uncompromising struggle against opportunists of every stripe. He took part in the hounding of Uglanov. Together with Sergo, he exposed and denounced the "right-wing" Communists at the Sixteenth Party Congress. And praised Stalin: "Our party is firm, united, and monolithic as never before, ranged solidly around its Central Committee and its leader, Comrade Stalin," he declared at the Sixteenth Congress.[60]

Devotion was always a good thing. But Koba killed people who were even more devoted.

If you look closely at the personalities of such assassins as Lee Oswald and Sirhan Sirhan and think about their behavior and actions, you notice something they had in common. They were all embittered misfits, people with something lacking, physically and psychologically incomplete. That's what Leonid Nikolaev was like too.

Various legends circulate about the man who committed what is sometimes called "the crime of the century."

Son of a hopeless alcoholic, Nikolaev was born deformed. He couldn't walk until he was fourteen. Crooked legs, short stature, and an enormous resentment against humanity—such is the portrait of the sixteen-year-old who joined the Bolshevik Party in 1920. He took part in the grain-requisitioning units' forays into the countryside and subsequently mastered the skills of a drill-press operator, but factory work was hard for him. This

*The Ryutin affair, which involved an opposition program calling for Stalin's removal, is described in the next chapter.—TRANS.

perennial malcontent, whom fate had passed by, envied the party official-dom and sought to win some sort of administrative position, however lowly.

In 1930 he found a place in the division of the Workers' and Peasants' Inspectorate concerned with prices. His ten-year membership in the party helped. It was not bad as a first step, opening up some possibilities. To consolidate his position, Nikolaev began to attend a party school in the evening and completed the course of instruction there.

Because of his lack of any real practical ability, however, he was forced to leave the important institution in which he had ensconced himself. That happened in January 1932, at a time when a mass party purge was getting under way. Nikolaev was not expelled from the party, but it was only with difficulty that he found a second-rate job in the archives of a district committee of the party. One more painful pinprick to his morbid self-esteem.

But to balance that, in the party purge, which picked up steam while he was at his new job, Nikolaev felt he was in his element. Invariably he sat in the front row of the meeting hall and pelted loyal Communists with tricky questions. What a delight—to see the party brass squirm on the stage in front of you, their eyes darting nervously, with none of the usual aplomb of "important leaders."

Then a mobilization of party members for railroad work was an-nounced, and Nikolaev's name appeared as one of the first on the list. The end of his career! Nikolaev complained to the district committee, then to the city committee. No use. He wrote to Kirov personally. But his memo was forwarded directly from Kirov's reception room back to the district committee—the well-oiled bureaucratic machine was working smoothly. Nikolaev felt he was at the end of his rope. He flatly refused to do his duty on the labor front. And for that, naturally, was expelled from the party.

The only thing left him was this: Back to the factory. Back to the drill press. Start over from scratch. Even worse, actually. Because now he was an *ex–party member!* Nevertheless, he fought to have truth and justice restored. For him that meant securing important party work, the chance to be a leader and enjoy all the privileges of rank. Neither the district committee nor the city committee "understood" him. All they could sug-gest was that he renew himself amid the class whose hegemony rules Soviet society—that is, back to the drill press, back to the factory.

Fortunately, Nikolaev had never forgotten that in Moscow, in the Kremlin, lived a man who was all-knowing, all-comprehending, and all-powerful. He would not allow people to make a mockery of an honest Communist.

Nikolaev wrote to Stalin. He told the Leader his trials and tribulations. He unmasked the cold-hearted, callous bureaucrats and especially reviled Kirov, who had not even had the decency to reply to a deserving party member.

"Dear Joseph Vissarionovich! They have brought me to the point of desperation by unjust persecution. I am now capable of anything."

O you vast tribe of party secretaries, whose merits have not yet been immortalized. Will a Shakespeare ever be found to do you justice?

Some purebred dogs have a remarkable sense of smell; they are able to detect a scent up to twenty-five points on a scale. What scale can measure the secretary's olfactory powers? There is none. There never could be. The keenness of the secretarial nose surpasses all bounds.

Who was the irreplaceable secretary that smoothly and unobtrusively picked one letter out of the hundreds that came to the Gensek every day? Who placed that ordinary-looking envelope sealed with hate upon the Boss's desk?

Nikolaev waited for an answer. He was growing poor, but still he would not go back to the factory. The former NKVD officer Orlov reports that a denunciation came in against Nikolaev as a person dangerously embittered by adversity. And that the Leningrad "secret section for political cases" placed him under surveillance as a potential terrorist.[61]

Nikolaev sent further declarations, each more biting than the last. Finally, on orders from the center, Nikolaev was restored to party membership, but he was given a severe reprimand as a warning for breaking party discipline. In Nikolaev, Stalin saw an instrument for his design. Stalin could sniff out a criminal miles away.

It so happened that there were two brothers named Orlov in a Leningrad jail at that time. On death row. When it came to dirty business, they knew a thing or two. They were approached by certain unnamed persons, who had been sent from higher up. Make an attempt on Kirov's life, they were told, and if you succeed, your lives will be spared.

Late one night the Orlovs were brought to Kirov's house. The guard outside had prudently been removed, and the brothers went up the back way without interference. Kirov was still awake, visiting with guests. The two goons began trying to break down the locked door. Sophia Lvovna (Kirov's sister-in-law) was afraid the door would give under the heavy blows. But when the Orlov brothers heard several men's voices inside, they took off. Soon after, they were executed. But if they had been "successful," would they have been pardoned? Hardly. The law of the criminal world is the same whether in a prison cell or in the Gensek's office: "You today, me tomorrow." (The investigation made after the Twentieth Congress confirmed the participation of the NKVD as the ones giving orders, and of the Orlov brothers as the ones following orders, in the nighttime assault on Kirov's apartment.)

The next attempt was made in the summer of 1934 in Kazakhstan, where Kirov was sent as the Central Committee's authorized representative for grain procurements. An accident was skillfully arranged: the car carrying the Politburo member went flying down an embankment. Fortunately, no one was hurt.

Now a new opportunity was presenting itself. It must not be missed. But to whom should this "capable of anything" Nikolaev be entrusted?

Filipp Medved wasn't suitable for the role. Too friendly with Kirov, too loyal to him. And changing the leadership of the Leningrad NKVD would arouse suspicions. The best thing, probably, was to put your own man in as first deputy to Medved. Stalin went with that plan.

The first thing was to get rid of Karpov, who had been working with Medved for a long time. A reassignment was arranged for Karpov—from Leningrad to Voronezh, to the NKVD's transportation division.

Medved took pains to have his long-time colleague provided with his own railroad car, and went to the station himself with two baskets of oranges for the trip. Karpov was sure his former chief was responsible for the transfer. So he was puzzled. Why this masquerade?

"Believe me," Medved assured him, "I don't know who arranged your new assignment. You and I are used to each other, we've had a good working relationship. Please don't think it was my doing."

Karpov's replacement was Zaporozhets. Why did Stalin choose this particular man? At one time Zaporozhets had been a member of the Left Socialist Revolutionary Party. His government work began with the Cheka. In 1920 he infiltrated Makhno's command staff.* In the NKVD he had been deputy chief of the information division.

Tall, broad-shouldered, a "fine figure of a man," Zaporozhets was a joker and a wit, the life of the party at picnics and outings, and a connoisseur of wine and women. Full of the joy of life, he was. He loved to live with style, and he knew how. Also how to kill with style.

Filipp Medved did not know Zaporozhets. The few scraps of information he managed to come by did not dispose him to feel much confidence, however. That's why Medved asked Sergei Mironovich to spare him this unasked-for deputy. Kirov called the Boss. Stalin hit the roof.

"What are your people up to, there in Leningrad? The appointment has been made. Zaporozhets was recommended by the Central Committee. Decisions of the Central Committee are binding on everyone. Tell your Medved not to try dictating personnel policy to the CC."

Zaporozhets settled in, moved his family to Leningrad. His wife, Proskurovskaya, joined the staff of the party's provincial committee.

Zaporozhets got busy with Nikolaev right away, placing him under the charge of a trusted assistant from the secret section. Zaporozhets was present in person several times, in the role of a visiting staff member in civilian clothes, when Nikolaev was being interviewed in someone else's office.

A standard technique of the tsarist Okhrana.

It wasn't hard to convince the failed civil servant Nikolaev that casehardened bureaucrats like Kirov were destroying the party from within. Already full of bile, Nikolaev conceived a violent hatred for Kirov, and

---

*Nestor Makhno, during the Russian civil war of 1918–20, led a peasant army in the Ukraine which opposed both the Soviet Red Army and the counterrevolutionary Whites. They called themselves "Greens."—TRANS.

focused his insatiable thirst for revenge on the Leningrad leader. When they proposed that he "save the party" by freeing it from this dangerous enemy, he agreed without a moment's hesitation.

They gave this "enacter of the party's will" a pistol and a black leather briefcase with a specially made flap in the top, so that, on the right occasion, he could easily reach the pistol without opening the case. They also began to take Nikolaev for target practice at a restricted firing range. In all other respects he was ready. Even to die in the attempt, as long as his name lived after him.

Nikolaev wrote in his diary, "I came into this world as a new Zhelyabov.* I will perform a deed of liberation and save Russia."

On one of the sheets in his diary Nikolaev marked off the route Kirov took on his walks. Sergei Mironovich lived not far from the party offices at the Smolny Institute and often walked to or from work, while his guards fanned out behind him in a semicircle, covering the rear and both flanks. In October Nikolaev began to follow along after the ring of guards. He usually stayed back a good distance, but he did not go unnoticed. Twice a suspicious individual was detained, carrying a briefcase in which a gun and some notes were found. Twice he was let go by order of Zaporozhets.

Kirov's bodyguard Borisov and the other agents were indignant and were about to appeal to Medved. But Zaporozhets called them into his office, took their party cards, and locked them in his safe.

"That man you don't touch," he ordered fiercely.

Thus all the steps leading up to the final act had been thoroughly rehearsed. Nikolaev was prepared, the day was set, and Zaporozhets went off for a vacation in the south. A distant resort would make a good alibi.

On December 1, 1934, a meeting of the active party membership of Leningrad province was to be held in the Tauride Palace. Kirov was at home completing the outline for his report. Remembering that he had left some necessary statistical material in his office, he called the garage for his car and gave notice he was going to Smolny. It was about four o'clock in the afternoon.

Nikolaev had been furnished with a pass to the Tauride Palace and was awaiting Kirov's arrival. Suddenly he was notified that the chief was going to stop at Smolny first. It would be *better* there. No pass was needed; a party card was enough. Nikolaev was quickly brought to the provincial committee building. With his black briefcase he entered, went up to the third floor, and hid in the bathroom. From the bathroom window the main entrance was visible.

Nikolaev knew his way around Smolny quite well. The division of the Workers' and Peasants' Inspectorate, in which he had worked earlier, was located on the first floor. He knew that the third-floor hallway took a sharp turn to the left at the first secretary's office.

*Zhelyabov was the leader of the People's Will, the terrorist group that assassinated Tsar Alexander II in 1881.—TRANS.

Here came Kirov's automobile. Sergei Mironovich entered the building and went upstairs. At that moment the usual guards at the head of each flight of stairs were missing. No one was on duty on any of the floors. Instructions were for Borisov always to accompany Kirov. He was constantly on duty outside of Kirov's office and was in charge of the inside guard of the building. Borisov had managed to warn Kirov about Nikolaev and of the peculiar favoritism shown him by Medved's deputy.

Borisov wasn't there that day. He had been detained at the NKVD building. Nikolaev opened the door slightly and saw Kirov through the crack. He was walking down the hall alone; the guard had not caught up. Nikolaev left the bathroom, came within two meters of Kirov, pulled the pistol out of the briefcase, and, as Kirov turned the corner, shot him in the back of the head. Then he shot himself and fell alongside the stricken leader.

In the office of Mikhail Chudov, second secretary of the provincial committee, an editorial commission was at work preparing a draft resolution for the party membership meeting. A member of the commission named Tikhonov, head of the commerce administration of the provincial executive committee, ran out when he heard the shots; then he called the others. At first they thought the murderer was also dead, but it turned out he was unharmed; the bullet had gone into the ceiling. Chudov put his coat under Kirov's head and said, "Stay back. Don't touch anything. It could be evidence for the investigation."

Chudov went back into his office and called Stalin.

The Gensek gave orders at once: "Cancel the membership meeting. Surround Smolny with NKVD troops. Wait for further orders."

About six o'clock in the evening, Aleksandr Poskrebyshev, Stalin's personal secretary, called and dictated the text of an official communiqué from the Central Committee:

"On December 1 in Leningrad an outstanding leader of our party was struck down by the treacherous hand of an enemy of the working class," etc., etc.

The communiqué was capped by an appeal to the people:

"Root out once and for all the enemies of the working class!"

The investigation had not yet started. The body of the murdered man was still not cold, but the Central Committee knew everything: who had done the killing, where, and why. And how this onslaught by the class enemy should be answered.

An express train reached Leningrad early the following morning. Arriving with Stalin were Molotov, Voroshilov, Zhdanov, Vyshinsky, and Yezhov. Yezhov was the Central Committee official in charge of the NKVD, the procuracy, and the judicial agencies. Stalin brought him along to Leningrad to try him out, just as a mother wolf sics her cubs on the half-dead rabbit she has dragged into the lair.

Maybe the Master was already preparing to replace Yagoda as head of the NKVD. Yagoda was still walking around, breathing, giving orders, but to Stalin he was a corpse. He knew too much. After that would come Yezhov's turn. But for the time being Stalin put Yezhov in charge of the investigation.

A second train arrived from Moscow with a punitive detachment. (Among the new arrivals was the investigator Lyushkov, who in later years, after fleeing the country, would publish information exposing Stalin's role in falsifying the history of Kirov's death.) The Politburo members established themselves in Smolny.

Stalin knew whom to bring with him to Leningrad. Molotov, Voroshilov, and Zhdanov (who was already a candidate member of the Politburo) were absolutely obedient to his will and—no less important—capable of any crime. He had already tested them.

Stalin decided to question Nikolaev in person. He hoped that in his presence the fanatic would not dare name the real murderers and, with a foretaste of eternal "glory," would take it all upon himself. The arrested man was brought to Smolny.

Stalin asked, "Did you kill Kirov?"

"Yes, I . . ." Nikolaev started to answer, falling to his knees.

"Why did you do it?"

Nikolaev pointed at the officials standing behind Stalin's chair in NKVD uniforms. *"They* made me do it. They gave me four months of target practice. They told me that . . ."

Two men with stars on their lapels stepped from Stalin's side and hammered the loudmouth's head with the butts of their revolvers.

Nikolaev began to slump forward, but Stalin, with a blow from his boot, laid him out on his back.

If Nikolaev had said he was carrying out the orders of Zinoviev or Bukharin—let's take the ideal case—would Stalin have stayed the hand of his Oprichniks? He wouldn't have had to. The men in his service had fine intuition.

The bloody scene played out in Smolny on December 2 is so important that the names of all the witnesses must be given. Several have blessed history with their reminiscences. In addition to the men from Moscow, Mikhail Chudov, Medved, and the provincial procurator Palgov were present. Chudov was convinced that Nikolaev was finished off that morning and that the man questioned at his "trial" was a double. He expressed these suspicions to a comrade. Medved told his friends in the camps about the scene of Nikolaev's questioning, giving the same details. Medved's account stuck in several people's memories. In particular, Nikolaev's cry was remembered: *"They* kept at me for four months. They said it was necessary for the party."

Palgov told a friend the details of how the assassination was prepared. Then he committed suicide. Decent people cropped up even in those circles.

Stalin was quick to extract maximum political advantage from the Kirov assassination. Without waiting one hour, he gave the order by telephone to Moscow to publish the resolution of the Presidium of the Central Executive Committee on the struggle against terrorism.

Special bodies were authorized to conduct investigations at an accelerated pace in cases of terrorism, and sentences were to be carried out at once, because the Central Executive Committee would not consider pleas for clemency.[62]

The resolution was signed December 1. That means Stalin had drafted it in advance. The Master was not about to trouble himself with the proprieties. The Politburo and Central Committee, after all, were merely instruments of *his* will. Not long before the Kirov assassination, another man organized the Reichstag fire and used that political provocation as a signal for mass terror.

These two men at work—or, rather, serving the people, in Germany and in Russia—perhaps, without ever suspecting it themselves, were really twin brothers.

On December 3 an open-backed truck was driving down Voinov Street toward Smolny. In the back was Borisov, Kirov's bodyguard, and two other guards. On the right, the high blank wall of a warehouse without any windows stretched past. At this point the man next to the driver grabbed the wheel and cut it sharply, but the driver managed to straighten it. The NKVD man tried again and steered the truck up over the sidewalk into the wall. Crash; the truck stopped. No one was hurt, it seemed at first. However, in the back, the second phase of the planned operation was completed with lightning speed. One blow from an iron crowbar crushed Borisov's skull. The guard struck a second time, just to be sure.

Neither the driver nor the man next to him received even a scratch in this "accident." Only the truck's right fender was dented. The driver turned the truck around and drove back to the garage.

Borisov was an upright type, who couldn't be bought, and was genuinely devoted to Kirov. He might mess up a second round of questioning, the way Nikolaev had the first round at Smolny the day before. It came out later that the men who did away with Borisov were members of the Gensek's personal guard. Carrying out His will.

The death certificate stated that Borisov had died as a result of an automobile accident. (In 1956 the surviving doctors would show that death had been caused by blows to the skull from a blunt metallic object.)

Then they got rid of Borisov's wife. In such cases any witness is one too many. What if she knew something from remarks her husband had made? They put her away in a psychiatric hospital, just in case. And there they poisoned her.[63]

The wife of Chudov, a long-time party member by the name of Ludmilla Shaposhnikova, was sent to the camps, sentenced to eight years as a "member of the family of a traitor to the motherland." She was in a special compound for wives of enemies of the people at the prison in Tomsk. In 1938 she was summoned for a trip to Moscow. As she said good-bye to her friends she remarked: "Obviously the camp isn't enough for me. We won't see each other again." They killed her, just as they had her husband.

The driver of the truck that was taking Borisov to Smolny was the only one who managed to outlive Stalin—an extremely rare case when you consider that he was sent to the death camps. (The man who killed Borisov was prudently erased within a few weeks.) After the Twentieth Congress the truck driver told the Politburo commission investigating the assassination what he knew.[64] By the beginning of the Twenty-second Congress the Politburo had a thoroughly verified picture of the crime and the elimination of witnesses. If Khrushchev had wished to, he could have exposed the chief organizer of the Kirov assassination in full.

In the prison hospital they soon brought Nikolaev around. Once he had recovered, some experienced arm-twisters took him over. Beatings, prison conditions designed to break his will, a little bit of chemistry—all the usual things. And for a type like him, threats alone would have sufficed. Soon Nikolaev was crushed and ready to confess that he had belonged to a counterrevolutionary terrorist Trotskyist-Zinovievist center and had acted on its instructions.

Tormented by awful doubts, Nikolaev tried once to smash his head against the cell wall. An NKVD agent had to be put in with him. The name of this cellmate was Katsafa, an experienced comrade with the rank of lieutenant commander. Katsafa kept his uniform on, and perhaps that rare move—prison authorities playing it straight with one of their wards—made Katsafa's job easier.

Nikolaev soon came to trust Katsafa and asked his advice. Should he "expose" the fancied terrorist center or not? The investigator promised his life would be spared if he did. The investigator said—and the head of the investigations division confirmed it—that Nikolaev would be given a trifling sentence, three years or so, would be transferred quickly and conveniently to a labor camp, and there would be given a job in cultural-educational work. Nikolaev hesitated. What if it was a trick? But he decided to go ahead.

Stalin and his retinue returned to Moscow December 4. The Gensek called in the men who worked at the NKVD's central card file and asked for the cards on everyone who in the past had been an active oppositionist. In those days the file keepers were ordinary staff members. By the time of the Twentieth Congress they wore colonel's insignia. These colonels told how they had carried out the Gensek's assignment.

Stalin had taken a sheet of paper and drawn a line down the middle, dividing it in two. On the left side he put the heading "Leningrad Terrorist Center"; on the right, "Moscow Terrorist Center." Then the Master took from them several dozen cards and quickly filled the two columns with names. At first he wrote Zinoviev and Kamenev's names together on the left-hand side; then he crossed out Zinoviev's name and moved it to the right-hand column. (This sheet of paper was found intact in the personal archives of the deceased Leader. Handwriting analysis, done by experts after the Twentieth Congress, confirmed that the document was written by Stalin.)

But let us return to 1934, which was already nearing its end.

The investigation into the Kirov assassination, as we have said, was headed by Yezhov. One member of Yezhov's team was Lev Sheinin, an investigator for especially important cases working for the public prosecutor's office of the USSR under Vyshinsky. In Moscow, Vyshinsky had grabbed Sheinin and brought him along to Leningrad. Sheinin, who has since passed away, had some interesting things to tell about the whole business.

On the second day after Kirov's assassination, Leonid Zakovsky arrived in Leningrad. He was the former commissar of internal affairs for Byelorussia. Stalin put him in to replace Medved, who had "messed up." Earlier, Zakovsky had worked in Vinnitsa, Odessa, and Minsk. Stalin had been especially impressed with his style. By 1934 he had successfully mastered and applied the "latest" methods—fabricated cases, refined tortures, lavish promises, and cruel punishments.

"If Karl Marx himself fell into my hands, he'd soon confess to spying for Bismarck," Zakovsky liked to brag. Alas, he wasn't just blowing his own horn. During the four years when he ran Leningrad, Zakovsky reaped more than one bloody harvest. Then Stalin put an end to him as a British spy. This was to happen under the new NKVD commissar, Beria.

Within days after the Kirov assassination arrests began among leaders of the Leningrad Young Communist League (YCL). One of the first names on the "Leningrad Terrorist Center" list was Ivan Kotolynov. In the 1920s he had been secretary of the Vyborg district committee of the Young Communist League and a member of the YCL Central Committee. He had opposed the violence and arbitrariness of the Stalinists in the YCL and in 1934 had taken part in discussions on a project for a book about the history of the League. In the interrogators' offices these meetings were transformed into secret gatherings of terrorists, with Nikolaev allegedly in attendance.

Since the "counterrevolutionary" activity of Kotolynov and others had begun in the 1920s under Zinoviev, Stalin had no trouble turning the investigation in the necessary direction. At the same time he linked the exiled Trotsky with the affair as the one who supposedly exercised "overall leadership" of the conspirators through an unnamed foreign consul. Nikolaev was supposed to have received money from this mythical diplomat. That at least is what was said in the indictment published on December 27, 1934, over the signatures of Vyshinsky and Sheinin.

One of the first to be arrested was Grigory Yevdokimov, a former secretary of the Central Committee. Then Ivan Bakaev, who had headed the Leningrad GPU under Zinoviev. On December 15, Zinoviev himself was hauled in, and after him, Kamenev.

Stalin skillfully prepared the party for these police measures, and whipped the population into a state of hysteria through the press, the radio, and the use of mass rallies. On his order, in strict compliance with the new "law," tens of thousands were shot in the first days of December as White Guards, Trotskyists, and terrorists in general. Their names were dug out of the records of party congresses and meetings held long ago, or wrenched from lips that had turned pale from torture under "questioning." *Pravda* called for "the lives of the leaders to be safeguarded the same way we protect our flag on the field of battle."[65]

Everyone knows that on the field of battle they shoot. Against this background the arrest of Zinoviev and Kamenev, Lenin's comrades in arms, who had shared power in the party with Stalin for so many years, went smoothly. And the shooting went on and on and on. The kettle was boiling. Stalin ordered: "More wood on the fire!"

On December 22 *Pravda* presented Stalin's foul concoction to the public. Nikolaev's pistol had been aimed at the heart of the party by the Leningrad Trotskyist-Zinovievist center. It was very important for Stalin to bring Zinoviev and Kamenev into it—as the "inspirers of terrorism." And the readers of *Pravda* swallowed it, along with the news that the former Politburo members and their "accomplices" had been arrested.

Accompanying all this were certain rumors, which we must assume did not originate on some village bench. First, the rumor that Nikolaev had been torn apart by an angry mob on the way to prison. "Eyewitnesses" even appeared. Then the rumor that Nikolaev had killed Kirov out of jealousy. Wasn't it through the same keyholes that other rumors crept concerning Yagoda (in 1938)—that he was getting ready to flee the country and was caught at the airport with a suitcase full of gold in his hand? It's hard to tell when this art of "gendarme folklore" sprang up in Russia; but that Stalin made the genre flourish—of that there can be no doubt.

Stalin's great wish was to organize a public trial. But it was one thing to draw up two lists assigning good Communists to two different "terrorist centers"; it was something else again to extract "sincere confessions" from them. For that a good deal of time was needed. And the Soviet people were impatient. Listen, for example, to what the workers were saying at turbulent mass rallies.

"Dear Joseph Vissarionovich, we know that in the person of our dear Kirov you lost not only your loyal disciple and fighting comrade in arms but also your dear and close friend."

This is from a declaration addressed to Stalin by 200,000 workers of the Kirov district of Leningrad. They promised "to keep a sharper eye out, to increase our revolutionary vigilance and alertness, and to struggle ever more firmly to destroy completely, down to the very roots, the last remnants of the class enemy."

And again: "Long live the wise leader and teacher of the world proletariat, our Stalin!"[66]

Wise? A clumsily arranged assassination and a clumsily constructed investigation. The indictment states that a certain foreign consul gave

Nikolaev five thousand rubles, forty-five hundred of which he passed on to Kotolynov. Nikolaev hadn't worked since March 1934; still, he lived comfortably in a three-room apartment and rented a dacha in Sestroretsk. All this on the miserly sum of five hundred rubles. The authors of the indictment told the public that Nikolaev and Kotolynov had jointly worked out the plan to kill Kirov. Through this act of terrorism they had aimed at arousing the entire Soviet people against the party and government.

The indictment was based almost totally on Nikolaev's fantastic "confession." There is no testimony from Kotolynov or other "leaders" of the terrorist underground.[67] No one bothered to try for believability. Stalin's subjects had no special craving for that. *Pravda* had called this phony indictment a "document of grim accusation." Wasn't that enough?

A cloudburst of popular indignation followed. After the workers, the intellectuals spoke up. Thousands of students and professors from the Rostov Teachers' Institute demanded "that all members of the counter-revolutionary terrorist organization be shot immediately."[68] The journalist Mikhail Koltsov published an article called "The Killers from the Leningrad Center." The author asked rhetorically, "And who put the murderer up to it?"[69] Who indeed?

In November an émigré newspaper published in Belgrade, *Za Rossiyu* (For Russia), had called for terror against the Soviet leaders. An article titled "What Are They Afraid Of?" had stated bluntly, "Kirov in Leningrad must be eliminated."[70] But Stalin hardly needed the urging of the White émigrés to murder his "dear and close friend." He did it entirely on his own. Then, responding to the ardent wishes of the workers, the Gensek reduced all legal formalities to the minimum.

As early as December 28 Nikolaev was brought before the Military Collegium of the Supreme Court of the USSR. The hearing, in Leningrad, was conducted by the perennial chairman of the collegium, Vasily Ulrikh. Although he was quite tall, Ulrikh didn't look it when he sat slumped behind the judge's bench. He was a stereotyped bureaucrat, gone to fat early in life. When he lifted his puffy face from his papers and, peering through his spectacles, drilled the next victim with his tiny eyes, the prisoner—alone and doomed—would be seized with dread. Ten years and death were the standard sentences, but in that court they rarely gave ten years.

The courtroom was filled with security agents. Ominously visible above the judge's bench was a shaved, yellowish bald head that came to a point at the top. Flabby folds hung at the neck. Ulrikh, a total misanthrope, stewing in his own juices. This bloodsucker sent tens of thousands of the best minds of Russia down his conveyor belt of legalized death. The flower of our people—he put their heads on the block.

Ulrikh was an indispensable member of the cutthroat crew: Yagoda, Yezhov, Beria, Shkiryatov, Vyshinsky. Quite an important little screw in the Stalinist death machine. And one of the longest-lasting.

We might never have known what went on behind the closed doors of that kangaroo court, but under Ulrikh's personal protection there happened to be in that courtroom an individual who was quite close to Ulrikh. He saw Nikolaev brought in, accompanied by his investigator and inseparable companion, Katsafa. Other NKVD agents were present, and of course guards. The proceedings bore no resemblance to the trial of a "terrorist center"—there were no other defendants and no witnesses. Only the perpetrator of the crime. The courtroom capacity was a hundred persons—not one was sympathetic to the victim.

Nikolaev began by denying that he belonged to the alleged terrorist center. In fact, he had not known of any "Center"; he had worked alone, convinced that he was helping the party. Then the officer of the court confronted him with the testimony he himself had given in the pretrial investigation and warned that false testimony would be regarded as counterrevolutionary sabotage.

Nikolaev tried to object, but Ulrikh methodically, remorselessly intensified the pressure, now appealing to his civic consciousness ("Your duty and your obligation is to assist the judiciary"), now threatening severe punishment. Nikolaev was wilting visibly. He was exhausted by confinement and crushed by the cross-examination. He was close to capitulation. The NKVD men closed in all around him. It seemed their cruel eyes would pierce him through. Ulrikh kept bearing down.

"How long have you belonged to the party? You know there is nothing more dangerous for the party than political deviation. And here the Trotskyists and Zinovievists have taken it into their heads to kill our leaders. By giving honest testimony you can help expose these inveterate enemies and prevent the deaths of the best sons of the people."

Nikolaev gave in, reaffirming his original "confession."

Yes, terrorist centers existed in Moscow and Leningrad. Yes, they had assigned him to carry out this act. Yes, the leaders of the center were also planning to kill Stalin, Molotov, Voroshilov, and Kaganovich. Ulrikh sighed. The *entr'acte* could now be announced—that is, a break in the session—and the others called in.

Nikolaev was conducted to a special cell adjacent to the collegium. Free for a moment from the pressure of the courtroom, he came to himself.

"What have I done? What a rotten scum I am. I've betrayed innocent people. They knew nothing about it, and I've dragged them into it." (Gusev, a soldier of the internal security guard who was then on duty, heard these cries.)

But the investigators took him in hand. "Why feel sorry for those counterrevolutionaries? You testified against them, remember, and now you're not going to be shot. You saved your own life." They had a special logic all their own, those guys. And their own ways of influencing people.

After the break the other defendants were brought into the courtroom, thirteen members of the "center": Kotolynov, Rumyantsev . . . but why go on with the list? There would be as much truth to it if we listed Thomas Münzer, Mark Twain, Admiral Nelson, Enrico Caruso, and Sergei Yesenin as members of the Leningrad center. And threw Isadora Duncan in to boot. But Stalin didn't have the creative imagination for that.

Nikolaev was seated off to one side, away from the rest of the defendants, with a solid ring of NKVD agents around him.

The performance continued without an audience, behind closed doors. This time Nikolaev "unmasked" those sitting on the distant bench, whose faces he couldn't see, without any prompting.

Not all the members of the mythical center obediently recited the lines they'd been given. Their "leader" Kotolynov protested, "This entire case has been fabricated from beginning to end!"

On the next day the trial was concluded. When the death sentence was read out Nikolaev exclaimed: "No! I've been tricked. They tricked me, the bastards. They promised me three years. . . ." He managed to hurl several curses at the organizers of the performance as he was dragged through the courtroom door.

Investigation, trial, execution—all at a blitzkrieg pace. Stalin had no time to lose. As in 1918, with the Martov affair: "No postponement for the summoning of witnesses."

The condemned men were executed that very night in a cellar on Liteiny Prospekt. A man named Medvedev, who was the military commandant of the building, directed the shooting. An executioner by conviction, he finished off many of the "enemies" with his own hand out of love for his profession.

Here too Kotolynov bore himself heroically. "The whole case was fabricated. We are dying for no reason," he managed to shout at the barrel of Medvedev's pistol.

And Lev Sheinin? He not only conducted the investigation but was also present at the execution. Technically, Vyshinsky was supposed to be there, but the assistant public prosecutor of the USSR shifted this honorable duty onto the broad, fleshy shoulders of his subordinate.

Sheinin later became a writer, a member of the Soviet Writers' Union, or as they then called them, an "engineer of human souls." I see nothing extraordinary in that. After all, the cop Nebaba, that deathless creation of Ilf and Petrov, managed to change his profession to music critic.

In accordance with a sound tradition established during dekulakization, all the relatives of the condemned men were likewise liquidated. Nikolaev's wife, Milda Draule, worked as a cleaning woman at a streetcar barn, but the investigators found it appropriate to include her in the terrorist center. She confessed that she had gone to meetings of the imaginary center with her husband. Milda was killed, and so was Nikolaev's mother.

Next in line were the NKVD agents involved. They were sentenced on January 23, 1935. Among the materials for the trial there wasn't even a hint of the true role played by Zaporozhets; nevertheless, the leaders of the Leningrad NKVD were accused of "criminal negligence." For this the strictest punishment was called for. These unwitting "accomplices of the terrorist center" were given only two or three years each. For the moment Comrade Stalin seemed to have forgotten that the terrorists were supposedly preparing an attempt on his sacred person as well. On the other hand, he remembered to have these jailbirds put up in the most comfortable quarters available. Yagoda sent Medved and Zaporozhets to the camps in a special railroad car with all the conveniences. They were supplied with everything they needed, and their families on the outside were given every attention.[71]

Filipp Medved, who ended up in Kolyma, refused the position of head of the records and assignments division which was offered him in the administration of Dalstroi, the largest camp complex in that vast empire behind barbed wire. "I bear the responsibility for Kirov's death and I don't deserve any privileges." Having said that, he went out to "general work" with everyone else, digging the soil.

In 1935 Lavrenty Kartvelishvili, first secretary of the Far Eastern territorial committee of the party, visited the gold fields. He happened to run into Filipp Medved in one of the prisoner compounds. The exiled Chekist recognized Lavrenty and said to him: "Listen, they let me keep my party card. What do I do with it?" What indeed?

But Stalin was not about to leave witnesses alive, let alone the instruments of his will. In 1937 he had Medved killed, along with all the other agents who had been involved, and also Berzin, the head of the Kolyma camps, and his subordinates. Stalin did away with all department heads of the Leningrad NKVD—Lobov, head of the special section, first of all.

Zaporozhets's turn came in 1938, when Stalin decided to rid himself of Yagoda. Although in the show trial of 1938 both men were "unmasked" as organizers of the Kirov assassination, Zaporozhets was not brought into the courtroom.

Two of Medved's former deputies survived the prisons and camps: Fyodor Fomin and a man named Petrov, who in 1934 had been in charge of matters concerning the military district of Leningrad. He, incidentally, refused to submit any statement in writing about that memorable December. It's hard to imagine, however, that he simply knew *nothing*.

In 1937–38 Stalin put an end to all of Kirov's former collaborators. For example, A. I. Abramov, head of the organizational department of the Leningrad provincial committee. Shortly before Kirov's death, Abramov had been sent as first secretary to Murmansk. In 1937 Stalin found him and destroyed him.

With the Kirov assassination Stalin achieved several goals. He removed his main rival. He discredited and later executed other prominent leaders. He intimidated the population by intensifying the "class struggle," and in all the uproar he began the annihilation of the Leninist Old Guard. In Kirov's blood he wrote himself a license for mass murder.

And to heighten the effect, he praised the murdered man. Kirov's name was given to factories, collective farms, mines, academies, schools, ships. Two provinces and seventeen cities were found worthy of this honor. On the map of the USSR appeared three Kirovsks, three Kirovskoyes, a Kirovgrad, a Kirovograd, and so on. Also some islands in the Kara Sea.

Lavish signs of Stalin's continued mourning. And daily reminders of the underhanded murderous Trotskyist-Zinovievist-Menshevik-Monarchist gang. (For them, the public show trials of 1936–38 would be held in reserve.)

What if Stalin had been elected to the Central Committee but at its first plenary session had not been elected to the secretariat, and Kirov had become general secretary? Wouldn't history have taken a different course? No. Kirov was too soft and too naïve for the part of leader. The express train of pseudo-socialism had built up such speed that no one could have stopped it, not a group, still less a single individual. Proof of this was to come later, with the brief reign of Khrushchev.

* * *

Stalin understood that many people, not just NKVD agents, linked him with the Kirov assassination. As he erected the monstrous structure of the show trials, his thoughts dwelt incessantly on the problem of blaming his surviving political opponents for the Kirov assassination. At the trials of 1936 and 1938, Trotksy was incriminated *in absentia* for the Kirov assassination, as were—one after another—Zinoviev and Kamenev, Bukharin and Rykov. The Soviet people heard such charges constantly reiterated.

Stalin operated on the principle: "It doesn't matter. They'll swallow anything." And was he wrong?

In 1936, when the trial of Zinoviev, Kamenev, and the others was under way in the Hall of Columns at the Central House of Trade Unions, I was a sixteen-year-old history student. My father was fifty-three. Kirov's death was a very hard blow for him. As public prosecutor of the Russian Republic, he was given a pass to the House of Trade Unions; he came home that evening gloomy and depressed.

He was a trusting man and pure of heart. How could he have doubted Stalin? Among the Old Bolsheviks only a few isolated individuals guessed. And they kept quiet, right up to the Twentieth Congress.

Not until 1956, three years after Stalin's death, were doubts as to the veracity of the official version of the Kirov assassination publicly voiced in the USSR. This was done by Khrushchev at the Twentieth Congress. Five years later, at the Twenty-second Congress, he raised the curtain on this vicious murder just a little bit higher. But he didn't have the courage to do more than make a few vague hints in the direction of the chief culprit.

Khrushchev already had at his disposal the materials of the Politburo's special commission to investigate the circumstances of the case. Khrushchev promised to make the commission's information and conclusions public. Hundreds of witnesses were questioned by the commission in

Moscow, Leningrad, and other cities. Mountains of documents were examined. The commission was given access to top-secret archives of the Central Committee (in the Kremlin cellar, guarded by people who had been assigned by Malenkov) and of the NKVD.

This was a huge job. And dangerous. "Aren't you afraid to get involved in a case like this?" a former NKVD man asked a member of the commission named Aleksei Kuznetsov. "Surely you realize how many little wheels you're going to start turning."

This "Communist" would have been glad to give all possible information concerning the Kirov assassination, if in 1934 he had been working not in the transport division but in the secret section for political affairs. His advice was to question the former agents in that department.

But who didn't know they had all been shot, down to the very last one, on Stalin's orders?

Another participant in the events, an associate of Zaporozhets who accidentally survived, tried to talk his way out of it.

"Tell me, what do you need to know all this for?"

Kuznetsov answered: *"Everyone* needs to know this. There's a very great need for it!"

This comrade had seen a lot. He wouldn't give in:

"But aren't you afraid you'll *get it?* They'll arrange a little automobile accident for you. . . ."

The well-meaning comrade warned Kuznetsov straight out.

"I'm telling you nothing. I still want to live."

In the winter of 1957 several members of the commission arrived in Leningrad. They asked a truck driver to take them toward Smolny by way of Voinov Street. There was the warehouse wall where, on December 3, 1934, Borisov had been killed. They stopped the truck. The driver smiled knowingly: "So . . . That means you're from that Politburo commission. . . . You're supposed to be investigating the Kirov murder. Hey, what's there to investigate? The whole of Leningrad knows Stalin killed Kirov."

And it was true. Back then, after the murder of "Mironych," as the factory workers affectionately called him, they were singing a little ditty all over working-class Petrograd (in a whisper, of course, looking over their shoulders):

> Hey, fresh tomatoes.
> Hey, want a cucumber?
> Stalin killed Kirov,
> Got him in the corridor.

The commission members stared silently at the spot where Borisov had died. They remembered that well-meaning warning. Even today, experienced comrades might be able to arrange a small natural-seeming accident. Not necessarily here; it could be done on some other street just as well. On the other hand, what was wrong with this place? It could be a kind of commemoration.

The materials of the commission were bound and all the volumes stored away in the archives. Ten years went by, new winds began to blow, and something unspeakable began to happen. The fat tomes were dragged out of storage, and certain party investigators, people who are called the "conscience of the party," began to summon all the individuals who had given the most important testimony to *that* commission. Witnesses who had exposed the real inspirer and organizer of the Kirov assassination were questioned once again, and this time were given a *real* third degree.

A GREAT BEGINNING

5

December 1934. That truly became the month of "A Great Beginning."* The verdict in the Kirov assassination case had not yet been announced. Still, the workers of the Baltic Shipyard were demanding that Leningrad be purged "of all 'former people' [Establishment people of the old regime], who have nursed the spawn of serpents in their bosoms, seeking to attack our party and our working class with their poisonous bite."[72]

But how to distinguish a "former person" from a "person of today"? And why should Leningrad be the only place purged? Stalin didn't ask himself such questions. He *knew* what he wanted.

The lead editorial in *Pravda* on December 25 was headlined: "On the Rotten Liberalism of the Dnepropetrovsk City Committee: On Revolutionary Vigilance." It was, of course, a signal for all city committees and provincial committees. A signal for a universal purge.

Everything before this was only a prelude to the Great Terror. By December 1934 roughly twenty million workers and peasants, killed by the famine or by bullets, could be credited to Stalin's account. That's leaving out those whose deaths in the civil war were his personal doing. Plus eight million deported peasants. The Virtuoso was just honing his ax.

Lady Astor, on a visit to Moscow in December 1931, had the rare honor of being received by the new Leader. During their conversation she asked a question no one else would have dared:

"How long will you keep killing people?"

Stalin's interpreter froze. But the Boss insisted on hearing the question and, without a pause, as though he had been expecting a question like

---

*"A Great Beginning"—title of a July 1919 article by Lenin praising the initiative undertaken by Soviet workers who had begun to do voluntary labor without pay on "Communist Saturdays."—TRANS.

that, replied to the naïve lady that "the process would continue as long as was necessary" to establish communist society.[73]

This butcher's theory of building communism on a pile of corpses lacked any philosophical foundation and therefore came out looking pretty bedraggled. But Joseph the Builder didn't bother trying to work out a more scientific concept. With childlike directness he declared that the closer socialism came, the sharper the class struggle would grow. Therefore, it followed logically that mass murder was indispensable for the victory of Communism. Here the theory and practice of the Stalinist interpretation of Marxism blended perfectly. Elegant and simple, as with any butcher really worth his salt.

But there was a problem: not every Communist had learned to catch Stalin's meaning from a word or two. His philosophical dabblings were not to everyone's taste. Listen to what Bukharin said at the April 1929 plenum of the Central Committee:

"This strange theory elevates an empirical fact—the intensification of the class struggle at present—into some sort of inevitable law of our development. According to this strange theory, the further we advance toward socialism, the more difficulties will accumulate and the fiercer the class struggle will become, so that at the very gates of socialism we apparently will have to start a civil war or else lay down our bones and die of hunger."

In his eagerness to expose the Gensek as the faulty "theoretician" he was, Bukharin resorted to hyperbole. But Bukharin's arguments proved all too prophetic. The hyperbole came true. Bukharin apparently never heard about another utterance of the self-styled Leader: "Better to start a small case of smallpox. Then there won't be a big one." These words dropped by Stalin over a bottle of Imeretian wine in the privacy of his home were like an aphorism from Machiavelli. Terror as preventive medicine against a popular uprising. This dots all the i's and crosses all the t's, as Bukharin might have said.

But the terror was not only, and not *so much*, in 1937. Not even in 1935, when Stalin opened the sluice gates after killing Kirov. Nineteen thirty-seven is for the philistines, whose name is legion. Terror as a means of building socialism originated in the lawlessness that prevailed even while Lenin was alive. It grew out of the system of one-party dictatorship. In 1917 Lenin at first included representatives of the SRs* and Mensheviks in the Soviet government, but he was unable to keep them at his side, because none of them would go along with the antidemocratic policy of restricting liberties. During his lifetime Lenin could have preserved dem-

---

*SRs: the usual designation in Russian and Soviet political literature for the Socialist Revolutionary Party, a major leftist party founded at the turn of the century. In 1917 it split into left and right wings, which became separate parties. The **Left SRs** formed a coalition government with the Bolsheviks in November 1917 but went into opposition again in the spring of 1918; the **Right SRs** remained in opposition to the Soviet government throughout. —TRANS.

ocratic procedures, an atmosphere of equality, and equal opportunities for other parties. The Americans call this "fair play."

But Lenin didn't play fair with anyone. In 1918, when Stalin began hounding Martov with unconstitutional methods, Lenin held his tongue. In 1920 the investigative agencies processed a case involving a certain "tactical center." As a result of this case Martov's brother Vladimir Levitsky was arrested and sent to Siberia.

The Cheka began to persecute all dissenters openly, anyone who dared to discuss facts, history, or philosophy in terms other than those dictated by the barracks—that is, in front of everyone and under the surveillance of party functionaries, instructors, and propagandists. Those who discussed things among themselves, in their own circle, with friends, were looking for trouble. There are many examples. Here is one. G. D. Zalmanovskaya, along with her friends and companions, eighteen-year-old Young Communists, took part in a discussion of Marxist books in the early twenties. In 1924 they were all rounded up—both those who read and those who listened.

On January 20, 1922, Trotsky gave a report to a youth conference and, in touching on the New Economic Policy, explained that the NEP presupposed "the use of capitalist forms and methods for building socialism." One of the listeners, the eighteen-year-old student L. Gurvich, "argued that we have returned to capitalism and that Lenin has openly acknowledged that fact in speaking of state capitalism." That is how Trotsky described the incident in his "top secret" January 21 letter to Lenin. He urged Lenin to come out with an explanation of this controversial question. Lenin, who was unwell at the time, answered immediately:

Comrade Trotsky,
    I have no doubt that the Mensheviks have now intensified and will go on intensifying their most malicious agitation. I think, therefore, that there is need to intensify surveillance over and repression against them. I have already spoken about this with Unschlicht and request you to find ten minutes or so for a conversation with him, not by telephone. As for the substance of the matter— I think I agree with you. I am now getting the urge to write a short article on topics close to those you mention; nevertheless I will hardly be able to do so any earlier than two weeks from now. Therefore it would be extremely useful if you would enter into open battle in the press, name this Menshevik by name, explain the vicious White Guard character of his speech, and insistently call upon the party to pull itself together.[74]

Lenin's militant orthodoxy imperceptibly shaded over into a policy of harsh repression. The chief of state referred the dissenting youth's remarks to none other than Unschlicht, who was then deputy chairman of the Cheka.

In late 1921 and early 1922 a number of opposition groups consisting of veteran working-class members of the party emerged in the Russian Communist Party.

As early as 1922 the authorities began to arrest opposition-group members and to hold them "with care and solicitude" in special isolation prisons for political offenders *(politizolyatory)*. It was easy to round up the Mensheviks. During the civil war they had gone to the front lines as volunteers, and in 1923–24 the old military mobilization lists were used to track them down.

In 1923 a prohibition was introduced against residence in any major city by "alien elements." The prohibition covered Moscow, Leningrad, Kharkov, Kiev, Rostov, and Odessa. It was called the "minus six clause" —referring to the six main cities. Later sixteen cities were included, and after that even more. The "minus clause" was usually applied after a person had been in prison or internal exile. In 1925 a continuously operating conveyor belt for dissidents was set in motion: the "political isolator" for three years; internal exile for three years; then the "minus clause," plus having to register regularly with the police. After a while a new arrest would come, and the same conveyor belt would take over again. Living under the "minus clause" meant showing up once every two weeks at the GPU commandant's office. A person subject to repression could not change residence or take a job without permission.

Beginning in late 1922 they began hauling in the Mensheviks with great deliberateness. The Mensheviks' "Forward" Club on Myasnitskaya Street in Moscow was closed. Even earlier, in August 1920, a group of Menshevik youth had been apprehended, and in February 1921, 150 people at this club were arrested. As many as three hundred socialists of different tendencies were collected at Butyrka prison. On April 25, 1921, the prisoners in Butyrka were beaten *en masse* by the guards. In February 1922, as a result of the correspondence between Lenin and Trotsky and the conversation with Unschlicht, twenty-five people, the nucleus of the Menshevik youth group in Moscow, were arrested. They were all sent to the Lubyanka, where the conditions were so strict they were driven to protest. They were sentenced to exile in a remote area. A hunger strike followed and their sentences were "reduced."

This is just a brief extract from the chronicle of early terror against youthful and well-intentioned critics of the system.

"For there must be heresies among you, so that they which are approved may be made manifest among you"; such was Saint Paul's exhortation in his letter to the Corinthians.[75]

Now, if Saint Paul had fallen into Stalin's hands, if Stalin's bone breakers had even caught a *glimpse* of that apostle . . . Under Lenin, though, what would they have done? "Simply" exiled him, right?

The roots of the Stalinshchina—the total terror—lay in soil that was carefully prepared and rich with manure.

A few years after Lenin's death, the restricted scale of the terror against the Mensheviks and SRs began to weigh on Stalin's mind. He liked to do things in a big way. In the mid-twenties he had made a clean sweep of the Georgian Mensheviks. In Leningrad the left oppositionists established their own underground print shop. On Stalin's suggestion the GPU got involved in this operation through one of its agents, who in the investigation was presented as a "White Guard officer." In this whole business you sense the guiding hand of an experienced provocateur.

In January 1928, "by decision of the Politburo," Trotsky was exiled to Alma-Ata. As the GPU brigade was breaking down the locked doors of his apartment, Leon Davidovich managed to drop a message out the window with the following lines of farewell:

"They are deliberately provoking us to make protests. Stalin is intentionally trying to goad us into a renewal of oppositional struggle. He knows that we will not become silent philistines and will not silently and indifferently surrender our persecuted comrades to their fates. They are prodding us on purpose to have an excuse to intensify repression, which will become harsh, merciless, and shameless. Stalin wants not only to continue the struggle against us, but to physically exterminate the opposition."[76]

Stalin had a satanic hatred of Trotsky and at the same time feared him. He feared Trotsky's indisputable authority as a leader of the revolution and the Red Army and his great popularity within the party and among the people. Stalin had already made the decision to exile Trotsky to Alma-Ata, but his agents brought word that crowds of people had gathered at the Kazan Station to see off the disgraced leader. The Gensek changed the departure time to the next day. The GPU carried out the operation in the most up-to-date fashion. This time Trotsky was taken to his train secretly and by force the day before the officially announced day of departure. This was followed by a slander campaign inspired by Koba, accusing Trotsky of having "sold himself" to the international bourgeoisie.

A year or two went by. The terror began to grow in breadth and depth. It became *qualitatively different.* In Georgian prisons they begun to beat arrested persons. Not much, but a beginning . . .

The Supreme Executioner's talent flowered definitively during all-out collectivization, with the mass slaughter of peasants. And during the first five-year plan, with the slaughter of engineers. In general, he always felt uneasy around specialists. During the civil war he eliminated numerous "military specialists," former tsarist officers who had served loyally in the Red Army. Now there were engineers and other bourgeois technical specialists getting in his way. He decided to fabricate an organization of "wreckers," with the help of an old friend, Yefim Yevdokimov, who had made his way into the GPU Organs. For three months, May-July 1928, the Shakhty trial attracted the attention of the contemporary world.

By 1928 Stalin was firmly in the seat of power in the party. But it was not his way to rest on his laurels. He wanted to instill his subjects with a lasting phobia. Fear of the word Trotskyist was not enough. Every party member, every citizen of the land of the Soviets must know and remember that a Trotskyist is an *enemy.* Supporters of Trotsky were agents of imperialism, spies, wreckers, saboteurs. A little later on, this "truth" would be taught, along with others of the same caliber, in all the schools, higher educational institutions, and party study groups. Into minds filled with dogmas, like jars with pickled cucumbers, Stalin shoved one more dogma: "The Trotskyists are enemy number one."

In order to give this dogma the weight of official truth, proof in the form of victims was required. Stalin filled the cells of Butyrka prison with such proof in 1929. Supporters of Trotsky, temporarily left at large by the Gensek, were granted the opportunity of recanting publicly in the newspapers.

By 1930 all activity by the Red Cross in defense of political prisoners had completely died out under pressure of the authorities. In the twenties political exiles had received a subsistence allowance from the GPU and additional aid from the Red Cross, an organization left over from tsarist times. Yekaterina Pavlovna Peshkova had worked with the Red Cross since February 1918. Peshkova had formerly been a member of the SR Party and had given assistance to all political prisoners without distinction. Dzerzhinsky, as head of the GPU, placed full confidence in her, allowed her to visit prisons, admitted her to his office once a week, and offered her assistance. (Gorky tells about this in a letter to Dalmat Lutokhin dated September 27, 1925.)

But in 1930 it all came to an end. Money could no longer come from abroad unofficially, and in Moscow fewer and fewer people were willing to engage in this self-sacrificing work. The attitude of the GPU changed drastically. Yagoda, the new GPU boss, refused to see Peshkova or receive petitions from her. Peshkova still kept up the semblance of an information bureau, but she could no longer provide substantial assistance to anyone. After 1935 the institution of aid to political prisoners died out completely. Hundreds of thousands and later millions were proclaimed "enemies of the people," i.e., political criminals. Any aid organization was bound to drown in that flood.

A day in January 1930. Into his office the Gensek calls Vsevolod Balitsky, chairman of the GPU of the Ukraine. Stalin paces up and down his office, listening to Balitsky's report on the "political situation" in the Ukraine. The Leader's pipe puffs loudly, somehow expressing disgruntlement. So Balitsky throws in new information—resistance by kulak elements, remnants of Makhno's gangs and the Petlyuraites.* Stalin stops him.

"No, not that, not that. My dear fellow, you're not looking in the right direction. Most likely Skrypnik, before he was removed from his high position, had his own political organization. Do you know that the Ukrainian Academy is behind a counterrevolutionary deal with Pilsudski? You didn't know that?"

Balitsky returned home with instructions to expose and bring to justice immediately—but whom? Academician Litvitsky? Or Hrushevsky, the president of the Ukrainian Academy of Sciences and the author of the

---

*Petlyuraites: followers of Semyon Petlyura, right-wing Ukrainian nationalist leader who fought against the Soviet government in the civil war of 1918–20.—TRANS.

famous three-volume history of the Ukraine? In 1917 he had headed the Central Rada and then had emigrated. Later he returned and become a Soviet academician.

Stalin gave orders not to touch Litvitsky or Hrushevsky. He displayed special concern for Hrushevsky, presented him with a dacha near Moscow, and forbade any testimony against him in court.

The "organization" was given a resounding title—Soyuz Vyzvolennya Ukrainy (Union for the Liberation of the Ukraine), or SVU for short. A magnificent show was prepared, the trial of the members of the SVU. The only thing lacking was the voice of some authoritative Ukrainian figure who could denounce the "contemptible hirelings" of Pilsudski. Stanislav Kosior, who was then the first secretary of the Communist Party (Bolshevik) of the Ukraine suggested, "Wouldn't Litvitsky speak out against the SVU?"

In 1911 Litvitsky had given Lenin a memo on the principles of socialist construction in the countryside. He was one of the first to propose the collectivization of agriculture. However, Litvitsky had remained unaffiliated with any party. As a result his voice would be all the more authoritative at the trial.

A comrade from the Central Committee arrived at Litvitsky's apartment. All the Ukrainian papers were cursing the members of the anti-Soviet SVU, who had sold themselves to the Polish dictator Pilsudski. Litvitsky didn't have to be persuaded.

"Only a peasant slave could lick the boots of Pilsudski," he flung out angrily and agreed to make a statement for the press. Now everything was ready: the script, the scenery, the props, and the actors. Stalin called Balitsky in again, this time along with Panas Lyubchenko.

"Who will we put in as public prosecutor?" the Gensek asked. And decided the question himself: "I propose Panas, chairman of the Ukrainian Council of People's Commissars."

And some final instructions for Balitsky:

"Be sure to organize it so that all the defendants get tea with lemon and pirozhki during the trial." The director in chief didn't miss a trick.

The trial of the "traitors" was held in Kharkov in March and April 1930. The defendants' bench was filled with academicians. They "confessed" to everything and, stirring their tea with lemon, eagerly gave the details exactly according to the script.

Among the accused were academicians Andrei Loboda and Vladimir Perets. *Loboda* in Ukrainian means "garden orache," an Asiatic herb similar to spinach. *Perets* means "pepper." On this occasion the official humorists wrote:

> They sowed Loboda
> And reaped Perets.

The leaders of the SVU turned out to be ultra-nationalists who had sold out not only to the Polish ruler Pilsudski but also to Germany, under

whose protectorate they intended to establish a monarchy in the Ukraine
to serve the capitalists and landowners. Forty-two prominent figures in
Ukrainian science and culture were tossed into this salad seasoned with
the vinegar of espionage.

In 1930 the central apparatus of the GPU as such, in its interaction
with the Gensek, was still in the warm-up phase. On one occasion Stalin
handed Yagoda a list of thirty-six people he personally disliked, covered
with the usual "Trotskyist" dressing:

"These are hidden enemies of the party. Some of them are even open
enemies. A trial must be held. Arrest all of them, and they'll tell the truth
about their Trotskyist activity. Then the people will be able to judge
them."

But Yagoda didn't want to assume such a responsibility:

"I can't do that, Comrade Stalin. Maybe the Central Control Commission could investigate their anti-party activity and pass on the material
evidence to me?"

Stalin pretended to retreat. That was his customary maneuver. He
had a reliable person in reserve—Ivan Akulov, former secretary of the
Donetsk provincial committee. The Gensek had installed him as public
prosecutor of the USSR. He was a totally compliant bureaucrat whom
Stalin intended to place in charge of the Organs. But to begin with, some
information had to be pried out of Yagoda about foreign intelligence
networks, and Yagoda was no fool. Akulov couldn't get it. Then Stalin gave
the ticklish assignment to Bulatov, who was in charge of GPU cadres. But
he too failed. (The same fate awaited all of them—Yagoda, Akulov, and
Bulatov—but first the Gensek would squeeze what he could out of them,
like a slice of lemon with tea.)

In late 1932, two prominent party figures, Mikhail Ryutin and Aleksandr Slepkov composed a document in which, with full justification,
they named Stalin as the one to blame for the economic crisis and the
source of anti-Leninist policies within the party. The Communists who
signed the "Ryutin platform" demanded that the peasants be freed from
the yoke of compulsory collectivization, that the pace of industrialization
not be forced to an extreme, and that all members who had been expelled for "opposition" be returned to the party. Ryutin's supporters
criticized the "right-wing Communists" for their alliance with Stalin,
who was destroying the gains of the October revolution for the sake of
his personal power.

That was the wheel of their platform which the Gensek grabbed hold
of, their personal attack on him. He charged Ryutin with a desire to
murder the sacred personage, the party's Leader, and to carry out a
counterrevolutionary coup. The question of executing "terrorists" could
now be posed point-blank. But Stalin wasn't able to convince the Central
Committee or the Central Control Commission, which was then headed
by Rudzutak. Likewise, the majority of Politburo members wouldn't agree
to the Gensek's proposal that the insolent critics be eliminated. (Stalin hid

the two-hundred-page seditious platform safely away. From then on, severe repression followed for reading this document.)

For the time being, the Ryutinites were only expelled from the party, and Ryutin himself was only arrested.

Here again Stalin displayed that capacity for patience which is so important in high politics. If the time was not yet ripe for the execution of oppositionists, he could console himself with a mass weeding-out of the party. The Gensek put Georgy Malenkov in charge of the bone-jarring operation, backing him up with a pair of party Oprichniks who had long careers ahead of them—Shkiryatov and Yezhov.

One of the main points in the specially issued questionnaire for this cleansing of the party ranks was the question: "Did you ever belong to an opposition and if so, which?" But an exception was made for the Military Opposition. An official communication from the Central Committee urged that the Military Opposition not be regarded as an opposition. That was perfectly logical. Otherwise they'd have to purge the chief inspirer and organizer of that opposition—Stalin. Along with his lieutenants Voroshilov and Yaroslavsky.

Shkiryatov and Yezhov worked smoothly in tandem. The purge ended in 1935 with an exchange of party cards, after which Malenkov could boast at a Central Committee plenum that they had succeeded in discovering and exposing 300,000 "alien elements" in the course of the purge. The October plenum of the Central Committee in 1935 passed a resolution, based on Yezhov's report, on the results of the purge (this campaign was shamefacedly called "a checking of party documents"). It was reminiscent of a military order to combat banditry. *Alien elements, class enemies, enemies of the party, criminal practices, alien people,* and *people in the party by accident*—the resolution was saturated with such expressions. The Central Committee reproached the party organizations five, six, ten times over for their lack of Bolshevik vigilance and demanded as many times again that all enemies be exposed.

During the purge of 1933–34 the Organs succeeded in disarming a vast number of "spies." Where had they come from? Let's take one case. Aleksandr Milenin headed a technical agency in the Commissariat of Heavy Industry. He was arrested in 1934 and brought to the Lubyanka. He was supposed to have been close to a woman, who in turn was close to a German engineer. To avoid being tortured, Milenin admitted that he was guilty of spying for Germany. To make the confession more convincing, he referred to a number of secret documents with invented code numbers such as F-2, F-14, X-4.

An appeal from Ordzhonikidze helped save his life. Instead of shooting the "spy," they gave him ten years. His wife came to see him in a remote labor camp and managed to bring back an appeal written by her husband and addressed to Stalin. She entrusted this paper to P. Semushkin, assistant to Ordzhonikidze, the commissar of heavy industry. Sergo passed it along to the Master. Stalin's resolution followed: "Comrade Ye-zhov, investigate and report."

Among those Milenin mentioned in his statement was his old front-line comrade Rudakov (at any rate, that's what we'll call him). Being summoned to the Central Committee was a surprise for him. Yezhov was at that time in charge of top management personnel for the Central Committee and oversaw the activities of the GPU. He was sitting in his large office on the third floor of the Central Committee building on Sta-raya Ploshchad (Old Square), behind an immense desk. Milenin's dossier lay open on his desk. Yezhov asked for a character reference on Milenin and was given a first-rate report commending him as an honest and self-sacrificing front-line commander. In those days, before the Kirov assassina-tion, it was sometimes possible to state one's views candidly without fear of the consequences.

"Do you want to see Milenin?" Yezhov asked. "They're bringing him here now."

But Rudakov was in a hurry to get back to work and decided to leave, knowing he would see his friend the next day under different circum-stances.

In taking leave of Rudakov, Yezhov warned him about the strictly confidential nature of their discussion. Rudakov held his tongue for thir-teen years. He told his boss that he'd been summoned to the Central Committee about an old school chum recommended for work in the Central Committee apparatus and that he had endorsed the recommenda-tion. This version even reached the ears of Yagoda.

Milenin was freed but not restored to party membership. After all, you couldn't free someone on the grounds of being totally innocent. The charge of "moral corruption" was left hanging over him just in case. He fought in the Great Patriotic War under this cloud, commanding a divi-sion, but no awards or decorations came his way.

* * *

In the campaign against present and former oppositionists the theme of spying and having foreign connections was heard more and more insist-ently.

The death penalty in fact could be imposed merely for "intention to flee the country." Stalin also introduced the practice of exiling the rela-tives of arrested persons. The system of hostages had existed in Georgia back in the times of King George Saakadze. Stalin began to use this system in the first years of his reign. Blackmailing his victims with the threat of reprisals against their relatives and loved ones and venting his unquencha-ble anger upon the families of those he arrested—that was his element.

It suited history to synchronize the activities of the two dictators Hitler and Stalin. On June 30, 1934, the Fuehrer wiped out the supporters of his rival Röhm. Hitler's Night of the Long Knives served Stalin as a model for his own throat-cutting operation after the Kirov assassination. In Leningrad alone the Stalinist Oprichniks annihilated forty thousand veteran Communists. Altogether in that city, the cradle of the October revolution, and in Moscow, 180,000 "enemies of the people" were "unmasked."

The year 1935 is famous for one other case of mass carnage. No sooner had the Soviet share of the Chinese Eastern Railway been sold to Japan than the employees of that Soviet institution were deported to their homeland, and soon the prisons and camps were filled with an army of fifty thousand "Japanese spies." How many of them survived? What happened to their children? In the official histories there is not one word about this. Or about Stalin's personal responsibility for it.

The mass terror had to have people to carry it out, more and more of them, a constantly growing number. A mighty battle-ready army of killers and marauders had to be constructed in a hurry. Out of the central and local detachments of security-police plunderers who had gone through the great school of liquidating the kulaks and hunting the first round of political witches.

The minds and hearts of the peasants and workers could not be affected by the artificially whipped-up enthusiasm aimed at "builders of socialism." They didn't think in party dogmas but in terms of real life. Stalin had not forgotten 1921, when the workers' unrest surfaced in Petrograd. He also remembered Kronstadt. And wanted no repetitions. The backward workers and the peasants, lacking in class consciousness, had to feel the firm hand of the GPU Organs ever at their necks.

If the Leader had set himself the modest task of bringing the party to its knees, how much more important to do the same with the workers and peasants, that is, the people, the masses, or whatever you want to call them. The official historians have not yet given full credit to Stalin for his leading role in organizing an army of search-and-destroy experts. At its highest point this army numbered more than half a million "people." This estimate, made by specialists, includes the personnel of all the commissariats of internal affairs and security administrations of the national republics, provinces, and large cities, and of all the local police departments and transit police. These were highly qualified experts who had accumulated a wealth of experience in conducting searches and investigations and using torture. As for tracking people down and rounding them up—that was a minor matter under Stalin. They took anyone and everyone and usually didn't trouble the public prosecutor with the annoyance of writing out arrest warrants. There was also a palace guard, the so-called internal troops of the NKVD.

Who says the civil war ended in 1922? That was just a dress rehearsal for the real fratricidal war. After a brief interval of six or seven years, civil war was renewed in Russia with hurricane force. It was given various names: dekulakization, collectivization, industrialization, the struggle against the opposition and other "enemies of the people," the lesser terror, and the Great Terror. The essence remained the same.

GETTING PERSONALLY INVOLVED

6

On a summer evening in 1926, a group of young people on the Central Committee staff of the Young Communist League (YCL), having finished their work for the day, were heading for the elevator on the third floor of the building where the Secretariat of the party Central Committee was also located. In those years the "Big Central Committee" was in the same building on Staraya Ploshchad as the "Small Central Committee" (of the YCL). A short, fussy individual came running up to the Young Communists. It was the commander of the guard, Trachtenberg.

"Hold the elevator. Comrade Stalin's coming."

The young people waited, and into the elevator stepped the Gensek, his coat thrown over his shoulder, his hands in the pockets of his semimilitary tunic. "How are things with the youth?" Stalin said in a cheery but patronizing way.

"Things are good. Everybody's feeling fine," someone answered for them all. One of the Young Communists had a Mauser in his pocket, left over from the war. Twenty years later, dying of starvation in one of Stalin's camps, how many times he would think back to that moment in the elevator.

* * *

In 1937 the Secretariat and the Orgburo were moved to the Kremlin, but the rest of the Central Committee apparatus remained at Staraya Ploshchad. The first thing Stalin saw to at the new location was the bugging of telephone conversations. The technology had improved and he was provided with the latest models. After the Kirov assassination and the show trials there was no telling what kind of conversations party leaders and apparatus officials might be having. It seemed that everyone had learned how to hold his tongue and observe secrecy. Life itself had taught them all. But not everyone. The Master would listen in, twirling his tobacco-scented mustache. The Lubyanka would do the untwirling.

By this time Stalin had succeeded in revoking the right of party members to carry weapons. He himself never parted with his revolver and was surrounded by numerous personal guards. The Big Chief was taking the warpath against a helpless, unarmed people—his own.

The institution of a personal bodyguard for each member of the Politburo was established in 1928, after an unsuccessful attempt on the lives of the activists in the GPU. On a summer day in 1928 some evildoers had placed two bombs in the GPU building on Lubyanka Square. One of them had gone off and the other hadn't. All forces were thrown into the investigation. Success in catching the terrorists went to Pyotr Kolosovsky. For this he was given the title Honored Chekist.

At that time a special department for guarding members of the government was established under the auspices of the Administration for Secret Operations. Later Stalin devised a separate administration for bodyguard services, headed by Nikolai Sidorovich Vlasik, with powers more or less comparable to those of the Politburo. The name of Vlasik made Central Committee members, people's commissars, and even the most trusted confidants of Stalin tremble.

Every member of the Politburo was assigned his own special commissar (!) as the head of his personal bodyguard.

A Georgian by the name of Rustam Odzelashvili served as the chief of Napoleon Bonaparte's personal guard. This highly important post Stalin entrusted to a Hungarian named Karl Viktorovich Pauker, a former hair stylist for the Budapest opera. Pauker made a career for himself under Menzhinsky. A pushy, two-faced individual, he quickly wormed his way into Stalin's good graces and was able to "make friends" with even a misanthrope like Ulrikh. Pauker was soon given the post of chief of the operations department of the GPU. He was always to be found at the Master's side.

The monarch's private office was guarded by special troops, similar to the Chapars under the Georgian kings. Stalin spent many a year picking out people to serve in his immediate presence, people incapable of a single independent act. Still, it was possible that the carnage and bloodletting in the country might provoke someone to try an act of desperation. Stalin's motto was: "God protects those who protect themselves."

The time had come to think about broadening the scope of the terror. On July 29, 1936, Stalin sent a secret letter from the Central Committee to all local areas. According to this letter, despite the great successes of the vigilance campaign, some imprisoned enemies of the people had nevertheless managed to hold on to their party cards. (A resolution of the December 1935 plenum of the Central Committee had referred to people expelled from the party who still had their party cards.) The Central Committee called for greater revolutionary vigilance and a resolute struggle against the hidden enemy within. Thus, a second impetus was given to the mass terror that Stalin had unleashed after the Kirov assassination.

* * *

In those years Stalin exterminated, one after another, his own relatives and a number of comrades who had worked closely with him for many years. One was his brother-in-law Aleksei (Alyosha) Svanidze, who had raised Koba's first son, Yakov, in his own home. The Master arrested Svanidze along with his wife, Maria Korona, a soloist at the Tbilisi Theater of Opera and Ballet. The husband and wife, after being "exposed" (for what?), were sent by Stalin to different labor camps. The outbreak of the war found them in the political isolation prison at Oryol. A certain agent from Stalin visited them at that location. On the Master's behalf the agent urged Svanidze to repent and confess all his sins. If he did, the agent promised, their lives would be spared. Svanidze answered: "I know of no sins I've committed against the party. There is nothing for me to confess."

The stubborn pair were executed. They couldn't be broken, even with threats against their three sons. Stalin was later to speak of Svanidze with pretended admiration: "What a hero! Went to his death without even asking for mercy." But Svanidze had certainly hoped for mercy. Otherwise he wouldn't have gone to Stalin in 1937, back before his own arrest, to beg for the life of Yenukidze:

"We all know Yenukidze perfectly well. He couldn't be an enemy."

"They'll give him a good working over," answered the Leader, "and then you'll see. He'll confess to all his crimes."

Stalin had shared the dangers of underground party work with Abel Yenukidze in the early years of the century. But in 1930 Yenukidze had gone and written a pamphlet in which, among other things, he described the organization of the underground print shop in Baku. Without including Koba. He had also told about Stalin's intrigues.[77] And in the early thirties he had naïvely repeated the truth in articles for the press. In 1935 the Gensek demoted Yenukidze from secretary of the Central Executive Committee to second secretary, creating a whole new job category for the occasion.

Yenukidze had been the first to find Stalin's dead wife, Nadezhda Alliluyeva, with the marks of the killer's fingers still on her throat, in November 1932. In general Yenukidze knew too much. And was too sympathetic and forgiving. The charges that figured in "the Yenukidze case" (other than the masterminding of the Kirov assassination) were that he had planned to seize the Kremlin by force and intended to do away with Gorky and Kuibyshev. Lastly, he was planning to poison the Leader (with the help of some great ladies from the old regime who had managed to penetrate the staff of the Gensek's personal library). In addition Yenukidze was charged with monarchism, political and moral corruption, links with the Tukhachevsky group, with the "right-wing" Communists, and with the Italian far-left extremists of the Red Brigades. No, the last item wasn't there, but all the rest were.

After Yenukidze was killed, the exiled Trotsky published an article about him on the theme, "Cain-Stalin, where is your brother, Abel?"[78]

A cobra reacts sensitively to heat. It can sense a living thing even at a great distance, or in the dark, and will strike unerringly. Koba detected his victims by their intelligence and talent. Most of all, however, he feared people of strong will. Someone else's will was an enemy will. With serpentine acuity he sought out strong-willed people. And killed and killed and killed.

Stanislav Redens was the brother-in-law of Nadezhda Alliluyeva. He had married her sister Anna. At one time he had charge of the Transcaucasian GPU, when Beria ruled the party organization there. Redens had been one of Dzerzhinsky's loyal collaborators and his personal secretary. He was capable of decisive action but, hobbled by his party prejudices, couldn't bring himself to raise a hand against the general secretary. When it came his turn to taste the gruel of Stalin's prisons and the whiplash in the Lubyanka cellars, Redens kept his courage. But Stalin couldn't stand stout-hearted people; he yearned to see each and every revolutionary turn into a coward in the face of his torture machine.

How he rejoiced at every betrayal committed by a former Leninist in prison. If an arrested "enemy of the people" refused to sign the GPU's concoctions, however, the Master grew restless, couldn't sleep. The omnipotent Leader would start to lose faith in his own powers.

When he learned that Redens had rejected the demands of the interrogators and that they couldn't break him with torture, Stalin sent for Anna Alliluyeva. He promised freedom for her husband and safety for her and her children if Redens would confess to counterrevolutionary activity.

What could the poor woman do, the mother of three?

She was brought to Lefortovo prison and put in the same cell as her husband, who was emaciated from his tortures. She threw herself upon him and begged him to give in, to sign everything the Gensek wanted. "Koba has promised to let you go right away."

Redens tried to explain to her that the man could not be trusted in anything. But she kept insisting, begging him. Redens went to the door of the cell and starting banging on it. The jailer appeared. Redens asked that the duty officer for that wing of the prison be called. When the duty officer came Redens demanded, "Take this fool woman away."

Those were the last words she heard from her husband.

After Stalin's death Anna Alliluyeva fought long and hard to have her husband rehabilitated. When at last she saw "justice" done, she lost her mind. I put justice in quotes on purpose. It was none other than Redens who had scourged the active party membership of Moscow and, later, the leadership of Kazakhstan.

* * *

Grigory Broido had been an attorney and a member of the Menshevik Party's Central Committee. In 1918 he was a deputy to Stalin as people's commissar of nationalities. Blessed with a good mind and a clever wit, this capable and efficient worker took a substantial share of the worries of office off Koba's shoulders. Broido was elected a candidate member of the Central Committee at the Seventeenth Party Congress. At one time he was in charge of the party publishing house and worked as a secretary for the Central Committee of the Communist Party of Turkmenistan. If Stalinist standards were applied, the one-time commissar of nationalities who had later become the Gensek should have been jailed for collaborating with and showing favor to a man who in the past had been an active Menshevik. (In the Lubyanka, Broido would confess to engaging in hostile activities during the years after socialism had triumphed.) Instead they arrested Broido. He served his seventeen years in the camps, managed to win his rehabilitation, and died in 1970.

* * *

In 1937 Stalin wiped out the philosopher Yan Sten, who had spent three years teaching him Hegelian dialectics. Sten had a rare opportunity to sound out his pupil's most secret aims and desires. "Koba will organize things," he told his close friends in 1928; "that'll make the Dreyfus and Beilis cases look like a picnic."

Sten's prophecy began to come true not many years later. Sten himself, a veteran Communist, was put to death on Stalin's personal orders.

* * *

Several of Kerensky's colleagues whom Lenin had pardoned appear among the endless rows of Stalin's victims. One of them was Pyotr Palchinsky, a mining engineer who gave the years of his youth to the revolution. As an émigré before the revolution, he had befriended the old anarchist leader and theorist Prince Pyotr Kropotkin. In the fall of 1917 Palchinsky had been governor general of Petrograd and in October had headed the defense of the Winter Palace. Did I say he had been pardoned by Lenin? That's not exactly right. He was arrested several times in the first few years of Soviet rule. But he served loyally, worked hard, and wrote several valuable books. Back in 1905 a tsarist court sentenced him to hard labor, but he managed to flee the country. Under Stalin things were simpler. In May 1929 this patriot, guilty of nothing, was shot as an "unreconstructed enemy of the revolution."

Another man whom Lenin had spared was P. N. Malyantovich, minister of justice in Kerensky's government, and a long-time member of the Social Democratic Party. In July 1917 Malyantovich had issued the order for the arrest of the Bolshevik leader. Dzerzhinsky also allowed the former justice minister to remain at large.

Vladimir Antonov-Ovseyenko encountered Malyantovich three times. First in 1907. After escaping from prison in Sevastopol, he found refuge at the apartment of a Moscow lawyer—Malyantovich. Ten years later, after taking the Winter Palace, Antonov confined the minister of justice along with other members of the Provisional Government in the Peter and Paul Fortress. Their last encounter came nearly twenty years later, in 1936. Malyantovich came to Antonov-Ovseyenko, who was then public prosecutor of the Russian Republic, with a personal request. Antonov, afraid he might be denounced and accused of "complicity" with a former Kerenskyite, received this old acquaintance in his office in the presence of two members of his staff. Not long after, Antonov-Ovseyenko was sent to Spain. Later, both of them were seized: the former people's commissar of Lenin's first government and the former minister of Kerensky's government. (It's really true: extremes tend to meet.)

The beginning of 1937 was marked by an event that proved to be a watershed—a Central Committee plenum. In the official history it's customary to glorify almost every Central Committee plenum or party congress as "historic." But you hear no such thing about the February-March 1937 plenum. Mostly they keep quiet about that one, though it deserves the weighty epithet "historic" more than any other.

By 1937 Stalin had succeeded in getting rid of a number of his inconvenient contemporaries. Gorky had been especially annoying. He was poisoned in the most primitive fashion. The Moor had done his duty by giving his blessing to the terror: "If the enemy does not surrender, he must be destroyed." Now the Moor could go.

The circumstances of Valerian Kuibyshev's sudden death in 1935 remain a mystery to this day. Some historians number him among the leftists, for some reason. It's true that Kuibyshev sometimes dared to oppose the Gensek for his excessively drastic measures—following the lead of Kirov and the other "liberals"—but on the whole he was sufficiently unprincipled and obedient to Stalin. Kuibyshev was virtually the only Politburo member whose dacha Stalin himself visited and with whom the Gensek would while away leisure hours over a bottle of wine.

The most difficult case was that of Grigory ("Sergo") Ordzhonikidze. This faint-hearted Stalinist commissar committed suicide on February 18, five days before the plenum opened, thus weakening the already timid "front" of those who were unhappy with the carnage. Stalin prepared the ground for the plenum with great care. His report and the reports of Yezhov, Molotov, and Zhdanov differed only in outward detail. Their essence and aim was the same—to justify and intensify the terror. True to his long-standing custom (it had become his political mode of operation), Stalin waited till the very end of the plenum to present his report, which denounced the "Trotskyists and other double-dealers." Trotsky was still alive in foreign exile and his articles and books laid bare before the entire world the gangster essence of Stalin's rule.

"Present-day Trotskyism is no longer a political current in the working class movement but consists of an unprincipled gang, devoid of ideology, wreckers, diversionists, intelligence agents, spies, and murderers, a gang of sworn enemies of the working class, working in the employ of the intelligence agencies of foreign powers." In keeping with these "guidelines" every party member was obliged to regard any oppositionist first of all as a wrecker and a spy. This new style in politics was announced by the Gensek for the year 1937. It is a style that has long outlived its creator.

Then came the general instructions: "Today the weakness of the people on our side consists not in technical backwardness but in political immaturity, blind trust in those who hold party cards by mistake, failure to test people not by their political pronouncements but by the results of their work." Expanding on this "idea," the Gensek warned: "A genuine wrecker has to show success in his work from time to time because that is the only way he can maintain his position as a wrecker, worm his way into people's confidence, and continue his wrecking activities."[79]

Illogical? Possibly. Ingenious nevertheless. From now on it was possible, in fact obligatory, to round up everyone, both those who failed to meet their quotas and those who overfulfilled their quotas. The plenum passed the appropriate resolution. It noted the lamentable passivity of many of the economic institutions and condemned the attempts to put the brakes on the campaign to root out all "Trotskyist wreckers." (This was a reference to the late Sergo Ordzhonikidze, all of whose deputies and administrative chiefs had been hauled in just before his suicide.) The NKVD had been trying and trying, sparing not one drop of its own sweat or other people's blood, but industry and transport still failed to show the necessary initiative and energy in fulfilling the party's demands.

Thus the terror was given new impetus for the third time since the Kirov assassination. The plenum opened all the sluice gates. Wide open.

The ten days of the plenum were ten scenes from a stage production for a highly restricted audience. One of those scenes, the hounding of Bukharin and Rykov, two of Lenin's closest associates, was played out on February 27. Too bad that Tomsky had already shot himself. Nevertheless, Tomsky's final act of hostility toward the party was suitably denounced in the press. As for those who thought like Tomsky, Stalin contented himself with purely verbal abuse for the time being. He let his yellow eyes roam greedily as he watched his Central Committee claque do the expelling.

First Bukharin and Rykov were removed from the Kremlin Areopagus.

Bukharin tried to voice his doubts about the correctness of the NKVD's activities. He was interrupted by rude shouts from the assemblage.

He tried to demonstrate his innocence.

"If you're innocent, prove it in a prison cell."

Bukharin couldn't hold back his tears.

"Shoot the traitor. Off to prison with him!"

The doomed men were led from the room. Once outside they were taken in tow by a prison-guard unit.

On behalf of these rejects some other doomed men tried to intervene —Postyshev, Rudzutak, Eikhe, and Chubar. But Stalin wasn't inclined to encourage improvisation in this club of suicides. As always, he knew his opponents' intentions. So Postyshev was going to play the ringleader? Well, we'll clip his wings. . . .

Stalin began a campaign to discredit the Kiev provincial committee and the Ukrainian Central Committee in January. Postyshev was demoted from first secretary of the provincial committee to second secretary of the Ukrainian party's Central Committee. Kaganovich went off to Kiev. Stalin's emissary quickly had Postyshev relieved of his burdensome post in Kiev. For three weeks in February the Organs rounded up Postyshev's coworkers in the Ukraine, as *Pravda* kept up a hue and cry, pasting the label "Trotskyist" over dozens of names, veteran Leninists included.

Do you think Stalin could deny himself the pleasure of playing cat and mouse? While everyone condemned Postyshev, the victim-to-be, the Master remained kind, indulgent, and forgiving. He drew back as if to say, You can't do this. . . . Give the man a chance. . . . Maybe he'll think it over and repent.

Meanwhile the ax had been thoroughly sharpened.

* * *

The time had come to reorganize that army of shock workers, the NKVD. First of all, remove Genrikh Yagoda. At the plenum Stalin accused him of a number of blunders and oversights. Traditionally this would be followed by "organizational measures." And the audience wasn't kept waiting long. Yagoda was reappointed commissar of postal and telegraph services. (In the same way, Yezhov was transferred to the Commissariat of Water Transport when the right time came. With Beria, the Master tried a new variant: promoting him to the Politburo and stripping him of direct command over the Organs.)

What was Stalin up to in such cases? Although he had picked out the next victim among his top lieutenants, he didn't feel he could send yesterday's favorite to the netherworld just like that. Two strangely antithetical traits coexisted in Stalin—adventurism and circumspection, the daring of a street apache and the timidity of a downtrodden shopkeeper.

Yagoda had not simply known too much; he had helped *do it*. It is difficult to establish exactly whether he hastened the deaths of Frunze, Dzerzhinsky, Menzhinsky, Gorky, and Kuibyshev, but it is enough to read his testimony at the 1938 trial to guess the role of Stalin's commissar in the political murders committed by the Master.

Within two weeks of the Central Committee plenum, on March 18, 1937, the deputy commissar of internal affairs, Nikolai Yezhov, had already branded Yagoda a traitor. Only on April 3 was Yagoda's arrest announced, only on April 5 was Yezhov made people's commissar of internal affairs, and only on April 18 was the "unmask Yagoda" game completed. Truly the ruling cabinet of Stalin's great state resembled a bunch of paralyzed rabbits in a cage, fallen into the hands of a drunken gamekeeper.

As far back as March Yagoda was branded, but then only as a criminal and a "degenerate." His astonished colleagues learned that he had worked for the tsarist Okhrana since 1907 and after the revolution had been recruited by German intelligence. (In putting this provocation together, Stalin surely knew that in 1907 Yagoda was only sixteen, didn't he? Of course he did. But the autocrat also knew that *they*—that is, the people —would swallow it.) Someone circulated the rumor (how timely) that Yagoda had been arrested right at the airport with a suitcase full of gold in his hand. He was getting ready to flee the country, but the glorious security police . . . and so on and so forth. (I wonder if they had a special division for rumors at the Lubyanka? Or if the *provocateur*-activists made them up during off hours.)

After Yagoda's arrest a "nest of traitors" was found in the very heart of the Security Organs. Stalin was obliged to arrest and destroy almost all officials of the NKVD. Thus, our wealthy clotheshorse managed to change his outfit every season. And throw out the old one.

Since Yagoda's staff had turned out to be full of wreckers, then all the cases should have been reviewed, shouldn't they? Ah no, Stalin had his own special logic, beyond the ken of ordinary mortals.

Alexander Orlov gives an account of the executions of Yagoda's former colleagues and the suicides of many. The suicides I doubt. Two or three cases out of a central apparatus of many thousands is not very significant. Not one of the really high-ranking officials of the Lubyanka was so quick to depart this life. For that, courage was required, and firmness of will. Where were those wretches to find such qualities?

Yezhov's team hadn't been working for even a year when the twentieth anniversary of the Cheka-OGPU-NKVD arrived—December 30, 1937. For the hard-working exterminators there came a flood of articles and books, poems and songs, medals and honors. And a triumphal celebration in the Bolshoi Theater with an honorary presiding committee consisting of the Politburo at which, after a speech by Mikoyan, Yezhov was appropriately given a gold star with white wings.

Stalin didn't appear at the theater. He knew how to maintain distance. But in the afternoon he held a private dinner for the directors of the Organs. He was even photographed with the people's commissar. The child Yezhov is sitting in a chair looking endearingly up at the Master standing behind him. Stalin leans over the "favorite of the entire Soviet people" and rewards him with one of his touching fatherly smiles of the day.

The Cheka was born at the end of 1917. For twenty years the child of the revolution grew, matured, and under the never-resting tutelage of the Gensek developed full-blown into the hired assassin of its mother.

It was well-established custom in the Politburo for each member to oversee a certain area of governmental concern. But to say that Stalin "oversaw" the Organs is to say nothing. He was constantly preoccupied with these agencies and never for one moment let the activities of the people's commissar of internal affairs and the deputy commissars out of his sight.

During the trigger-happy years (especially 1936–38) the Organs became the fundamental instrument of Stalin's policy, if we can use the word "policy" for what he did. His days and nights were spent in the cares and woes of trying to preserve the unity of the party and maintain the highest standards of justice.

> Hasn't justice always been
> A multiplication table,
> Where corpse is multiplied by corpse,
> Murder by murder,
> Evil by evil?

The poet Maksimilian Voloshin asked that question. Stalin tried to answer with maximum precision.

In his job of supervising and providing direction for the Yezhov team, Stalin placed no limits upon the butchers' appetites, nor was he stingy in granting signs of the highest approval. Tenderly he nurtured the chiefs who would run the Organs, centrally and locally. The commandant of a labor camp was more important to him than a people's commissar in charge of vital economic matters. The slave army of forced laborers in the camps passed the ten-million mark and kept growing. Reinforcements substantially exceeded in number the "natural losses."

The saturation point was reached in the summer of 1938. People simply *got tired* of killing each other. When something like that happens in a war, the soldiers on either side organize a cease-fire. If things had gone much further, the number of "enemies of the people" in the land of October, warmed by the sun of the Stalin Constitution, would have exceeded the number of "friends." The people would have been left with no choice but to beg that they all be thrown in prison.

Stalin had a surprisingly acute feeling for the moment when events peaked, when the time had come to acknowledge "political excesses." Zealous local officials, don't you see, had exceeded the authority entrusted to them by the Soviet government. Well now, we will have to correct these comrades, point out their errors to them and forgive some magnanimously while punishing others as an example. (Can you smell the smoky incense as the demagogic curtain rises upon the spring of 1930, when the Great Collectivizer tossed the people his "Dizzy with Success" article to divert their rage?)

The simulated change of policy in 1938 deceived many. Many, but not all. Fyodor Raskolnikov wrote to Stalin on August 17, 1939: "To the gullible you make yourself out as a lover of simplicity, who for years has been led around by the nose by some sort of monsters in carnival masks. 'Go seek and find some scapegoats,' you whisper to your confidants, and you reward your victims after they have been caught and condemned to infamy, you reward them with the sins of your own commission."

In the fall of 1938 Stalin set up a special subcommittee of the Central Committee to check on the activities of the NKVD. It consisted of several highly competent individuals—Molotov, Malenkov, Beria, and Vyshinsky. This quartet submitted a memo to the Gensek about "excesses in investigative work" and the need for re-examination of some cases. Two resolutions from the Central Committee followed. The first dealt with inadequacies in the procedures for arrest, investigation, and oversight by the procuracy. The second was entitled "On the Recruitment of Honest People for Work in the Security Agencies." So *honest* people were needed? And the ones in there before, what kind were they?

An *honest* people's commissar was needed. On a motion by Kaganovich, Beria was appointed to the post of first deputy of the NKVD. (Lazar had a record of sniffing out the Master's intentions just a little bit too often.) Even a cretin like Yezhov must have guessed what the Gensek was up to.

For the sake of appearances a start was made in putting some people on trial for "excesses." Some cases were set aside for re-examination, and were actually freed. In 1939 the Organs let about 200,000 framed "enemies" go, including a number of officials from the apparatus of the Moscow city committee and the Moscow provincial committee. But none of those released were veteran Communists from the time of the revolution.

* * *

I remember well that brief thaw in the spring of 1938. Stalin had just let fall those words, "The son does not answer for the father." As a seventeen-year-old student in the history department, I had just been expelled from the Moscow City Pedagogical Institute and from the Young Communist League. Before the local YCL bureau I had refused to acknowledge my arrested father as an enemy of the people. I appealed to higher levels —the district committee, the city committee, and so on—but not until I reached the YCL Central Committee did a member of the commission repeat the words of the Leader about the son of an errant father and help me get reinstated.

The demagogic furor whipped up by the Gensek and intended for simpletons did not hamper him. In fact it helped him carry out his real plans. In 1938 Stalin continued to fan the flames of repression with truly inexhaustible energy, urging on any of his myrmidons who might have grown reluctant. To the capitals of the national republics and the major provinces of Russia the Gensek sent special assistants and instigators with extraordinary powers personally authorized by him. When they arrived in some locality, they openly and publicly declared that they were acting on Stalin's orders. Among the members and candidate members of the Politburo and other prominent Central Committee officials, Lazar Kaganovich distinguished himself, as usual, by wiping out the entire active party membership in Smolensk, Ivanovo, and the Kuban.

At the same time, Georgy Malenkov outdid himself in Minsk and Armenia.

Many who perished then in Yerevan are on the conscience of Anastas Mikoyan.

Andrei Andreyev cut the throats of the leaders of Uzbekistan.

Andrei Zhdanov had the leading party and government cadres of Leningrad shot. To immortalize this feat Zhdanov's name was then given to various streets and districts and even to Leningrad University.

In the Northern Caucasus another practiced Oprichnik was at work —Matvei Shkiryatov.

And in Georgia, Lavrenty Beria, the Little Pope, in imitation of the Big Pope, held show trials of the "Trotskyists" in those parts.

This list may be filled out with the names of Nikita Khrushchev, who scourged the Ukraine, Pavel Postyshev, whose arena was the former province of Samara, and Yakov Yakovlev, who made a name for himself in Byelorussia. The last two soon fell beneath the ax themselves.

Without any fear of being rhetorical, we ask: Why, after all, did Kaganovich, Malenkov, Zhdanov, and company keep killing high-ranking officials just like themselves? One day the secretary of a provincial committee or a city committee would denounce some "enemies of the people" at a meeting or in the newspapers, and the next day he himself would be thrown into the cellar. Everyone in the local apparatus would go too. On what charge? Collaborating with an enemy who hid behind a pretended devotion to Stalin.

It's hard to explain that behavior simply by some psychological need to kill, or a blind desire to serve the Master. They sowed fear of the Kremlin dictatorship in the hopes of strengthening it and simultaneously rising higher in the court circle. Another thing. They saw clearly that there was an unwritten order: *All* party members of long standing were to be exterminated, the entire Old Guard of Lenin's time. But Stalin's vision extended much further. By the late thirties those who had taken part in the revolution were already over forty or even over fifty. The generation that had lived under the tsar was passing from the scene. These older people had seen a lot and knew a lot and had something they could compare the present with. Stalin set himself the general task of hastening the departure of this whole generation, along with the "thin layer" of Old Bolsheviks.

The regime that had been overthrown had regulated the carnage in its day. Under the tsar one had known exactly which sections of the population were subject to extermination. Stalin had his own special dialectics of slaughter. When he had to kill, everybody went, regardless of political affiliation. He slaughtered them in the name of "friendship and equality" between all peoples.

"Kill them all. The Lord will recognize his own," said Arnold Amalric, the papal delegate, when the crusaders asked him how to tell the heretics from the right-thinking Catholics. It was according to this same vivifying formula that the crusader in the Kremlin was to destroy thirty or forty million people. Not the easiest task in the world. But Stalin hoped to perform it in a brief historical time, relying on the enthusiasm of the broad masses. Fate had blessed Russia with a great optimist.

The time had come to settle accounts with the delegates of the Seventeenth Party Congress. Their criminal design for dumping the Gensek in the Central Committee elections had been divined and crushed in the egg. But despite all his leniency and permissiveness, that was something Stalin could not forget. He took pains to see that none of those delegates would ever take part in voting again. It's true, of course, that he didn't kill every last one of them. Out of the 1,961 delegates, perhaps two dozen survived.

The higher a Communist stood on the party or government ladder, the greater the chances of a quick demise. Stalin wiped out four chairmen of the Council of People's Commissars of the Russian Republic in a very short time. They were Rykov, Syrtsov, Sulimov, and Rodionov.

Not all the local leaders understood what was going on. Not all were able to sense the brilliance of the Leader's design. The plan for the production of oil, coal, grain—that was something clear and familiar. But planned quotas for the arrest of "enemies of the people"—something about this confused the Organs and threw them off balance. A *signal* had to be sent to Moscow for clarification. But not many local leaders could bring themselves to do that. The isolated provincial-committee secretaries and local procurators here and there who tried to stop the illegal acts of repression and to appeal for help to the Central Committee, or to the Gensek personally, were pitilessly rubbed out by Stalin. And when apologists for Stalin nowadays mutter, "He didn't know anything about it; the bloody deeds were done by others behind his back," I answer with certainty: "He knew. At every moment. Every hour of the day or night. Who was to be arrested, when, and how. He knew. He did the planning. He gave the orders."

In June 1937, on the eve of the regular plenum of the Central Committee, several veteran Communists gathered at an apartment for evening tea, among them Pyatnitsky, Kaminsky, and Filatov. A conversation started about Stalin, his leadership methods, and the intolerable situation in the party. The names of Lenin's comrades who had been killed so far were mentioned with pain. All agreed on one thing: Stalin had to be removed from the leadership. At the Central Committee plenum a condemnation of the policy of terror had to be carried and Stalin had to be replaced as general secretary.

The Master heard about this conversation, which was called "the cup of tea." Filatov informed on his comrades. Stalin subsequently wiped them all out, including the informer. In July 1938 Pyatnitsky was sitting in cell No. 96 in Lefortovo prison and told his cellmate V. V. about their conversation over tea that fatal evening. He was brutally beaten, and in the last month of his life, he underwent eighteen torture and interrogation sessions. They broke his ribs, gave him severe internal injuries, and mutilated his face. The investigator was Langfang, one of the few who were tried and condemned after the Twentieth Party Congress, a party member and a former official in the Zamoskvorechye district committee of the YCL. Among other things, a personal confrontation for Pyatnitsky was arranged with one of the witnesses against him, Bela Kun, former leader of the Hungarian revolution of 1919. Kun's life ended in the same cellar, only a year later, on November 30, 1939.

In 1963 Pyatnitsky's cellmate had the following recollections:

Pyatnitsky taught me a small lesson. He put on a double layer of underwear. When he came back he couldn't take the underwear off by himself. He raised his arms and I pulled the undershirt off him. His face was bruised and cut—the marks of a belt buckle.

The mutilated Pyatnitsky could no longer read, so I read to him out loud. It was a book by Saltykov-Shchedrin. Many pages had been torn out by the local censors. The writings of the great satirist gave them something to worry about, that's for sure.

Pyatnitsky was accused of the following crimes:

"(a) In selecting cadres in the fraternal Communist parties, he had placed a provocateur in every one.

"(b) He inserted Trotskyist formulations into the texts of books translated into foreign languages and into works by Marx, Engels, Lenin, and Stalin.

"(c) He had appropriated 30,000 rubles from one publishing house."

Those were the charges brought against a man who had spent his whole life at Lenin's side, through whose hands hundreds of thousands of gold rubles had passed during his travels abroad.

At the Seventh Comintern Congress, Stalin was photographed with the members of the presiding committee of the congress: Pyatnitsky, Dimitrov, Cachin, Thorez, and Pieck. This photograph can be seen in some books published quite recently.

* * *

Rudzutak, an old-timer in the party who had spent ten years at forced labor under the tsar, including three years in irons (the official record of this was preserved in his dossier), was accused by the Lubyanka hacks of ties with the tsarist Okhrana! And of organizing a plot against the life of Comrade Stalin. It was made known at the Twentieth Party Congress that Rudzutak had managed before his death to tell the "court," after totally refuting all the charges, that there undoubtedly existed in the NKVD some sort of secret central office devoted to the task of exterminating all of the Leninist Old Guard.

What was the Leader thinking about in destroying Rudzutak? He knew of Lenin's dying wish to see Rudzutak take the post of general secretary. Lenin regarded Rudzutak as a man capable of holding the dynastic passions of the party leaders in check. However, Rudzutak had no aspirations for personal power and had not intrigued against Stalin. On the contrary, at the Sixteenth Party Congress he had given Stalin a boost by speaking out against the platform of the "Rights."

"There are not only protests against the existing party machine, there is also outright slander against the party, outright slander against Comrade Stalin, against whom they try to make accusations of trying to establish one-man rule in our party."

Did Stalin hesitate and weigh these factors and considerations? Are you kidding? Rudzutak belonged to the Leninist Old Guard. That's all that mattered.

* * *

Another one of the doomed was Vladimir Zatonsky, who had been a member of the first Soviet government of the Ukraine and a revolutionary activist for many years. Back during the Tenth Party Congress, in 1921, he had warned the party against deviating in the direction of great-power chauvinism. The most consistent supporter of such a deviation, the Georgian Dzhugashvili-Stalin, also remembered Zatonsky's part in revealing the machinations in the voting at the Seventeenth Congress. Remembered it and entered it in his account book. Payment fell due in 1937.

At the September meeting of the active party membership in Kiev, a housebroken Stanislav Kosior reported on the discovery of a "counter-revolutionary gang of bourgeois nationalists" on Ukrainian soil. Zatonsky, who was commissar of enlightenment for the Ukraine, was forced to present some tales of political fantasy in the same genre. He admitted that his commissariat and many schools were "littered with enemies."

But statements like this and even willing self-denunciations in public were not enough to propitiate the Gensek. To begin with, on some flimsy pretext the Leader refused to allow Zatonsky, or his Moscow colleague Andrei Bubnov, to attend the regular Central Committee plenum in October 1937. Then, after letting Zatonsky taste all the pleasures of anticipation, he ordered him arrested and eliminated.

The Master could not refrain from executing Boris Sheboldaev, who in 1918 had been deputy commissar of war in the Baku Commune and had worked closely with Stepan Shaumyan (Stalin's rival). Sheboldaev died at the same time as several other prominent party figures—Abel Yenukidze, Mamiya Orakhelashvili, and Levon Karakhan.

* * *

David Ryazanov was sixty years old when he died. One of Lenin's contemporaries, he had done an enormous amount to establish Marxist scholarship in Russia. In 1918 he organized the Socialist Academy of Social Sciences under the All-Russia Central Executive Committee of the Soviets. (In 1924 its name was changed to the Communist Academy; in 1936 it was eradicated.) Ryazanov did invaluable service for the party by acquiring many of the archival papers of Karl Marx in Western Europe and laying the foundations for the future Institute of Marxism-Leninism. He published works of great value and edited important editions of the works of Marx and Lenin. He was a sparkling polemicist, in whom there lived an irrepressible spirit of free thought and independent action. Back at the turn of the century he had fought against Lenin's *Iskra*. After the victory of the revolution he argued for including the Mensheviks and SRs in the government. In protest against the signing of the Brest-Litovsk peace treaty, he resigned from the party. He constantly clashed with Lenin and had an ironic and contemptuous attitude toward Koba. There was a sharp exchange between them once at the Tenth Congress. After Ryazanov had spoken, Stalin remarked: "I respect Ryazanov a lot, but I respect Marx more." Ryazanov parried from his seat: "Koba, don't embarrass people. Theory is not your strong point." Years later, after Stalin had banished Trotsky and Rakovsky and was severely harassing them, Ryazanov continued to contract with them for scholarly work on the volumes of Lenin's and Marx's writings.

Stalin first brought charges against Ryazanov in connection with the case of the so-called Menshevik Union Bureau in 1931. He was charged with the crime, among other things, of stubbornly refusing to hand over a letter Darwin had written Marx, which Ryazanov had obtained from the relatives of the great scientist. They had stipulated that the letter could not be published, and Ryazanov had given his word. This struck Stalin as so odd and suspicious that he decided to banish the obstreperous scholar and thinker to the Saratov region, just in case. And a few years later he had Ryazanov done away with altogether.

* * *

Slandered and lawlessly suppressed, many prominent Communists wrote to Stalin personally, begging him to investigate what was going on and save the party from destruction. Many letters reached Stalin's desk from those about to die—Eikhe, Bukharin, Rudzutak, Radek, Rakovsky, Bulatov. And what happened? Either he rerouted them to their "proper destination," the NKVD, or he left them where they sat. It amounted to the same thing. Without Stalin's knowledge no one dared arrest or kill any of the prominent party or government leaders. The most important right, the right to kill, he reserved for himself. Lengthy lists of the proscribed, bearing notations deciding their fates, in Stalin's own handwriting and that of his lieutenants Molotov and Kaganovich, have been preserved.

Stalin was lazy by nature, but in organizing the terror and working out its technology and procedures, he displayed enviable application and persistence. To him belongs the honor of inventing this dynamic formula: Arrest—smear—torture—obtain a confession—try—condemn—execute (= send to a death camp).

Only one of these operations was done in public—smearing the victim as an "enemy of the people." The rest were carried out in deepest secrecy. Without the slightest reference to the law, the rights granted under the Constitution, or other paper props. The Master saw to the maintenance of secrecy most diligently, for the criminal feared publicity worst of all. The public show trials were a special case. He personally stage-managed them.

In the civil war, the Finnish campaign, and then World War II, Stalin demonstrated his worthlessness as a strategist. He made up for it in the war at home. Here he was at his best. The operations for exterminating unarmed subjects were planned and directed by the Master himself. Eagerly he went over all the technical details and took great pleasure in participating directly in "unmasking" enemies. Confronting them personally gave him particular pleasure. He indulged himself more than once in such truly diabolical performances.

History has preserved some precedents for this. Empress Catherine (the "Great") personally directed the investigation of the freethinker Radishchev, "an insurrectionist worse than Pugachov." Tsar Nicholas I supervised the investigation of the Decembrists. Similarly, Stalin condescended to give orders to the interrogators, encouraged the use of torture, and personally cross-examined "witnesses" in his Kremlin office.

Having decided to eliminate Panas Lyubchenko, the chairman of the Council of People's Commissars of the Ukraine and one of the top leaders of the Ukrainian Communist Party, Stalin personally conducted a confrontation between Lyubchenko and a certain party official brought directly from the Lubyanka. This was in September 1937. In the presence of Kosior and Yezhov this "witness" testified to the treason of the distinguished old revolutionary.

Later came Kosior's turn. Stalin arranged a personal confrontation between Kosior and Grigory Petrovsky, chairman of the Central Executive Committee of the Ukrainian Soviet Republic. The confrontation was preceded by a meeting between Petrovsky and Yezhov. Petrovsky's oldest son, Pyotr, a hero of the civil war, had been killed not long before on Stalin's orders. Pyotr Petrovsky had been a personal friend of Kirov's. Petrovsky senior knew he couldn't count on mercy, but he remained firm.

Yezhov: You knew that Kosior was an enemy of the people and that he was contemplating treason?

Petrovsky: I knew Kosior as a man of exceptional honesty and purity.

Yezhov: Do you think that just because the party has forgiven you for the sins of your Trotskyist son, nothing more is required of you?

Petrovsky: My son Pyotr was also a loyal Bolshevik. He disagreed with some things about the general line but he was never an enemy of the party.

Yezhov: Your son was convicted as an enemy of the people. There's no use your being stubborn. You can't talk that way with the party.

When Stalin summoned Petrovsky to his office for a personal confrontation with Kosior, the Gensek decided to teach the stubborn old Village Elder of the Whole Ukraine a lesson and at the same time have the pleasure of witnessing the humiliation of Kosior, who had finally been broken completely.

Yezhov: Prisoner Kosior, tell us about Petrovsky's participation in the counterrevolutionary plot.

Kosior: Grigory Ivanovich Petrovsky and I established connections for criminal purposes in 1934.

Yezhov: For what purpose?

Kosior: We decided to fight by all possible means to have the Ukraine separated from Soviet Russia.

Yezhov: By what means exactly? Please be more precise.

Kosior: Terrorism, preparations for an armed uprising, espionage.

So far everything had gone smoothly. Half alive, his eyes glazed, Kosior repeated in a monotone all the phrases drilled into him by his torturers. Yezhov obligingly threw him all the right questions at exactly the right places in the script. But Petrovsky wouldn't sit still for it.

"Stasik, why are you slandering yourself and me?"

Kosior nodded his head. Yezhov had the prisoner removed immediately.

The Gensek was in a fury. He went up to Petrovsky and spoke these words very distinctly, one by one, at the same time drawing his finger across Petrovsky's face right under his nose:

"You know, we're going to hang all the spies. Do you think your serving in the Duma is going to save you?"

How many personal confrontations like this did the Gensek have in his office? How many times did he order his closest collaborators and Politburo members brought in? He would listen to the testimony of the "witness," closely observe the reaction of the accused, refute his objections, urge him to confess, promise forgiveness and guarantee full personal safety, threaten, turn to the witness again, throw meaningful glances at his straight man Yezhov, and get so involved in his role that perhaps, in the heat of the moment, he himself would start to believe in the correctness of what he was doing. Even his party comrades, the Gensek's victims of today and yesterday, got the impression that Comrade Stalin believed these provocations. Certainly he hadn't contrived them himself. And maybe they weren't provocations after all, but the actual truth? Perhaps people had simply confessed under the weight of the evidence, and that's all there was to it. . . .

Joseph the Builder counted on such ninnies and simpletons in the party in his plans for constructing his own model of socialism, with which he would astound the world.

Here we encounter a historical paradox. On the one hand, the deeply muffled secret work of the Organs. Secret investigations, trials, secret participation by Stalin in exterminating the party and the people. On the other hand, public trials with foreign correspondents attending, accompanied by a noisy media campaign in the newspapers, over the radio, in films, and in public meetings.

Why were these show trials needed? There was an entire complex of reasons for them. It was not enough for Stalin to justify his totalitarian terror in the minds of the "working masses." Voiceless and bound by intangible shackles, they learned by heart the cry of full-grown idiots for all occasions in life: "Hurrah." The Leader needed the show trials as powder and makeup for his pockmarked face. He wished to appear before the public—at home and abroad—as perhaps harsh, but nevertheless a just keeper of his flock. His was a complex nature. Police Chief Stalin desperately wanted to look respectable in the world arena.

Exactly like Catherine II. She sentenced Pugachov to be drawn and quartered. But on December 10, 1773, she wrote to Sievers that the "whole affair would end with a hanging." Above all she was concerned lest "Europe think we still live in the age of Ivan the Terrible."[80]

Stalin too was worried about European opinion. The show trials were meant to calm Western fears. At the same time accounts could be settled with some people on a totally legal basis. And all the failures of the leadership written off, including one's own personal blunders, as the work of "spies and wreckers."

By accusing Trotsky, Zinoviev, and Kamenev, and later on Bukharin and the "Rights," of having planned terrorism against Lenin, Stalin the scenarist was equating his own person with that of Lenin, one the object of terror in 1918, the other in 1936–38. Thus in passing he increased—or, more accurately, multiplied—his political capital. After all, Stalin's alleged role in the events of 1917 and 1918 as a leader of the revolution, Lenin's loyal disciple, and sole continuator—all that was still just a legend in the eyes of people who knew.

How pleasant it was, then, to hear from the lips of a ferocious enemy of the party the following forced expression of rapture over the thousand-year fortress of power erected by him, Stalin. (These lines, incidentally, were inserted in Kamenev's confession in the Gensek's own handwriting. He did not shun even the meanest, dirtiest labors.)

"The leadership of Stalin is made of too hard a granite to expect that it would break apart by itself. Therefore it must be broken."

In these words you will find all of Stalin, with his undying faith in his own star of destiny—and his uncertainty as to the stability of his absolute rule over his people and time. Along with that, a childishly bombastic style and grammar worthy of a seminary dropout. With his screenplay drama-tizing the vicious and insidious struggle of countless enemies against the party of Lenin and Stalin, the Gensek hoped to strengthen the impression in the minds of his audience of the granite strength of his rule.

He also wished to gratify himself with the abasement of Lenin's for-mer comrades, who at one time had allowed themselves to regard him so condescendingly. Now they were on their knees and everyone could see it. And on their knees they would crawl right out of this life.

Catherine II's grandson, Nicholas I, wrote this about the execution of the Decembrists: "The vile wretches died vilely without any dignity." Stalin forced grown men to take part in a political striptease. At the 1937 trial, Karl Radek made a remarkable admission. They, the enemies of the people, he said, by their own silence, lying, and stubbornness had tortured the hard-working and self-sacrificing Soviet investigators, these humane and sensitive friends of all prisoners, these devoted instruments of the party's will.[81]

In the October Hall of the House of Trade Unions in Moscow, where the trial of Kamenev and Zinoviev was held in August 1936, Antonov-Ovseyenko saw the Military Collegium of the Supreme Court at work, headed by Ulrikh, that tried-and-true protector of Soviet legality. Less than two years were to pass before my father would himself appear as an "enemy of the people" before this Gorgon in the uniform of a military attorney.

But for the time being the hearing continued, and Public Prosecutor Vladimir Antonov-Ovseyenko sat among the spectators dumbfounded by the perfidy and baseness of these counterrevolutionary plotters. So this was who had guided the hand of Nikolaev, Kirov's assassin, plotting to restore capitalism along with Judas Trotsky. The present evil-doings of this gang were no accident. Back in 1917 Lenin had branded them as strike-breakers of October.

Before the trial began, under the fresh impression of the irrefutable "evidence" and established "facts," Antonov published a virulent article in *Izvestia* with the characteristic title "Smash Them Completely."

Gray from his years of battles, the old revolutionary cursed the Trotskyist-Zinovievist gang, this "special detachment of fascist diversionists," the worst enemies of the people, with whom "there's only one way of talking—shooting." Antonov was recanting for his past. From 1923 to 1927 he had tried to reconcile Trotsky with Stalin. Now Antonov was in raptures over the farsightedness of the great Stalin, surrounded by the "ardent love and devotion of all the toilers."[82]

"I am ashamed for Antonov-Ovseyenko's gray hairs," Nikolai Bukharin remarked when he received this letter of my father's for publication.

But Stalin gleefully rubbed his hands. Truly Antonov-Ovseyenko had said exactly the right thing. He had compared the USSR with a mighty granite cliff, called the Trotskyist-Zinovievist bandits direct agents of the Gestapo, and had not failed to mention "the first and indispensable condition for victory—the iron Leninist unity of the party in unrelenting struggle against the agencies of the class enemy." Moreover he had noted with full justification the decisive role of Comrade Stalin, whose "eagle eye" had seen far ahead and ensured this unity.

So, he had not spent all those long nights in vain hunting for ways to destroy his rivals on the road to supreme power. His strategy had even won the hearts of Lenin's fellow fighters, or so it would seem if he had succeeded in pulling the wool over the eyes of as politically experienced a man as Antonov-Ovseyenko. That means people had *believed* the performances staged in the House of Trade Unions.

We have not forgotten the professional skill with which Stalin conducted the performances he called party congresses. In the production of the show trials, the incomparable talent of this home-grown Kremlin genius reached new heights of directorial brilliance. He labored with youthful enthusiasm to put on the plays composed by the Lubyanka dramatists. As for the 1937 play, he displayed his daring innovativeness as a director and his unwavering democratic spirit by having Karl Radek write the script, although Radek had already been arrested as an "enemy of the people." And was to take part in the show himself. Rehearsals were held right in the Lubyanka, and there too, under the supervision of Assistant Director Yezhov, the actors learned their parts so well that there was no need for a prompter. As the show went on, the Lubyanka delivered the partly finished materials—the disemboweled, physically and mentally exhausted defendants and witnesses, drugged by poisons and terrified by the impending retribution. A few days before the opening of the performance they were quickly made up to appear human. Then it was, "Get ready. You're on."

Stalin took great pains to try to clothe his revenge in the decorous garb of legality. This was a difficult task since the charges were based exclusively on the confessions of the accused. In his final statement Bukharin had the nerve to call this practice a "medieval juridical principle."[83] At the Fifteenth Congress, in December 1927, as he was starting the first round in his deadly hunting expedition against his party rivals, Stalin declared, "Soviet legality is not an empty phrase."[84] Ten years later, as the prison roofs bulged from the excess of prisoners, Stalin would begin publication of a journal with the reassuring title *Socialist Legality*.

* * *

Catherine II spared Radishchev's life. Nicholas I pardoned many of the Decembrists. The Kremlin usurper did not stain his reputation with a single act of mercy. As for Rakovsky and Sokolnikov, in the trials of 1937 and 1938 they were given "only" twenty and ten years in labor camps, respectively, by way of exception. However, they were rubbed out in compounds behind barbed wire, by criminals specifically assigned and paid for their services by the Lubyanka. This operation was carried out under a special code name and number, and its traces remain in the financial records of the NKVD. Thus, the unworthy suspicion that Comrade Stalin had a momentary lapse of humaneness is removed. Karl Radek, composer of remarkable political jokes and of a no less remarkable trial script, a man whose works were still valued by Stalin during their author's eight years in prison, was killed by having his head smashed with a brick.

* * *

Is there any need to demonstrate that Stalin never regarded any of the "enemies of the people" as real enemies? Apparently there is. For even today many of our contemporaries have a strange view of the period when Stalin was on the rampage. They look at it from this angle: "Well, if people were arrested, they must have done something. . . ."

To refute this infamous formula, it is enough to observe that Stalin actually freed a great many condemned "enemies" the moment their services were needed. Here are a few names from a very long list: the engineer Leonid Ramzin; the airplane designer Andrei Tupolyov; the physicist Lev Landau; the epidemiologist Pavel Zdrodovsky.

But there is not one prominent party figure on this list. Stalin did not bring back any of the Old Communists ("We can do without the old loudmouths"). Scientists, inventors, design engineers—that was a different matter. These "spies and wreckers" could be used for building socialism.

At the beginning of the war, when the army that had been bled white by Stalin's terror was reeling under the blows of the Wehrmacht, Stalin released several thousand commanders who had survived in the camps and prisons. However, only a few of the highest-ranking military leaders were still alive—Meretskov, Gorbatov, Sandalov, Rokossovsky, Podlas.

Without delay Stalin sent them to the collapsing front lines. There were regiments waiting with no one to lead them.

Stalin knew better than anyone that they were about as much enemies as the nineteenth-century geographer Miklukho-Maklai or the still-flourishing ballerina Galina Ulanova. Then there was the episode involving Otto Kuusinen, the Finnish Communist leader and a member of the Executive Committee of the Comintern. Stalin asked him why he didn't petition for his son's release. Kuusinen bowed submissively before the sultan: "Apparently there were substantial reasons for his arrest." The

Great Humorist guffawed. A day later Kuusinen's son was freed.

Pavel Filippovich Zdrodovsky, a scientist with a reputation throughout Europe, had headed the Institute of Epidemiology in the thirties. It so happened that Deputy Commissar of Defense Tukhachevsky had summoned him three times in connection with epidemics in the Red Army. In the investigator's free way of interpreting things, this came out as an enemy plot aimed at poisoning the entire army. In the Ust-Vym camps, where Zdrodovsky served his time, a postcard came from Aleksandr D. Vishnevsky senior: "Pasha [short for Pavel]—we haven't forgotten you and are looking after your family."

"Who's this postcard from?" the camp security officer asked Zdrodovsky. But the scientist played dumb. (Vishnevsky, a surgeon, was a prominent figure in the Soviet medical world.)

One day just before the war broke out, Zdrodovsky was called to the guardhouse with his things and sent under reinforced guard to Moscow. Everyone assumed they were taking him for retrial, and this time would give him the "highest form of punishment" (being shot).

But Vishnevsky had won out. Taking advantage of a critical situation, a bad epidemic that had started in the garrison of Irkutsk, he had appealed to the people's commissar of defense: "What's going on! Our Red Army men are dying while the best specialist in fighting epidemics is sawing wood in a labor camp." Neither Beria nor Stalin had any objections to releasing the "case-hardened diversionist."

No, no matter what they say, the Master always released the people he needed. Naftaly Frenkel, the legendary organizer of the camp system, was freed from Lubyanka prison in 1939. A railroad had to be built in a hurry to the Karelian Isthmus for the delivery of munitions to be used against the stubborn Finns. So yesterday's convict Frenkel became today's head of GULZhDS, the Chief Administration for Railroad Construction, a vast prison-camp empire that stretched from Leningrad to Vladivostok.

OUT BY THE ROOTS!

7

Stalin had long nurtured his plan for the extermination of the Leninist Old Guard. The final decision was made in 1934, at the Seventeenth Party Congress, when he almost lost his seat as general secretary. But after the Kirov assassination he still could not come down full force on the veterans of the party. Any military operation requires preparation. Even he understood that.

On May 25, 1935, the Society of Old Bolsheviks, headed by that most humble subject Yemelyan Yaroslavsky, was dissolved. A month later the Society of Former Political Exiles and Hard-Labor Prisoners was given the same treatment. What a thing to have as part of your name, a reference to tsarist hard labor. We'll give you something to chew on. Compare *our* labor camps! Then maybe you'll be a little more modest, you bearded old fools.

If you live through it.

On March 24, 1922, two years before his death, Lenin wrote with obvious concern that "the proletarian policy of the party is not determined by the character of its membership, but by the enormous, undivided authority enjoyed by that very *thin layer* which might be called the Old Guard of the party. A slight conflict within this layer would be enough, if not to destroy its authority, at all events to weaken it so much that decisions would no longer depend on it."[85]

Stalin tried to do everything that *depended on him* to turn Lenin's fears into reality. The history of the ensuing years is an unbroken series of political intrigues set in motion by Stalin with enviable ingenuity. And once the internecine conflicts in the Central Committee had decisively weakened the authority of that "very thin layer," he began to exterminate them, to the last one—oppositionists and orthodox Communists alike.

The Kremlin sportsman was careful, at least at first, to do his shooting of Communists selectively. Long before the Great Beginning, Noi Zhordania asserted that Stalin already had his lists of the proscribed ready, that the Gensek knew who was to be put out of the way, when, and how. Zhordania had seen Comrade Koba at work many times. That was the source of his astonishingly accurate prediction.

It is the Seventeenth Party Congress. At the speaker's stand is Artemyev, representing the gunmakers of Tula: "We brought some samples of our output to show our leaders, especially Comrade Stalin, our brilliant teacher." (That was how they were glorifying the Victor already.) Artemyev then handed a sniper's rifle to the Gensek. Stalin looked through the sights and aimed the rifle at the audience. The delegates to the congress broke into an ovation.[86]

Stalin's sniper fire at the party didn't stop until his death. As for ovations, even the death of the Great Sniper didn't stop those.

Only a few years would pass after the Seventeenth Congress before the Old Guard layer would be so thinned out that not one, literally not one, would have any say any longer. Everything would depend from then on on one man, who in the most imperious way referred to himself as "the continuator of Lenin's work."

* * *

The delegates to the April Conference of the Bolshevik Party in 1917 elected nine members to the Central Committee: Lenin, Sverdlov, Nogin, Stalin, Zinoviev, Kamenev, Milyutin, Smilga, Fyodorov. The last five lived into the thirties. Stalin killed them all. He concerned himself as well with the five daughters of Fyodorov, who had headed the metalworkers' union in the year of the revolution.

The Central Committee elected at the Sixth Party Congress in August 1917 consisted of twenty-seven people. They were not all outstanding revolutionaries; nevertheless this Central Committee of 1917 could be considered the nucleus of the Leninist leadership. Based on the results of the secret balloting, Grigory Ordzhonikidze referred to the following four men as the *leaders* of the party: Lenin (133 out of 134 votes), Zinoviev (132), and Kamenev and Trotsky (131 each).

Three of these four leaders turned out subsequently to be "enemies of the people." Who can say? Maybe Ilyich died just in time. In the first few years of Soviet rule, enemy bullets cut short the lives of three Central Committee members—Shaumyan, Dzhaparidze, and Uritsky. Disease carried off Sverdlov; disease or something else, Dzerzhinsky. The seventeen members who survived to the period of 1935–38 were struck down by the hand of Stalin.

Stalin had a fierce, irrepressible hatred of Lenin, however well he concealed it. When the time came to settle the score for the "humiliations" he had suffered in the early years of the revolution, he destroyed the trusted lieutenants of the deceased leader without mercy, including those who had saved the life of the party's founder in 1917. Them first of all.

Aleksandr Shotman, a member of the Central Committee came from a family that had been industrial workers for generations. When the party had to go underground in the summer of 1917, he was Lenin's liaison man and organized Lenin's move from the Petrograd suburb Razliv to Finland. Stalin got rid of Shotman in 1939. In 1938 he killed Gustav Rovio, who as chief of police in Helsinki in 1917 had helped Lenin hide from the Kerensky government. Rovio was arrested by Stalin while serving as first secretary of the party committee of Karelia province. Jacob Hanecki, a prominent figure in the party, had been instrumental in having Lenin released from an Austrian prison in 1914, and in the spring of 1917 had helped arrange Lenin's return to Russia. In 1937 he died in Stalin's torture chambers. Nikolai Gorbunov had been a secretary of the Council of People's Commissars and Lenin's personal secretary. Stalin put an end to him too in 1937.

Then there's the case of Fritz Platten. When Lenin returned to Russia in April 1917, he was denounced by the bourgeois press as a German spy who had arrived in a sealed train. Twenty years later the Swiss Communist Platten, who had organized Lenin's return to his homeland, was accused by Stalin of having been a German spy in 1917. Did the Lubyanka interrogators notice, as they were torturing Lenin's old comrade, the mutilated wrist on the "spy's" right arm? On January 1, 1918, a group of terrorists fired at the car in which Lenin and Platten were sitting. Platten had thrown up his arms to cover Lenin's head. Fritz Platten took up residence in the USSR in 1923 and founded one of the first agricultural communes,

OUT BY THE ROOTS!

near the city of Ulyanovsk, where Lenin was born. That's where he was arrested. He died in the Kargopol camps in 1942.

Nikolai Yemelyanov provided Lenin and Zinoviev with a hiding place by the lake in Razliv. Vladimir Ilyich paid tribute to him as one of the best and most reliable Petrograd workers. In those dangerous times Yemelyanov's sons rowed Ordzhonikidze and Sverdlov out to see Lenin and kept him supplied with newspapers. The boys also brought Comrade Koba more than once to the hunter's shack where Lenin was hiding.

Could Stalin forget or forgive something like that? Krupskaya pleaded with the Gensek for the life of the old worker Yemelyanov. The Leader commuted his death sentence to twenty-five years in the camps. After Stalin died, Yemelyanov returned to his home, having done time for sixteen years. Of his three sons, he found only the youngest, Kondraty, among the living.

* * *

Stalin showed his hostility toward Nadezhda Krupskaya even while Lenin was alive. After the Bolshevik leader's demise Stalin placed the widow under close surveillance. The Gensek kept a record of all her contacts with Lenin's old comrades. She lived in the Kremlin but was denied any telephone communication with the city. Stalin installed a woman to serve as Krupskaya's personal "guardian." This was Vera Dridzo, the youngest daughter of the prominent revolutionary Solomon Lozovsky. (His eldest daughter maintained surveillance over the Krzhizhanovsky couple, who had also been close friends of Lenin.)

On one occasion Nadezhda Konstantinovna was standing in line outside a movie theater when one of her friends came by.

"What's this, Nadezhda Konstantinovna? You're alone?"

"My gendarme's out of commission," Krupskaya answered with a smile. Dridzo was ill that day.

Vera Dridzo was given wide-ranging powers. She was placed on the staff of the Marx-Engels-Lenin Institute and was assigned by the directorate of the institute to oversee publication of Krupskaya's manuscripts. Every line Krupskaya wrote about Lenin or the party had to pass through the fine sieve of Vera Solomonovna's vigilance. She decided what to keep quiet about (i.e., delete), what to correct (i.e., distort), and what to place on her boss's desk.

For many years Krupskaya lived in the same place as the son of Dmitry Ulyanov (Lenin's younger brother) in the suburban district of Domodedova near Moscow, a spot called Maloye Arkhangelskoye. She had two small rooms on the grounds of the Zootechnic Institute. In later years she put on a lot of weight because of a metabolic disorder. She ate at the Kremlin dining hall and was prescribed a meat cutlet three times a day. Not a very sensible diet for a person with her illness.

In 1939, Krupskaya was getting ready to speak at the approaching Eighteenth Party Congress, to object to the intolerable regime Stalin had created in the party. At this decisive moment the old underground fighter's sense of danger failed her. In conversation with some close friends she made her intention known. Someone commented that she might simply be denied the floor. She flared up: "I'd like to see them try to stop me from speaking. I'll take the floor at the congress and demand the right to speak. I have been in the party forty years and I have the right to tell the congress what I am concerned about."

Margarita Fofanova recalled this conversation of early February 1939. Krupskaya's most trusted comrades were present. Which of them informed on her? Probably we'll never know. But Krupskaya's name disappeared from the speakers' list drawn up by the organizing committee for the congress.

On February 26, 1939, Krupskaya celebrated her seventieth birthday. The Gensek had a cake delivered to the celebrant's table. As soon as Nadezhda Konstantinovna, stricken with poison, arrived at the hospital, she was taken for some reason to the top floor, to the operating room. There she died without ever regaining consciousness. The coroner's report gave the cause of death as an abdominal embolism. (Fofanova had been at Krupskaya's place just before her death. There had been no sign of illness then. They had been planning to take a trip to Leningrad together a few days later.)

Krupskaya's remains were carried to the Kremlin wall by Stalin and Molotov. There were a few words about dear Nadezhda Konstantinovna, who had headed the publishing division of the People's Commissariat of Enlightenment. That was all. Then a prolonged silence, for almost twenty years, during which the name of this veteran revolutionary was hardly ever mentioned.

* * *

The argument that although Stalin may have been a little rough at times, those he destroyed were dangerous oppositionists and his only aim was to preserve the Leninist unity of the party—that's a lot of unholy nonsense. The murder of oppositionists, and the less bloody battle he waged against the opposition in the earlier years, simply served to conceal his true aims. What was his real attitude toward dissenters? No one has answered that question better than Stalin himself. In April 1917 he made this accurate observation: "Without disagreements there can be no party life."

In 1924 Fyodor Raskolnikov, who was then Soviet ambassador to Afghanistan, returned to Moscow from Kabul. At Stalin's apartment in the Kremlin he found Semyon Budyonny. On the table there was wine and fruit. Raskolnikov passed along the latest news.

"No doubt you've heard that the leader of the opposition in Turkey has been poisoned. . . ."

Stalin gave Budyonny a poke in the ribs: *"That's the way to stop political discussions."*

This was at home, over a bottle of wine.[87]

A few days later, at the Thirteenth Party Congress, the Gensek would observe that the policy toward former oppositionists had to be *exceptionally comradely*.

* * *

On a list of two hundred prominent party figures felled by this "fighter for the party's purity" we find barely twenty who had belonged at one time to the opposition. Boris Semyonov was one of the hard-core working-class Communists of St. Petersburg. A member of the party since 1905, he had been secretary of the provincial committee in Lugansk and then in the Crimea. In the twenties he energetically opposed Zinoviev. In 1937 he was wiped out as a member of the "Trotskyist-Zinovievist gang." How many of these Semyonovs were there who upheld the Leninist line of the party all their lives and perished in Stalin's dungeons and barbed-wire camps?

But shooting people for some trivial role in an opposition, or, more often, for *allegedly* being in an opposition, was not much consolation. There were still the annoying scoldings and pleadings from Krupskaya one moment, Bukharin another, Sergo Ordzhonikidze another, and then that "great proletarian writer" Gorky. "Would he have been great without me, Stalin?" Such was the Gensek's thinking as he commanded the Organs from then on to charge all arrested Communists, without fail, with espionage, terrorism, wrecking, or simply counterrevolutionary activity in general. Or maybe "working for the tsarist Okhrana."

Back when he was in exile in Turukhansk, Koba had circulated rumors that Sverdlov was an agent of the tsarist secret police. The Duma deputies who came to the exile colony vouched for Sverdlov's honesty. Koba turned around then and accused another honest man, Grigory Petrovsky, of provocation.

In Karl Radek's final statement at the 1937 trial, as printed in *Pravda*, someone inserted the following words:

"All the Old Bolsheviks were essentially Trotskyists—if not completely, then halfway, and if not halfway at least a quarter or one-eighth."

In the stenographic record of the trial, published in 1937, the text of Radek's remarks is different. There he says: "There are in the country semi-Trotskyists, one-fourth Trotskyists, one-eighth Trotskyists, people who helped us." Since we know that Stalin personally arranged with the arrested Radek to write the script for the trial, promising to spare his life in return (we've seen how he kept that promise), the question of who "edited" the text disappears.

Radek's statement, published in millions of copies, struck just the chord the Gensek needed for his reign of terror. It was now acceptable to haul in anyone, even those most devoted to the Father of the Peoples, for every one of them was a little bit crooked at heart, maybe only one-eighth crooked, but still . . .

Stalin was devoured by vindictive hatred of Trotsky, overlapping with his hatred of Lenin and the Leninists. In some cases he could not abuse

Lenin's old comrades as he would have liked or send them down the Lubyanka conveyor belt. Having no sense of responsibility toward the Gensek, some of them, you see, had gone and died before the advent of the glorious era. In such cases Stalin, who of course had divined their hostile intentions, loosed his caged fury upon their relatives.

Pyotr Zaporozhets was arrested in 1895, along with Lenin, in the case of the St. Petersburg Union of Struggle for the Emancipation of the Proletariat. By taking the main responsibility, he saved Lenin from a heavier sentence. After his term in penal exile Zaporozhets fell ill and died in a hospital, in 1905. In 1937 Zaporozhets's brothers were arrested on Stalin's orders—Viktor, a mining engineer, and Anton, an agronomist. Also his sister Maria and her husband and children. The men were shot but the sister's life was "chivalrously" spared. The same fate befell the relatives of Uritsky, who was killed at the beginning of the civil war in 1918.

It was a rare party veteran who departed this life without being labeled a "spy." A first-rate school of international espionage could have been put together from the list of inmates of the Lubyanka. The prison cells were teeming with Japanese, Iranian, Turkish, Romanian, Polish, German, American, and other spies. But the label that Stalin pasted onto Lenin's old comrades with the greatest glee was *"British* spy." After all, hadn't those accursed Britishers shot the twenty-six Baku commissars years ago, robbing him of his rightful prey? He had just been aching for his chance to settle accounts with Stepan Shaumyan, Prokofy Dzhaparidze, Meshadi Azizbekov, and the rest.

How did he treat the heroes of October, the leaders of the armed insurrection in Petrograd? In the forties Grigory Petrovsky was working in the Museum of the Revolution, one of a handful of surviving party veterans. Stunned by the deaths of all of Lenin's old comrades, someone asked Petrovsky:

"What's going on, Grigory Ivanovich? Explain it to me. What's happening?"

"Read the history of the great French revolution," answered Petrovsky.

The man who asked the question was fairly well informed, but he reread the history of the French revolution and compiled some statistics. Here's what he found: of the twenty top leaders of the French revolution, including Robespierre, Danton, Saint-Just, Couthon, and Barnave, seventeen were guillotined within a few years of the revolutionary outbreak. The rate of butchery for the French revolution, then, was 85 percent.

The data for the October revolution had to be taken after 1935. In the Russian revolution eighteen years passed before Thermidorian terror began. Some people, of course, managed to die before that. Others perished in the fighting during the revolution and civil war.

Nevertheless, out of the twenty members of the Petrograd Military Revolutionary Committee, which led the insurrection, only one came through the Stalinist terror unharmed. That was Nikolai Podvoisky, who was mentally unbalanced and incapable of holding a job. No one from the Moscow Military Revolutionary Committee survived.

Only one member of the Presidium elected by the Second Congress of Soviets, which proclaimed Soviet power and adopted the first Soviet government decrees, survived—Aleksandra Kollontai. Stalin not only destroyed Lenin's closest collaborators, such as Trotsky, Zinoviev, Kamenev, and Rykov, and all three members of the first Soviet government's Committee for Army and Navy Affairs—Antonov-Ovseyenko, Krylenko, and Dybenko—he also killed the leaders of the Left SRs who were elected to the Presidium at the Second Congress of Soviets—Maria Spiridonova, Vladimir Karelin, and Boris Kamkov.

Twelve members of the first Soviet government lived to see 1937. Stalin wiped out eleven of them, and he himself was the twelfth. A 100-percent record. This was an advance over the French counterrevolution. He achieved a substantially higher rate of butchery—95 percent, as against the 85 percent achieved in Paris. (Meanwhile, we should keep in mind the 100-percent record in relation to the Central Committee elected at the Sixth Party Congress.)

The first and most immediate aim of Stalin's campaign was to eliminate those who had made the revolution and defended it in combat. His ultimate aim was to transform the party, bled white and paralyzed with fear, into the central stronghold of his personal dictatorship. The statistics on the various Central Committees elected at party congresses illustrate plainly the process by which he destroyed the central core of party activists. I will leave out the earlier congresses and begin with 1925.

YEAR	CONGRESS	NUMBER ELECTED TO CENTRAL COMMITTEE	NUMBER KILLED IN 1936–38
1925	Fourteenth	106	80
1927	Fifteenth	121	96
1930	Sixteenth	138	111
1934	Seventeenth	139	98*

*This figure was given by Khruschchev in his secret speech to the Twentieth Congress. Some Soviet historians, including Roy Medvedev and Pyotr Yakir, have placed the figure at 110.—TRANS.

On the average, three out of four were cruelly murdered. And what a group it was! For example, out of the 121 Central Committee members and candidate members elected at the Fifteenth Congress, 111 (or 92 percent) had joined the party before 1917.[88] The Central Committee delivered a steady stream of Lenin's fellow fighters to the Lubyanka. There was no more regular clientele for the Lubyanka torturers.

The Great Woodcutter not only selected the mighty oaks and pines to be felled; he also attended to the underbrush. He was not too proud for that.

Nothing delineates his nationwide tree-cutting spree so clearly as the plain black-and-white of statistics. These figures are taken from the reports of the credentials committees at twelve party congresses.

YEAR	CONGRESS	NUMBER OF PARTY MEMBERS (IN THOUSANDS)
1918	Seventh	170
1919	Eighth	313
1920	Ninth	611
1921	Tenth	732
1922	Eleventh	612
1923	Twelfth	532 (after the party purge)
1924	Thirteenth	736
1925	Fourteenth	643 (after the purge)
1927	Fifteenth	887
1930	Sixteenth	1,261
1934	Seventeenth	1,872.5
1939	Eighteenth	1,589

The Eighteenth Congress was the only one the party came to with such losses—300,000 Communists. That's how many were purged in 1934. However, approximately two million new members had joined in the intervening five years. Thus, well over two million Communists disappeared between 1934 and 1939. These same statistics give us a no less important qualitative picture of the extermination campaign.

Invariably delegates who had joined the party before the revolution, or at least during the civil war, predominated at all congresses until the Eighteenth. The president of the credentials committee at the Fourteenth Congress, Konstantin Gei, reported that the number of party members with prerevolutionary records was declining on the average by 3 percent from one congress to the next, which in view of the age of these veteran members was a natural development. At the Fourteenth Congress he reported a decline of 3.6 percent.

Here are the data for subsequent congresses.

At the Fifteenth Congress, delegates who had joined the party before 1920 constituted 71 percent.

At the Sixteenth Congress, they constituted 82 percent.

At the Seventeenth Congress, 80 percent.

At the Eighteenth Congress, 19 percent.

The main blow fell on them, the Leninist cadres.

At Frunze's funeral, in 1925, Stalin made the melancholy comment: "Perhaps this is exactly the way, so easily and simply, that all the old comrades should go to their graves." The "simplicity" became contagious. This is the only campaign in which millions of honest people suddenly became criminals. No one had to hunt them out. Nobody cried out their names in the central square. They all waited at home in a disciplined and politically conscious way, within the family circle, for the Stalinist emissaries. None of these good comrades complicated matters by fleeing or resisting. And the older they were, the more disciplined they proved to be.

For many years the congress delegates were considered the flower of the party, and the party veterans the living embodiment of Bolshevik traditions. They were the ones at whom Stalin directed his fire. We're not dealing here with elemental outbursts of blind fury but with the planned and deliberate destruction of an entire layer.

"Where is the Old Guard?" asked Fyodor Raskolnikov. "It's no longer among the living. You have shot them all, Stalin. You have corrupted the souls of your associates. You have forced those who go along with you to wade with anguish and disgust through pools of their comrades' and friends' blood."[89]

But perhaps Raskolnikov exaggerated the horrors of the Stalinshchina? Perhaps "Academician" Pyotr Pospelov was right when he said that in those trigger-happy years, thanks to Stalin's farsightedness, the "fascist fifth column of traitors and enemies of the people" in the Soviet Union was destroyed.[90]

* * *

The cells of the smaller prison at the Lubyanka were full to overflowing. The new arrivals were shoved out into the corridor, where a crowd had been standing for several days. It was so jammed that if you took your hand out of your pocket, you couldn't get it back in. There were two children here as well, girls of twelve and thirteen. The prisoners took turns resting. Among those lying on the floor was an Italian Communist. Young and attractive.

She said in French, "You've had a fascist coup."

"That's not right," they answered her.

"What else if they're arresting Communists?"

"What are you saying? The Communist Party is still in power."

The Italian woman turned up her almond-shaped eyes. "Why are you trying to trick me? This is a fascist coup for certain. I know what one looks like."

Now *that's* a person Pospelov ought to meet—and talk with on equal terms, in a prison cell. Maybe then he'd see the light. No, the Pospelovs never see the light. They only do their job.

The Italian woman was shot in 1936. That was the year the end came for Zinoviev and Kamenev too.

Stalin was apparently afraid the death penalty might not actually be carried out against his two former allies. He sent Voroshilov to observe. This is what Voroshilov reported.

They stood up in front of Stalin's executioners.

Zinoviev (shouting): This is a fascist coup!

Kamenev: Stop it, Grisha. Be quiet. Let's die with dignity.

Zinoviev: No! This is exactly what Mussolini did. He killed all his

Socialist Party comrades when he seized power in Italy. Before my death I must state plainly that what has happened in our country is a fascist coup![91]

On April 6, 1919, the anti-Soviet Cossack ataman Grigoryev entered Odessa with his army-sized division, a well-armed, unruly mob, bent on plunder. Three days before Grigoryev revolted against Soviet power, there arrived in Odessa a certain Ivan Shafransky, a former commissar of the Tarashchansky regiment. He wore his hair long like a holy man, and had none of the look of the military about him. The top command of the Ukrainian Front had appointed Shafransky as Grigoryev's political commissar. In the very first days he won the ataman's respect. The brief acquaintanceship was fated to end quickly: "Listen, commissar, I like you. Tomorrow I'm coming out against the Soviets and I might kill you. Hop a railroad car and get out of here. God be with you. . . ."

When Stalin decided to come out against the Soviets and against the heritage of October, he could have allowed all the honest old revolutionaries to leave, or expelled them from the country. But he did that only with Trotsky, and later, bitterly regretting it, sent a hired killer to set things straight. The world knows how much effort (and how many millions of dollars) Stalin expended to organize the assassination of Trotsky. He was driven by thirst for vengeance multiplied by insatiable ambition. He could not forgive anyone for escaping his reach—neither inside the country nor beyond its borders.

Under old Georgian law a runaway serf who managed to hide for seven years was considered free. He had the right to choose a new master. Under Stalin there was no statute of limitations. With impatient lust he lured back Old Bolsheviks who were serving in diplomatic posts during the most important years, when the Soviet Union was gaining international recognition. Lured them back from abroad and killed them.

Stalin began his efforts to bring Raskolnikov back in late 1936. Raskolnikov, who was then Soviet ambassador to Bulgaria, was offered diplomatic posts one after another in Mexico (although diplomatic relations had not then been established with Mexico), Czechoslovakia, Greece, and Turkey. Finally, in April 1938, after turning over his affairs, Raskolnikov set off for Moscow. He had not yet reached the border when he learned from foreign newspapers that the government had decided to remove him from his post as ambassador. He did not wish to imitate Saint Denis, who placidly held his head in his own hands. He refused to bring his head home to be laid on the butcher's block. Raskolnikov remained abroad, but in no way discredited the title of Communist or Soviet citizen. He asked the reason for his sudden replacement. But Stalin denounced him and ordered him immediately convicted as an "enemy of the people."

After publishing two open letters to Stalin, Fyodor Fyodorovich suddenly fell ill. His wife, Muza Vasilyevna, placed him in a private clinic near Nice. The preliminary diagnosis was a brain tumor. During the last two

weeks of his life his temperature stayed at about 40° C. His wife kept watch
at his bedside for about twenty days straight, without a break. One night
she decided to get a few hours' sleep, went home, and slept until morning.
That night he met his end. No autopsy was performed.

When she placed her husband in the clinic, Muza Vasilyevna had
warned the doctors:

"Stalin has a long reach."

"Madame, you are in France. . . ."

* * *

The party placed great confidence in Stalin, entrusting him with the
highest and most honorable positions. And great services were rendered
to Stalin personally by Lenin, Trotsky, Zinoviev, Kamenev, Bukharin.

At the end Stalin badgered Lenin terribly, hastening his death. With
the help of Zinoviev and Kamenev, he removed Trotsky. With the help
of Bukharin and the other "Rights," he cleared Zinoviev and Kamenev out
of the way, and finally, after the "Rights" had served his purposes, he killed
them. A simple pattern, it would seem. But how much thought and inven-
tiveness went into it. Simulated retreats, demonstrations of strength,
feigned weakness, sudden blows, and long periods of watchful waiting.

This blueprint—copyright Joseph Stalin—served just as well for his
reprisals against the leaders of the union republics. In 1928 Stalin had to
face the fact that the Ukrainian Communists would not tolerate Lazar
Kaganovich as the first secretary of their Central Committee any longer,
and so he recalled him to Moscow. Stalin had to accept the choice of
Stanislav Kosior, but as insurance the Gensek sent another emissary, Pavel
Postyshev, to Kharkov in early 1933. With his direct help Stalin drove
Nikolai Skrypnik to his death. Skrypnik, one of the founders of the Communist Party of the Ukraine, committed suicide in July 1933. Then Posty-
shev, as second secretary of the Ukrainian Central Committee, began to
dig a hole under Kosior. The bell tolled in turn for Postyshev at the Central
Committee plenum of February-March 1937.

In place of another deceased Ukrainian leader, Panas Lyubchenko
(who also committed suicide), a new man was appointed on Beria's recommendation—Mikhail Bondarenko. Within a month Bondarenko was arrested along with other "upstarts." They were accused of forming a counterrevolutionary organization.

In 1938 Stalin rounded up all of them—Kosior, Postyshev, and Postyshev's replacement, Mendel Khatayevich. The entire Politburo and government of the Ukraine were shot. Along with all the secretaries of provincial committees and secretaries of district committees. Then all the people
who had replaced them. Then the same thing again.

All local government bodies underwent the same kind of havoc. Of
the 102 members of the Ukrainian Central Committee, three survived by
a miracle, including Grigory Petrovsky. These results were even higher
than those achieved with the deadly purge of the Central Committee in
Moscow.

A similar pattern, following the same blueprint, emerged in the other republics. People talk about Georgian nationalism and about the Georgian people's strong devotion to their country, which they call Sakartvelo. Georgia has given the world many remarkable names over the many centuries of its history. Dzhugashvili-Stalin didn't leave Sakartvelo untouched. He drowned the Georgian Republic in blood.

They talk about the vitality of national diversity in Georgia. For centuries the different nationalities there have maintained their separate identities—Abkhazians, Svans, Adzharians, Mingrelians, Imeretians, Lezghians. The important task of wiping out the party cadres of Georgia was entrusted by Stalin to the Mingrelian Beria. He knew what he was doing. Beria was a confirmed criminal type who had pursued his calling by serving the secret police under various political regimes. With meticulous cruelty he massacred the party veterans in the other Transcaucasian republics as well—Azerbaidzhan and Armenia. As early as 1931 Stalin placed Beria at the head of the Transcaucasian territorial committee of the party. In the two years that marked the high point of the slaughter, 1937–38, the Little Pope, with the blessing of the Big Pope, exterminated all the Georgian party leaders. Many of them, of course, had known the real Koba-Dzhugashvili.

Beria held several "public" trials modeled after the Moscow trials, with prepared scripts, professional agents provocateurs, "spy" defendants broken by torture, and—representing the "public"—crowds of security police.

At last the cherished dreams of the vengeful Gensek came true. Choking with impatience, he devoured the cream of the Georgian people. Later Beria was to tell his boss how he had gloated over Mamiya Orakhelashvili, one of the true founders of the Bolshevik organization in Transcaucasia. Everyone had loved the kind and sincere Mamiya, president of the Council of People's Commissars of the Transcaucasian Republic. He was a powerful man, tall and handsome. They killed him in front of his wife, Maria, also a member of the Georgian party's Central Committee and at one time Georgia's commissar of enlightenment. (Many years later, after the execution of Beria, the children of those who had been killed were invited to a judicial session in Tiflis. Mamiya's daughter fainted when she heard the details of her father's death.)

When Lavrenty Kartvelishvili, first secretary of the party's Far Eastern territorial committee, was seized in Khabarovsk, Beria demanded that his old rival be brought to Tbilisi. In his torture cellar he forced the old party veteran to dance the Lezghinka to the blows of his club. Two years before that, on Stalin's orders, Beria had settled accounts with the leader of the Adzharian Communists, and also with the favorite of the Abkhazian people, Nestor Lakoba. Lakoba had been friends with Ordzhonikidze, Dzerzhinsky, and Kirov—a first-rate recommendation for the other world.

Room was found in the overcrowded prison for Budu Mdivani as well. Stalin had wanted to rub him out back in 1923, when Lenin was still alive, but hadn't been able to. Lord, what labels the Gensek hung on him now, this former president of the Council of People's Commissars of Georgia. Terrorist, deviationist, British spy . . . The mere confession of this arrested "enemy" was not enough to crown Stalin's long-postponed pleasure. Our thanks must go to the person who kept alive and brought down to our day the courageous reply of this old Georgian revolutionary to his interrogator:

"I have known Stalin for thirty years. Stalin won't rest until he has butchered us all, beginning with the unweaned baby and ending with the blind great-grandmother."[92]

These words should be printed and posted in all the schools and on all the streets and squares of Georgia, along with the names of all the Social Democrats, Bolsheviks, scientists, scholars, musicians, artists, writers, and poets of that mountain republic who died in torment. Perhaps then the Georgians would remove the Stalin buttons from their jackets, and the pendants with his likeness worn around children's necks. And perhaps at last the shameful Stalin monuments that still exist in the city squares of Georgia would be removed.

HIS PEOPLE
8

It is hard to think calmly or write coherently about the Lubyanka, that eight-story building at No. 2 Lubyanka Square in Moscow. It doesn't look that big, and yet it ground up an entire people. It became the focal point of Stalin's malevolence and embodied all the horrors of his inhuman regime. All of his power over the government, the party, and the people was concentrated in the Organs of the NKVD.

Under Peter the Great, the Holy Synod passed a decree obligating the clergy to report to their superiors "if anyone during a confession reveals to his spiritual father some act of thievery not yet committed but intended, even more so an act of treason or rebellion against the ruler or the state."

Under Stalin, who abolished religion and destroyed the church, the function of spiritual shepherd passed to the investigators of the secret police. In the police offices, believers in Joseph of the Kremlin confessed to the uncommitted sins and "evil intentions" ascribed to them by their Lubyanka pastors. And informed on their neighbors.

In medieval Europe the forerunners and spiritual fathers of the Lubyanka interrogators put witches on trial. They came up with a collective method of interrogation and execution. They had their victims confess in a chorus and go to the bonfire in a chorus. Who knows? If not for Stalin's early demise, our home-grown Inquisitors might have reached such heights as well.

This was the only form of industry in which Joseph the Builder undeniably outdid all others. Say what you will, Russians by nature are very poor organizers. Still, the Lubyanka fulfilled its work assignments, handed down from above. It couldn't have done that without the help of the so-called people, without its slavish submission.

Formally speaking, the Military Collegium, under the perennial chairmanship of Vasily Ulrikh, was considered a subdivision of the Soviet Supreme Court. In fact it was a second-rate appendage to the dictator's personal chancery. Its procedure was as primitive as the headsman's ax. After a brief hearing of three or four minutes, Ulrikh would announce, "The court will retire for consultation." The guards would lead the first victim off to a cell called the "phone booth." In the consultation room the collegium members would sign the prearranged verdict and return to the court room. The second victim, then the third, would be brought in. They too would pass before Ulrikh's three minutes of mumbling and be led away. Only then would the first be summoned and have the verdict read to him. Going to his death, the victim would think that at least they had spent ten minutes on him, a lavish gift considering how busy this lofty institution of justice was.

The Politburo showed great concern for those who toiled in the institutions of the judiciary. A special Politburo resolution established a three-man body—Beria, Vyshinsky, Shkiryatov—"for the preliminary examination of cases." Thus the Stalin machine had two kangaroo courts, and both were secret. The Supreme Court, unlike the Politburo's super-supreme "threesome," had the status of an official institution. But since no one was able to penetrate into its depths, not even the mother of tomorrow's corpse, it became the legal counterpart of Stalin's three.

The top officials and investigators of the security police were hand-picked by Stalin. One of these people, the investigative judge Rodos, was summoned in 1956 to appear before the Central Committee Presidium. Khrushchev described him in his "secret speech" to the Twentieth Congress as "a vile person with the mental horizon of a chicken and morally a complete degenerate." Yet this protégé of the Master interrogated such leading figures as Kosior, Chubar, and Kosarev.

Stalin needed people like Rodos in the central apparatus of the Organs in Moscow, and also in Leningrad and as plenipotentiaries from the Lubyanka to major provincial cities, such as Odessa and Rostov, Tashkent, and Khabarovsk. He selected hardened thugs and scoundrels who were born sadists but who, for all that, were as devoted to their benefactor as only a member of an outlaw gang can be toward his chief. All the dregs of society rose to the surface. The Criminal was recruiting criminals.

At work in the Ukraine in 1937 was a certain Lieutenant Ivan Dolgikh. The tab of his uniform collar then had only two cube-shaped insignia.

He was famous for the fact that during torture-and-interrogation sessions he made arrested members of the Central Committee drink their own urine. His resourcefulness and zeal in rooting out "enemies" were noticed. Dolgikh earned the shoulder straps of a general of the Organs and became irreplaceable. So much so that even after Stalin's death he headed the Chief Administration of Corrective Labor Camps (Gulag). The new government appointed him deputy minister of internal affairs.

"A Chekist must have a warm heart, a cool head, and clean hands." That injunction was bequeathed to us by Feliks Dzerzhinsky. The hangmen of the 1935 enrollment bore little resemblance to the pure knight in the revolutionary posters. They were people of a different make-up altogether. Tracking down and persecuting honest party workers, reading people's mail, tapping their phones, engaging in blackmail, acts of provocation, violence, the corruption of minors, refined torture, and executions in cellars—all this and much more was required by the NKVD of its employees. By way of personal initiative, they also gave themselves over to the systematic plundering of their victims.

In 1918 Dzerzhinsky drew up instructions on how to make searches and arrests.

> Let all those who are assigned to conduct searches, take people into custody, and imprison them behave solicitously toward those being arrested or searched. Let them be much more courteous even than toward close friends. Let them remember that the incarcerated cannot defend themselves and that they are in our power. Each and every one must remember that they represent Soviet power, the workers' and peasants' government, and that any verbal abuse, rudeness, injustice, or impropriety is a blot upon the Soviet power.[93]

Splendid instructions. Only one thing is unclear: to whom were they addressed? For the Chekists of the Stalin school operated according to quite another set of instructions. They had great respect for Dzerzhinsky, though. Didn't his expressive portrait grace the walls of the torture rooms—alongside the immortal visage of the Leader?

Dzerzhinsky's instructions remind me of the fall of 1937. The Soviet counsul general in Barcelona, Antonov-Ovseyenko, was recalled to Moscow at the end of August. In the lobby of Building No. 2 of the Council of People's Commissars, Vladimir Aleksandrovich met the frightened gaze of the elevator operator. Nearly every door of the seven-story building was sealed with the large wax seal of the NKVD. Sulimov, premier of the Russian Republic, had been arrested and was now an "enemy." Also Krylenko, Antonov's comrade in the battles of October 1917. Tukhachevsky and the other glorious commanders had perished.

A week passed, then another. Each morning you got up with nothing to do and spent the day aimlessly, and the long night, waiting—for what?

Stalin called Antonov to the Kremlin on the thirtieth day after his return to Moscow. The Master began with some reproaches. It seemed that Antonov had functioned too independently in Spain, didn't coordinate his measures with the Soviet Commissariat of Foreign Affairs. Many complaints had come in.

Vladimir Aleksandrovich explained: "It was sometimes necessary to make risky, audacious decisions on the spur of the moment, as required by complicated battle conditions." Apparently his interlocutor was convinced. For his appointment as commissar of justice came a day later. However, in the gray building on Bolshaya Dmitrovka, in an office on the fifth floor, Public Prosecutor Vyshinsky had already prepared the arrest warrant for the new people's commissar.

It was late at night on October 11. D. I. Vasilyev, assistant director under Mikhail Romm on the film *Lenin in October*, didn't want to say good night to Antonov. The hero of October had such interesting details to recount. Romm had been given permission to present only a few leading figures on the screen—Lenin, Stalin, Dzerzhinsky, and Sverdlov. That was the will of Stalin himself. Even so, they needed Antonov's information.

Toward morning Vasilyev finally left. And within half an hour, men in NKVD uniforms arrived. Rude shouts, cynical abuse (what were Dzerzhinsky's instructions to them?), things thrown around . . . Antonov-Ovseyenko was taken off to the Lubyanka. All his papers were taken too. Those that survived found their way subsequently into the state archives, but access to those documents was not permitted until forty years later.

Document No. 463 is one that remains—an inventory of confiscated property, drawn up on January 22, 1938. Here are some items and their estimated value.

NUMBER	ITEM	QUANTITY	PRICE
4	Waistcoat with tails	1	27 rubles, 50 kopecks
5	Suits	4	50–70 rubles each
24	Wool sweaters	2	3 rubles, 50 kopecks
32	Polar-fox boa	1	50 rubles
109	Satin quilt	1	12 rubles
110	Down filled silk quilt	1	22 rubles
116	Cotton sheets	4	6 rubles
224	Russian-language records	—	—
245	Table service (7 items)	—	—
294	A water color	—	1 ruble, 50 kopecks
297	Various perfumes	3 bottles	1 ruble, 50 kopecks
305	An old briefcase	—	2 rubles, 50 kopecks
(Items of furniture:)			
	Oak buffet	1	60 rubles
	Ottoman	1	17 rubles
	Sofa	1	18 rubles

I can personally testify that my father's apartment in no way resembled the used-clothing shop suggested by this inventory. He had a very valuable collection of books, as you'd expect of an active writer fluent in several European languages. But his library was not placed on the list. The same with the original etchings by famous artists, the typewriter, the phonograph with eight albums of records, his wife's jewelry, her squirrel coat, expensive French perfumes purchased in Paris on the way home from Spain, and much, much more.

Antonov was not the only one robbed by the Lubyanka marauders. They robbed prisoners, they robbed the people, they robbed the state. They confiscated scholarly and scientific papers, poetry, novels, plays, inventions. And how many irreplaceable things of value were burned as "not relevant to the case"?

* * *

They scrounged everything from the "enemies of the people"—personal possessions, wives, apartments. By 1939 all the best buildings in Moscow, Leningrad, and other cities were occupied by NKVD employees or their relatives and friends. They even took over the names of towns—didn't they deserve immortality? At one time the capital of Cherkessia, Batalpashinsk, was given the name of Sulimov, premier of the Russian Republic. After his murder the town was called Yezhovo-Cherkessk, in honor of the chief of the Organs. When Stalin removed Yezhov, a new name appeared on the maps: simply Cherkessk. This was just one of many geographical metamorphoses during the Stalin blight.

There he goes, down a street in Gorky, the power-gorged Boris Berman, former chief of Gulag. (Later he was a people's commissar of the Byelorussian Republic. His brother, Matvei Berman, oversaw the extermination of countless "enemies of the people" in the building of the Baltic–White Sea canal and briefly held the post of people's commissar of communications.) Boris Berman's fat breasts are weighed down with medals. His hands are adorned with rings bearing precious stones. On his left middle finger is a long, exquisitely curved claw.

Another mandarin of the Lubyanka comes to mind: Colonel Benenson, chief of the investigations department. How he flaunted himself in front of his subordinates, who had been unable to make me confess to terrorist activity. There was a snob in full bloom, a typical representative of the new *gendarme caste* (Mayakovsky's phrase).

Stalin provided them with all of life's blessings: special stores closed to the public, limitless funds, box seats at the theater, trips abroad, luxurious apartments, and villas by the sea. When the workers take vacations in the former palaces of the tsarist nobility, that can be seen as historic justice: it was their hands that built the architectural masterpieces. But butchery experts in the princely palaces? It's disgusting.

* * *

Moscow, 1929. Yagoda is head of the Organs. A young woman, confined in one of the cells of the Lubyanka, spreads her expensive sealskin coat right on the dirty floor and invites a prisoner who had done hard labor under the tsar to lie down beside her. And tells this story:

"The coat's done for anyhow. And I'll never get out of here. They give us these coats as work clothes. At first they tell you at the district YCL committee office that they trust you to do important government work. And they send you to the GPU. There they explain, 'We have to help the country disarm its enemies. You're young and good-looking. It'll be easy for you to hang around the restaurants.' They give you chic clothes and tons of money. And don't ask a damn thing in return. You only have to meet with someone, remember something, talk, even flirt. Then report on what was said.

"An encounter with a foreigner was my undoing. He was the son of a match manufacturer. We fell in love, and I went off to Berezniki with him. After a little while they expelled him from the country and I was left alone. They arrested me and tried to make me put down in writing that I was pregnant by him. I refused. Then they forged a letter themselves, trying to extort foreign exchange from him."

* * *

Saratov, 1935. A dying nineteen-year-old girl was brought into the city hospital. She had just married a military man. He hadn't told her he worked for the Organs. (And if he had, would she have turned away?)

Not long after their marriage the "husband" invited her to come to the Red Army recreation center with him. There he let his friends have their way with her. (Among professional criminals this is called "running the dame under the streetcar" or "taking turns.") After this inhuman violation she drank corrosive sublimate and died in agony.

* * *

Rostov-on-Don, 1939. According to some of the young women who ended up in the prison there, a bordello had been organized in Rostov around that time for the party mandarins. It was a very modern establishment, with a madam, photo albums of young beauties, European cooking, fine wines, silk underwear, special lighting effects. . . .

Having abolished houses of ill repute along with the other institutions of bourgeois society, could Vladimir Lenin have imagined the flowering of such individual initiative in the near socialist future?

* * *

The Cheka and OGPU had provocateurs from the very beginning. They infiltrated the Mensheviks' print shop, the headquarters of the Tambov peasant rebellion, and the Irpen conference of Social Democratic youth in 1923. In the prisons they occupied every cell; in the camps every barracks.

My provocateur in the Lubyanka was Aleksandr Spirkin. He had been a graduate student at the Lenin Pedagogical Institute (the Andrei Bubnov Institute until 1938). But before I was transferred to the cell he was in, three to four months of uninterrupted interrogation went by—empty, tormenting. I was accused of terror and anti-Soviet agitation.

"Tell us about your terrorist activity."

"Tell us about your terrorist connections."

Every interrogation session, with slight variation, began with those questions. Later they came to their senses and dropped the charge of terrorism against a person who was half blind. As for agitation, they could establish nothing in that respect, having no evidence.

Apparently that's why they decided to put me in with a provocateur. Their calculations were simple. Spirkin was a graduate student and a writer, jailed under Article 58, points 10 and 11 (group agitation). I was a historian. Therefore we would get into conversation. What we talked about I have no recollection. But I do remember very well the confrontation with him that my investigator arranged a month later. Spirkin said that I had told him about a plan to engage in espionage for fascist Germany. It was a repulsive scene. Spirkin kept his greedy eyes turned away from me. The investigator cut short my expression of outrage over the provocation.

This meant that I had escaped the charge of "terrorism" only to get caught on the hook of "espionage," which also carried the death penalty. After the confrontation they took me to a different cell. I don't know who they served up to Spirkin after me. (Before my encounter with Spirkin I was inclined to place a somewhat higher value on my life. I now give thanks to prison, where I was freed from such harmful pride.)

Today Spirkin's name is found on the distinguished list of corresponding members of the Soviet Academy of Sciences. He is a philosopher, the vice-president of some society, and the author of some highly moral tracts. Like any respectable scholar, he has a hobby. In the pages of *Nedelya*, the weekly supplement to *Izvestia*, he instructs readers on the rules of good socialist manners.

During the excitement-filled time when he was penetrating the academy and installing himself there, Spirkin, holder of a candidate's degree and later a doctor's degree, shamelessly courted the celebrated academician Fyodor Konstantinov, a loyal armorbearer of the Stalin Establishment. At Konstantinov's suburban dacha in Otdykh, outside Moscow, Spirkin busied himself as volunteer gardener and groundsman, with hoe in hand.

And here are some of the products of his pen.

A Course in Marxist Philosophy (two editions)
Materialist Dialectics (coauthored with Glagolev)
In the World of Wisdom (editor)
Problems of Cybernetics (consulting editor)
The Origin of Consciousness
Consciousness and Self-Awareness
Theory Transforming the World
The Further Development of Marx's Philosophy by Lenin
The Comprehensive Study of Man and the Well-Rounded Development of the Individual

Several of Spirkin's philosophical treatises have been published in foreign languages by Novosti Press and Progress Publishers. One of his most recent books was *The New Society and the New Man,* issued in 1976.

But that's enough about Aleksandr Georgievich Spirkin, the new man of the new society.

As for my investigators, where they are now and what they are doing, I do not know. They did not use physical torture on me. They only sent me to the punishment cell from time to time, when I tried to protest. I would like to take this opportunity to express to them my prisoner's gratitude.

* * *

Among the flood of investigators who poured into the Organs in the thirties there were many accidental elements hastily trained for government service. Some were taken from factories and scholarly or scientific establishments, through party or YCL mobilizations. Others came from the higher institutions for legal training. A few, when they realized the nature of their peculiar assignment, could not accept the shameful role intended for them. But those who became agents of the all-powerful Organs no longer belonged to themselves. They couldn't transfer or resign or simply take sick leave.

Under Stalin, in the years of the bloody harvest, the staff of Lefortovo prison was wiped out entirely four times. Everyone went—prison guards, investigators, and intelligence personnel. The most resourceful, having a premonition of the inevitable reprisal, tried to go into hiding abroad. Experienced intelligence agents disguised themselves skillfully and hid in Switzerland, Belgium, Africa, and America. That was something the Master could not tolerate. A special section was established under Yezhov to hunt down and destroy the "nonreturners" on every continent. Thus the Organs became a trap for the trappers themselves.

It was necessary to adapt somehow. Everyone wants to live. Imperceptibly, the new recruit would get into the swing of it. After arriving at the Lubyanka with a diploma in the humanities, he would gradually acquire the skills of bone breaker, first class, and would reach the highest levels in—something his superiors especially appreciated—"applied psychology." And methods of provocation.

As in any criminal undertaking, though, it was very hard to stop. The Lubyanka experts began informing on one another, arranging slick provocations against their own colleagues. In addition, from time to time, in the depths of the central extermination apparatus, lists of proscribed employees would develop like ripened fruit. Such a list is an impressive thing to see. A long column of names, a hundred or more. And at the bottom, the investigator's comment:

"Would recommend shooting."

Next to that, on the right, the official stamp of the head of the department and the words:

"I agree."

Toward the top, in the left-hand corner, an impressive flourish by the head of the administrative unit:

"Approved."

And at the very top, impinging on the caption and the date stamp in the corner, the crucial decision by the deputy people's commissar: *"Shoot."*

Then, the culminating brush stroke appears—the notation by the NKVD commandant:

"Sentence carried out."

(Incidentally, I would not propose that provocateurs like the philosopher Spirkin be shot out of hand. But I suggest that it would be extremely valuable—for both my generation and younger generations—to publicize the names of the butchers, provocateurs, and informers. Everywhere. Indoors and out, at work and at meetings.)

Power over the life and death of others has a certain attraction. The lowliest of specimens begins to feel omnipotent sitting in the interrogator's chair. Many took part in arrests, then in torture. Soon they became skilled at falsifying evidence and working up cases, learned not to bother with facts, laws, individual rights, and to content themselves modestly with the suspect's confession. The extraction of confessions was the skill they learned above all. An investigator earned a bonus of two thousand rubles for each confession. Every petty thief, sadist, or climber was free to go at it as hard as he liked. Nowadays, when people discuss the problem of why prisoners confessed, I have to ask them, "You aren't really serious, are you?"

* * *

How to Hold Up Under Questioning—that was the title of a pamphlet published in 1906. The author, Vladimir Akimov-Makhnovets, urged his fellow fighters to refuse to confess to anything. Aleksandr Mikhailov, a member of People's Will, wrote in his testament: "I recommend that you refuse to make any statements for any investigation, no matter how plain the evidence or testimony might be. That will spare you many errors."

And so the "political gentlemen" in the tsarist era refused to give evidence. And the gendarme gentlemen did not dare insist. Strange people they were in Russia at the turn of the century. The revolutionaries and the Okhrana and, it seemed, the tsar himself vied with one another in naïve benevolence. Under the new criminal code of 1904, courts were obliged to hear all political cases in open session. And those who wished to overthrow the existing system openly called for revolt, in the presence of a crowd of people. The prosecutor, gendarmes, and "upright citizenry" listened to these seditious speeches with loathing, but they did listen. The judges would send the offender off to penal exile, sometimes to hard labor, very rarely to the executioner. But everything was done in public. Where has all that gone to? Lost in the swift currents of Lethe.

Vladimir Levitsky, Martov's brother, was arrested (for the nth time) in 1937 and accused of belonging to an "SR-Menshevik-monarchist organization." (Logical charges were not the Lubyanka's specialty.) Levitsky announced a hunger strike to the death. Being sentenced to a term in camp meant losing the status of political prisoner. Was a prominent journalist, former editor of *Nasha Zarya* (Our Dawn) and contributor to *Golos Sotsial-Demokrata* (Voice of the Social Democrat), to be placed in the same bunks and on the same level as the dregs of the criminal world? This moral torture was mixed with physical—the torments the politicals were subjected to in the cells, during transport, in the camps. And the guards encouraged the criminals.

As for torture, Stalin personally gave orders for it to be used, just as the deadly routine in the camps was organized on his direct orders. Here are some examples of what his torturers accomplished.

In 1938 Maria Davidovich, a member of the YCL Central Committee and secretary of the YCL committee in Moscow's Zamoskvorechye district, was arrested—right after Aleksandr Kosarev and other top YCL leaders. Ten years earlier she had been sent to do underground work in Poland, where she was caught and sentenced to ten years at hard labor. She had served eight years before the International Red Aid managed to trade her for someone Poland wanted.

In Lefortovo she found herself in a cell with an Armenian Communist named Mikaelyan. Both women held firm, rejecting the wild charges against them. The investigator flew into a rage.

"So you have nothing to confess, huh? Well, Zinoviev and Kamenev didn't want to confess either. But when we ran an electric jolt across their asses, they 'fessed up soon enough."

The arrested women stood firm. They were taken to the first floor. From there the cries of those being tortured in the cellar could be heard. Electric shock torture? How many days did they spend in that cell? Each morning Mikaelyan noticed another strand of gray hair on Maria's head, though she wasn't yet thirty. By the time they left Taganka prison for transport to the camps, Maria had gone completely gray.

There is probably no need to describe all the horrors of a Lubyanka affiliate in the Moscow region—Sukhanovka, with its infamous torture chambers. Its experts surpassed even those at Lefortovo. No one withstood the pressure there.

Torture made People's Commissar of Finance Grigory Grinko confess that as early as 1923 he had conspired with the Ukrainian writer Vasil Blakitin to start an armed uprising against the Soviets.

The satirical poet Ostap Vishnya told his cellmates he had signed the interrogation transcript under hypnosis, without even looking at it, and when he came to himself, demanded it be brought back. But the machinery of the Lubyanka did not have reverse motion.

The investigators obtained their confessions by any means and at any cost. They had a very tempting and noble goal before them—to report "mission accomplished" to Yezhov or Beria, or even—dare we say it?—to the Master Himself.

One investigator complained to a colleague: "Damn, I'm tired. I had to slave over Bukharin three days and nights in a row before he'd sign the materials against Rykov. Now I'll take a break and then start work on Rykov—get him to give evidence against Bukharin."

The quality of the confession—their efforts were not aimed at quantity alone, as you might have guessed—depended on the subject's threshold of pain. Some had a very high threshold: Kotolynov, Uglanov, Redens, Kosior, Blyukher. Some could be broken with threats against their children or others close to them. Those who were broken were also killed.

* * *

Not until ten years after Stalin's death did Soviet scholarship dare to begin serious research and systematic publication of documents relating to the reign of Stalin's favorite tsar, Ivan the Terrible, and his organ of terror, the Oprichnina. For example, the collection *Studies in the History of the Oprichnina,* edited by S. B. Veselovsky, was published in Moscow in 1963. (How many decades will we have to wait for an unbiased history of the Stalinshchina?)

Unlike Ivan the Terrible, the later Russian monarchs refrained from persecuting the families of their political opponents (with some exceptions). Let us recall that although Lenin's older brother, Aleksandr Ulyanov, was executed for being involved in a plot on the life of the tsar, his family was spared.

Stalin was not so lenient. He made use of Ivan's old recipe: don't just eliminate your political rival; wipe out the entire clan. He killed secretly and suddenly. The places where the murdered are buried are not known *to this day.* Even in the case of revolutionaries to whom monuments have been erected, grave sites are unknown. And in the camps, where millions of innocent people perished, no graves were maintained. There is nowhere that you can pay your respects to the deceased.

Stalin showed that it is possible to go further than Ivan the Terrible. He not only eliminated all relatives of an arrested "enemy," but also destroyed all books, papers, letters, photographs, and personal effects. All traces of his existence on this earth. And before doing so, he exposed his victims to desecration from all party pulpits, at mass meetings and in all the newspapers. And the fanatical practice of posthumous denunciation comes from the Great Benefactor as well, although those who did his bidding share the blame.

Within the party and the Organs there were people of potential honesty. Some even tried to protest. But they did not save anyone and only hastened their own end. And frightened others from following their example.

In 1936 a certain Drovyanikov spoke out at a meeting of the active party membership of the Leningrad NKVD: "Comrades, we are not uncovering conspiracies; we are fabricating them. We are persecuting and killing people on the basis of unfounded and slanderous charges. I know what faces me, but I cannot remain silent about what is being done now in the NKVD."

NKVD agent V. A. Kandush later recalled how fiercely the chairman of the Leningrad Soviet, Ivan Kodatsky, struck back at the "accomplice of the enemy" at that meeting: "Drovyanikov's speech is evidence that enemies of the people have penetrated the NKVD as well. They must be ruthlessly eradicated." They were both "eradicated." Drovyanikov that very night, Kodatsky a year later.

In 1938 six "enemies of the people" were sitting in a cell in the Lubyanka. One of them we will call Pavlenko. He had been an official in the party committee of the Northern Caucasus territory. He was one of the lucky few who survived a hearing before the Military Collegium. Pavlenko had just been brought to Moscow from a camp. He had the honor of being interrogated by Beria himself. It turned out that not long before, Mikhail Litvin, a former chief of an NKVD regional unit, had shot himself in Leningrad. He had left a suicide note: "I can no longer take part in the murder of innocent people and the fabrication of spurious cases." The contents of Litvin's note became known to many people. Beria decided he had to discredit the dead man at all costs. Pavlenko had known Litvin personally, for Litvin had often visited the offices of the Northern Caucasus territorial committee in Rostov on inspection trips, as Yezhov's deputy.

Beria was sitting in an office at Lefortovo prison, holding a device consisting of a steel spring attached to a wooden handle. The guards seated Pavlenko on a chair off to one side. Beria told the prisoner to give evidence against Litvin, to testify that Litvin had forced Pavlenko to retract his confession in front of the Military Collegium in order to discredit the Organs. But Pavlenko had not encountered Litvin during his investigation. Beria then *urged* Pavlenko to remember a conversation with Litvin, playing ominously with the spring. He wanted so badly to report to the Master that Litvin had shot himself in fear of being exposed.

When Mikoyan, a member of the Politburo, heard about Litvin's suicide, he muttered, "at least one honest man was found among that gang."

Only a year before, at the celebration of the Organs' twentieth anniversary, Mikoyan had gone into raptures over the glorious labors of the NKVD and had urged his listeners to "study the Stalin style of work by the model of Comrade Yezhov, for he has studied and studied the model of Comrade Stalin."[94] Mikoyan was not alone. Everyone lived and worked under the sign of the two-faced Janus in those years.

Artur Khristianovich Artuzov (real name, Frauchi) had held the post of chief of counterintelligence back under Dzerzhinsky. A quiet, unassuming man, he did not wear any badges of distinction and looked like a kindly village schoolteacher. "Artuzov is a splendid worker. I trust him as I do myself." That was the kind of reference Dzerzhinsky gave about him.

At a meeting of NKVD activists in 1939, Artuzov spoke bitterly about the "sergeant major's" style of leadership that had come in since the death of Menzhinsky. Artuzov recalled Dzerzhinsky's warning:

"Beware of becoming a simple technician of the apparatus with all its bureaucratic insufficiencies. That would place us on the same level as the despicable political police of the capitalists."[95]

Stalin strode over the obstacle represented by Artuzov with as much ease as he had over Dzerzhinsky, Menzhinsky, and all the Chekists of the old school who tried to observe some of the proprieties during the bloody terror. Artuzov was arrested, of course. Before he was shot, he wrote on the wall of his cell: "It is an honest man's duty to kill Stalin."

Perhaps the reader has not forgotten Palgov, who was public prosecutor for Leningrad province under Kirov. The windings of his thread of fate are a separate issue. What concerns us here is this: In January 1939, as he was seeing off an Old Communist who was on his way to Moscow and who had not given in to the provocations of the Organs, Palgov warned: "Don't go into the dining car, no matter what. That gang might throw you out the window of the moving train."

Everyone knew that the NKVD was a gang of killers. Everyone kept quiet. Everyone assisted them in their work. Reports of isolated instances of protest did reach Stalin's ears, but on the whole the process of corruption of the officials of the NKVD, the judiciary, and the procuracy went along smoothly. Of course several dozen prominent Chekists of the Dzerzhinsky school had to be shot, party members of long standing with honorable records. The list of those victims is well known.

* * *

In 1826 the Turkish Sultan Mahmud II slaughtered tens of thousands of Janissaries, even though they had served him faithfully. The Kremlin sultan never trusted his Janissaries either and slaughtered them by the thousands. But these periodical prophylactic purges did not prevent the Organs from fulfilling and overfulfilling their plan. The country's main assembly line never stopped for a moment.

The deeds of the Lubyanka Janissaries deserve to be recorded in many volumes. A number of solid books, rich in factual material, have already appeared. I will select only three colorful figures from the army of Stalin's stalwarts. (But don't forget that we are not dealing with "the despicable political police of the capitalists.")

* * *

At one time a certain Genrikh Lyushkov was active in the OGPU central apparatus under Yagoda. He rose fairly rapidly to the post of deputy chief of the secret political section, the weightiest administrative unit in the Lubyanka.

In December 1934 Lyushkov was a member of Yezhov's team investigating the circumstances of the Kirov assassination. And in 1937 he was appointed head of the NKVD for the Azov–Black Sea territory. His seat of operations was Rostov-on-Don. In a short time he was able to uncover and eliminate, one after another, *three* counterrevolutionary "Right-Trotskyist centers." Hundreds of Communists, the entire active party membership of the Don region, were shot on his orders. For all this Lyushkov earned Stalin's personal thanks and an Order of Lenin—"for carrying out in exemplary fashion the most important tasks set by the party and government."

In August 1937 Stalin had Terenty Deribas, chief of the Organs in the Far Eastern territory, killed. Who to put in his place? A special decision of the Politburo assigned the outstanding toiler Lyushkov. He was allowed to select his own staff of assistants, two hundred field-tested experts.

Lyushkov had miraculously escaped the fate of Yagoda's close collaborators. But the time had come for Stalin to eliminate Yezhov's team. The miracle wouldn't happen twice.

As the new chief, Lyushkov had barely "started the work rolling" in the Far East when a telegram came from Moscow. He was being summoned to NKVD headquarters. Lyushkov didn't show the telegram to anyone and decided to look out for himself. He left for a border inspection with a group of agents. They arrived on June 13, 1938. Half a kilometer from the border with Japanese-occupied Manchuria, near a bridge over a river, Lyushkov stopped the car.

"Stay here. I'm going over the bridge. A top-secret Japanese plant is supposed to meet me here. No one can see him but me."

Lyushkov showed the border guards his papers and crossed into Manchuria. Three days afterwards, the newspaper *Yomiuri* printed the defector's statement. Later Lyushkov spoke over Harbin radio, and people learned how one of Stalin's favorites, one of many, had slaughtered party and government cadres. (In an empty typewriter case Lyushkov had taken with him some highly classified documents giving the locations of border posts, military units, air bases, and military plants.)

Lyushkov had prepared in advance for the border crossing. He divorced his wife and sent her and their daughter to Moscow. Later, in a Lubyanka cell, his wife told Valentina Pikina that her husband had insisted, saying only, "It's necessary." The traitor's wife was brought back to the cell after interrogation on a stretcher. They simply tore her apart. Then they liquidated his parents in Odessa. And all his relatives.

In 1948 in the settlement of Abez, capital of the Northern Pechora camps, a new contingent of prisoners arrived. Among them was a Japanese general, former chief of staff of the Kwantung army.

We asked him, "What ever happened to your number-one agent?"

"What agent?"

"Lyushkov, of course."

The general was surprised. How could it be that in a camp compound thousands of kilometers from Manchuria they were asking him about Lyushkov?

Here's what he had to say.

"We in Japan do not trust traitors. We don't like them. If he betrayed his homeland, what was to prevent him from also betraying the state that granted him asylum? Lyushkov brought documents with him which were valuable only at first. After three months they weren't worth anything. We gave him the highest salary in the intelligence service. At first he enjoyed great honor among us. But as the information he brought lost its freshness,

his stock began to fall. Two years went by. All that time we supported him.
I personally paid him every month. One day he came to collect as usual.
We talked a little. I gave him his pay envelope and said good-bye. I had
a big office. Before he reached the door I had time to put a bullet in the
back of his head with my Colt. I ordered my adjutant who came running
in: 'Get that repulsive mess out of here.' "

* * *

We will begin the story of Aleksei Nasedkin in 1934, when he was
deputy chief of the NKVD unit in the central Volga region. Remember
the secret chemical complex near Samara where the enthusiasts of the first
five-year plans died amid poisonous fumes? One day Ordzhonikidze, the
people's commissar of heavy industry, summoned the director of the complex, whom I will call Lutsky.

"Tell me, please, do you need good specialists?"

"Of course we do, Comrade Sergo."

"I will give you some first-rate specialists. But keep in mind that they
are well-known wreckers. They were involved in the Ramzin case, members of the Industrial Party.* If you welcome them humanely and they feel
you trust them, you'll find no better workers."

Thus Lutsky obtained three "wreckers." One was the power engineer
Yakovin, whom he would remember for the rest of his life. In the mythical
anti-Soviet government supposedly projected by Ramzin, Yakovin was
given the post of deputy premier by the Lubyanka playwrights. At the
chemical complex Yakovin was given a modest post as head of the heat and
power plant.

The complex embraced eleven plants. The special needs of explosives
production required a continuous supply of electric power, and an unexpected breakdown at the power plant could cause an explosion. Something like that had happened a little earlier at plant No. 7.

An anxious telephone call came one day to the director's office. There
had been an accident at the power plant. One of the three turbines had
stopped. Lutsky found Yakovin on the spot, pale and distraught. The head
of the power plant knew only too well what this could mean for him
personally. The local plenipotentiary of the Organs came up, a complacent
blockhead with two stars on his uniform collar. He pulled at the director's
sleeve but Lutsky waved him away. The big lug insisted. In an ominous
whisper he demanded an immediate audience, eye to eye. In a separate
office the lug showed the director a list of eighteen "diversionist wreckers"
subject to immediate arrest. The star-studded officer had succeeded in
exposing a wreckers' organization endangering the state.

"Why don't you go straight to hell," Lutsky responded in a flash of
temper. "Are you going to run my turbine for me?"

The director returned to the plant floor, got the engineers together,

---

*In frame-up trials involving mythical organizations of "wreckers" in the 1928–31 pe-
riod, many technical specialists serving the Soviet regime were victimized. One trial, in 1930,
involved the so-called **Industrial Party**, supposedly led by Professor Leonid **Ramzin**, a prominent engineer. —TRANS.

headed by Yakovin, and called them into his office. The NKVD man said he was very busy and didn't appear. Yakovin drew up a list right then and there of the specialists and the materials he would need to reactivate the turbine. A coded telegram went to Moscow immediately, to Ordzhonikidze. Sergo answered a few hours later: "Plane flying out with materials and five specialists."

Vladimir Shubrikov, a candidate member of the Central Committee, was working then as the first secretary of the party committee in that region. He called Lutsky in and said that the representative of the Organs had already filed a complaint.

Lutsky's next visit was to Foma Leonyuk, chief of the NKVD unit in that region. Leonyuk wasn't out for anyone's blood and refused to sanction the arrests. Nasedkin, Leonyuk's deputy, favored repression, but made no move against his boss.

Within a week the turbine was reactivated. The "wrecker" specialists saved everyone from a real disaster. That was 1934.

Then came 1937. Yezhov called in Leonyuk. "Why haven't you exposed a single enemy center? Why haven't you jailed anyone? You've got military plants in your region. They must be full of wreckers." But Leonyuk didn't want to kill the innocent, and up to that point he hadn't.

Yezhov got rid of Leonyuk, and Nasedkin found himself in charge. He soon got the kind of work going that Stalin liked. Before long all the prisons were overflowing with members of "counterrevolutionary centers." Shubrikov, the first secretary of the territorial committee, ended up behind bars. So did Aleksandr Levin, the second secretary, and Georgy Polbitsyn, the president of the Soviet executive committee of the region, and Filipp Ksenofontov, secretary for agriculture in the party's territorial committee and the real author of the book *Problems of Leninism*, for which Stalin took credit. (A special order came concerning Ksenofontov, and he was killed during interrogation.) All heads of plants and chief engineers at the chemical complex were shot. They were reminded of that "wrecking action" back in 1934.

Nasedkin's zeal did not go unnoticed. At Yezhov's recommendation the Politburo sent Nasedkin to Byelorussia to be people's commissar of internal affairs. But who can guess the fate of a Stalin Oprichnik? March 1939 found Nasedkin in the inner prison of the Lubyanka. He had interesting things to say before he died. For example:

One day Yezhov gathered all the people's commissars of internal affairs of the non-Russian republics, Nasedkin among them. "Now, in the Ukraine, that's the way work should be going. It can serve as a model for everyone. Twenty thousand Polish spies have been unmasked there."

What was Nasedkin to do? He didn't have any Polish spies in Byelorussia. He didn't have any spies at all. He tried hauling in all the heads of industry. But the minute he took one factory manager, Ordzhonikidze interfered. Sergo wouldn't let his cadres be mistreated. Nasedkin arrested the director of an enterprise in the food industry. Mikoyan, commissar for light industry, immediately demanded an explanation. And he was a Politburo member.

So Nasedkin would have been done for as people's commissar if he hadn't remembered the Jewish shopkeepers. In a short time he arrested twelve thousand of them. Fewer than his Ukrainian colleague but still . . . The "material" proved to be tractable. Everyone confessed right away to spying. And no one intervened in their behalf. So things went smoothly.

Nasedkin was summoned to Moscow, where the Politburo heard his report "On the Political Situation in Byelorussia." They praised the commissar. He was fighting the enemy splendidly. Warmed by the Kremlin sun, Nasedkin returned to Minsk and sent all his victims through the local OSO.* When only eight hundred "enemies" were left an urgent telegram arrived from Moscow: "Meet commission. Halt repression."

Again something wrong? Nasedkin decided to commit a forgery. He changed the time of receipt of the government telegram from 1:00 A.M. to 9:00 A.M. And had all the remaining "spies" shot that night. Now he could face any commission.

Stalin's strategy of mass execution paused now and then, when the Dispenser of Destinies gave the order to punish one or another of his overly zealous Oprichniks as an example. The conveyor belt didn't actually stop. The propaganda organs simple sent another flashy diversion into orbit, proclaiming the concern shown by the Father of the Peoples for the strict observance of socialist legality.

That's how Nasedkin ended up in the Lubyanka, as a committer of "excesses." During the first months they took him for questioning quite often. One night the cell was awakened by an unusual commotion. A group of prison supervisors rushed in and surrounded Nasedkin's bunk. He had opened his veins. The parquet floor was covered with blood. They took him away and put the others in "boxes" immediately. Then they made each sign a statement not to reveal what had happened that night. They were returned to the same cell. Five days later Nasedkin was brought back. A bed was placed in the middle of the cell. On a stool next to the bed they put meat, milk, cutlets, and other food absolutely unheard of in prison. Vinokurov, the warden of the inner prison, called on him every day. Apparently the testimony of the former people's commissar was very badly needed by someone. (The circumstances of Nasedkin's execution became known only in 1954, and even then to a very small circle of people. The families of the many thousands of "spies" he killed have been told nothing to this day.)

* * *

Yefim Yevdokimov, our third Lubyanka Janissary, held a special place in Stalin's cohort of hangmen. He had every reason to welcome 1917. A

*OSO: Osoboye SOveshchanie, or Special Board, an NKVD court used for trying political cases without witnesses, attorneys, or the public.—TRANS.

repeat offender and professional criminal, he was freed from prison by the revolution. He soon sided with the victors, and when he came under Stalin's command on one of the fronts of the civil war, Stalin immediately singled him out for promotion.

Later, in the formative years of Stalin's dictatorship, he assigned Yevdokimov as his personal escort when he went to the Caucasus for vacation. The Master soon appointed him OGPU representative for the Northern Caucasus, and Yefim the Chekist, as Stalin called him, enthusiastically plunged into his native element of robbery and violence.

Yevdokimov's sharp nose as a professional criminal led him earlier than everyone else to the profitable business of hunting for "wreckers and diversionists." The Shakhty trial of 1928 was his dirty work. It was he who reported to Moscow the existence of a powerful, widely ramified "wreckers' organization" and who denounced the fifty Soviet and three German technicians and engineers. When Menzhinsky, head of the OGPU, demanded proof, Yevdokimov cited some mysterious "letters in code." Menzhinsky wasn't convinced. But Yevdokimov knew that to retreat would be to expose himself to retaliation. So he turned to his old friend Joseph. And Stalin, using his authority as Gensek, gave Yefim the Chekist carte blanche.

Returning to Rostov, Yevdokimov immediately arrested all the alleged wreckers and sent a telegram to the Master warning that objections might be raised in the center. When Kuibyshev and Rykov tried to intervene in defense of the veteran specialists the Gensek showed them the telegram from his emissary in Rostov.

The Shakhty concoction, brewed in Stalin's kitchen, served as a model for the later trials. The great beginning made by Yefim the Chekist was duly noted. He was the first GPU man to be awarded honorary orders four times, and in 1934 he was made a member of the party's Central Committee. A year later Stalin made him first secretary of the Rostov provincial committee (later the Azov–Black Sea territory). His position as absolute ruler of the region placed him under great obligation. In the summer of 1937 he arrested tens of thousands of enemies throughout the Northern Caucasus. The prisons of Rostov and Grozny didn't have room for all the Russians, Chechens, Ingush, Jews, and Ukrainians hauled in. Warehouses, garages, even schools were brought into service.

What was sooner or later bound to happen came about in the fall of that year. The cell Yevdokimov occupied in the Lubyanka was shared by a prominent journalist, Vsevolod Rakitsky, a man of considerable wit and talent who had formerly worked on *Izvestia*. Rakitsky survived Stalin and the camps. The story of Yevdokimov survived with him. (Rakitsky, incidentally, was sent up for a quip he was overheard making on Red Square at a parade. As he watched Stalin's image being borne on high by balloons, he said: "Bewhiskered angel." That "angel" cost him ten years.)

Yevdokimov, according to Rakitsky, had been spotlighted by the Leader so many times and shown so many signs of His august favor that he assumed he could only have fallen victim to envious rivals. No doubt they had accused him of stealing valuables. Fear of the terrible end that awaited him bared his filthy soul. He stood by the wall with an imaginary telephone to his ear and, glancing around suspiciously at Rakitsky, began moaning and complaining:

"Comrade Stalin? It's me, Yefim the Chekist. You remember me, don't you, Comrade Stalin? Listen, I didn't do anything. I'm not guilty. All I took was one little medallion. Yes, that's right. Before the party I swear, I'm clean. Listen to me, Comrade Stalin, please. It was only a little medallion, a tiny little medallion. Comrade Stalin, it's me. Me. Yefim the Chekist."

* * *

Lyushkov, Nasedkin, Yevdokimov—not quite enough to fill a gallery. But that's what most of His People were like. Perhaps these three sketches will bring us closer to an appreciation of the true portrait of Stalin.

THE TYRANT AMUSES HIMSELF

9

A person's character is shown in his actions. Stalin's main activity, and his favorite form of diversion, his real calling, was murder. No other tyrant, from Nero to Hitler, compares with Stalin in numbers killed.

But he wrote his name in history not by blood alone. This consummate performer's idea of fun and relaxation was to do some more playacting. Stalin was good at scenes of friendly sympathy for people condemned to death, and he performed them with style, relishing every detail. He was building up a legend for the future. As an old trouper, he knew how to control his movements on stage and never forgot about audience reaction. Let some official who had been his close collaborator yesterday but now was being denounced in public, go off to the torture rack with a picture in his mind of a kind, just, and cheerful Koba. Let everyone think that Yagoda, Yezhov, or Beria had acted on his own and deceived the Leader, or that these were the intrigues of Molotov or Kaganovich, or, if you like, Zhdanov, Malenkov, or one of the others. Let the entire population think—now and tomorrow—that Stalin knew nothing. The legend has had surprising vitality. He calculated far ahead, this man who thought by dark of night.

The mark of shame has not yet been removed from the foreheads of the "right-wing Communists," Bukharin, Rykov, and Tomsky. The story of how Bukharin was persecuted, "exposed," tried, and executed recalls the game of cat and mouse.

In August 1936 Pravda published a statement by Vyshinsky. On the basis of confessions by some of the accused, the public prosecutor's office had begun an investigation into the counterrevolutionary activity of Uglanov, Radek, Pyatakov, and the "Right" grouping. Two weeks later *Pravda* reported that the case involving the "Rights"—Bukharin, Rykov, and Tomsky—had been closed.

Neither the prosecutor's office nor the newspaper, of course, acted on its own. They were merely extras in this cat-and-mouse performance.

At the end of 1936 an unofficial plenum of the Central Committee was held. (There is indirect evidence of this plenum, but the media suppressed all news of the event.) Kaganovich, Molotov, and Voroshilov hurled wild accusations at Bukharin. The Gensek listened to his flunkies as though he were an impartial observer, then intervened authoritatively and wisely. He had never suspected that the comrades were so ill-disposed toward "the favorite of the party," as Lenin had called Bukharin.

"I think, comrades, that we shouldn't be hasty in the case of Bukharin and Rykov," Stalin went on in his well-rehearsed conciliatory, benevolent tone. "Evidence has also come in against Tukhachevsky, but we have sorted it out, and now Tukhachevsky can do his work without cause for concern. I propose that no decision be made for the time being and that the investigation be continued."

Of course, behind that narrow forehead, the fates of Tukhachevsky, Bukharin, and Rykov had been decided long before. But do you think Stalin was going to deny himself the pleasure of putting on his fatherly-sympathy act once more?

A month passed. On January 23, the first day of the Pyatakov trial, Bukharin, Rykov, and Tomsky were named as co-conspirators. Still Stalin didn't arrest or remove them from their posts. Now let us look again at the February-March plenum of 1937. Bukharin had decided at that plenum to warn the comrades about the NKVD. Something incomprehensible was going on inside the Organs. He personally had the impression that Yezhov was engaged in a plot against the party. Bukharin proposed that the Central Committee assign a commission to check into the functioning of the Organs.

"I do not believe in the existence of documents revealing counter-revolutionary activity by Lenin's comrades in arms," said Bukharin, looking straight in the Gensek's narrowed eyes. Stalin had a vicious retort: "So we'll send you personally to the NKVD. Where you can check into everything."

On the Gensek's motion, Bukharin and Rykov were expelled from the party, and the question of their "enemy activity" was turned over to the Organs for investigation. Had the cat at last sunk his claws into the prey? No, of course not. The game went on. On March 13, *Pravda* published an

article about the antiparty activity of the "Rights." Still Stalin refrained
from giving the order: "Take them away."

* * *

Red Square. November 7, 1936. Bukharin is on the reviewing stand
with foreign guests. Suddenly an NKVD agent comes over. "Comrade
Stalin has sent me to ask you to join him. Your place is on the main
reviewing stand."

What did Nikolai Ivanovich think, standing next to the Politburo
members atop the Lenin Mausoleum? Perhaps he remembered the first
years after October, when all the leaders lived in the Kremlin as one big
happy family. They had mock wrestling matches then, in which he, Nikolai Bukharin, would pin his friends' and comrades' shoulders to the
ground, Koba among them. "Bukharchik"—Stalin used to call him by that
affectionate nickname, and in their conversations they had used the familiar form of address.

Koba looked at Nikolai amicably. The divisions marched by across the
square in measured pace. Meanwhile, in the Lubyanka, the next trial was
already in preparation. Bukharin's "co-conspirators" were already being
tortured. The Gensek would dedicate the new trial to his dear friend
Bukharchik.

In the spring of 1937 they began calling Bukharin into the Central
Committee offices for "consultation." Usually they called him in the evening and kept him there until dawn, when he would be released. That
went on for almost two weeks.

Stalin made his victims, tomorrow's corpses, live with the taste of
death in their mouths—at party congresses, in Central Committee meetings, and in their own offices. Sensing that death would come soon, Bukharin wrote a final letter, his political testament. He asked his wife to learn
it by heart, then burned it. Anna Mikhailovna Larina preserved it in her
memory. With her, it survived seventeen years in the camps.

"In these days," Nikolai Ivanovich wrote, "the newspaper with the
sacred name 'Truth' is printing the foulest of lies, charging that I, Nikolai
Bukharin, wish to destroy the gains of October and 'restore capitalism.' "

Pravda had denounced the "bourgeois hireling," but Koba still put off
Bukharchik's arrest—until the Lubyanka had finished the last few lines in
the scenario for the coming show trial.

* * *

In 1937 Stalin arrested all the deputies of Lev Maryasin, chairman of
the board of the State Bank. Maryasin went to see a close friend of his and
was about to put an end to himself right there in his friend's office, but the
friend grabbed the pistol and took it away from him.

"Why stop me?" Lev Yefimovich reproached him. "You know what
kind of horror stories they make you write *there*. They make the tales of
Poe sound like a picnic."

At the Central Committee plenum, during a break, Stalin put his arm
around Maryasin's waist and said amiably:

"You're one of ours, a true Soviet banker. You wouldn't do any dirty work for that filthy enemy, Sokolnikov. You're one of ours. . . ."

Within a month "our Soviet banker" was taken away and charged as a wrecker. He died in torment in the Lubyanka.

The last of Maryasin's deputies to be arrested was Alyosha Svanidze, the brother of Keto, who had been Koba-Dzhugashvili's first wife. After a little while, Koba let him go. Later he was arrested again.

The same old game of cat and mouse. Stalin didn't invent it, but he became very good at it; it was his favorite pastime.

* * *

Stalin's order for the arrest of Central Committee member Dmitry Bulatov in late 1936 was carried out by the Organs with some hesitation. Bulatov had been in exile with Stalin in Solvychegodsk, later had headed the organizational department of the Central Committee for almost ten years, and in the most recent period had supervised the selection of NKVD personnel. They put the man in Lefortovo prison but refrained from torture, collected "testimony" against him from twenty-seven people, and waited for orders.

Bulatov was very anxious about his family and wanted to write to the Master. But his cellmates advised against it. They had experienced on their own tender skins how responsive the authorities were to such appeals. Nevertheless Bulatov wrote the letter, in which he reminded Stalin about Solvychegodsk, where he had rendered the future Leader many a service. Much to everyone's surprise, Bulatov was soon summoned. He was told that his case was being re-examined. Bulatov returned to his cell on the wings of joy, although he felt a little awkward about his cellmates' unhappy lot. Perhaps the systematic extermination of all party veterans was continuing, but at least in regard to this one old comrade, Stalin's conscience apparently bothered him. That very evening Bulatov was summoned from his cell and told to bring his things.

Several years went by. On a July day in 1941, in one of Butyrka prison's "general cells," large enough to hold two hundred people, two friends met, two old-time party comrades. Bulatov was unrecognizable: deathly pale, weak, barely able to move. It turned out that they hadn't freed him from Lefortovo prison but transferred him to the "villa of torture"—Sukhanov prison. The promised re-examination began. And was very quickly completed: instead of the testimony of twenty-seven people, Bulatov was confronted with that of seventy-three. He had once worked briefly as secretary of the Omsk provincial committee. At Beria's request all seventy-two secretaries of the district committees under him testified about his "counterrevolutionary activity." The seventy-third witness was the former NKVD commissar Yezhov. Yezhov's is a separate story. As for Bulatov, the morning of his hearing before Ulrikh's team became his last.

* * *

When Stalin sent Nikolai Krylenko to his death, he took no account of Krylenko's many years of service in the organs of justice. From the earliest period of Soviet rule Krylenko had actively assisted in the eradication of innocent people (and not only he, not only he). Unfortunately we can't speak the consoling phrase in regard to him, "He knew not what he did."

Krylenko knew very well. He played a key role as public prosecutor in the first frame-up trials, in 1928–31. In 1918 he had called for the death penalty in the case of an innocent man—Admiral Aleksei Shchastny, the officer in charge of the Baltic Fleet.[96] While acknowledging that capital punishment had been abolished, Krylenko stated that the tribunal could nevertheless condemn Shchastny to be shot on the grounds of "the revolutionary conception of the law."

The year 1937 found Krylenko in the post of people's commissar of justice. At the first session of the Supreme Soviet, Dzhafar Bagirov, one of the most perfidious of Stalin's lieutenants, went after Krylenko with the stupid accusation that he was overly involved in sports. The people's commissar was indeed a devoted mountain climber and loved to play chess. But what of it? The signal had been given, however, and Krylenko was arrested. He spent five days turning his affairs over to Nikolai Rychkov, a divisional military attorney who until then had worked for Ulrikh. Then Krylenko went off to his suburban dacha.

An unexpected call from the Kremlin. Stalin's voice: "Listen, Nikolai Vasilyevich, don't get upset. We trust you. Continue with the work you were assigned to on the new legal code. . . ." That same night NKVD agents surrounded his dacha and arrested the former commissar.[97] Whether Stalin was basing himself in this case on the revolutionary conception of law cannot now be determined. But he did wipe out Krylenko.

* * *

Joseph Astsaturov was a cousin of the prominent revolutionary Bogdan Knunyants. Astsaturov was a construction engineer who in 1937 arrived in Moscow for the session of the Presidium of the Supreme Soviet, where he was awarded the Order of Lenin for completing construction on a bridge ahead of schedule. Though he was not a party member, the engineer was granted a rare honor: he was received by Stalin. The Master's manner toward him was exceedingly cordial. He congratulated him on his new award and deigned to show a lively interest in his plans.

Inspired and entranced by this royal reception, Astsaturov descended to the first floor of the Central Committee building and went into the cloakroom. They were waiting for him there. He was escorted to the Lubyanka. From there he was sent to the Krasnaya Presnya transit prison and shipped home to Armenia in a Stolypin car.* Visited by his relatives in Yerevan prison, he managed to slip his sister a letter addressed to Stalin. Once the Leader learned how he had been treated, he would be freed at once and the guilty would be punished.

---

*A railroad car especially adapted for transporting prisoners, modeled after those used after the 1905 revolution in Russia, under Prime Minister Stolypin.—TRANS.

His sister went to Moscow, delivered the letter to the Central Committee offices, and waited for justice to be done. Her brother was tall, strong, handsome. The death they dreamed up for this Hercules of the Caucasus was a savage one: they hanged him by the heels from the ceiling of his cell until he died.

* * *

Aleksandr Milchakov was recommended for the post of first secretary of the Young Communist League Central Committee by Grigory Ordzhonikidze. The candidacies of Kosarev and Chaplin were being discussed (this was in 1933) but Sergo said: "We have plenty of Kosarevs and Chaplins, but we have only one Milchakov. We recommend Comrade Milchakov."

Thus Sasha Milchakov, the son of a worker and, formerly, the first secretary of the Ukrainian YCL Central Committee, was elected first secretary of the All-Union YCL Central Committee. The Master favored him. Otherwise Milchakov would not have been elected a delegate to the next four party congresses and would not have been appointed as head of the Communist Youth International. After completing a course in Marxism-Leninism, Milchakov was promoted to a job in the Big Central Committee—deputy chief of the organizational department. He developed a good working relationship with Bulatov. But the Master suddenly decided to bring new blood into the entire central apparatus. Heads rolled everywhere as the reshuffling began. Just then there chanced along a decree of the Central Committee concerning the organization of a production complex called Vostokzoloto (Gold of the East), and Milchakov was sent to Irkutsk to become its deputy director. Another candidate for the next world was working there already—Aleksandr Yakovlev, also a long-time party member.

Milchakov got sick of office work and he asked to go into industry. He was appointed director of the Darasun gold-mining enterprise. But it's rather awkward to run a big operation like that without special training, and Milchakov, whose only education had been four years at a nonclassical secondary school, went back to Moscow to the Industrial Academy.

It was a fair September day in Moscow in 1937. Milchakov was sitting in the waiting room of a certain Comrade Korotkov, first secretary of the Bauman district committee of the party. Milchakov was about to be brought before a party bureau meeting and have his party card taken away. This was the final step in the procedure by which the decision of a primary party organization to expel an "enemy of the people" or an "enemy accomplice" was confirmed.

Suddenly Korotkov came out of his office and took Milchakov by the arm.

"Sasha, my friend, let's go."

"Where?"

"Come on quick. Stalin has called for you."

They arrived at the Kremlin. Korotkov gave Milchakov a shove into the office, while he himself stayed in the waiting room.

In the office were two people. Pacing up and down the carpet with a pipe in his teeth was Stalin. Lazar Kaganovich was sitting in a chair, an unusually troubled look on his face.

Stalin warmly embraced Milchakov.

"Sasha, my friend, how did this happen?"

Turning to Lazar, he continued with a dramatic ring in his voice.

"What's going on in the Moscow organization? What have we come to? Expelling a man like this from the party!"

Back to Milchakov: "Sit down, my dear fellow, sit down. What have they done to you? Ay-yay-yay . . . But we'll straighten it all out. Now, my dear fellow, we have an important assignment for you from the Central Committee. Take this excerpt from the government's resolution. You're being appointed deputy director of the Chief Gold Administration, Glavzoloto. You know Serebrovsky, the director. One of the most vicious enemies of the people, it turns out. Imagine. Delivered fifty million in gold ingots to Trotsky. Vicious, no? He's going to be arrested tonight, at two A.M. Take this mandate and go to Serebrovsky's office and don't take one step out of there. Don't leave until two A.M.

"If Serebrovsky goes to the lunchroom, you go too. If he goes to the bathroom, you go to the bathroom. If he goes home, you go with him. . . . At two A.M. they'll come for him, so you better be there. And at nine A.M. they'll bring you the document making you head of Glavzoloto. The Central Committee is relying on you. So get going."

Milchakov knew Serebrovsky as an honest Bolshevik whom Lenin had trusted, and a sincere, intelligent man, who had put great effort into the organization of heavy industry. But how could Sasha disbelieve in the Leader's sincerity? Meanwhile Stalin laid it on thick. Strings of curses aimed at the "vicious traitor" alternated with embraces and kisses for Milchakov in the best Caucasus tradition.

Overwhelmed by these signs of the Master's affection, Sasha went to the offices of Glavzoloto. Serebrovsky was glad to see him. Sasha had worked at Darasun and had plenty of organizational experience. The director didn't let his new deputy out of his sight, introduced him to all aspects of the job, ate with him, and stayed with him all evening—as though he himself knew of Stalin's plans.

Exactly at 2:00 A.M. they came for Serebrovsky. At 9:00 A.M. they brought Milchakov the promised document. But two months later, in February 1938, they came for the new head of Glavzoloto himself.[98]

* * *

At a stone quarry in Norilsk, Sasha Milchakov broke stone along with thousands of other *zeks* (political prisoners). Who needed this stone? What was going to be built here? What kind of construction project was this?

These questions were asked of the director of the camp subsection by a member of a Central Committee subcommission that came there some time after the war.

"No one knows," answered the director. "We were ordered to make sure all the enemies of the people were sent out for heavy work—a hundred percent. Why they opened up the quarry I don't know. There are no technical specifications or any other instructions."

The director of construction for this "industrial complex" was Avraamiy Zavenyagin, one of Ordzhonikidze's former deputies in the Commissariat of Heavy Industry. The Master had called in the prisoner and said, "Build the industrial complex at Norilsk and you'll get your freedom."

At Turukhansk, airplanes were grounded for a long time. The weather didn't permit any flights. The pilots had gone to the members of the commission and explained, "The airport at Good Hope can't take us."

Someone asked with surprise: "What does the Cape of Good Hope have to do with it? We're flying to Norilsk." V. A. Barabanov, a prominent official of Gulag, has related that after Stalin made his offer to Zavenyagin, the chief of the construction project named the local airport Good Hope. A major metallurgical complex was supposed to be built in this polar region. And the deadline was three years.

The labor force of humble zeks did not always remain submissive. Not long before the commission's arrival, Milchakov tells in his memoirs, a group of prisoners had sent up some kites to scatter leaflets. What did they call for? No, not for opposition to the Kremlin's arbitrary rule. They called for normal food rations and the right of prisoners to correspond with their relatives.

To suppress this "uprising" the guards shot 150 people. The commission was charged with the task of investigating the circumstances and, in passing, were supposed to check on the conditions at the Norilsk women's camp. Five thousand women "spies" had been brought there, but there was no work appropriate for women. The commission could find only 137 appropriate job descriptions. (As though women weren't used for heavy labor . . .)

Someone who had known Sasha Milchakov personally asked Zavenyagin about him. It turned out that when the director had run across Sasha in the quarry he had him transferred to work in an office as an economic planner. Sasha turned out not to be in camp section No. 7, where he was supposed to be. In section 3 they reported that Milchakov had been transferred to section 5, and in that section they learned that he had been sent to Moscow on the personal order of Kruglov, the minister of internal affairs.

In Moscow the commission suggested first of all that the women's camp be evacuated from Norilsk. Kruglov asked the Central Committee for a delay, but the brain center of the party was in a determined mood, and the minister was obliged to remove the women, although it was wintertime and the roads were impassable. Needless to say, the detachments of prisoners had arrived in Norilsk only during the brief summer, when the waterways were navigable. Who knows what the MVD boss thought up, but the order was carried out on schedule.

One evening in Kruglov's office the conversation turned to Milchakov.

"You know Stalin as well as I do," Kruglov began. "One time, after I'd given the usual report to Stalin, he said: 'Listen, I hear that Sasha Milchakov is still alive.'

" 'I don't know, Comrade Stalin, I haven't heard anything about him.' "

" 'If he's alive, bring him to Moscow. We have to give him some work.'

"I made a note of it, followed up with the necessary inquiries, and, when I learned that he was in Norilsk, gave the appropriate order. In Moscow he was placed in a solitary cell at Butyrka prison. If he'd been sent to Lefortovo, as you know, they might have broken his bones by mistake.

"I couldn't bring myself to report to the Boss about Milchakov's arrival. It was always better not to go to him with just one question. I prepared a whole lot of material and asked for an audience. When Stalin received me I reported on several different matters and then, as though I had just remembered something, I asked Stalin:

" 'You ordered me to bring Milchakov to Moscow, didn't you? I understand that he's here now.'

" 'And where has he been?'

" 'Norilsk.'

" 'Norilsk?' Stalin acted surprised. 'What foolishness. He knows all about the gold-mining industry. Send him to Kolyma. . . .' "

And that was how, for the second time, the Master *found work* for Sasha Milchakov.

CONCERN FOR THE CHILDREN

10

The degradation of the people began at a very early age, among the many millions of the Pioneer organization—that is, the one that is sponsored and helped along by the Young Communist League. No, come to think of it, it began even earlier—in the kindergartens, where the poor simpletons, as they left the dinner table, would recite in unison, "Thank you, dear Stalin, for our happy childhood."

On the playroom wall hangs a portrait of Grandfather Stalin with a little black-haired girl in his arms. The girl in the photo, six-year-old Gelya, had just presented the Leader with a bouquet of flowers. Among the guests had been her father, Ardan Markizov, people's commissar of agriculture for the Buryat-Mongol Autonomous Republic. Several years later Gelya's father suddenly turned out to be an "enemy of the people" and was exterminated.

The children look tenderly from time to time at the mustached portrait. And no one tells them the fate of the little girl's parents. Forty years pass. How many generations of children have passed through those kindergartens? But still no one tells them the truth.

You wonder, how was it that Stalin, always so busy finding new, striking, and effective methods for exterminating the adult population, found the time for children? On April 7, 1935, he published a decree in the name of the Central Executive Committee establishing twelve as the age of criminal liability. On that historic day, children in the land of socialism began to be judged on an equal basis with their parents. And punished on an equal basis—up to and including execution.

Well, there must have been a reason.

There was: OZAR. This counterrevolutionary terrorist organization, whose codelike name came from the Russian words for "We Will Avenge Our Parents" (*O*tomstim *ZA R*oditelei), was dreamed up by some middle-ranking official who had the overpowering urge to rise higher. Twelve children of deceased "enemies of the people" were listed as members of OZAR. I can name two of them: Leonid, the son of David Krimsky, head of a department of the party's Moscow city committee; and Anatol, son of Solomon Rabin, an official in the Commissariat of Forestry. Those two the interrogators were unable to break. The others confessed to belonging to the mythical OZAR. All ten were processed through an OSO, but not all survived the ITL. (OZAR, OSO, ITL—we're talking Martian and hadn't even noticed.)*

* * *

The Leader showed particular concern for the children of his comrades in arms. He arrested Mikoyan's sons, Sergo and Vano. At the request of Ashkhen Lazarevna, the mother of the arrested boys, Nikolai Bukharin called up Koba:

"What were the boys jailed for?"

"For being a pair of freethinkers, that's what," the Gensek snapped.

A forerunner of Joseph Stalin, Joseph Volotsky, burned freethinkers alive. But that was in the fourteenth century, under Tsar Ivan III. No one would venture to charge Stalin with the burning of heretics. He simply sent them to the camps—grown-ups and children alike. And it wasn't his fault if not all of them knew how to survive.

The public prosecutor authorized Ashkhen Lazarevna to send her children a sausage once a week, and soon, from lack of evidence, he decided to drop the case. When the Boss found out, he hit the ceiling. "*Apolitical,* that is!"

---

*ITL: *ispravitelno-trudovoi lager,* corrective-labor camp. A grim pun of the prisoners turned this into "*istrebitelno-*trudovoi lager," *destructive*-labor camp. —TRANS.

At the next session of the Politburo Stalin proposed that the case of the young freethinkers be turned over to Vsevolod Merkulov, deputy commissar of the NKVD. (As we can see, the Politburo did not consider itself above such minor matters.)

The number of children arrested can be expressed in a seven-digit figure. How many millions were torn from their families and homes and stamped with the initials ChSR?* How many lived through it? It is not within the power of statistics to give the dimensions of the tragedy. But Stalin's personal part in the extermination of the children is an indisputable fact. After annihilating the prominent cohorts of Lenin, our Beloved Father never failed to show his special concern for each and every one of their children. Valerian Osinsky's son, Dmitry, was arrested twice: the first time, along with Andrei Sverdlov; the second time, with his own father. On the same day, Dmitry's wife returned from the maternity ward with their infant son. I have already mentioned Lenin's comrade Pyotr Zaporozhets, who died in 1905, long before the mass purges. Stalin killed his children. A similar fate befell Lucia, the only surviving daughter of Prokofy Dzhaparidze, one of the twenty-six Baku commissars. In 1937 Stalin had her arrested and sent to a camp.

* * *

In the summer of 1918 the Bolshevik-led government of Soviet Baku decided to abandon the city, faced with Turkish intervention. The people's commissars set sail aboard the ship *Kolesnikov,* but the local authorities of Centro-Caspian returned them by force to Baku. Boris Sheboldaev alone managed to save himself. He jumped overboard and was able to swim to the island of Zhiloi. After a month, the commissars were miraculously released from Bailov prison and sailed from Baku a second time. Against their orders, however, the crew changed course and docked the vessel at Krasnovodsk, where British military forces seized the twenty-six commissars. They were shot on September 20.

Sheboldaev got out alive. But in 1937 a man was found in the Kremlin who undertook to correct history's error. Sheboldaev was then the head of the party committee of the Northern Caucasus territory. He was arrested at Rostov-on-Don and sent off to Moscow, to the Lubyanka. Right behind him came his wife and children, two little boys, a four-year-old and a two-year-old. World War I had brought Boris and Lika together in 1916. Lika had been a nurse on the Turkish Front. Later, the young Sheboldaevs had fought to defend Soviet power on the southern fronts.

After the arrest of Lika's husband, her sisters Valentina and Antonina accompanied her to the capital. They could not abandon Lika in her last month of pregnancy. At the maternity home an Armenian midwife they knew gave her name to the newborn child. So, unknown to the authorities,

*ChSR: Chlen Semyi Repressirovannogo, member of the family of a "repressed person" (i.e., one victimized for political reasons). —TRANS.

a third son, Sergo, was born to the Sheboldaevs. The naïve attempt of the women to hide with the children in the village of Petushki near Moscow was immediately and decisively brought to a halt by the Lubyanka. They arrested Lika, and picked up the courageous midwife as well.

Evidently, Boris Sheboldaev proved to be fairly tough. Stalin insisted on "confessions," however, so the butchers started in on Lika. The Oprichniks descended on Petushki one bright autumn day. They grabbed the infant and one of the little boys. Aunt Valya had managed to hide the oldest boy in a neighboring hut. But a newborn, you see, needs tending and swaddling, no matter what. So Aunt Valya gathered up a bundle of linen and demanded she be taken along, virtually forcing her way into the automobile with the children.

The car picked up speed. The road entered a forest. They threw the woman out without slowing down.

Now we see Lika Sheboldaeva being interrogated. In the adjoining room—the door has been thoughtfully left ajar—she hears a child's cry, the cry of her baby.

"Those are your children. Recognize them? Either sign or . . ."

How many such torture-interrogations did the mother endure? Who kept count? Lika went out of her mind. She managed only, with a last effort of will, to tell her cellmate what had happened. This turned out to be Lilya Ivanovna Rudzutak, niece of the Old Bolshevik and comrade of Lenin's.

It's the summer of 1937. Boris Sheboldaev is no longer alive. Lika sits in a Butyrka prison cell, rocking an imaginary child in her arms. He is so small, the infant Sergo, only four months old. During walks in the prison courtyard Lilya Rudzutak sings arias from operas. That is all the good her voice lessons in Milan did her. . . . It seems to Lilya her uncle is alive; he is in that corner tower, he can hear her.

Lilya and Lika ended up in the same prisoner transport. But in the prison hospital at the Kotlas camp they were separated. The demented Lika was put in a special cell on a bunk enclosed by iron mesh. Beneath this meshwork tent she ended her days. Like something from an exotic tale.

In Moscow the aunts went searching for the arrested infants. They searched for a year. They went to every *otokhmatmlad* (in ordinary language, a department for the protection of mothers and infants). Then they made the rounds a second time. They left the last department crying. Behind them they heard footsteps. A tall, thin woman came down from the porch and caught up with them. An inspector, she made them vow not to give her away. The children, she said, were being kept out on Yaroslavl Highway at a placement center for orphans. They'd been given the name Vorobyov.

The indefatigable sisters rushed to the Yaroslavka and announced that the Vorobyov boys were their nephews; the older one was three and the younger was one. The younger was there under the name of Alec; the bright idea had been to rename the older one Sergo. Aunt Valya and Aunt Tonya scooped up the boys and left with them for Uryupinsk, south of Tambov. Telling no one the address.

During the war the older one was killed by a stray bomb, the middle one died from scarlet fever. Only the youngest, Sergo, survived. He is now teaching at an institute that, through the blasphemous irony of fate, has only recently stopped bearing the name of Stalin, the murderer of Boris and Lika Sheboldaev.

Sergo Sheboldaev is looking for someone who can tell him about his mother's last days.

* * *

But perhaps Stalin was capable of compassion for the children of his close relatives? At least for them?

When he arrested Alyosha Svanidze, he had Svanidze's eleven-year-old son Vano brought to the Lubyanka. They wanted evidence from the child against the father. After Svanidze was killed at Oryol prison in 1941, Stalin put sixteen-year-old Vano in the psychiatric prison-hospital at Kazan, where the young man spent five years. From there they sent him to a destruction camp. He served a term at hard labor in the copper mines of Dzhezkazgan.

The probability that Vano would try to avenge his father, given the existing system of surveillance, was no greater than the probability that the Kremlin would disappear into the netherworld, with all its prophets, hangmen, and bailiffs. But the probability existed in Stalin's cowardly imagination. And he saw to it that Vano remained out of the way, in eternal exile.

Vano did not return to Moscow until 1956, having spent nineteen years in confinement. Life on the outside worked out for him this way: After graduating from the history department of the university and doing postgraduate work, Vano Svanidze entered the Africa Institute. He married (you never know what's going to happen next) Stalin's daughter, Svetlana Alliluyeva.

* * *

To whom did he show mercy, the Great Friend of Children? To no one. There was no system. Only all-consuming hatred. More than enough of it, in fact, to take care of the entire Young Communist League (YCL).

Aleksandr Milchakov was virtually the only secretary of the YCL Central Committee to survive, by some miracle. If you consider seventeen years in the destruction camps a "miracle." The real story of the YCL has yet to be written. How so? Milchakov himself explained in the foreword to his book *The First Decade:*

"It wasn't by chance that Stalin and his henchmen annihilated almost all the honest Leninists who had headed the YCL during its first decade,"[99] Among them were five secretaries of the "Small Central Committee" in the twenties and thirties: Oscar Ryvkin, Pyotr Smorodin, Lazar Shatskin, Nikolai Chaplin, Aleksandr Kosarev.

Of the four Chaplin brothers, only the youngest, Viktor, a student at Leningrad University, survived the terror. In 1937 he had just turned twenty.

Nikolai was the first to be taken. He had helped suppress the Kronstadt revolt, then served in the navy. After graduating from an aviation school in Koktebel named in honor of Leon Trotsky, he was sent to Finland as a resident intelligence officer. The typical biography of a YCL leader.

At a confrontation in prison with his younger brother Sergei, Nikolai was brought in on a stretcher; tufts of gray hair on his head, teeth knocked out, ribs broken. Was it so long before then that everyone had admired this strong young man, a regular Hercules?

At first Nikolai didn't even recognize his brother, half blind as he was from the torture, with his face swollen from severe beatings. When he did, he had this advice for Sergei: "Seryozha, sign everything they put in front of you. Or you'll end up the same way I am."

But confessing didn't save Sergei. They sent him to Magadan. There they brought an additional charge against him—plotting armed insurrection—and shot him. His wife, Vera Mikhailovna, has recounted Sergei's fate. On their way to the camps, Sergei and Vera were thrown together briefly at a transit prison.

The oldest Chaplin brother, Aleksandr Pavlovich, a former colleague of Lunacharsky's, also died in the camps.

* * *

The list of those who perished seems endless. Here are the names of secretaries of the YCL Central Committee and members of the Executive Committee of the Communist Youth International who found themselves behind bars or barbed wire in the Stalin years: Oskar Tarkhanov, Rimma Yurovskaya, Vladimir Feigin, Pyotr Petrovsky, Andrei Shokhin, Dmitry Matveyev, Georgy Ivanov, Rafael Khitarov, Husein Rakhmanov, Ignaty Sharavyev, Pavel Gorshenin, Sergei Andreyev, Dmitry Lukyanov, Vasily Chemodanov, Sergei Saltanov, Valentina Pikina. Only a few lived to see rehabilitation. A novel could be written about each—no, a tragedy. For each one, to the extent of his or her abilities, served the tyrant and helped raise a generation of moral cripples.

As a leader of the YCL, Aleksandr Kosarev carried out a purge of the Leningrad youth organization on Stalin's orders in December 1925. He literally destroyed the YCL committee of that city. Stalin lavished favors on this diligent flunky and nominated him to the post of first secretary of the YCL, to replace Milchakov.

The thirties, however, demanded of the YCL Central Committee a different kind of work, and on a larger scale. Kosarev didn't catch on right away that it was no longer enough just to be the party's loyal helper. You had to become the instrument of the Organs—to expose and exterminate enemies everywhere—in schools, institutions of higher learning, factories, on collective farms. And the more the merrier. In the plan for the transformation of the country into an immense prison barracks, the four million YCL members were assigned the role of auxiliary spies and punitive troops.

Clearly, Kosarev was not able to grasp the Gensek's epoch-making design at the outset, or to respond effectively. Stalin decided to "straighten out" his young comrade. Stalin called in the three secretaries of the "Small Central Committee"—Kosarev, Pavel Gorshenin, and Pikina—and in Yezhov's presence reproached Kosarev: "The Central Committee of the YCL is not helping the Organs to expose the enemies of the people." The Gensek then enlightened the YCL leaders with the appropriate categorical directives.

This took place in the Leader's office on July 21, 1937. A year later, after Beria had installed himself in the Lubyanka, Stalin decided that the time had come to replenish the YCL leadership, which had shown itself unequal to the main task of the day. (But, my God, hadn't they tried? How many local YCL organizations had they beheaded in just one year. . . .)

An emergency plenary session of the YCL Central Committee convened on November 19, 1938, at which, on the Gensek's orders, nearly the entire gang appeared—Molotov, Malenkov, Zhdanov, Shkiryatov. The soil had been worked over superficially only, but in full accordance with the Gensek's wishes. As an instrument of provocation Stalin this time chose an official of the YCL Central Committee, Olga Mishakova. She appealed to the Leader for help against Kosarev's domination. At the same time, Mishakova accused the first secretary of the YCL Central Committee of liberalism: when he had been in Gorky, Kosarev hadn't exposed a single Trotskyist, she said; thus he had used his authority to cover up for the enemies of the people. Receiving this alarm signal, the party's Central Committee decided to send Mishakova to Gorky. She was able to track down and unmask hundreds of "inveterate Trotskyists," who had wormed their way into the Gorky YCL organization.

Such were the circumstances leading up to the emergency plenary session.

Stalin might, after all, have dressed in mourning for the imminent funeral of the "Small CC," but he preferred his usual semimilitary attire. The Gensek sat a little off to one side, smoked his pipe, and listened to the furious attacks of his subordinates—inspired by him—on the YCL leaders who had shown such criminal indulgence toward the enemies of the party. During the discussion, one of the speakers declared that Kosarev hadn't been able to detect the traitors on his own Central Committee. Zhdanov, with well-fed indignation, remarked from where he was sitting:

"How come Kosarev couldn't detect them?"

"Maybe he didn't *want* to detect them," the Gensek put in quietly but with meaning.

After this planned bit of dialogue the debate took the necessary turn.

The YCL Central Committee—the "Kosarev gang," that is—was annihilated in its entirety within a few days.

They rewarded the provocateur Mishakova with the position of secretary of the YCL Central Committee. And Young Communist heads rolled. In those days they had a name for it: "strengthening the leadership."

AN ARMY WITHOUT COMMANDERS

11

Stalin's war of extermination against his own people could not pass over the army, leaving it untouched. He feared the military command as a force capable of leading a rebellion. Quite often cowardice and ferocity are combined in the same person. Stalin's fearfulness, compounded by his suspicious nature, had prompted him long before to prepare to move against the army.

The operation had to begin in the summer of 1937, no sooner and no later. By then the people had been warmed up enough by the spy hysteria to accept it. Delaying the destruction of the officer corps meant risking everything that had been achieved. The mass arrests of veteran party leaders might shake the confidence of even the most loyal officers. It would be one thing if Gorky interfered (the "Stormy Petrel" had been removed in timely fashion), or Bukharin, or that hysterical old woman, Krupskaya. It would be quite another if the military leaders started to grumble. It wasn't so long ago, was it, that the generals had revolted in Spain? Now they couldn't be removed by force, because they themselves were a greater force.

No. It was better to cover yourself on this flank. Here was a chance also to give vent to a long-festering envy of talented strategists.

So . . . this Tukhachevsky plays the violin? Let's see what sort of performance he can give in the Lubyanka.

Tukhachevsky had every count against him—his personal abilities, his culture, his decisiveness, his intelligence. Above all, his aura of military glory. Stalin's inferiority complex, if you will, came into play here, as it had in the case of Mikhail Frunze. He couldn't tolerate such able men around him. It was only types like Voroshilov that he felt comfortable with. That's why the Gensek didn't put Tukhachevsky in as people's commissar of defense. And even in his role as chief of staff of the Red Army, Stalin and Voroshilov treated him with contempt, often to the detriment of the work.

The Red Army was considerably behind the strongest Western armies, especially in modernization of weaponry and mechanization. But Stalin and Voroshilov persistently blocked any sensible proposals Tukhachevsky made. Worn out by the pressure from these case-hardened intriguers, Tukhachevsky asked to be relieved of his post. For three years he commanded the Leningrad military district. The marshal became friends with Sergei Kirov. He would have to pay for that too.

Stalin's international ambitions demanded a strong modern army. But who was to carry out the reorganization of the armed forces? Joseph the Builder had to appoint Tukhachevsky as deputy commissar of defense. Under Tukhachevsky's able leadership, the army was re-equipped, and a well-trained officer corps built up. Once this was done, it was time to get rid of him. Stalin wasn't satisfied with destroying Tukhachevsky alone. He liquidated all of Tukhachevsky's colleagues in the Leningrad military district as well—Iosif Slavin, Ivan Fedko, and Boris Feldman. No one was overlooked, not even Tukhachevsky's friend, the musician Nikolai Sergeyevich Zhilyaev, or the marshal's daughter Svetlana.

In less than two years, Stalin sent virtually the entire high command and almost all the senior officers to prisons and labor camps. Later, General Aleksandr Todorsky, who himself spent many years in Stalin's camps, put together some figures. If you add up all the officers lost in wars by the various belligerent countries over the past two centuries, this comes to only half the number of officers murdered by Stalin. Lefortovo prison alone ground up fifty-three corps commanders in the course of two years —more than all the country's wars together. Of the five Soviet marshals, Stalin liquidated three—Tukhachevsky, Blyukher, and Yegorov. Out of four fleet commanders, he also liquidated three—Vladimir Orlov, Mikhail Viktorov, and Aleksandr Sivkov.

In October 1957, Marshal Malinovsky said, at a meeting of the party activists in the Ministry of Defense, it was as though the *Beria clique* had picked up a giant crystal vase containing 82,000 of the best, most experienced, and qualified commanders and political workers in the army and navy, and smashed it on the rocks. "On the eve of the war, we found ourselves decapitated," Malinovsky concluded.

That is what happened, all right. But Beria was only one of those who carried out the orders. He was included, along with Yezhov, Vyshinsky, Shkiryatov, Mekhlis, Shchadenko, Ulrikh, and the more notorious figures —Molotov, Kaganovich, Malenkov, Zhdanov, Voroshilov, and Mikoyan— in the Big Clique, Stalin's.

In 1937, Cavalry Commander Oka Gorodovikov, happened to run into Marshal Budyonny. Gorodovikov said: "Semyon, look what's happening! They're taking everybody, one after another."

Budyonny replied: "Don't worry, they won't touch us. They're only taking the smart ones."

The marshal's answer was only partly true. Stalin let Budyonny and Voroshilov live, not only because of their total lack of intellect, their complete incapacity for strategic thinking. He needed them for their propaganda value: Budyonny, the peasant's son, and "Klim" Voroshilov, the locksmith from Lugansk. That was a good front for the "masses." Let the people console themselves with the illusion that the government represented them. The two had other valuable qualities. They were no threat as rivals. Along with a doglike loyalty to the ruler, for which the only parallel was the groveling of the lifelong serf before the lord of the manor, they had a visceral hatred of intellectuals. For a soft job surrounded by honors, they were ready to do anything vile. Proof of that is scattered along the entire career of Voroshilov, climber and intriguer, first-class.

Few of those who had been officers in the Red Calvary during the civil war suffered from the purges. Stalin did not touch such former division commanders as Iosif Apanasenko and Semyon Timoshenko, whose military capabilities were on the same level as Voroshilov's and Budyonny's.

As he set about destroying the brains of the army, the Gensek encountered several unplanned early deaths among prominent commanders. In 1929, Jan Fabricius died in Sochi while rescuing a pregnant woman. In 1936, the former commander in chief Sergei Kamenev died. He had been a great irritant to Stalin in 1920, so this was an especially unpatriotic act: he could have waited another year to meet his death. But the long arm of Stalin's law reached him even in his grave by the Kremlin wall. A role in this business was played by Aleksandr Svechin, chief of staff under General Brusilov during World War I and author of the book *The Art of Commanding Troops*. After the revolution he took up service in the Red Army, later heading the Military History Commission.

On one occasion, Sergei Kamenev asked him: "Comrade Svechin, what do you think about the possibility of using the works of Clausewitz at the military academy?"

Svechin replied: "Whatever you say, Sergei Sergeyevich."

But this obliging attitude did not save Svechin in 1937. He was arrested as a participant in a monarchist plot, no less. In the Lubyanka, Svechin was forced to make a statement that Sergei Kamenev had committed "treason." Svechin was shot. Kamenev's name vanished from history.

The campaign of destroying the high command of the Red Army was a great success. Military men, after all, were not party men. You could deal with them in a more direct way. You could even venture to make a personal appearance at the scene of operations. . . .

On June 1, 1937, Stalin staged a two-week performance in the Kremlin, with all members of the Revolutionary Military Council and the Politburo taking part. Some 120 commanders and military commissars were invited. Everyone was searched at the door; weapons were left in the cloakroom. Each person was given a *blue folder* containing copies of depositions revealing the treason of Tukhachevsky, Uborevich, Putna, Primakov, and others.

From these blue folders many learned of their own involvement in spying and plotting against the Kremlin.

The presiding committee consisted of the Politburo, headed by Stalin. The Leader was flanked by Voroshilov and Yezhov. One after another the speakers stigmatized the traitors. As the show went on, NKVD employees brought in new folders with fresh depositions by those just arrested. Yezhov would lean over to the Master and whisper the names of the newly exposed traitors. A barely noticeable, imperial nod of the head would follow, and another "traitor" would be taken from the hall. Then another. And another.

Those who remained hotly reviled the newly exposed enemies and just as hotly swore their loyalty to the Leader. Who would be the next speaker? Everyone rushed to be first on the list. On the Master's face was a mixture of severity and triumph. Where were those flabby intellectuals now who had nagged him about his cruelty? Now everyone could see: the plotters had built their filthy nest in the very heart of the army. Yes, his day had come, his, Stalin's. The insidious foe would be liquidated by the righteous hand of the people. The Master seemed sunk in mighty thought. But no, he was watching everything, noting down everything. His incomparable mustache twitched. He said: "I don't see Comrades Bulin and Slavin on this list."

Anton Bulin, an old St. Petersburg Communist, was deputy chief of the army's Political Directorate, and Iosif Slavin was head of the political department of the army schools. Neither of them could bring himself to take part in the humiliation of the commanders of the civil war.

The Master continued: "Those who come to us and tell us themselves about their criminal ties with the enemies of the people can be forgiven. But if anyone thinks he can deceive the party, he has only himself to blame."

More speeches, more anathemas, more vows. Pavel Dybenko takes the floor. He rages at those who only yesterday were his comrades and have turned out to be spies. Side by side with them this Baltic sailor, at one time chairman of the revolutionary Central Committee of the Baltic Fleet (Centrobalt), and later a people's commissar, had defended Soviet power during the civil war. Now the slogan is "No mercy to the enemy."

"That Gamarnik!" Dybenko says with outrage. "He pretended to be as pure as Jesus Christ. Never had an extra stick of furniture in his house . . . We've been saying all along these bluebloods were sticking together. Wouldn't give us a chance to move up."

But before another year passed, Stalin liquidated this loud-mouthed sailor who was so loyal and so credulous. Liquidated him with no regard for his hatred of the "bluebloods," timely as it was.

The master of cunning used the scenario that had served him so well in the twenties: divide and conquer. The court that was set up to condemn Tukhachevsky, Yakir, Primakov, Putna, Kork, Eideman, and Feldman included Budyonny, Blyukher, Belov, Alksnis, Shaposhnikov, Dybenko, Kashirin, and Goryachev. Stalin liquidated them all, first the "traitors," then the "judges" (with the exception of three, it seems).

When they were trying Jonah Yakir, he demanded that Stalin be called to the court session. "Hey, Jonah," Primakov chided, "I thought you had some brains. Who do you think planned this farce if not Him?"

But the civil-war hero Yakir simply could not accept the awful truth. The day before his execution, he wrote: "Every word I say is honest. I die with words of love on my lips for the party and the country, with boundless faith in the victory of Communism." At the moment of his execution, as the curtain fell, he managed to cry out: "Long live Comrade Stalin!"

They told the Master about this. He smiled. "What a hypocrite that man was. . . ."

Who could have dreamed that the Gensek himself had planned the great executions? That he, Stalin, was directing this murderous scenario? That the "judges" and "defendants" alike were doomed?

In the winter of 1939, Corps Commander Konstantin Rokossovsky was taken to Butyrka prison. He was a convinced Communist, having joined the party in 1919 and made a record for himself as a brave soldier and able commander. In his cell, he met a prominent Bolshevik.

"Even you have ended up here, old man! What's happening? I don't understand anything. This is worse than when artillery fires on its own troops. . . . My friend, you are older than I am. Tell me, explain it to me, help me unravel it. . . . Can it be that this is *necessary* now? . . ."

Rokossovsky was lucky; those who investigated him were not so bad. As a native of Poland, he could have had the charge of spying pinned on him and been shot, but all they did was send him to a prison camp. He ended up in Knyazh-Pogost, north of Kotlas. He was released from there in 1940. His prison experiences left an indelible mark on him. He couldn't stand NKVD people around him and kept military men only as personal guards. After the war, against the marshal's own wishes, Stalin made him minister of defense for Poland. In Warsaw, Rokossovsky was the target of several assassination attempts by Polish patriots. He understood a lot of things, but he was slow to grasp the main thing—who gained from the slaughter of the military command in the 1930s.

* * *

Stalin knew better than anyone that there could not be even one spy among the commanders he liquidated. The fact that the documents planted by Hitler were skillful forgeries was not doubted for an instant by the provocateur in the Kremlin. He held back the folder of Tukhachevsky's "letters" because he did not want to risk compromising the June performance. But once Tukhachevsky had been executed, the folder of documents fabricated at the Alexanderplatz in Berlin was tacked onto the Tukhachevsky case. Stalin let the legend circulate about correspondence between Tukhachevsky and the German general staff, and this legend served him well for sixteen years.

The marshal spent two weeks on death row. Stalin sent confidants to him who called on him to repent. As always, Stalin was not satisfied with taking a person's life; he wanted to see the victim grovel. But Tukhachevsky spent his last days working. He was hurrying to finish an important work on strategy. In 1956, General Todorsky happened to read the three-hundred-page manuscript. Before his execution, the marshal wrote:

"Fascist Germany will attack the Soviet Union in the spring of 1941 with up to 200 mobile divisions."

The fact is that in Hitler's "Plan Barbarossa" the campaign was scheduled to begin in the spring of 1941. The number of divisions that took part in the offensive launched in June was 180.

Thousands of commanders were arrested in connection with the Tukhachevsky case. Military academy graduates who "had the good luck" to receive diplomas signed by the marshal were dispatched to prison in whole classes. And in less than a year, Stalin was to liquidate all the investigators and prosecutors who had fabricated the case against Tukhachevsky and the other commanders. The procedure is familiar.

* * *

True to form, Stalin interpreted the suicide of Yan Gamarnik, the head of the political directorate of the army, as the cowardly act of "an enemy who got entangled in his own web," and that is how it was explained to the people. After that, "without further ado," as the saying went, the entire top staff of the directorate, eighty-two people, were jailed. Nor did the Master forget about his beloved Red Army band. In 1937, the band musicians played in Paris. The leading musicians were arrested as soon as they returned home to Moscow, right in the railway station.

In early 1938, after liquidating 82,000 commanders (a mere trifle on the scale of totalitarian terror), Stalin could stop and catch his breath. He indicated to the few commanders who still survived (for how long?) that his thirst for blood had been appeased to a certain extent and that the mass arrests were over. Pavel Dybenko, the commander of the Leningrad military district, was echoing the Master when he assured party members at the artillery academy in a meeting at the end of January that from then on the NKVD would not arrest any member of the military without a careful investigation. Dybenko himself was seized a month after this meeting. In a forty-eight-hour period, they arrested nine hundred commanders and political workers in the Leningrad military district.

One day in February, Marshal Yegorov, who had served with Stalin throughout the civil war, came to visit the Gensek.

"You have shot all the commanders. If there is a war, there will be no one to carry out the plan for mobilization. In our division, first lieutenants have taken over the commanders' roles. We can't work this way any more. Life is impossible."

"Does that mean you've gotten tired of living?" the Master asked.

An enemy attack was the last thing Stalin was concerned about. Yegorov's fate was decided that very day.

In that period Stalin succeeded in liquidating almost all leaders who had any local importance—the Central Committee secretaries of the republics, of the districts, regions, and cities. The Central Committee had to organize cram courses to prepare new party leaders.

It was Slavin, the very one who could not bring himself to purify his soul by anathematizing the "traitors," and who happened to survive by luck, who was assigned to prepare exercises for those attending these special courses on this theme: "the leading role of the party in the Red Army command." In August 1938, Voroshilov summoned Slavin to give a report. Stalin's commissar handed him a blue folder containing a confession by the "spy" Marshal Yegorov (implicating Slavin): "Comrade Stalin warned you," the people's commissar remarked. Slavin hadn't taken the clear hint.

They helped clarify things for him in the Lubyanka, where he was taken on October 5. There, the Communist Slavin came around. As a loyal member of the party, he took the correct position toward Army Commissar Slavin, accomplice of the enemy.

Having planned a counterrevolutionary coup, could Stalin have let the commanders who had defended the revolution live? The Revolutionary Military Council of the Republic that had existed at the start of the civil war remained a constant irritant to the all-powerful Gensek. Neither he himself nor his right-hand man Voroshilov had managed to become part of that body. Now, in 1937, like a sharpshooter knocking off ducks in a row, Stalin brought down one by one all the members of that RMCR who hadn't been smart enough to die first—Vladimir Antonov-Ovseyenko, Konstantin Mekhonoshin, Vladimir Nevsky, Aleksei Okulov, Fyodor Raskolnikov, and Ivan Smilga. The last to fall was Leon Trotsky, former chairman of the RMCR. Thus the body that had led the defense of the Soviet Republic turned out to be a collection of traitors. The public was presented with the myth that it was not Trotsky, Frunze, Tukhachevsky, Yegorov, Blyukher, Raskolnikov, Mekhonoshin, Uborevich, Primakov, and Antonov-Ovseyenko who had won the civil war, but Stalin and Voroshilov.

Stalin's remarkable memory served him well. In October 1918, after the courageous assault of the Steel Division led by Dmitry Zhloba had saved Tsaritsyn, Stalin, speaking in the name of the Politburo and the Soviet government, had grandiloquently promised that the deed would never be forgotten. Zhloba later commanded a corps and an army and, after peace came, worked in the Northern Caucasus. In 1937, Stalin remembered his promise and sent Dmitry Zhloba to a dungeon in the Lubyanka.

By the end of 1938, Stalin had not left a single proven commander alive. At the head of the armed forces stood the puppets Voroshilov, Budyonny, and Timoshenko, along with some hangmen from the establishment on Lubyanka Square, such as Frinovsky (people's commissar of the navy). Beneath them were Kulik and Shchadenko, participants in the destruction of the command staff. Finally, there was Lev Mekhlis, who had managed to become an old hand in political executions (the liquidation of the command staff of the Army of the Far East was his work, his and

Frinovsky's). Stalin put him in charge of the political department of the Red Army.

That was the general staff.

A few commanders survived purely by chance.

Aleksandr Todorsky, the commander of the Fifth Corps, ended up, along with other military men of the same rank, in Lefortovo. A special "three-judge tribunal," a sort of military equivalent of the NKVD's OSOs, efficiently dispatched one corps commander after another. There were a few minutes of trial ceremony, a short deliberation, a death sentence, and in the next room the victim was felled with a sledgehammer blow to the head. The bodies were thrown into the basement, where those who exhibited excessive vitality were given the coup de grace with a bullet.

Todorsky's turn came. Luckily, one of the three judges turned out to be an officer who had served with him. He asked the corps commander, "Is that you, Aleksandr Ivanovich?"

The tribunal was thrown into confusion. They consulted together, then handed down an extraordinary sentence—fifteen years in prison.

General Aleksandr Gorbatov, author of published memoirs in which he did not fail to speak of his years in prison, was saved by Budyonny. The marshal's intervention was a unique case, but it enabled the corps commander to survive.[100]

Only Stalin could have saved Vasily Blyukher. But since Stalin had given the command to liquidate the marshal, no one could save him. The Gensek had intended to kill him in the summer of 1937, but the military conflict in the Amur region got in the way. The blow suffered by the command staff of the Army of the Far East had encouraged Japan to reassert its claims to the borderlands. So, the following summer, Japan launched an attack in the Khasan Lake region. Blyukher was still needed. But the fighting ended, and on August 18, Blyukher flew to Moscow.

At the meeting of the Revolutionary Military Council, Blyukher was criticized for the military campaign he had just conducted. He was accused of letting it drag on. Moreover, he was supposed to have allowed heavy losses of men. The Politburo members, headed by the Master, attended this meeting. For the very first time Stalin remained silent; for the first time he failed to come to Blyukher's defense. Vasily Blyukher was removed from the council and from his post as commander of the Army of the Far East.

After the meeting, Klim Voroshilov tried to smooth things over.

"Vasya, come to my villa in Sochi, take a rest. Later we will find proper work for you."

Blyukher put his savings in his wife's name.

"Now anything can happen to me. . . . Let them bury me in the earth of Volochayevka, where my heroic soldiers fought and fell."

Vasily Blyukher "rested" for a month and a half at Klim's villa in Sochi. What did he, a peasant's son, have to answer to the party for? He was the first in the country to get the Order of the Red Banner. And he had gotten three more since. There were the battles of Samara, Chelya-binsk, Tobolsk, Kakhovka, Perekop, Volochayevka.... And China—hadn't he, the chief military adviser of the revolutionary Soviet government, helped Sun Yat-sen build an army?

The marshal was arrested on October 22. In the Lubyanka, this "Japanese spy" was savagely tortured.

How many minutes does it take to get from Lubyanka Square to Theater Square in Moscow? Five? Ten? Today in the Hall of Columns at the Central House of Trade Unions, Lidia Ruslanova is performing. Her repertoire is Russian folk songs, old familiar songs. Then she begins to sing a marching song, a song of the soldiers of the Army of the Far East, Blyukher's favorite song:

> Over the hills and through the valleys
> Forward our divisions marched . . .

The singer waves a green gauze scarf, like a flag.

That was the romance of the partisan campaigns. But what about the everyday life here and now of the prisoners in the Lubyanka? The hangmen tore out one of Blyukher's eyes and put it in his palm.

"If you don't talk, we'll tear out the other."

Proof of this episode is recorded in the documents of the public prosecutor's office. With regard to the commander's final hour, only oral accounts remain. Taken to Beria's office, Blyukher lunged at the hangman and was shot down on the spot.

Years passed. After spending eight years in prison camps, the marshal's widow, Glafira Lukinichna, went to find her daughter. At the age of five, the child had been put in an orphanage. Glafira Lukinichna arrived at night at Krasnoyarsk Station in the remote Siberian town of Kemerovo. One of the local people, seeing the woman wearing a prison-camp jacket, said:

"There are a lot of hoodlums in this town. You shouldn't walk around alone. I'm going that way myself. Let's walk together."

They talked as they went along. The man accompanying her turned out to be an auto mechanic. Yes, he knew that orphanage. "Isn't that where they keep the children of executed enemies of the people?"

"The girl's father was shot."

"Pardon me, what's your family name?"

The mechanic fell to his knees in front of the widow of the murdered marshal. He embraced her ankles, which were wrapped in ragged prison-camp leggings.

The sound of an approaching vehicle. The mechanic ran out into the road and stopped the truck. The woman was carefully helped into the cab. They reached the place in the early morning.

The director of the orphanage brought in the girl. She was thin, small for her thirteen years. She hesitated a second, and then threw her arms around her mother's neck, stammering with emotion.

"Ma-ma!"

Then, as soon as she had gotten control of herself, she complained: "Mama, yesterday they took away my doll."

Suddenly, the bare waiting room darkened. The heads of curious children had blocked the windows. After so many years, the first mama. The first mama!

"KISS THE VILLAIN'S HAND"

12

In the fall of 1928, the expropriation of the peasants reached a crescendo, and the triumphant music was swelled by the exultant fanfares for the first five-year plan. The thoughts of the Supreme Maestro directing the orchestra of the Great Change turned to a section that was failing dismally to contribute to the chorus of general rejoicing—the Academy of Sciences. For a start, Joseph the Builder decided to infuse some new blood from the party into this scholarly body. He carried out what his Chinese colleagues were to call a "cultural revolution."

For almost a hundred years, since 1836, the charter of the Russian Academy of Sciences (soon to be renamed the Soviet Academy of Sciences) had remained in force. It guaranteed the scholars certain rights limiting the intervention of the authorities in the work and administration of the academy. The institution was accorded the following rights.

The right to nominate and confirm candidates for membership.

The right to publish its studies without censorship.

Exemption from postal fees.

The right to receive foreign publications without interference by the censors.

The right to procure books, equipment, and collections outside the country without interference or payment of duties.

The right to transfer academy property abroad (including manuscripts) freely.

Exemption from customs inspection at the border.

The right to its own official stamp.

Could the Gensek leave a charter like that alone? He changed the charter three times until even the last prerogative, the academy's right to an official stamp of its own, was eliminated. According to the new charter, for the first time in the history of world scholarship the "broad public" was supposed to participate in the selection of candidates. Translated into plain language, that meant the candidates were to be appointed from above. Henceforth the party apparatus was to decide who was, and who was not, a scholar.

The second step forward was the April 3, 1928, resolution of the Council of People's Commissars increasing the number of seats in the academy to eighty-five. This provided the opportunity for the selection of forty-two new members. Academician Aleksei Sobolevsky appealed to his colleagues in a letter, calling on them to save the academy from destruction. He asked them not to vote for "Marxists." Here was the only *man* in this assemblage of intrepid researchers.

Eight candidates were nominated in the humanities section. They all passed the first stage (on December 12, 1928). But in the general assembly, three of them—Abram Deborin, Nikolai Lukin, and Vladimir Friche—had an ample number of blackballs cast against them. In an emergency session, the presidium (Karpinsky, Joffe, Krachkovsky, Krylov, Oldenburg, and Fersman) decided to call another general assembly, including the candidates just elected, and to hold another vote on the three rejected candidates. The decision of the presidium was supported by Academicians Marr, Kurnakov, Platonov, Komarov, and Tarle.

In all, fifteen academicians voted for the three rejected candidates. After the declaration by the presidium and the five who had added their names to it (this took place on January 12, 1929), it became easier to solve the equation for the problem entitled "Who had dared?" There were only five whose positions were not known.

No, no matter what they say, cowardice and treachery did not begin in 1937.

In 1929, there were still some stout-hearted people. Nine academicians protested against a repetition of the voting. These included Lyapunov, Levinson-Lessing, Karsky, Lavrov, Borodin, Petrushevsky, Vladimirtsov, and Sakulin. The last three had just been elected to the academy. The ninth protester, Ivan Pavlov, became a special case. The most famous and "protected" of the lot, he proved the most stubborn. In its special illustrated feature on the academic scandal, the magazine *Chudak* discreetly left Ivan Pavlov's portrait out of its gallery of academician-oppositionists.[101] But Ivan Pavlov stood his ground. On January 17, in the general assembly, he protested sharply against the arbitrary action of the party officials. He was admonished by Platonov and Krylov. The venerable mathematician, mechanical engineer, and ship designer Aleksei Nikolaevich Krylov made this homey remark:

"What the hell, old fellow, go ahead and kiss the villain's hand."

Thirty-seven of the seventy-eight academicians were absent from the general assembly. Of those present, twenty-eight voted for the presidium resolution and nine against. There were four abstentions. On January 31, the academy petitioned the Council of People's Commissars "as an exception" and "a deviation from the charter" to grant permission for the vote to be taken again.

Molotov reported to Stalin on the situation. The Gensek brought to bear the full power of his propaganda machine. Rallies in the factories, a storm in the press, appeals—to punish, expose, forbid, reorganize. There's no denying that Stalin had acquired some experience by then in organizing campaigns of political baiting. In this chorus of newborn Black Hundreds the collective voice of the Communists at the Leningrad "Communist University" stood out.

"The obscurantist scholars should be given notice that the working class, which is advancing under the banner of the fusion of science with labor, will not hesitate to march over them for the sake of this fusion. And if the present Academy of Sciences does not deal with these obscurantists, the working class will march over the academy too."[102]

That was the voice of the future.

On February 13, the balloting was finally held. Fifty-four academicians participated. The voting had been prepared so carefully that only two or three dared cast blackballs. The ironic fate of the three unwelcome new academicians is instructive. Friche died a year and a half after the vote. It was a wise move. He avoided hearing himself denounced as a representative of the school of *vulgar sociology*. Deborin was subjected to a withering barrage of criticism, charged with "Menshevizing idealism" and failure to grasp fully the Leninist stage of philosophy. He even earned the dubious honor of being named the founder of a new "deviation"— Deborinism. Academician Lukin participated to the fullest extent of his powers in the persecution of dissidents. But this did not save him from sharing the fate of the thousands of scholars who were stricken from the rolls of the republic of knowledge in the 1930s as "enemies of the people."

All in the spirit of the times.

How could I fail to note here the words spoken by Krzhizhanovsky on that memorable day of February 13, 1929: "We are entering the Academy of Sciences as a column of Marxist dialecticians."

Dialecticians . . .

And of those who were unwilling to develop flexible, dialectical spines, five left the world of the living within the next two years—the Slavist Lavrov, the botanist Borodin, the literary scholar Sakulin, the Byelorussianist Karsky, and the Mongolist Vladimirtsov. Before all of them, however, Sobolevsky went to his grave. (This early martyrology was drawn up by I. Voznesensky. He notes that only the historian Dmitry Petrushevský maintained his independence all the way up to 1942, when he died.)

Aleksei Krylov was to become a Stalin Prize winner, a Hero of Socialist Labor, and the holder of three Orders of Lenin. He kept on nuzzling that hand until he reached a very old age. He died in 1945, eighty-two years after his birth. Krylov traveled a bitter road to reach the embrace of the villain. Under the tsar, he had held the rank of rear admiral. He saw the October revolution as a mob rampage. Krylov's son died in the civil war, fighting on the side of the Whites.

* * *

In the post-October period, the scholarly world underwent three campaigns of destruction—1917–23, 1929–31, and 1936–38. The first came when Lenin was still alive and Stalin was only gathering up the keys that would open his way to supreme power. In 1923, under Lenin, the Soviet government liquidated the traditional democratic rights of the universities (and some institutes)—that is, academic autonomy. In the previous century, the tsars had not infringed on this ancient prerogative of the universities.

After he clawed his way to power, Stalin wasted no time on niceties in dealing with any university or institute. Every year higher educational institutions turned out tens of thousands of specialists, future commanders of production, and scientists. Most of them quickly fell under the ax of the Great Terror. Did Stalin's right hand know what his left was doing? It knew. For the sake of instilling fear and servility it was possible (in fact necessary) to skim off the cream of the population. Above all, the cream.

From time immemorial, the Russian muzhik had looked with mistrust on "educated people," nearly all of whom came from noble families, after all. Stalin carefully fanned this antipathy; he encouraged the workers to hate the intelligentsia, especially the scientists. In the late 1920s, Stalin started an undeclared war against the country's scholarly community. With the help of his experienced right-hand man Molotov, Joseph the Builder turned the Academy of Sciences upside down. The period of terror proved rather short, two years in all. But the Academy of Sciences came out of it transformed. In this period, the scholars learned the science of silence and the execution of the Master's grand designs. Arm twisting was used on stubborn ones. The most rebellious were ejected. The ambitious realized that you could stay on this ship of science only at the expense of your less well adapted fellow scholars. And they acted accordingly.

"The Academy of Sciences Case"—that was the name given the case of the historian Sergei Platonov, which began in 1930. At that time our celebrated Chekists were uncovering counterrevolutionary "centers," "parties," and other "organizations" in all spheres of the economy. There were millions of "enemies of the people" in the schools and kindergartens, in the commissariats, in the hospitals, in the fire departments, and in the opera halls. Could the Academy of Sciences lag behind in this great national movement? The academicians turned out not merely to be thinking about forcibly overthrowing Soviet power; they had already formed an underground government. While awaiting the overthrow, they kept busy with ideological diversions and outright sabotage. One scholar, Vladimir Beneshevich, a professor of ecclesiastical law and a historian, had actively opposed the election of the Marxists to the Academy of Sciences. According to the prosecutor's brief, he was to be minister of religion in Platonov's cabinet. The portfolios in this mythical cabinet were assigned in Lubyanka prison by the investigator Albert Stromin.

They began rooting out academicians, along with their families. Before arresting Platonov, they grabbed his daughters and sent them to a camp. The father was deported to Saratov province, where he died two years later.

Academician Yevgeny Tarle, the author of outstanding works (he was a specialist in the history of the nineteenth century), was deported to Alma-Ata. He was one of the few "fortunate ones" granted the right to die peacefully in his own bed. After his deportation, he eventually returned to academic work and even had some of his writings published. But henceforth he was only Professor Tarle. When Stalin heard about this he feigned surprise: "Isn't Tarle an academician?" The venerable scholar was immediately restored to the rank of academician—without having to be elected or wait for a vacancy.

The new subordinate position of scholarship and scholars found its expression in the charter adopted in 1930. According to Article II, only those scholars could be elected to the honor of membership who "contributed to the socialist construction of the USSR." Article XVI posed an additional condition. Eligible for election were "those scholars who have enriched human learning with works of worldwide importance, with the exception of those who have shown a hostile attitude toward the revolutionary movement of the proletariat."

Thus there was not a single internationally recognized scholar—no matter whether English, German, Persian, or Ukrainian—who could hope for the distinguished title of member of the Soviet Academy of Sciences unless he or she publicly expressed joy at Stalin's usurpation of power. (But why was the "revolutionary movement of the proletariat" mentioned? Doesn't everyone know that, besides his other positions, Stalin was "Leader of the World Proletariat"?)

In order to ensure full control over the Academy of Sciences, Stalin introduced a new "revolutionary" system of elections. Articles XIII–XVIII of the 1930 charter denied the Academy any say in the nomination of candidates. Furthermore, in order to swaddle tightly this unruly infant left over from the old regime, the officials defined the tasks of the Academy of Sciences in the following advanced utilitarian spirit. Henceforth the Academy was to "aid in the elaboration of a single scientific method based on the materialist world views, systematically orienting the entire system of scientific knowledge toward the satisfaction of the needs of the socialist reconstruction of the country and the further development of the socialist order."

If they wanted to survive, scholars had to assume new tasks. For those slow to understand, an article was kept in the charter providing for expulsion from the academy for "activity harmful to the USSR." Anything could come under the purview of this article. How many scholars were accused of "harmful activity"? How many perished?

Get to work, old fellow, to work. Take the mathematicians. They gathered in June 1930 at their conference and—one shudders to think of it!—refused to send greetings to the Sixteenth Party Congress. And Professor Yegorov, recently removed from his post as director of the Mathematics Institute (he stubbornly refused to join the union of mathematicians), dared publicly declare: "The really harmful activity is the attempt to impose a standardized world view on scholars."[103]

This "head of the reactionary Moscow school of mathematics" was a church elder. Moreover, he thought that this was in no sense worse than being the secretary of a party bureau.

Stalin unleashed the full power of the party, the governmental apparatus, and the propaganda organs against such unrepentant scholars as Yegorov. "Wrecking activity in science and scholarship" became the most fashionable theme in the press. Everyone came under the gun—the physicist Frenkel, the biologists Gurvich and Berg, the psychologist Savin, the geologist Vernadsky, the mathematicians Bogomolov and Luzin, the Sinologist Alekseyev. Those who got it worst of all were the historians and philosophers. These "Machists," "Vitalists," "Menshevizing Idealists," "vulgar sociologists," and various "shortsighted empiricists" were branded as purveyors of reactionary theories and opponents of Bolshevik policy in the area of science and scholarship. They were accused of "ideologically clouding the minds of Communists."[104]

Somewhere we have read about something like that. Oh, yes: the protocols of the Spanish Inquisition.

The medieval inquisitors were practical people. They were not content just to anathematize the heretics. Stalin also preferred deeds to words. He set in motion the process of deporting scholars and scientists from intellectual centers and liquidating recalcitrant ones. (This actually started in 1922, with the deportation of three hundred historians, philosophers, and literary scholars from the country.) In the thirties the number went into the thousands. And they were not deported from the country but to those beauty spots beyond the Volga, beyond the Urals.

Some scholars Stalin only banished from their profession—and only for the time being. The linguists Derzhavin and Obnorsky, the physicist Lazerev, the physiologists Beritashvili and Leon Orbeli, and the agronomist Pryanishnikov found themselves without jobs. Political accusations were raised against Pryanishnikov by the "red academician" Viliams. Colleagues exposed and defamed one another. Sometimes it was hard to distinguish "our own people" from the "alien elements."

Party official, "philosopher," and "literary scholar" Ivan Luppol forced Zhirmunsky and Shishmarev out of the academy. In 1939, Luppol was "elected" to the Academy of Sciences, and a year later was arrested. The liquidator perished in May 1943.

Scholar betrayed scholar.

Divide and conquer.

Then too, after being thoroughly defamed, an academician would be dragged before the Master for the final accounting. And the Master would decide what to do with the traitor, depending on his or her authority (did he or she have an international reputation?) and usefulness (could his or her discoveries substantially increase the economic or, better yet, the military potential of the country?). The accused might be sent to a camp, deported far from Moscow, or simply denied employment.

The world-famous American geneticist Hermann Joseph Muller first came to the USSR in 1922, to attend the celebrations of the hundredth anniversary of Mendel's birth. Muller was offered a Guggenheim fellowship to work in Germany. With Hitler's rise to power, a witch hunt started against geneticists, and the neurological institute where Muller worked was dissolved. The scholar was arrested. But for the intervention of Krupp, Muller would have become a victim of the New Order: he was incautious enough to have been born with "impure" blood.

The chairman of the Soviet Academy of Sciences, Sergei Vavilov, knew the prominent geneticist personally and invited him to Moscow. Muller came. On February 2, 1933, he was elected a corresponding member of the academy in the foreign section. In Moscow, the Institute of Genetics was set up, and Muller, full of hope, occupied one of its laboratories. Shortly thereafter Muller published a book in which he acknowledged the services of the Stalin regime to science. But, failing to understand the nature of the political processes at work in the country, Muller began disputing with the Lysenko gang, exposing these ignorant "colleagues."

The fatal hour struck for Soviet human genetics. The director of the Medical-Genetic Institute, Solomon Levit, who had, unwisely, been studying the chromosomes of various ethnic groups, was declared an enemy of the people. All the prominent genetic scientists were seized and thrown into jails or camps to be exterminated. The "false science", was liquidated, the institute turned into a rest home for military men. Now no one could doubt the total victory of what was called "creative Darwinism."

Miraculously, Muller survived. He managed to get out of the country and participated in the revolutionary struggle of the Spanish people against fascism. After World War II he won the Nobel Prize.

Hermann Muller survived. But how many didn't?

Besides genetics, Stalin stripped bare and liquidated many branches of science and scholarship. The place of the exiled and liquidated researchers was taken by pseudo scientists who had understood the main formula for success in the field—"betray your colleagues before they betray you."

Here is another achievement of the Stalinshchina, the corruption of the Academy of Sciences. The physiologist Ivan Pavlov, who experimented with monkeys and dogs in his Koltushi laboratory, used differentiated diets on his experimental animals. In providing for scientists and scholars, Stalin likewise divided them into three separate categories: members of the academy's presidium, regular members, and corresponding members. The appropriate quantity and quality of caviar, meat, and desirable kinds of fish went to each group. The same with apartments, salaries, medals, villas. Against the background of the persecution of cosmopolitan "hangers on," against the background of the starvation existence of the rest of the citizenry, such benefits for scientists and scholars were quite effective.

Unfortunately, the scientists and scholars didn't just kiss the Benefactor's hand. They forged weapons for him, with which he was to enslave half of Europe.

And what did Stalin do to the ethics of scientists and scholars? In the world of scholarship, the name of Fyodor Shcherbatsky, an expert on Buddhism and the founder of an Institute of Buddhist Culture, was well known. Under Stalin this institute was destroyed, its director liquidated. His manuscripts suffered a common fate: they were appropriated by respectable scavengers among the ruins of scholarship and science. The philosopher Yan Sten, who taught Stalin the basics of logic, perished in prison. The "academician" Mark Mitin, one of the authors of the fairy-tale biography of the Leader, published Sten's work under his own name.

Openly and confidently, pirates invaded the fields of science and scholarship. The academicians and corresponding members of the academy by the grace of Stalin, the legions of fake doctors and professors, panting with impatience, rushed to steal and destroy.

If one were to make a list consisting only of the discoveries, inventions, and studies that are now known to have been stolen by the "learned" Oprichniki, it would fill a huge volume.

After unleashing the Great Terror in 1935, Stalin could no longer tolerate academic "free agents." Some sort of suspicious foreigners were traveling back and forth, writing something, thinking something, making discoveries. Who were they working for? It was useful to the world bourgeoisie to have its agents in the very heart of the Great State. Here we are, feeding them, giving them the best apartments and laboratories. Why, their very presence is having a corrupting effect on our splendid scholarly and scientific patriots. Under the treacherous tsars, foreigners swarmed around the Russian Academy in St. Petersburg. The working class won't tolerate this any more.

In short, in 1937, the meager trickle of international genius that had been reaching the Soviet Union was cut off.

Nothing and no one contributed so much to the lag of Soviet science as that distinguished academician Joseph Stalin and the Stalinshchina school. By the end of his life, this lag had become catastrophic.

"Let us drink to science—to the science we need, not to the science we do not need." In 1938, when Stalin made that not very comprehensible toast, the science to which he did not want to drink, and the scientists, no longer existed. The only ones who remained were those most quick to kiss the villain's hand.

WHO WAS SPARED

13

Ivan the Terrible, in one of his letters to Prince Kurbsky, wrote: "We are *free* to have mercy on our slaves, and we are free to put them to death."

Stalin was free to put to death or to have mercy on whomever he wished. He was the freest man on his giant latifundia. Most convenient would be to spare no one, but who would there be to work then? And who would go into raptures over the Leader's benevolence? Not only that: if you liquidate every last one of the Old Communists, the Gensek might be accused—you never know—of totalitarian terror.

Thus, necessity and caprice came into conflict. Some people had to be left alive, but the Master wouldn't have mercy on just anyone who chanced along.

In Georgia there were only two prominent party members he did not destroy—Filipp Makharadze and Mikha Tskhakaya. They had known Koba—the real one, not the fictional version—from their youth, but they turned out to be more manageable than the murdered Georgians Kartvelishvili, Orakhelashvili, and their comrades. . . .

In Kiev, Moscow, and Leningrad Stalin spared several well-known Bolsheviks. The political record of Dmitry Manuilsky, from the point of view of orthodox Bolshevism, looked suspiciously mixed: as an émigré in France he had bordered on Menshevism; in 1917 he hadn't supported the Leninist platform right away and he had been close to Trotsky. Just one of these deviations would have sufficed to have Manuilsky listed in the enemy camp. However, he had shown himself to be quite an energetic supporter of Stalin at party congresses in the twenties. After Lenin's death Stalin put Manuilsky on the presidium of the Comintern's Executive Committee. He fully justified the Gensek's confidence, exposing many a so-called opportunist. Following World War II, Manuilsky played the operetta role of minister of foreign affairs of the Ukraine. He rose to the position of deputy premier of the Ukraine and outlived the Benefactor in Chief by six whole years.

The diplomat Maxim Litvinov was a party veteran who, in contrast to Manuilsky, tried to maintain an independent stance. A figure of much higher caliber, Litvinov was not a submissive instrument of Stalin's will. This was revealed in the critical year 1939, when the Leader abruptly changed his foreign-policy course and entered into collusion with Hitler. Litvinov was removed as people's commissar of foreign affairs and nearly all of his staff was arrested. Litvinov waited, expecting arrest. He waited a year, two, three . . . but Stalin simply did not touch the disgraced diplomat.

The caprice of a despot? Undoubtedly. However, his ambition as a ruler also forced him to take other human lives into account. What would people say? In particular, what would they say over there, in the West? Opinion abroad was hardly a matter of indifference to Stalin. Then too, Litvinov might come in handy again as a diplomat.

Litvinov was one of two prominent associates of Lenin to whom Stalin graciously granted life. The other was Grigory Petrovsky.

Why didn't Stalin deal with Petrovsky as he did Lyubchenko, Kosior, and other leaders of the Ukrainian Bolsheviks? In the spring of 1939, when all of them had been imprisoned or killed, the plenary session of the Central Committee of the Communist Party of the Ukraine relieved Petrovsky of his post as chairman of the Supreme Soviet of the Ukrainian Republic, in connection with his appointment as deputy director of the Council of the Union. Everyone knew that no such post existed and that you're not appointed to the council; you're elected (formally, at least). Nevertheless, the respected senior Communist was escorted to Moscow with all the honors.

In the capital, Petrovsky found himself without an occupation. People were afraid to talk with this old comrade of Lenin's. Even Klim Voroshilov wouldn't see him. Petrovsky was awarded a pension—eighty rubles a month—and forgotten. A paltry pension, no apartment.

This member of the party's Central Committee wandered aimlessly around a city that had suddenly turned a deaf ear to him—until he ran into Fyodor Samoilov, director of the central Museum of the Revolution. From 1912 to 1914 they had represented the Bolsheviks together in the Fourth State Duma. Samoilov offered Petrovsky a job as deputy director of the museum's cleaning and maintenance department, and hoped that the Zeus in the Kremlin wouldn't come down on him for taking such a liberty. Petrovsky moved into the attic of the museum and devoted himself passionately to collecting historical documents of the revolution.

Why, when all is said and done, didn't Stalin destroy the old Leninist? Was it only out of respect for a former Duma deputy? In the confrontation with the "enemy of the people" Stanislav Kosior, arranged by Stalin with the assistance of Yezhov, Petrovsky had conducted himself bravely. Once, twenty years earlier, in exile at Turukhansk, Petrovsky had slapped Koba in the face for certain intrigues and fabrications. In prison a bullying criminal would leave one of the "suckers" alone, if the sucker dared to stand up to him. Doesn't the explanation for the strange "clemency" shown by the tyrant lie in this paradox of the hoodlum psyche?

(Some parenthetical comments on the Petrovsky case are in order here. Stalin's "clemency" had its limits. Two members of Petrovsky's family were killed: first his elder son, Pyotr, then S. A. Zager, husband of his daughter Antonina. Zager had at one time directed the Industrial Bank of the Ukrainian Soviet Republic and later had been president of the Soviet executive committee of Chernigov province in the Ukraine.

After Stalin's death and the denunciation of him at the Twentieth Congress, Grigory Petrovsky gained a new lease on life. For days on end he traveled to factories, schools, and institutes and, in discussions about Lenin and the revolution, revealed the face of Stalin, the bloody usurper, to people thirsting for truth.

Khrushchev gave the old revolutionary an apartment on the Frunze Embankment in Moscow. When Petrovsky died, in 1958, Khrushchev happened to be away from the capital. The party brass didn't know what to do—at which level, where in the hierarchy, should Petrovsky be buried? For three days the remains of the deceased lay in his Moscow apartment. Petrovsky's friends turned to Khrushchev's wife, Nina Petrovna. Instructions soon came through from the new Boss, and the body of the Old Bolshevik Petrovský was laid to rest at last in a place of honor, the Kremlin wall.)

Stalin's "benevolence" extended to several dozen senior members of the party who had not made their mark in any big way during the revolution. He needed them to create the appearance of a Leninist entourage around his person: their constant glorification, their composition—on suitable occasions—of welcoming addresses, their presence on the presidium at congresses and conferences. And the rewriting of party history. In this respect, Yemelyan Yaroslavsky proved to be an especially useful servant and errand boy.

The Gensek noticed Yaroslavsky when Lenin was still alive, brought him into the central apparatus, and entrusted him with the editing of the party's leading publications. Yaroslavsky was in charge of the "Short Course" history of the party and the short biography of Stalin. An outstanding mediocrity, Yaroslavsky displayed a rare diligence in the field of falsifying history. He combined within himself the traits of party bureaucrat and prodigious weaver of fantasies—an astonishing product of the times. To the care of this throne-room scribe and rewriter of history the Master entrusted the Society of Old Bolsheviks.

Stalin first liquidated the society, then liquidated the Old Bolsheviks. But he spared Yemelyan, spared him and honored him with the highest distinction—put him on the Central Committee at the Eighteenth Congress, in 1939.

Nikolai Podvoisky was another highly useful extra in the Stalin theater. In 1917, as a member of the military organization of the Bolshevik Party, he joined the Petrograd Military Revolutionary Committee (MRC). Podvoisky proved to be one of the most tireless careerists. At every opportunity he would sign his name on behalf of the president of the MRC, pushing the elected president, Pavel Lazimir, out of the limelight. The position of president did not at that time have any great importance. There were dozens of MRC members who signed documents for the president during October and November 1917.

Podvoisky was one of those to whom applied the saying: "Plenty of ambition—but short on ammunition." Maybe that's why he wasn't included among the Bolsheviks prosecuted by the Kerensky government.* Likewise, Stalin's poleax did not reach out to strike him. On the contrary, after all the active leaders of the October armed insurrection had perished, Podvoisky was quickly elevated to the important rank of "a leader of the revolution." They awarded him, long after the events, the titles of president of the MRC, president of the party's military organization, and first people's commissar of war. In reality, Lenin—giving in to Podvoisky's demands—appointed him deputy people's commissar on November 11, 1917.[105]

Under Lenin, from 1918 to 1924, Podvoisky did not become a delegate to a single party congress. Lenin had a great many opportunities to convince himself that Podvoisky was completely unfit for the work of leadership. The head of the government did not give him effective command of any troop units and soon insisted on his removal from the position of responsibility he held.[106]

Stalin wasn't thrown by facts and documentary evidence. He even disregarded the nervous disorder from which Podvoisky suffered. So what if all the heroes of October had turned out to be "enemies"—the "president of the MRC" was still alive and well. See, there he stands!

Encouraged by the Gensek, Podvoisky's relatives put out a series of memoirs in the genre of fantasy à la Yemelyan Yaroslavsky. The firm of Yaroslavsky, Podvoisky, and Sons—and daughters and sons-in-law and company—filled the Augean stables of Soviet historiography with such piles of dung that a legion of Herculeses would be needed to clean them out. That's apparently why those stables remain untouched to this day.

Who else did Stalin allow to die quietly in his or her own bed? The Gensek bestowed that gift upon two women—Yelena Stasova and Aleksandra Kollontai—and upon several other comrades of Lenin's. Nadezhda Krupskaya cannot be numbered among them. Her death too greatly resembles "elimination."

* * *

Power without bloodshed? It doesn't happen. And glory without blood isn't glory. But what about the great poets? They had won worldly fame without shedding anyone's blood. How did they manage that? Stalin felt a certain superstitious deference toward poets. Within limits, of course.

Osip Mandelstam, Yegishe Charents, Marina Tsvetaeva: these he put to death (Tsvetaeva went by suicide). Anna Akhmatova and Boris Pasternak: these he spared. And yet the latter two were among the most recalcitrant. Pasternak dared to refuse his signature on an appeal for the execution of the "Trotskyist dogs." And another thing. Hadn't Bukharin, that "contemptible hireling of the world bourgeoisie," extolled Pasternak at

---

*After the semi-insurrection of July 1917 for which the Bolsheviks were blamed.—
TRANS.

the First Soviet Writers' Congress, in 1934? Still, something held Stalin back from taking reprisals against Pasternak.

Vladimir Mayakovsky did himself in rather early. But if he had lived, he could not have escaped Gorky's fate. He was not suited to the role of some minor Kremlin official. But there's no point speculating. What we know for certain is that on one death list presented for the Master's approval, he struck out Lily Brik's name with the words: "We will not touch the wife of Mayakovsky."[107]

As for Gorky and how he died, one thing can be said for certain: executing him as a spy (for Italian fascism, right?) would have been far too scandalous. That was why Stalin had him removed "quietly."

Another well-known writer, Ilya Ehrenburg, remained alive, thanks precisely to his fame in Europe. A unique case: an author whose books were "arrested" (withdrawn or banned) but who was left unharmed. This fact can't be explained by Stalin's respect for the writer. The Gensek was absolutely devoid of any concept that a person has inherent worth. In fact, the slightest display of independent thought or creative individuality simply drove him wild. Ehrenburg's relatively happy fate doesn't fit into any logical framework. (Stalin also spared Sholokhov—the polar opposite of Ehrenburg in literature and in life. However, they both served the Master well.)

In 1944, when the Soviet army entered German territory, Stalin uttered with satisfaction: "Well, Ehrenburg's articles have done their job." His novel *The Storm* was recommended to the Stalin Prize committee by Stalin himself. "If such a universally known writer as Ehrenburg is in favor of Soviet power," the Master deigned to remark in private to some of his right-hand men, "that means it is strong."

At a Writers' Union discussion of *The Storm*, Ehrenburg reproached Sholokhov:

"It is impossible to be silent in these times. It is unpatriotic."

Sholokhov, who'd been on a bender as usual, answered:

"Yes, I'm not writing. That's true. And maybe it's even unpatriotic. But I donated my Stalin Prize for the construction of a kindergarten. Ehrenburg put his in his bank account. I live in Veshenskaya, in the Cossack country, while Ehrenburg has his villa in Paris."

Others took the floor and blasted *The Storm*. Then came the author's turn to speak:

"I don't know. Maybe your views are justified. But permit me to read you another opinion."

Ehrenburg read a note from Stalin:

"Congratulations on your novel *The Storm*. I wish you new creative successes and good health. Joseph Stalin."

The cannibal's compliment carried the day.

* * *

Let us recall two other polar opposites—Tolstoy and Bulgakov. Count Aleksei Tolstoy wrote a servile opus—*Bread*. Mikhail Bulgakov wrote

caustic, half-concealed satires of the dismal present. They became enemies, the court novelist Tolstoy and the great wit Bulgakov. Tolstoy tried
to bring the Organs down on the unaccommodating playwright by informing on him. As a result, Bulgakov was trounced in the press. But the Master
took it into his head to preserve Bulgakov, author of the popular play *The
Days of the Turbins*. He was also the author of the seditious play *Kabala
Svyatosh (The Cabal of the Hypocrites)*. This splended work—scenes from
the life of Louis XIV—was immediately banned. From 1929 on, for forty
years, the censorship suppressed Bulgakov's play, which dared to touch a
forbidden theme, the interrelation of power and art: what does power
receive from art, and art from power? It was a play about the dramatist
and Stalin. In the twenties Bulgakov had been able to anticipate the
evolution of the Stalinshchina, with its apparatus of power, its society of
hypocrites.

Stalin dragged the disgraced dramatist back out of poverty and obscurity and returned him to the Moscow Art Theater. But now it was: Kiss the
villain's hand. Bow down, bow down. Now, then!

And Bulgakov set to writing a play about the Leader's youth—*Batum*.
Molière was humiliated. And Bulgakov was humiliated. But his life was
spared. Thus, the Master reduced those polar opposites in literature, Tolstoy and Bulgakov, to their common denominator. One more phenomenon of those terrible times.

Among the genuine writers whom Stalin spared was Konstantin Paustovsky. Yet Paustovsky avoided complimenting the despot—a heroic action in times like those. Why did the Master have mercy on him?

Stalin also left Emanuel Lasker, the world chess champion, untouched. What was at work here, of course, was not only and not so much
the respect of the pariah for a powerful intellect. It was Stalin's reluctance
to stain his own reputation by persecuting the world-renowned grand
master. But what a paradox, really: Lasker fled from Hitler to Moscow—
into the protective embrace of Stalin.

Stalin didn't wipe out every last cultural figure, or every tenth one,
as with hostages in wartime. He acted selectively. And unlike Gogol's Viy,*
he didn't ask that his eyelids be raised, so that he could thrust a finger at
the victim. Stalin knew with his eyes closed who was next.

Present at one reception in the German embassy were actor Vasily
Kachalov, ballerina Galina Ulanova, violinist David Oistrakh, and a theater director. Several days later the director was arrested on suspicion of
espionage and convicted. The others weren't touched. The others were in
great favor with the Master.

In the realm of science and technology, repressive policy was subor-
dinated to the same "laws"—that is, the Master's whims and considerations of prestige. Stalin usually didn't touch the valuable specialists, and

---

*Viy is a fiendish creature, in Gogol's tale of the same name, who has the power to detect
a person made invisible by a sacred charm. Viy's eyelids hung down to the ground. When
they were raised, he poked the victim so that the countless monsters and demons searching
for the victim could find and destroy him.—TRANS.

when he did, he let them live and quite often returned them to their scientific work. This too was out of hypertrophied ambition.

The academicians Yevgeny Tarle and Ivan Maisky, historians, remained alive—although they had devised no new types of weapons. Maisky, moreover, bore the stigma of his Menshevik past and his participation in the Samara Committee of the Constituent Assembly, which opposed the Bolshevik government in the civil war. The repression struck them both, but they survived and returned to Moscow from internal exile.

Stalin did not arrest Ivan Pavlov, but praised and gave his protection to the world-famous psychologist, though Pavlov had never accepted the October revolution and had opposed the dictatorship of latecomer bigshots over the Academy of Sciences. Like Ivan Michurin, Pavlov became a standard display item in the publicity showcase of science "flourishing" in the USSR.

But if Pavlov was widely known in the world, having been invited to join the Swedish Academy of Sciences during the early years of Soviet rule, the physiologist Aleksei Ukhtomsky was known only as an aristocrat who had been close to the throne of Tsar Nicholas. His brother Aleksandr had been Bishop Andrei of Ufa in the Russian Orthodox Church. Aleksei Ukhtomsky did not just remain in one piece; he joined the Soviet Academy of Sciences at the very time of the pogrom against it. In 1932 he was elected a corresponding member; in 1935, an academician. Those were the years when Stalin, with Molotov's help, was wiping out physiologists in whole batches, scientists with highly satisfactory social origins and completely loyal political views—none of your Prince Ukhtomskys. Why?

Stalin had to utilize the good minds at his disposal; he couldn't let all of them have it, the way he'd have liked. It was because of this that Academician Abram Joffe came out alive, even though this world-famous physicist—something totally unheard of—had a direct conflict with the tyrant.

So any search for a political principle in the campaign of mass terror is a vain effort. Stalin's aim was simply to intimidate and crush.

But a useful person could be left to live on.

THE CASE OF THE MISSING CENSUS

14

We will begin this chapter on statistical matters with Valerian Osinsky (Obolensky), scion of an old aristocratic Russian family. He joined the Bolsheviks in 1907. Though he was only twenty years old, this revolutionary's great erudition set him apart. Over the years he had frequent disputes with Lenin, but the Bolshevik leader trusted him and after the revolution assigned him to highly responsible duties. He was made director of the State Bank, then chairman of the All-Russia Supreme Council of the National Economy (Vesenkha). From 1921 to 1923 he was deputy commissar of agriculture. In the late twenties and early thirties he continued to hold important posts—as a member of the presidium of the State Planning Commission (Gosplan), head of the Central Statistical Bureau, and then head of the Central Administration of National Economic Accounting.

In 1925, as the first chairman of the Soviet highways administration, Osinsky visited North America at the invitation of Henry Ford, Sr. Ford had, of course, introduced the Taylor system to rationalize production processes (the assembly line, etc.) and was happy to acquaint Osinsky with his vast automotive operations. At the end of Osinsky's visit, the American millionaire personally drove the Soviet representative to his ship and then presented Osinsky with the car as a gift. Back in the USSR, Valerian Valerianovich could be seen driving his Ford all around Moscow.

Under Osinsky, the Soviet motor-vehicle industry flourished. Construction began on the first Soviet auto plants: the old AMO plant in Moscow was refurbished and a new auto plant built in Gorky, under contract with Ford.

But nothing Valerian Valerianovich did pleased Stalin. Nor was Osinsky particularly eager to please the Leader: he was one of the first to comment on the disastrous state of agriculture. So Stalin sicked Mekhlis on him.

As head of the Central Statistical Bureau, Osinsky published an article in 1933 citing the disastrous decline in the number of cattle (the result of the peasants' slaughter of livestock to protest "collectivization"). Mekhlis blasted Osinsky and accused him of harmful activity, "wrecking." In 1933 you could still argue without risking your neck. But in this case there was no real argument. Mekhlis didn't try to disprove Osinsky's statistics. He just heaped lies on Osinsky's head. In *Pravda* (The Truth), of course.

Lev Mekhlis rose with terrible swiftness as one of Stalin's assistants in the early twenties; his skills lay in gathering information and writing speeches for the Gensek. In the Great Terror of the thirties Mekhlis had a hand in the destruction of hundreds of thousands of devoted party officials. During the Nazi-Soviet war, as the traveling representative of the High Command (Stavka), Mekhlis did everything he could to disrupt operations in the battle on the Kerch peninsula in 1942. His genuine wrecking activity, as an "administrative-political" overseer, cost several hundred thousand Soviet soldiers their lives.

Osinsky lived until the beginning of the war, but in prison. It was people like him whose blood fertilized the fiendish crops of the thirties. As a first step, Stalin ordered the arrest of Osinsky's son, Dmitry. In 1937 he arrested the father. In 1941 Valerian Osinsky was among those in Oryol prison who were shot in the prison yard before the city was surrendered to the Germans.

Another victim of incautious statistical reporting was Turar Ryskulov, a founder of the Communist Party of Kazakhstan. At one time he worked as a deputy to Aleksei Rykov, the Soviet premier. After investigating the situation in Kazakhstan, Ryskulov drew up an official report for the Central Committee (in 1932).

Collectivization was a genuine tragedy for the Kazakhs, a nomadic people. Not only all their sheep and horses but even their herd dogs were socialized. The Kazakhs didn't want to surrender their goods and possessions, so they slaughtered their sheep and ate the meat. Many actually died of overeating. Soon there was nothing to eat, and famine came. It was no less harsh than the famine in the grain-rich Ukraine. Ryskulov's top-secret report described the situation. To it he appended photographs documenting cases of cannibalism (not isolated cases either).

Ryskulov's concluding statement was this: "Kazakhstan began collectivization with a population of about 10 million and ended with about 8 million." (These data relate to the total losses for the period 1928–32. Allowing for the natural growth of population in Kazakhstan—approximately one million every five years—we must place the figure of three million against Stalin's account in this case. This is the Kazakhs' share in the overall total of twenty-two million slaughtered by the Peasant Fighter. It could have been worse; Stalin didn't deliberately organize a famine in Kazakhstan.)

In 1937 the Great Collectivizer reminded Ryskulov about those statistical computations that no one had asked for. The time had come to take a closer look at statistics in general, which had to be hitched to his wagon more efficiently. The ace in the hole in the Gensek's new game was the census.

The first Soviet census was taken in 1920, the second in 1926. The population figure reported then was 148.8 million. The demographers estimated the yearly "natural increase" at 2.3 percent, with the rural districts accounting for between 2.7 and 2.8 percent and the urban districts between 1.7 and 1.8 percent. (As I have said, the Soviet population was predominantly rural.)

The third census was carried out in January 1937. Stalin placed great hopes in it. To show the world one more great achievement of the land of socialism. The natural increase since 1926 should have been about 37.6 million. (Calculating simply, without compounding the percentage: $11 \times 2.3\% = 25.3\% = 37.6$ million.)

But the 1937 census results were shattering. There were only about 156 million citizens in our great socialist state after all. The increase had been only 7.2 million. A deficit of 30.4 million. How many of those deaths should be attributed to the prisons and camps and how many to the famine? It's difficult, in fact impossible, to tell.

Should the census results be announced? Wouldn't it be better to denounce them as the product of sabotage and "wrecking"? That's exactly what Stalin did. On September 26 *Pravda* published a communiqué of the Council of People's Commissars. It seems that "extremely crude violations of the most elementary principles of statistical science" had occurred in the census taking. Therefore the government was declaring the census results unsatisfactory.

The data were immediately confiscated and destroyed, but the figures were still being carried around in the heads of statistical agency chiefs. The first head to fly off its shoulders was that of Ivan Kraval, head of the Central Statistical Bureau. He had been close to Dzerzhinsky, under whom he had headed the labor and wages department of the Chief Economic Administration of the Supreme Council of the National Economy. Kraval had graduated, in his day, from the Institute of Red Professors and was regarded as a disciple of "the Bukharin school." When the time came to denounce Bukharin, however, he had been forced to join in with all the rest.[108]

All of Kraval's deputies disappeared with him. No, I'm wrong—one of them survived. Aleksandr Popov. For some reason they put off arresting him; they even sent a special commission to his home town of Yaroslavl to see if he had "alien social origins."

Aristarkh Kvitkin, head of the census bureau, was considered the best demographer in Russia. He cut a rather striking figure: hair down to the shoulders, always a cigarette between his fingers, discussing matters with staff members as he strode through the hallways of the Central Statistical Bureau building. Kvitkin was seized immediately upon delivery of the seditious census data.

Among others arrested was Ivan Balashov, secretary of the party organization at the Central Statistical Bureau. He had surprising good luck: instead of being shot he was sent to a destruction camp. The inmates of Butyrka prison were later to recall the stocky figure and the open, direct gaze of this very simple, typically Russian personality.

It's 1955. Balashov is still alive. He has outlived Stalin. The cases of Central Statistical Bureau officials who had suffered repression are being reviewed. David Bozin, a statistician who accidentally survived, is invited to the offices of the public prosecutor of the USSR. He has the opportunity to look at the records on Balashov, who has just been found totally innocent by the Military Collegium. As he looks through the final pages of the thick volume, Bozin's eyes fall on one last document, "crowning" the case: an official report that Balashov has been shot and killed. He was killed *one week* before his rehabilitation. Someone wanted him out of the way.

Thus, the 1937 census became an *un-thing*. Yet it was awkward somehow to go without a census altogether, especially in the eyes of Western Europe. The Gensek set a new census for 1939. The results of this one were more like it. His subjects numbered 170 million—a two-year increase of fourteen million.

If we recall what kind of years 1937 and 1938 were, how bountiful in death, we observe a true miracle. However, the miracle fades when set against the 1926 census. An increase of 21.2 million over a period of thirteen years is not so great. It's only a 9-percent increase instead of the 29 percent that was to be expected.

There is a man who could tell what kind of pressure was applied, with the use of "corrective coefficients," to arrive at the comforting figure of 170 million, and how the unruly child, statistics, had its locks shorn. That man is Vladimir Starovsky, who was made the new head of the Central Statistical Bureau. Statistical manipulations brought him the title Hero of Socialist Labor and made him a corresponding member of the Soviet Academy of Sciences—an example and a model for his fellow researchers.

Stalin could now be content. He had removed everyone he had to, and no one would find out about the 1937 census. But at night there was no joy in the office of the Kremlin's Caucasian mountain man.* "Hm, the comrades tell me there are some sort of statistical yearbooks being published abroad and whole institutes are at work studying the state of affairs in *my land!* As if they don't have enough of their own damn imperialist problems to worry about! . . . But statistics, figures, you can't just pick 'em off the ceiling. Yes, statistics need to be watched over—vigilantly. We'll call it 'party control.' " Thus, Stalin placed statistics under lock and key. (Let us hope there will be a time limit on this measure of Stalin's.)

Now, what was he to do about people? The number of builders of socialism had become too small. Who was going to fulfill the plan? Great designs, even majestic designs, require people to carry them out.

Of course, one thing could be done—put an end to arrests and artificial famine and give the land back to those who worked it. But that would be capitulating to the private-property element. No. The shame of the capitalistic NEP would never be repeated. The party of Lenin and Stalin would never betray the principles of Stalinist socialism.

Then Stalin had an inspiration. Why not try to increase the birth rate? It was so simple. And—as always—ingenious. But how to implement this brilliant idea? Not by actually improving living conditions for the people. Announcing further improvements at party congresses was good enough for them. Let's wish the people all the best and continue with our thoughts. Probably the best thing would be to *prohibit* something? But what?

Whereupon our Leader Most Wise made abortion illegal.

Still the birth rate didn't rise. The number of arrests rose, however—gynecologists and amateur "physicians" who dared to violate the new law. And the number of women killed or disabled, or whose health was undermined.

The war prevented an exact calculation of the losses. And brought with it new losses and new ways of playing with statistics.

*An epithet for Stalin.—TRANS.

A PARTIAL BALANCE SHEET

15

The exact number of those who died in Stalin's prisons and camps remains unknown to statistical science. At the Lubyanka, after Stalin's death, all the records relating to executed people were destroyed. Only empty folders were left, bearing the names of those who had been investigated. In the camps the whereabouts of the huge pits where millions of corpses lay were hushed up. The sites were plowed under, so that no traces could be found. And how many cemeteries in towns and villages near former campsites were leveled and covered over with new earth?

Those who did the killing have been collecting their pensions for a long time now. Ordinary workers could never dream of such hefty allowances. The hangmen cultivate roses and pear trees in their southern villas. And their grandchildren have all the diamonds they want. Who would dare to call them murderers? Statistical science is also silent about the number of highly honored citizens of this type.

Back in the twenties, of course, the prisons were not empty. But the number of prisoners had not yet exceeded the number in the tsarist era.

The following table gives the average number of prisoners in various years. The data, in which all categories of lawbreakers are included, were compiled by Professor Yevsei Shirvindt, who in 1954 was appointed head of the research department of Gulag.

1905	85,000	1912	183,000
1906	111,000	1923	65,000
1907	138,000	1924	86,000
1908	171,000	1925	98,000
1909	175,000	1926	104,000
1910	168,000	1927	122,000
1911	175,000		

Unfortunately we do not have data for subsequent years. On the other hand, we do know the size of the population in the prisons and destruction camps in the year of the great wave, 1938—*sixteen million*.

In the extreme police terror after the revolution of 1905–07—which all the textbooks describe as "bloody" and "ghastly"—the tsarist prisons generally held 170,000–180,000 prisoners. There's no denying that it was a cruel period of history.

The statistical table above leads us to other reflections as well. After 1923 a clear tendency to increase is evident for the number of prisoners. By 1927 their number had doubled. After only ten years more, however, there would be *sixteen million*. This figure should be set against the population of the country. According to the 1937 census, the Soviet population was 156 million. In 1938, figuring in the expected yearly increase, the population should have been over 158 million—that is, nearly 160 million.

And so there were roughly sixteen million prisoners out of a population of 160 million. Every tenth person. And what if we subtract the children and the elderly?

On May 30, 1978, *Pravda* reported that Uruguay had seven thousand political prisoners, one out of every four hundred inhabitants. Almost as many as in South Africa.[109] In Chile, after Pinochet's coup d'état, from 1973 to 1975, one out of every forty inhabitants was behind bars. At the Twenty-fifth Congress of the CPSU a delegate from the Spanish Communist Party stated that in his country there were now 550 political prisoners, half of them terrorists. That was in a country where the Communist Party was still banned.

The scale of Stalin's "accomplishments" is easier to grasp if one goes back into history. Under Ivan the Terrible, when the Oprichnina devastated feudal Russia, four thousand boyars perished. This happened four hundred years ago. In Paris in 1871, the "men of Versailles" shot approximately thirteen thousand Communards. In Russia in 1874, during the "summer of madness"—when the radical youth, the Narodniks, "went to the people," that is, went out among the peasants with socialist propaganda—the gendarmes arrested fifteen hundred "agitators" in the villages. This was termed the "great persecution."

During the nineteenth century the technology of destruction showed a marked tendency to expand. The twentieth century became an age of wholesale slaughter. The casualties of war rose into the millions and tens of millions. Here too Stalin introduced something new, something exclusively his own. He demonstrated to an astounded world that an internal war, against one's own people, could kill twice as many as a war with other countries.

Did Stalin give preference to any nationality? Did he show particular mercy to one? The meager statistical data indicate that his murderous appetites were not selective at all; he was an omnivore.

In Azerbaidzhan in 1937 and 1938 out of a population of 2,215,000 the Organs arrested 28,000 people, approximately one out of every thirty adults. In Georgia the corresponding figures are three times greater— 63,000, although the population (3,542,000) was only one and a half times that of Azerbaidzhan.

Thus, every twentieth adult inhabitant of Georgia fell victim to the terror. That means that Dzhugashvili-Stalin was concerned not only with the Old Communists among his fellow Georgians. The complete data for the entire period of his rule present an even worse picture—one out of every ten compatriots of the Kremlin's man from the Caucasus was either tortured or killed.

A separate monograph could be written on the statistical results of the mass terror. Take, for example, the changes in the birthrate (per thousand inhabitants) from 1928 to 1940, as in the following table compiled by statisticians.[110]

1928	44.3	1935	31.6
1929	41.8	1936	34.3
1930	41.2	1937	38.7
1931	32.6	1938	37.5
1932	32.6	1939	36.5
1933	32.6	1940	31.2
1934	32.6		

The sharp decline in the birth rate, 9 percent in 1931, undoubtedly reflected the great victory of Stalin's regime in the war against the peasants. And the famine. As for the figure of 32.6 percent in which the birth rate remained unnaturally frozen for four years—what sort of abyss was this figure called upon to cover over? (According to unofficial data, in the years 1932–34 the number of newborn infants that died was 2.5 million.)

In 1936, when the country began to emerge from the food crisis and the results of the mass terror were not yet felt in full, the birth rate gradually began to rise. But a new decline began in 1939, and in 1940 the percentage fell to its lowest point. These glaringly obvious data did not, however, prevent one of the authors of the collection from which I took these figures from coming to the remarkable conclusion that the probability of someone's dying in 1938–39 (by comparison with 1926–27) was lower for all adult groups.

* * *

In a conversation with Sergei Eisenstein and Nikolai Cherkasov the Gensek once remarked: "Ivan the Terrible and Peter the Great didn't cut off enough heads."[111]

What number would have been enough? We should look at it from the tyrant's point of view. Cutting off heads one by one is a very time-consuming process. One must draw on substantial human and material resources and exert oneself enormously. The emperor Caligula, wearying of it all, was said to have exclaimed, "If only the Roman people had but one head." The Father of the Peoples would have liked that.

In 1956 came the thaw. The Politburo asked the Organs for statistics. Here are the data that the "internal" statisticians compiled. From 1935 to 1940 the number of persons who passed through the Lubyanka and its affiliated institutions was 18,840,000. Of these, seven million were shot in prison. The rest were sent to destruction camps. (Detailed tabular data, broken down by year, were provided to the Politburo.)

Nearly nineteen million. Is that a lot or a little? One-quarter of the adult population of the country, excluding children and the elderly. Almost all of them died.

* * *

Nicholas I once said to the Swedish ambassador at a diplomatic reception, "If necessary I would order the arrest of half the nation so that the other half might remain free of infection."

Stalin came very close to carrying out the tsar's modest aspirations. The civil war and famine of 1921–22 took sixteen million lives. Stalin's pogrom of the villages and the famine of 1930–32 brought death to twenty-two million. The terror of 1935–41 claimed another nineteen million.

Still, by the beginning of the war Stalin had not succeeded in killing or sending to the camps even one-fourth of the adult population. True, every arrest was accompanied by cruel and unremitting persecution of the heretic's relatives—both old and young. But a war with tens of millions of unnecessary casualties, and after it a new wave of repression, were still to come.

* * *

"What are you complaining about? Sure, there was terror, but Stalin was simply removing the party's bureaucratic upper crust, which had been corrupted by wealth and power." You can hear such arguments today even among Old Bolsheviks. Molotov continues to spread this popular legend. In his highly qualified opinion, the repression of the thirties was "historically necessary." If so, why didn't he submit his own person to this necessity instead of just his wife and a host of innocent people?

Among Stalin's many sententious and bloodthirsty observations, one recorded by Henri Barbusse stands out: "The problem of repression may be reduced to that of finding the minimum necessary from the point of view of the general forward movement."

In 1934, when he wrote his book about Stalin, Barbusse took an understanding view of this statement by the Soviet leader. The Bolsheviks, Barbusse explained, considered it necessary to "render *some* people harmless" only out of "respect for human life."[112]

Barbusse himself was "rendered harmless" in 1935. And after him "a few" more, two or three tens of millions. Keeping it down to the necessary minimum.

Now we understand what Stalin meant when he spoke of giving Russia a mild case of smallpox to avoid a severe one.

THE ATMOSPHERE OF AN ERA

16

And so the blessings of prison life descended on Russia.

From the heights of the Kremlin hill Stalin could survey what he had accomplished. In the life and consciousness of his subjects, fear and its traditional companions—venality and submissiveness—had taken root. This holy trinity helped his subjects to crawl without hurting their knees through their trouser legs. People finally learned the art of silence. They began to yearn for the saving grace of ignorance. They came to love the lie as the only truth to which they had access. They adapted themselves to breathing lies, as though part of the air. Lying became a civic virtue. Cruelty and treachery became model forms of behavior. And a fanatical, slavish devotion to the Leader emerged as the new religion.

The terror of the civil war years produced temporary fear. But it passed, and soon no one remembered those early experiments in bloodletting. In the thirties, when blood really began to flow, it became evident that the civil war had been merely a prelude. Over Moscow by night hung smoke from the bonfires of a new inquisition. In depositories and special book collections the archives of "enemies of the people" were being burned, their letters, their poems, their portraits, their novels.

In teaching his subjects the art of silence, Stalin took from them a right that should never be taken from anyone, the right to mourn. He denied children the option of weeping at the deaths of their parents. And to him that still seemed insufficient. He forced them to rejoice at the deaths of their loved ones and renounce them publicly. Also to send greetings to our splendid Organs, to praise them and to glorify the Father of the Country. Only for things like that could the universal silence be broken.

They killed Anna Akhmatova's husband and took away her son.

> Like the wives of the Streltsy I'll howl
> Beneath the Kremlin towers. . . .

No you won't, Anna; they won't let you. They won't let anyone.

Fear became a nutrient medium, part of the atmosphere you breathed. Everyone and everything was feared. The neighbors in your building, the caretaker in the building, your own children. People lived in fear of their coworkers, those above them, those beneath them, and those on the same level. They feared oversights or mistakes on the job, but even more, they feared being too successful, standing out. At the top they also lived in fear. A party or government post was something like a smoking crater in which someone had just been killed. A newly appointed minister, Central Committee member, secretary of a provincial committee, or president of a municipal Soviet executive committee would hunch down and work away in the fresh creater in the hopes that the theory of probability would not let him down: a second artillery shell shouldn't fall on the same spot. But Stalin didn't recognize the theory of probability. In general he didn't recognize any theory. In the thirties he sent three, four, or even more officials to the executioner's block from the same post.

"Don't try to be a government minister. They get shot."

Among the first to know about the removal of some lesser leader from his post were the inmates of Moscow's prisons. This paradox is easy to explain. The investigators would remove the portrait of some Politburo member from the walls of their offices. That meant one more party big shot had joined the Lubyanka's clientele.

Stalin wasn't able to instill the full dose of fear in the upper echelons of power right away. He had to keep working at it. He established round-the-clock surveillance over all of his top-ranking associates—and their wives and children.

On one occasion Yekaterina Kalinina, the wife of Stalin's puppet president, Mikhail Kalinin, unintentionally made an unflattering remark about the Gensek. Her friend Valentina Ostroumova, who at one time had been a stenographer for party congresses and then worked as a secretary for one of the party's city committees in Siberia, nodded her head in agreement. Not only did she nod her head, but she also said something along the same lines. They were not alone. There was a third person with them. The third one informed.

Ostroumova was arrested in the lobby of the Troitskaya tower in the Kremlin. She was called to the Kremlin on some pretext or other, and when she reached there, she was taken away. At the Lubyanka they presented her with the verbatim text of her seditious conversation. At first she denied it but the investigator kept the pressure on:

"Why be stubborn? Yekaterina Ivanovna has already confessed to everything."

What could Ostroumova do, poor inexperienced thing? She was sent to the camps hard on the heels of the president's wife.

* * *

What about the pangs of conscience? Did they feel at peace with themselves? Very much so, most of them.

One morning Yakov Brandenburgsky kept staring at his hands.

"Dripping . . . dripping . . ."

"Yakov, what's wrong with you?" His wife was alarmed.

"Don't you see it? Dripping from my fingers? Blood. Dripping. Dripping . . ."

They took him away. This member of the Soviet Supreme Court was no longer in his right mind. He died in a psychiatric hospital.

* * *

"The average person is a coward," said Mark Twain. That was a truth Stalin absorbed from life, not from any book. And Joseph the Builder based his policies on that. His only problem was how to bring the average coward to the point of hysteria.

People were so intimidated they stopped using foreign words. They were afraid to gather in groups, even in groups of two. They would huddle over a matchbox looking for the swastika on the label. I saw this with my own eyes.

Post-October Soviet history can be divided into three periods.

1917–24: people are guided by their political convictions.

1925–34: convictions and fear.

After 1935: only fear.

Hunger and poverty are not the only sources of suffering. Humiliation, depression, and fear are also. The evil afflicting society merged with the psychological suffering of the individual. Life under Stalin was more frightful than death. Those still able to think kept their heads above water only through the blind instinct of self-preservation.

What about those not disposed toward thinking? They were ready to howl from hunger and fear. But in that society of "total democracy" the only one allowed to howl was the gray wolf in the forest of Bryansk. (That was a favorite joke of the camp guards.)

Fear of the implacable state machine, alienation from people and nature, helplessness in the face of evil, and constant anxiety made the builder of socialism more of a lonely, isolated figure than any Russian had ever been, even in the darkest ages of our people's history. If through some happy accident some builder of socialism avoided falling into prison, he remained in a prison of social isolation. And this happened in a society based on "collectivism."

Years passed. One victorious five-year plan followed another. The slogans, the local leaders, the names of the enemies of the people all changed. Only the suffering remained the same. But people wanted to live, to be happy, and to have those close to them happy. Instead, the all-knowing leaders assigned them the role of fertilizer for some great harvest in the future. And the builder of the future paradise was powerless in the face of the mighty machine.

Constant fear in expectation of repression—that was the hallmark of the Stalin era. Arrests became part of everyday life, something like a late-evening meal. Once people became used to it, it was hard to imagine a different kind of life. Yesterday they took my neighbor on the left, today my neighbor on the right, tomorrow they'll take me. . . . The Americans call their country the land of equal opportunity. At least that's not excessively modest. In the land of Stalin each citizen had the opportunity to jail his neighbor, if he happened to covet the other's wife, apartment, or property. No other government has provided its citizens with such opportunities.

The people took itself by the scruff of the neck and dragged itself off to prison, to labor camps, to the executioner's block. Peasant robbed peasant, spied on him, hounded him, and arrested him, held him under guard, and brought shame upon himself. The newspapers were studded with messages of repentance, denunciation, and vile abuse. . . .

On May 21, 1937, *Izvestia* published a decree of the Academy of Sciences in column one announcing the expulsion of Nikolai Bukharin from its glorious ranks, since the above-named citizen had used his position in the Academy "to the detriment of our country," and by his struggle against the party and against Soviet power had "placed himself in the ranks of the enemies of the people." And in column four of the same government newspaper we find the signature of the editor in chief, Nikolai Bukharin.

After that who would dare to say that under Stalin there was no freedom of speech? There was complete freedom. Children denounced their parents, and parents disowned children arrested for "counterrevolutionary activity." Each denounced the other. Under Stalin the number of informers approached the number of inhabitants able to read and write. Or speak. Only the infants failed to denounce. Even in the kindergartens denouncing was encouraged. Soon every second person in the country was informing. The movement became so strong that some activists appeared who were ready to seize themselves and drag themselves off to you know where.

* * *

Emma Shif was the Young Communist organizer of our section of the history department at the Moscow City Pedagogical Institute. She sat there, never rising from her chair, keeping her hands beneath the desk (holding documents of some sort), leaning forward with the upper part of her body, and went on questioning our classmate Boris Markus about his past, went on trying to pry something out of him. He had previously studied at the Highways Institute, but something had happened to him there, and now he was studying with us in the history department. What had happened? Why had he changed institutes? Why was he hiding it from the concerned public?

Outwardly Emma was calm. Despite her youth (she was only twenty-five), she knew how to hold in the ardor of her devotion to the Organs. Boris was a tall, handsome fellow and a sharp one too. He understood. The time of universal denunciation had come, the time for investigating *everyone*. So wasn't it safer to denounce someone else in advance? But he wasn't a bad person. Nor was Emma. It was simply that the times were bad. Simply that everyone had fallen in love with the system of ironclad order and discipline.

In the eyes of the terrified philistine, terror is the same as law and order, as long as he or she is not touched, naturally. Everyone votes the same way at meetings—unanimously—everyone overfulfills the plan, everyone glorifies the Leader, everyone gazes approvingly at the rectangular prisons, residential buildings and barracks, stores, schools, hospitals, and the rectangular compounds of the labor camps. And on the collars of the agents of the security police were cubes and diamonds. The rectangle, the symbol of order. And the mass graves in which millions of bodies of violators of law and order would be dumped had the same configuration. The Lenin Mausoleum likewise. The air itself was confined in rectangles, furnished with gridirons—the air, the atmosphere of an era. People lived in prison and in constant expectation of prison for so many years that they no longer noticed the prison bars.

They loved it and rejoiced in it.

Since the universal rejoicing over the victory of "socialism" needed an outlet, the Leader let the people pour out their feelings on holidays in the city squares. He had a weakness for primitive patterns, and his henchmen eagerly formed all appropriate objects into the well-practiced rectangular shape—tanks, athletes, soldiers, industrial workers, white-collar employees, veterans of the revolution, children. Red Square in Moscow—and following its example, all the city squares in the country—were transformed into centers for the mass outpouring of devotion by all the people for their Father and Teacher.

Under Tsar Paul I things were much more boring on Palace Square in St. Petersburg: on public holidays the columns would file past the tsar carrying huge shields representing the sixty provinces of the country. Under Stalin, the coats of arms of the union republics were carried past him on Red Square.

Joseph the Builder had a special passion for elaborately worded greetings. He liked all the newspapers to publish greetings from miners and tractor drivers, scientists and writers, women and children, addressed to him personally and to his stooges. The Leader also liked to observe anniversary occasions for the great names of the Russian past. Something might spill over in his honor. And usually did.

On February 10, 1937, in that year of bloodletting, a grand celebration was held in the Bolshoi Theater for the hundredth anniversary of Pushkin's death. Stalin sat in his special bulletproof box seat. All eyes were on him. The poets read their verses for him. Aleksandr Bezymensky came on stage. He cited a line from Pushkin: "Long live the sun. Long may darkness be banished."

Then he read his verses for the occasion, about what Pushkin had longed for.

> He dreamed that
> all might be free
> forever.
> Both people
> and songs
> and work's inspiration.
> . . . We've brought to life
> And embodied his hopes.

This was followed with words about brotherhood, freedom, and "our Soviet happiness." At the end came this:

Long live the party's sunlike genius!
Long live Lenin! Long live Stalin!
Long live the sun, long may darkness be banished.

During the trial of Pyatakov, Serebryakov, and other innocent comrades, the poet cursed them publicly:

Give Pyatakov his five-cent payoff.
Polish off silvery Serebryakov.*

Sasha Bezymensky had fought in the October revolution and was one of the first Young Communists. He and my father were friends. It may be that he cursed my father too in the year of his death. I don't blame Bezymensky. We were all (or almost all) blind then.

* * *

In 1934 Stalin organized a major publicity event in the Arctic. Red Square wasn't big enough. This expedition by the steamship *Chelyuskin* was known to be impossible. The vessel was old and didn't have much power; it could do nothing in heavy ice. But if the *Chelyuskin* hadn't been trapped by giant ice floes, there would have been no one for Stalin's falcons to save heroically. And there would have been one less pretext for nationwide rejoicing.

The *Chelyuskin* rests on the bottom of the Chukchi Sea. But when will the historic shame of our country be sunk? Before me is a photograph of the triumphant welcome in Moscow for the rescued explorers. Here is Otto Shmidt, head of the expedition, with his impressive beard and the smile of victory on his face. Here are the ship's captain Voronin and the party and YCL organizers . . . and who is that over on the left, on the end, in a uniform—the uniform of the NKVD? We see him in profile. He's watching vigilantly from under the visor of his service cap. And in another photograph, standing on the platform atop the Lenin Mausoleum, we see him again like a watchful shepherd guarding his little flock of Chelyuskinites.

A play by Nikolai Pogodin called *The Man with a Gun* was performed in theaters all over the country during the thirties. The play is based on an episode recounted by Lenin. An old peasant woman encountered a Red Army man. And he helped her. For the first time in her life the old peasant woman was not afraid of a man with a gun. That happened during the civil war.

The symbol of the new era, its central figure, was a man with a revolver, guarding the people's total happiness. To this glorious epoch-making hero songs, odes, verses, and plays were dedicated. He became part of our life for good, this modest, hard-working member of the investigating army, this indispensable figure in the Stalinist shadow theater.

---

*The two lines of doggerel are virtually untranslatable puns on the names Pyatakov and Serebryakov. The first name suggests *pyatak*, a five-kopeck piece; and the second suggests *serebro*, which means "silver," or possibly a piece of silver, a *serebryak*.—TRANS.

* * *

In May 1937 a Soviet expedition landed on the North Pole. The ice-raft voyage of Papanin's four heroes began. Everything had been pre-pared far in advance—the people, the airplanes, the equipment, and the provisions. Then the *Izvestia* journalists interviewed some prominent polar explorers from Scandinavia. These foreign specialists unanimously rejected the airplane as a means of transport under Arctic conditions. Their comments were published, and a few days later the Soviet airplanes headed for the North Pole. Stalin would not again dream up such a marvel-ous publicity stunt in all the fifty years fate granted him.

The expedition was thoroughly equipped—in accordance with the requirements of international prestige. High boots of imported reindeer and sealskin, suits of fur, caps of various kinds suitable for any weather. Also food concentrates of meat, poultry, and vegetables, prepared by a special institute. Specially processed butter, sour cream, pressed caviar, and chocolate. Everything was provided for. Even a special ceremonial welcome for the conquerors of the Arctic. Nothing was forgotten.

Anything, so long as the people forgot about the millions of slaves in the camps, who wore *chuni* on their feet—rubber overshoes made from pieces of automobile tire put on over cotton socks and fastened with string —and whose "food" was a ladleful of *balanda*, the watery soup served in the camps.

* * *

A gang of thieves has gathered in the most out-of-the-way corner of the prison barracks. They are trying one of their own, who has violated the thieves' code. He is unable to clear himself of the charges, and now the obliging errand boy of the criminals slips the noose over the victim's neck from behind. The victim utters a choked cry, but all around him the criminals are doing their noisy tap dance on the floorboards and slapping their hands on their thighs. Rappa-tap-tap. The dying cries cannot be heard, and the next day the camp security officer won't be able to find out anything—not who did it or why or how.

In the thirties Stalin accumulated a certain amount of experience as a stage director. He had learned to make impressive sound effects. He knew that intensifying the contrast between light and dark, between good and evil, contributed to the success of the performance. During the trials of the "despicable enemies of the people" the newspapers published ac-counts of heroic flights by Soviet pilots, "Stalin's falcons," and the no less heroic achievements of the working class.

In the investigator's office a radio loudspeaker hangs on the wall. It reverberates with the cheering of enthusiastic crowds. Before the investi-gator sits a gray-haired revolutionary soon to be a corpse, Antonov-Ovseyenko. "Listen," says the investigator. "The people are greeting our Stalinist party and its glorious Chekists. Do you hear? I got a medal be-cause of you."

Father of the People

The Tyrant's Masks

The Peasant Fighter

Stalin flanked by Voroshilov (left), Molotov, and Kaganovich, with delegates to the Sixteenth Party Congress in 1930, during collectivization.

The Builder

Voroshilov, Molotov, Stalin, and Yezhov at the Moscow-Volga Canal, where many prisoners worked and died, 1937.

Performances

Yenukidze, Kirov, Badayev, Voroshilov, and Stalin in the Kremlin, *circa* 1933.

Greeting the leader of the Chelyuskin Arctic expedition, Otto Shmidt, 1934.

Mikoyan, Molotov, Kalinin, Stalin, Voroshilov, and Ordzhonikidze at a reception for Tadzhik and Turkmen delegates, 1935.

Performances

With Voroshilov, 1935.

With Voroshilov at Ordzhonikidze's
funeral, February 1937.

With Molotov, Kaganovich,
Ordzhonikidze, and Andreyev, as
pallbearers at Gorky's funeral, June
1936.

A Few Victims

Vladimir Antonov-Ovseyenko, 1917.

Marshal Blyukher, 1937, a year before his death.

Postyshev with Stalin, probably 1933.

A Few Victims

Ordzhonikidze with Stalin at a Kremlin reception, March 1936, less than a year before the former's death.

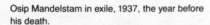

Osip Mandelstam in exile, 1937, the year before his death.

Yenukidze, Stalin, and Gorky on the steps of the Lenin Mausoleum, 1932.

Kirov with Stalin and Stalin's daughter, Svetlana, in Sochi,
August 1934, three months before Kirov's assassination.

Major-General Vasily Stalin (left), Stalin's eldest son, being
decorated by Shvernik, 1948.

Vasily Stalin, Zhdanov, Svetlana, and Stalin, in the 1930s.

The Gensek and his Politburo in 1937, the year of the great terror against the Communist Party.

His People

With Nikolai Yezhov, head of the secret police during the great terror, at the tenth anniversary celebration of the Cheka-NKVD in December 1937.

Lavrenti Beria, head of the secret police from 1939 to 1953.

His People

Matvei Shkiryatov, 1938

Lev Mekhlis, who as editor of
Pravda in the 1930s was a
leading manager of the Stalin
cult, 1940.

Stalin with Aleksandr
Poskrebyshev, long-time head of
his secretive personal secretariat,
1939.

His People

1947. Molotov and Andrei Vyshinsky, the Soviet Procurator who ran the legal system during the terror, including the Moscow Purge Trials.

Kaganovich and Mikoyan, 1935.

Malenkov, Khrushchev, and Shkiryatov, March 1950.

His People

Molotov, Stalin, Voroshilov, and Shkiryatov sometime during the great terror.

Stalin's commanders: Timoshenko, Voroshilov, Mekhlis, and Budyonny, July 1940.

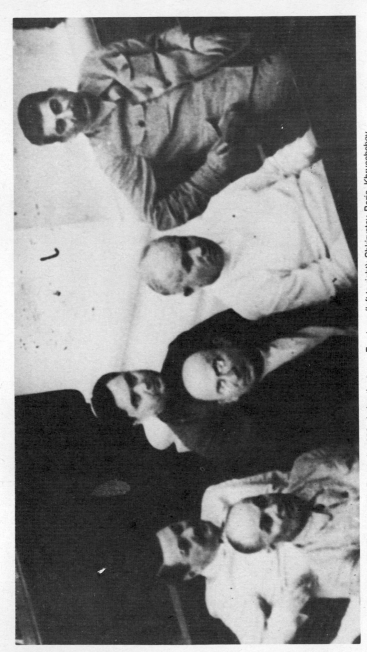

The Boss and His People in 1938, during the terror. Front row (left to right): Shkiryatov, Beria, Khruschchev, and Stalin. Back row: Zhdanov and Malenkov.

The Generalissimo

Stalin (in the white uniform) flanked by Molotov (left) and Marshal Zhukov at the Potsdam Conference, 1945.

Signing the Soviet-Polish friendship treaty, April 1945.

The Tyrant Grows Weary

Voroshilov, Shkiryatov, and Stalin, January 1949.

MOUNTAIN EAGLE

III

THE DEITY

1

In 1904 the young Bolshevik Sergei Basist was carrying on agitation among the sailors of Sebastopol. One of them asked him: "You say that under socialism everyone will be equal. But what if some bigwig like Tolstoy or someone even bigger decides he wants to take all the power for himself? What then?"

Basist hadn't expected a question like that, but he had no trouble answering it. Under socialism, he explained, leaders would be chosen in nationwide public elections. Therefore a personal dictatorship could not arise. Besides, who would let it happen? "Here you are, navy men, for example, the sons of workers and peasants. You're not about to saddle yourselves with a new tsar, are you?" The sailors laughed.

* * *

Thirty years later Alyosha Svanidze, brother of Stalin's first wife, was working as a deputy to the director of the State Bank. On Sundays it was the Gensek's habit to play billiards with Svanidze. One Monday Alyosha arrived at his office on Neglinnaya Street in a very depressed mood.

"What's wrong, did you lose at billiards yesterday?" an old friend asked him.

"What sort of monster do you think I am? If I won *one game*, he'd take it out on innocent people for the whole next week."

Svanidze was silent for a while, then spoke further.

"I just can't get over it. I couldn't sleep all night. Do you know what the Boss came out with? He chalked the tip of his cue and set it on the table. Then he said: 'You know the Russian people is a tsarist people. It needs a tsar.' That remark unnerved me completely. I couldn't finish the game. I just left. I'm not going to set foot in his presence again. I think that, without meaning to, he spoke his innermost, secret thought just then. Watch and see, he's got something in the works."

Two hundred years earlier, Russian peasants who dreamed of having a just lord and master over them proclaimed Yemelyan Pugachov tsar. They called him "Little Father," and later "Emperor."

"All that he does is just, like the deeds of a deity, for the Russians are convinced that the Great Prince of Moscow performs the Will of Heaven."

Quoting this observation of Herberstein's, the Marquis de Custine added his own comment: "I do not know whether the character of the Russian people produced rulers like this, or whether such rulers produced the character of the people."[113] The author of *Nikolaevan Russia* thought like a dialectician.

The first part of this formulation was brilliantly confirmed in the second quarter of the twentieth century, when the Soviet people began to deify a being with hardly more than an inch of forehead, and a pipe, always lit, held between two rows of black teeth. A little earlier, just before the revolution, wasn't Russia ready to see the reincarnation of Jesus Christ in a former horsethief, Grigory Rasputin? Wasn't Stalin of the same stock?

The deification of the party leader was by no means accidental. In the dawn of the Soviet era Lenin's comrades granted him the right of "unchallengeable" decisions (as Leonid Krasin put it at the Twelfth Congress). If it hadn't been for Lenin's asceticism and powerful intelligence, he too would have been ranked among the saints during his lifetime. And when the remains of the deceased leader were placed in a mausoleum in August 1924, a *precedent* was established.

The worship of leaders is akin to the herd instinct. Among the Mensheviks this phenomenon never appeared. "Leaderism" was alien to any sensible-minded socialist.

Gensek-Leader-Master-God. Such was the general line of the party's decline and the rise of the One and Only. The mutually reinforcing interplay between Stalin's aspirations and those of the "popular masses" are seen here most clearly.

The first "stormy, prolonged applause" in honor of Stalin burst forth at the Fourteenth Party Congress, in 1925. For the first time the stenographers recorded "applause swelling into an ovation." For the first time all the delegates *rose*. And after Stalin's summary they rose again. And repeated the ovation.[114]

The following year the workers of a sugar refinery presented our "iron, invincible" general secretary with a bas-relief portrait of himself carved out of hardened sugar. This "crystallization" was a harbinger of the future. On the other hand, an echo of the past was also heard at the congress: "Glory to our iron-fisted fighters—Comrades Rykov, Bukharin, Stalin, Petrovsky, Kalinin—glory!"[115] That kind of chant was not to be repeated.

In 1930, at the Sixteenth Congress, shouts of "Hurrah" rang out in honor of Stalin. The stormy applause swelled into a prolonged ovation. He was eulogized as the Leader. The vaulted ceilings of St. George's Hall in the Kremlin echoed with the slogan: "Long live our party in the person of Comrade Stalin."[116]

Four years would pass and Stalin would be dubbed "our brilliant teacher." At the close of that next party congress, Kalinin, to the roar of applause and more shouts of "Hurrah," would state: "Comrades, on behalf of the Seventeenth Congress the entire party greets its leader, Comrade Stalin."[117]

A modest beginning. Just half a year later *Pravda* would proclaim: "Today Communism is a great and unshakable material force, in the face of which the bourgeois world trembles to its deepest foundations. At the head of this great material force stands the great Stalin, the masterly leader of the Third International."[118]

Like a circus ventriloquist, the Leader began to utter eternal truths that the party repeated unquestioningly. Every word, every blessed bit of nonsense from the Gensek's lips, was immediately canonized.

Five more years went by. And what years! What was left of the party by the spring of 1939, when the Eighteenth Congress opened? A little something remained, of course. And that something was remarkable for its unexampled monolithism.

"The appearance on the speaker's platform of Comrades Stalin, Molotov, Voroshilov, Kaganovich, Kalinin, Andreyev, Mikoyan, Zhdanov, and Khrushchev is greeted by thunderous applause. A stormy ovation; all rise from their seats. From various parts of the auditorium come shouts in all the languages of the peoples of the USSR in honor of the *Great Stalin*. 'For the Leader of the Peoples, the Great Stalin—hurrah!' 'For our dear and beloved Stalin—hurrah!' 'Long live the Stalinist Central Committee!' 'Long live our leader and teacher, Stalin!' (In Ukrainian: 'Long live Stalin!') 'Long live the first marshal of the army of Communism—Stalin.' The attempts by the chair to call the session to order are drowned out by the unceasing and constantly intensifying ovations."[119]

That's how the *opening* of the congress is recorded. Is there any point in going on? We already have before us a clinically exact picture of the party's illness. And the people's.

Once Lenin was riding with his sister Maria Ulyanova in a car. A young worker jumped on the running board. "Let's go. I'll wave my cap and shout, 'Hurrah for the leader of the world revolution!' " Lenin carefully pushed the hysterical loudmouth off the running board. In telling about this peculiar event, Ulyanova remembered thinking that the man must be abnormal.[120]

Under Stalin the entire population became abnormal. And that was regarded as normal.

* * *

Of the multitude of possible secular professions Stalin had to choose one—the profession of leader. He possessed qualities that would have suited him for work as a prison guard, a police agent, or an actor, but he had to choose that other profession. At first he fastened onto the post of people's commissar of nationalities, a position dreamed up at the last minute when the Soviet government was being formed in 1917.

What capacities did he have? He knew how to intrigue, that's all. And to give incomprehensible speeches.

On April 24, 1920, an anniversary evening in honor of Lenin's fiftieth birthday was held by the Moscow party committee. Lenin himself stayed away. A reporter noted that not until after the intermission was he persuaded to make an appearance. Among the speakers were Gorky, Olminsky, Kamenev, Lunacharsky. "Now Stalin takes the floor, a Central Committee member of long standing, since the underground period, a

Georgian who doesn't know how to speak in any language. . . . The fact that Stalin *has absolutely no idea how to speak in public* makes his speech extremely interesting, even fascinating."[121]

At the Tenth Party Congress, in 1921, the delegates were openly contemptuous of Stalin's confused and empty report. They showed no respect whatsoever for the future Leader. Voroshilov was chairing the session. He had to appeal to the delegates: "I must announce that all walking around and reading newspapers and taking other kinds of liberties is totally out of order, because I have at least a dozen notes complaining that it's absolutely impossible to hear or to follow the proceedings of the congress."[122]

Stalin believed in his star of destiny, however. Hadn't he already made his way into the post of general secretary? Now a little glory wouldn't hurt either—Lenin shouldn't be the only one to enjoy that. And the Gensek surrounded himself with his own chorus of Arcadian nightingales.

No more than a year had passed after Lenin's demise when Valerian Kuibyshev proposed that Tsaritsyn be renamed Stalingrad. The rechristening of the city occurred on April 16, 1925. Tsaritsyn was blessed with the name of the man who during the civil war had sabotaged its defense so well. The following year the mining town of Yuzovka in the Donets Basin was renamed in honor of Stalin.

And so it went.

Around the same time the Old Bolshevik A. D. Sidorov made a proposal, along with a group of other comrades, to the Military Revolutionary Council of the Republic, headed by Voroshilov. A Lenin Memorial should be built in Petrograd or Samara. When the council petitioned the Politburo to that effect, the Gensek scribbled down his response: "I consider it inappropriate to establish a cult of Comrade Lenin."

Definitely. Who needs two suns in the sky?

* * *

Standing on top of the temporary wooden mausoleum erected for dear Ilyich, the Gensek was still overshadowed by the other leaders of the party. Temporarily. Soon a granite mausoleum replaced the wooden one, and Stalin appeared on it as *The* Leader. He took full revenge for having been in the position of number ten or even lower under Lenin. And for all other slights.

At the Twelfth Congress, in 1923, the Gensek, in a sly dig at the leaders of the Central Committee, compared them to the prophets of old. By 1939 those prophets were no longer among the living. And the new ones—Molotov, Kaganovich, Kalinin, Voroshilov, Mikoyan, Zhdanov, Malenkov—what kind of prophets were they? They had long since dissolved themselves into the mighty will of the Sovereign.

He, the son of a simple shoemaker, had managed to achieve what the pharaohs of Egypt had not. He was not only sole ruler of a vast country but also the supreme priest of his own cult. Stalin anointed himself as high priest, and zealously saw to the observance of his rites of devotion.

Samed Vurgun, an Azerbaidzhani poet, read his verses addressed to the Leader at a reception in the Kremlin.

He is the Bright Sun of my country; with his native-born smile
He warms the different peoples—and happy is the man
Who shakes his hand . . . and the high heavens,
Towering over the earth, envy the earth on which he walks. . . .

Samed the versifier fell on his knees and ended his ode this way, stretching his arms toward the Deity. Over his shoulder Stalin gave Kaganovich the word: "He's one of ours. See to it he gets support." The next day Vurgun was awarded an official order, given the title of People's Poet, and provided with a broad range of benefits. This represented payment for services rendered. And an advance on future work. And an invitation to other writers of odes.

In *The Importance of Being Earnest* Cecily writes admiring letters to herself. Stalin was much more modest. He was content merely to edit the biography of himself written by an obliging group of "academicians." With his own hand he inserted into the text passages such as this: "Stalin is the Lenin of today." And he selected some pointed epithets: for the oppositionists, "despicable spies"; for Comrade Stalin, "Great Leader."

Hardly noticed by his contemporaries, Stalin came to be on intimate terms, on a first-name basis, with immortality.

For three days the members of the Academy of Sciences, unable to express all at once their boundless joy over Stalin's election as a distinguished member, recounted the services of the Universal Genius of Mankind to world science. Ovation followed ovation. The fact that the Academy of Sciences managed to cope with this colossal task in just three days was an indisputable historical achievement for all its members.

The writer Leonid Leonov proposed a new system of numbering the years on the calendar—beginning with the year of His Birth. This was on the Leader's seventieth birthday. Stalin refrained from following this suggestion. It was true that his worldwide fame had long surpassed that of Jesus Christ, but it was better to leave the numbering of the years alone. From which we can conclude—to use party jargon—that on the modesty front, more solid gains were made by Comrade Stalin.

The trouble was, he was cursed with an uncomprehending population. The Leader wanted to be "simple and modest like Lenin," but the people, unable to control their boundless love and devotion, were constantly trying to eulogize him.

This was not an ordinary cult, not abstract, blind worship. Comrade Stalin was not simply the Leader; he was Leader of the World Proletariat. He was not simply a god, but a divine reincarnation of Marx and Lenin. Orthodoxy prescribed absolute nontoleration of all dissenters, of all who did not accept the cult. There was no point in trying to convert heretics. They had to be destroyed. Execution strengthens the faith. Thus, once the first batch of heretics were done away with, new ones had to be found.

The Biblical God was changeable, loving at some times, vengeful at others. At one moment He would forgive and at another destroy. The Kremlin God only hated and only destroyed. The church was satisfied with a tithe. Stalin took everything from the sons of the soil. The Bible ordered the faithful to free their slaves after seven years. The divine Stalin held his people in slavery for life. Christ endured torments to save humanity. Stalin condemned millions of people to ghastly torments for the sake of his personal power.

In one of his writings Antonov-Ovseyenko compared Stalin to a mountain eagle. This was written by a man who had devoted his life to fighting the monarchy. He wrote it sincerely, believing that fate had blessed the party by bestowing this Great Leader upon it.[123]

In *Hope Abandoned*, Nadezhda Mandelstam recalled the words of her deceased poet husband that "'they' were founding their party on authority, like a church, but that it was an 'inverted church,' based on the deification of man."[124] Along with other blind men, Antonov-Ovseyenko built this church. Many others knew what they were doing, however.

At the Ninth Party Congress, Timofei Sapronov, alarmed by the dangerous symptoms of bureaucratic degeneration in the party, bravely asked Lenin a question. (At that time it was still permissible to ask leaders questions.)

Objecting to the widespread practice of appointing local leaders, Sapronov inquired: "Who is going to appoint the Central Committee? . . . Obviously things won't go that far. But if we reach that point, the revolution will have been lost."[125]

Within less than twenty years, the Central Committee had been transformed into an appendage under the Gensek. And Stalin began unilaterally appointing the members of the Central Committee.

The work of deification was placed in government hands. It was provided with unlimited resources, and any scientist or cultural figure could be drawn into the work. Special success was achieved in the field of immortalizing the Leader's name. Two dozen cities, two provinces, a district, and a maritime bay were renamed in His honor. After the war Stalin's name penetrated the occupied countries and even embellished some foreign mountain ranges.

His ineffable profile was stamped on coins and medals. Artists labored over the narrow forehead. The image was dutifully woven into the patterns of rugs by the thin and callused fingers of Turkmen and Uzbek women. Fields were furrowed by tractors bearing the name "Stalinets."

Since he had all the attributes of divinity, how could he oppose the ardent and unquestionably sincere desire of his believers to embody his image in bronze and marble?

They were everywhere, those statues of the Leader—in railroad stations, city squares, auditoriums, village clubs, stadiums, ocean liners, schools, and kindergartens. They held sway over every city, town, and village. Their masses of gray and pink granite rose above rivers and canals, greeted subway passengers beneath the earth, and mountain climbers at the dizziest heights.

The remarkable fact is that all of this was done without special instructions from the Committee on the Arts or the Ministry of Culture. The singing of songs to Stalin became an everyday matter—in the kindergartens and schools, in the stadiums, on the streets, on stage, and at the circus —just as morning prayers are for the faithful. Then a new national anthem was composed to replace the Internationale.

> We were brought up by Stalin, to be true to the people;
> Toward great deeds of labor, he inspired our hearts.

A demonstration on Red Square. Something halfway between the festival of Athena, when the ancient Greeks brought gifts to the deity's sanctuary, and the Eleusinian mysteries. In ancient Egypt the fanatics carried sexual organs high above their heads. Stalin's subjects carried his portrait—made out of wood and metal, painted on canvas and paper. Since for some reason the Deity was unable to fly, hand-painted images of his countenance floated into the sky on balloons.

He stands on a little bench, the Gensek, canonized in his own lifetime. Holding up his hand in greeting, smiling down in his fatherly way upon the rejoicing crowds. On and on they carry his portraits before him, past the mausoleum. Better if they had done as the ancient Egyptians.

The pharaohs, you know, compared to modern rulers, were not all that hard to please. The divine Amenhotep IV had only six titles. Even the Dominican dictator Trujillo was content with twelve. For Stalin twenty-four weren't enough.

Great Leader of the Soviet People
Leader of the World Proletariat
Great Leader (simply that)
Great Friend of the Children (also Friend of Women, and the same for collective farmers, artists, miners, actors, deep-sea divers, long-distance runners, etc., etc.)
Continuator of Lenin's Work
Great Master of Daring Revolutionary Decisions and Abrupt Turns
Creator of the Stalin Constitution
Transformer of Nature
Great Helmsman
Grand Strategist of the Revolution
Supreme Military Leader
Marshal
Generalissimo
Standard-Bearer of Communism
Father of the Peoples
Father, Leader, Friend, and Teacher
Great Internationalist
Honorary Pioneer
Distinguished Academician

Genius of Mankind
Leading Light of Science
Greatest Genius of All Times and Peoples

Wherever the Kremlin miracle worker placed his hand, his name appeared—it was attached to the party, the epoch, the Constitution, the five-year plan, the banner, the tractor, airplane pilots, forestation plans, and the project for rebuilding Moscow.

The newspapers gleamed with epithets, praising a man who had killed millions and millions of his fellow human beings. Don't look for the word *cannibal* in the press of that incomparable era. To judge from a dictionary of word frequencies in modern Russian, the word *great* appears a hundred times more frequently.[126]

Soon there would not be a town left in the country, not even a group of summer cottages, without a street bearing his name. In Gagra, a small resort town in Abkhazia, there were only two streets. The one closest to the sea was called Stalin Street. What to do with the other one? It wouldn't do to give it the same name. But the Lord—that is, the Leader—is eternal. So they called the second one Dzhugashvili Street.

Lest any member of the Politburo reproach him with self-glorification, Stalin ordered his lieutenants memorialized. During their lifetimes. And soon the factories and collective farms, institutes, and—what are you talking about?—entire cities and provinces were gay with the many colors of his comrades' names. Monuments were erected to them, songs written, and postage stamps designed.

The culmination came in 1939, when the Leader completed his sixtieth year. He observed his birthday in a heathen manner, with human sacrifice—as several hundred thousand soldiers laid down their lives before the Finnish lines of fortifications.

A massive volume was compiled of the greetings addressed to Stalin from all parts of the country and all continents. There were special meetings, concerts, choral recitals, and orchestral performances. What the hell, though, he deserved this day. For on that memorable night in October 1917, amid the disorderly and discordant cries of "Hurrah," an older cry was heard: "Vive l'Empereur!" In the Bolshoi Theater two thousand people gave the sixty-year-old celebrant a half-hour ovation.

Mishka Yaponchik, renowned leader of the Odessa underworld, was also a lover of rites like these. In 1919, exactly twenty years earlier, Yaponchik had pranced down the streets of "free Odessa" on the back of a white horse, to the music of the Imperial Theater orchestra. Two thousand of "the boys" had triumphantly greeted the King of the Streets. . . .

Nevertheless, the high point in Stalin's life was not that anniversary in 1939. Was it the Eighth Congress of Soviets, which gave the people the Stalin Constitution? Or May 9, 1945—Victory Day?

No, not these . . . The high point of his life was that day in 1937 when Jonah Yakir, about to be executed, cried out: "Long live Comrade Stalin!"

* * *

The exhibit "Stalin in Soviet Fine Arts" opened in spacious pavilions along the Frunze Embankment in Moscow. I was a participant in this shameful display. By order of my superiors I had prepared an exhaustive guidebook, and I personally led hundreds of industrial and office workers, soldiers, and students of all ages through the exhibit areas. I stopped them in front of each painting featuring the Leader's image: Stalin at the rostrum, Stalin on board a cruiser, Stalin at a canal, Stalin in a locomotive, Stalin surrounded by workers, collective farmers, Young Pioneers, scientists. Stalin in his office, with a newspaper and without one. Stalin in his box seat at the theater. And everywhere his comrades in arms. I led my group to the sculpture exhibit, and everywhere saw Him, Him, Him. The same with prints and etchings. The same with the porcelain vases from the Dulyovo factory and the famous lacquered boxes produced by the skilled craftspeople of Palekh.

A year had not passed since the death of Antonov-Ovseyenko, and his son was glorifying his murderer. For me, a youth of nineteen, Stalin's name was sacred. As for the executions of enemies of the people, what could you say? The state had the right to defend itself. Errors were possible in such matters, but Stalin had nothing to do with it. He had been and remained the Great Leader. That is how I thought in those days. That was how I had been trained. What an ocean of suffering I had to go through before I saw clearly.

The summer of 1944 found me at the central transit prison of the Pechora camp complex. It was a big compound, holding about three thousand prisoners. Not having been sent out with a production column for heavy work, I was not yet enfeebled. And so it happened that I was assigned to decorate a flower bed next to a small shed, the "clubhouse," with a silhouette of Stalin. There were no flowers; they didn't grow there. The materials were gray sand, halves of old bricks, and bits of broken glass. And I supplied this modest flower bed with the divine profile.

Even in the camps the Deity remained the Deity. A vast army of guards saw to that. According to one prisoner's account (as retold by T. I. Til), camp security officers at a compound in Norilsk in 1938 uncovered the dangerous "Joffe group." Boris Joffe wrote poems. In one of them he had revealed the true Stalin, the butcher. They shot the whole group.

In the Pechora camps I chanced to meet a former stage manager from a theater. He was given ten years because he had taken a bust of the Leader backstage and turned its face to the wall. Thousands and thousands of citizens, party members and nonmembers, languished in the camps for even lesser offenses. Many ended up there on account of anecdotes. It was enough to hear one and not report it, let alone tell one yourself.

Sergei Lunin was in his fifth year of studies at the First Institute of Medicine. In the company of two classmates he told this anecdote: There's a collective farm meeting going on. The exemplary workers are being awarded prizes. The milkmaid Masha Ivanova is given a kerchief for her head. The swineherd Anna Sorokina gets a phonograph and records. And to the brigade leader Polina Roshchina goes a bust of Comrade Stalin. "Just what she deserves, the bitch," says one of Polina's friends.

Lunin was grabbed the next day. His friends had informed on him. The two of them had gone to the police together. How else? If only one of them had informed, both of the others would have been taken.

At the Lubyanka, Sergei Lunin was given special treatment. After all, he was a descendant of a famous Decembrist. Beria himself had Lunin brought to his office, lazily punched him in the face a couple of times. And had him sent off to Magadan.

BEHIND THE MASK

2

What was he really, behind the mask, deity or criminal?

"When a limited, crude, half-educated man who at first glance seems to be a third-rate fanatic but in reality is a petty tyrant, a cruel and bloody-minded lowbrow with a morbidly inflated notion of himself—when a man like that is called a god, the gods deserve a big apology."[127]

Since he lived in the West, it was easier for Vladimir Nabokov to discern the true face of the Leader beneath the thick patina. But the real Stalin was even more repulsive than he appears in Nabokov's pen portrait.

STALIN'S EARLY YEARS

An individual's character is formed, of course, in early childhood, in the first years of life. What did little Soso experience in his family, in his preschool years, and at school? Beatings, cruelty, rudeness, constant humiliation.

In the books about Stalin, even in his official biographies, why is there no portrait of Vissarion Dzhugashvili? Photos of his mother have been published, but not of his father. There is only a vague reference to his father as a "worker in a shoe factory"—that is all that is known about the male parent of the future Leader.

Apparently Stalin had weighty reasons to be reticent about his father. Various tales are told by the old Georgians about Dzhugashvili's real father. They say he was an influential tsarist official who had an affair with a young servant girl, Keto, from a peasant family in the village of Gambarsuli. Her full name was Yekaterina Georgievna Geladze. When it was no longer possible to hide the consequences of the liaison, a husband was found for Keto, Vissarion Dzhugashvili, from the village of Didi-Lilo in Tiflis province. A shoemaker's shop was bought for him, and he was married to the Geladze girl.

Today no witnesses are left, but back in 1954 the old Georgian Menshevik Nestor Menabde was still alive. Having served his second or third prison term, he was living in exile in the Krasnoyarsk region, and after Stalin's death he revealed a few things to his fellow exiles. For example, that nearly forty skilled craftsmen worked in Dzhugashvili's shoe shop. So there we have it, the petty-bourgeois social origin that would become the object of scorn and ridicule in the socialist future. And grounds for persecution. Menabde related that the master of the shoe shop took to drink and was soon killed in a drunken brawl. In the old days no one made a secret of it. But when the need arose for the Great Helmsman to have a spotless biography, the image of his stepfather was touched up, with the assistance of such experienced fabricators of party legends as Yaroslavsky and Pospelov. In the text of the official *Short Biography*, the writing of which was overseen by the Master himself, it is said that Vissarion Dzhugashvili was the son of a peasant and "a cobbler by trade, later a worker in a shoe factory."[128]

Stalin felt his parentage as a burden throughout his life. Once, in 1927, when he arrived in Tiflis and saw his mother among those waiting to meet him at the station, the Gensek exclaimed, "You here too, old whore?"

Two Communist women with long and distinguished party records served as companions to Yekaterina Georgievna. One of them, Cecilia by name, later recalled a similar episode. The women had been assigned to look after the Gensek's mother. The three of them traveled to the Leader's residence outside the city. Several miles up the mountainside from Tiflis the summer heat was less enervating. A little farther up the mountain, at a spot called Manglis, party activists studied and took courses in the summer.

Stalin's villa in Kodzhori was quite grand. In the spacious living room which connected to his office, the members of the entourage gathered. With Stalin in the office was Filipp Makharadze. Seeing his mother, Koba decided to make a "joke" at Makharadze's expense.

"What's this, Filipp, you still fucking that old whore?"

Makharadze spat and, knocking over his chair, left the office. In the living room full of guests he remonstrated: "What kind of a Gensek is that? He's nothing but a *kinto.*"

But the mischief-making *kinto*, the perennial hero of Georgian anecdotes and vaudeville shows, the fun-loving joker and prankster, is an honest-to-God angel in comparison with Koba.

Stalin never missed a chance to humiliate his mother publicly. Svetlana Alliluyeva's tale about Stalin's filial affections is nothing more than that—a fairy tale. Toward his father Soso* nursed a ferocious hatred. Vissarion Dzhugashvili, the drunkard and debaucher, used to beat this

*Georgian name for Joseph.—TRANS.

wayward son unmercifully. Soso's mother used to get it too. Among the scandal-ridden families of the town of Gori, where Stalin was born, the Dzhugashvili family was notorious.

Of course once Stalin had become the Leader and began manufacturing a legend about his childhood, he told the German writer Emil Ludwig that his parents hadn't treated him badly at all.[129]

* * *

In 1956 a former teacher at the Gori church school, the eighty-year-old Kh——li, stated that Soso was different from the other children: his was an unusually vicious character. A constant instigator of fights, he harassed and tormented the teachers with a skill that was not at all childlike. They frequently punished Soso. At home fresh beatings awaited him.

There was another violent and oppressive influence in his childhood. In those days the Russian language was made compulsory in all the schools of the Russian empire. Schoolboys caught conversing in Georgian could be beaten by their teachers, and often were.

Joseph Dzhugashvili's fate was guided by someone's firm hand. The fifteen-year-old adolescent son of a "cobbler" was accepted into the Tiflis seminary of the Orthodox church and was given a scholarship. Stalin studied there for five years, from 1894 to 1899. Even in primary school Soso displayed a passion for reading. In the seminary, where, along with the main subject, theology, ancient languages were taught, he first encountered illegal political books. In the seminary's conduct book Joseph Dzhugashvili's name was recorded thirteen times for violations of the rules. He was punished with detention a number of times for reading forbidden books. Searches, denunciations, spying, strict inspections by the monks, and a cruel rector in charge of the seminary—all this contributed to making an already vicious individual more so.

Stalin was only one year short of graduating from the seminary. The reason for his leaving (expulsion?) remains one of the many mysteries of his biography.

The dogmatism of the future general secretary had its origins in his churchly training. Also his hypocrisy, his refined artistry as a dissembler. The seminary's imprint lies on all of Stalin's actions. For example, his question-and-answer style of exposition, and his use of expressions like "the mere wafting of a hand," "would fain do," and "brothers and sisters." At the party rostrum he remained a seminarian.

In his formative years Stalin faced constant violence—beatings by his father and his teachers, compulsory and harsh methods of instruction, and oppressive tsarist laws. He experienced humiliation and oppression—national, social, and familial. He became convinced quite early in life that society's official truths were all lies, the truths taught by the church doubly so. The roots of Stalin's inexhaustible cynicism are to be sought here.

From his reading of forbidden books at the seminary the young Stalin gathered that the possibility of overthrowing the tsar was a real one. Even earlier he had absorbed a no less important fact—that a pariah like himself, who had got into the seminary only because of a good word from on high, could not go very far in the existing system. So down with the government! This proletarian truly had nothing to lose.

In his first year at the Tiflis seminary Stalin joined a Marxist study circle. This fact by itself is not very significant. However, as Joseph Ire-mashvili, one of the other members of the circle, notes, the seminarian Dzhugashvili absolutely refused to acknowledge anyone else's leadership, let along personal superiority. He tried to organize his own separate circle.[130] If we add to this the testimony of Silvester Dzhibladze, that the young Stalin had a peevish personality and was an intriguer who agitated not only against the tsar but against the local Social Democrats as well, a central trait of Stalin's personality emerges.[131]

It is extremely difficult to put together a clear picture, even in broad outlines, of the early phase of Stalin's political activity. The documents of that period have not been preserved because of the underground conditions. Minutes of meetings were not kept, and the revolutionary organizations did without membership lists. And researchers have not been able to look at the police documents. Stalin short-circuited the access routes to the archives.

Despite the absence of much documentation, the recollections of those who participated in the events—published and unpublished, written and oral—present a clear enough picture of the real Koba. No one knows what he did immediately after his expulsion from the seminary. It was not until the last days of 1899 that Joseph succeeded in getting a job as a clerk at the Tiflis observatory. And by March of the following year he had lost the job—probably the only real work he ever did in his life. The police found illegal books in the clerk's room. In the roundup that followed, dozens of Social Democratic activists were arrested. Only the "leader," Joseph Dzhugashvili, was left untouched.

The first decade of the new century was marked by an upsurge of revolutionary struggle in Transcaucasia. Koba-Stalin's part in this upsurge was quite peculiar.

1901: TIFLIS, BATUM

In 1910 S. T. Arkomed described an unnamed "young comrade" who arrived in Batum in the fall of 1901 and began to display a stubborn insistence on having absolute authority within the party organization, and to intrigue against the Tiflis committee. This person had opposed the co-optation of industrial workers into the Social Democratic Party committee in Tiflis on the grounds that the workers had not yet come up to the level of the intellectuals.[132]

Noi Zhordania's testimony is of the same sort. He reports that Koba literally exhausted the leaders of the Social Democratic movement with his intrigues and insinuations. Within the party organization Koba put together his own group, loyal to him personally.

In 1901 Lado Ketskhoveli and Abel Yenukidze were collecting money for an underground print shop. They needed from 100 to 150 rubles more. Abel made a trip to Tiflis, but Koba and Silvester Dzhibladze refused him the money. They wanted to have this project "under their own control and leadership."[133]

1902: BATUM

In the spring of 1902 Stalin went underground. In March he took part in some political demonstrations by workers in Batum. The first significant event was the arrest of thirty-two strikers on March 7. Koba was among the organizers of a protest demonstration the next day, March 8. The authorities arrested three hundred people, almost all of those who protested in front of the prison. On March 9, Koba gathered a crowd of about six hundred and led them in a new demonstration. The authorities arrested another five hundred demonstrators. In a gun battle with police, fifteen workers were killed and forty-five wounded. On March 11, Koba took part in a mass funeral for the victims of the clash.

This sequence of events might appear quite natural if it weren't for one circumstance: Koba wasn't arrested or harassed. It was only on April 5 that arrest finally came, thus saving his reputation as "leader" of the local Social Democrats.

1903

In July 1903, after fifteen months in prison, Stalin was sent to "eternal exile" in Irkutsk province. We know little about this period—his arrival in Novaya Uda, his life in exile, his receipt of some sort of "party program" from Lenin, and finally his escape in January 1904—beyond what we are told in the Leader's fabricated biography.

1904: BATUM

Once again Koba tries to subordinate the local committee to himself. And once again he fails. The embittered "Bolshevik" provokes the workers of Batum to engage in an unorganized action. Koba accuses the members of the Social Democratic committee of cowardice.[134]

The Batum Social Democrats decided to observe May Day at sea. They took rowboats for a "Sunday outing." The plan was for the boats to meet far from shore and hold a rally there. As the boats headed for the agreed-upon location people sang, joked, and kidded one another. Everything was going fine until someone made a joke at Koba's expense. He was twenty-five years old, but still held himself aloof and allowed no personal familiarities. In a cold fury, the insulted Koba tipped the rowboat over, and it sank. His "insulters" found themselves in the water. A police patrol boat came to their rescue, and that was the end of the May Day celebration.[135]

If things had gone much further, the scandals Koba stirred up would have paralyzed the Batum organization completely. However, Stalin left the city. He hadn't been able to establish a firm grip on the local committee. On the other hand, he had been able to foul things up to his heart's content.

Around this time a shift in his strategy may be observed. He had been close to the Mensheviks, who clearly predominated in Georgia in those years. Now Koba seriously began to size up Lenin. Stalin's extraordinary feel for power politics made him one of the first in Transcaucasia to perceive that Lenin was standing on the road to power.

1905: TIFLIS, BATUM, BAKU

In Tiflis Koba was the same as ever. He again became involved in maneuvers against the leadership of the RSDLP committee, in personal squabbles and anarchic escapades. On one occasion he even started a fight with Filipp Makharadze at Silvester Dzhibladze's apartment.

The local party leaders organized a court of honor to take up Koba's case and expelled him from the Social Democratic organization as an incorrigible intriguer. None of the participants in those events lived to see de-Stalinization, and no documents have been preserved. However, many party members heard about the action taken by that party court.

After a brief stay in Batum, where they knew him too well, Koba moved on to Baku.

Faronzem Knunyants (known as "Faro" for short) was then a young member of the Social Democratic Party working in St. Petersburg. She was caught and sent to prison. After her release, she returned to her native Caucasus. Mikha Tskhakaya sent her to get some propaganda literature from a member of the Baku committee, Comrade Koba. Here is her account:

> I found Koba in a small room. He himself was small, thin, and rather dejected looking. He reminded me of some petty thief waiting for a verdict to be handed down against him. He had on a dark-blue Russian peasant blouse and a tight-fitting jacket, with a black Turkish cap on his head.
>
> He treated me very suspiciously. After lengthy questioning, he finally handed me a stack of illegal books. I had my own copies of some of them, so I took only three of those he offered. My host saw me to the door, still with that guarded, mistrustful look in his eye.
>
> That evening, with the help of a school friend, I was able to attend the sessions of the high-school study circle led by Stepan Shaumyan, a leading figure among Baku socialist workers. . . . After the session Shaumyan and I left together. I decided to ask him about Comrade Koba.
>
> "Who in the world is he? I've never met a Social Democrat who made such

an intimidating and depressing impression. What a bad-tempered and suspicious person. Is he like that with everyone?"

"What are you talking about? He's an old comrade, very committed, very experienced," Shaumyan reassured me.

I soon found a place on Merkuryevskaya Street, at the home of a tinsmith who was quite old and poor. It was a common gathering place for the members of the party's Baku committee. There were thirteen of us, and we took turns chairing the sessions. Before the meetings we always talked loudly and joked. . . . It would be time to start, and Koba wouldn't be there. He always came late. Not very, but it never failed. It seemed as though clocks existed only for one purpose—for him to time his arrival just late enough. When he got there the atmosphere would change. It was not so much that it became businesslike as *strained*.

Koba would arrive with a book under his shortened left arm and sit somewhere to the side or in a corner. He would listen in silence until everyone had spoken. He always spoke last. Taking his time, he would compare the different views, weigh all the arguments, and, basing himself on the most practical and farsighted position, make his "own" motion with great finality as though concluding the discussion. Thus there was a sense of special importance to everything he said.[136]

1906: TIFLIS

At one party meeting in the capital of Georgia, Koba kept creating obstructions for Arsenidze, who was presiding. When Arsenidze rebuked him for behaving "indecently," Koba parried with the bright remark that he was not aware of having removed his trousers. Arsenidze countered that he was less like a man with his pants off than a "wanderer without drawers" (a popular expression for a streetwalker).

Stung to the quick, Koba left the room. It should be noted that the meeting was illegal and there was a guard outside. Suddenly a whistle was heard, the prearranged signal that meant police were coming. That was Koba's way of getting back at Arsenidze. And of course that broke up the meeting.[137]

1908: KUTAISI

One of the members of the underground party committee, a "Menshevik," was working in a bank. Through him the committee was able to maintain contact with other committees and receive transfers of money. This comrade also knew certain devoted and loyal Social Democrats in the city's military garrison, and in general did extremely valuable work for the party.

From Baku a representative of the party's Caucasus committee arrived. It was Koba. The members of the Kutaisi committee sat down to discuss matters of current concern with the comrade from the center. When he saw the "Menshevik" at the meeting Stalin demanded that he leave. Not only that. He should also be expelled from the committee. The underground activists spoke up in defense of their comrade. They considered him necessary to the organization. Then Koba assumed a dictatorial tone and in the name of the Caucasus committee demanded the Menshevik be expelled. The insulted comrades went to Tiflis to complain. A short time later Koba came back to Kutaisi. At a meeting of the committee he lashed out at the local party members:

"Why did you expel that Menshevik? What did you do that for?"

"Didn't you tell us to?"

"Me tell you?" Koba acted astonished. "I ordered you to hold on to that comrade because he was an exceptionally valuable activist. . . ."

One of the underground committee members present was Sergo Kavtaradze. He picked up a kerosene lamp and brought it down on Koba's head. The lamp broke, spilling kerosene all over the insolent "leader." (Once, many years later, when he ran into Sergo Kavtaradze, Stalin recalled the incident.)

The case of the expelled Menshevik was investigated by Filipp Makharadze. Koba succeeded in lining up one member of the committee, who gave false testimony on how Koba had conducted himself.

(In 1960 Kavtaradze told about his encounters with the Leader. He told about Koba's wild escapades—the May Day celebration in Batum and the things he did in Bailov prison and Kutaisi. About a dozen friends of Kavtaradze's were present—several Russians, the rest Georgians.)

1908, 1909: BAKU

In 1908 Stalin was arrested and sent to Bailov prison. In the same cell with him was a young Menshevik, Andrei Vyshinsky, son of a wealthy pharmacist. At that time Stalin's future right-hand man was receiving a large basketful of tasty foods from his parents almost every day. Koba immediately sucked up to this useful cellmate, even though he was a Menshevik. A basket of goodies was worth it.

In the fall of 1909, after escaping from exile for a second time, Stalin returned to Baku. Heated debates were going on at the time on the editorial board of the magazine *Proletary*. By a fortunate accident a letter from Stalin to Mikha Tskhakaya, "For Mikha from Ko," was preserved. In later years the Gensek was unable to destroy the letter before it was published, but he did put it on the list of proscribed party documents. In the letter Koba referred to the differences that had arisen in the party as a "tempest in a teapot." He called for unity among the opposing factions and for "smoothing over the sharp edges of Bolshevism," stressing the "good sides" of empiriocriticism and Machism. A resolution of the Baku RSDLP was drafted with Koba's participation along the same lines. The Baku committee protested against "having the supporters of the minority on the editorial board thrown out of our ranks" (point 7 of the resolution).

The year 1909 was a turning point in Koba's activities. The Caucasus had become too small for him. He wanted to try his intrigues on the leaders of Bolshevism and on Lenin. At the age of thirty Stalin was a full-fledged careerist politician.

HIS LUST FOR POWER

In studying the Gensek's gloomy interior, we cannot overlook Erich Fromm's contention that the lust for power is the most typical manifestation of sadism. For Stalin this wasn't some sort of irrational lust, some desire to become the richest man on earth. He needed power as a means of subjugating or crushing other people.

Among the innumerable figures of prominence in history it is hard to find one that so single-mindedly pursued personal power. In Stalin's hands power became a means of sadistic satisfaction and diabolic abuse of his subordinates, the party, and the people. Power meant omnipotence to him. As long as he had power, the rest—ideas (which were all phony to him) and both ends and means (for him any means were permissible)—all of that was secondary. As soon as he got his first taste of power, during the revolution, he could no longer stop himself. "Power corrupts and absolute power corrupts absolutely." This saying does not apply to Stalin; he was absolutely corrupt even before he seized power.

PROVOCATEUR

Vera Shveitser, an Old Bolshevik who served her term of exile in the Turukhansk region and who, with her husband, the Bolshevik leader Suren Spandaryan, was friendly with Stalin, recalled that many of the political exiles did not trust "Comrade" Koba and regarded him as an intriguer and provocateur.

Here is what Shveitser told Rosa Zemlyachka in 1931 in the presence of Vladimir Milyutin: "When Koba arrived in the Turukhansk region not long before the outbreak of the world war, we all decided to boycott him. He had a reputation as a confirmed careerist and intriguer, capable of any kind of anarchistic action. There was definite talk in party circles in Petrograd and Moscow about links between Stalin and the gendarmerie. Subsequently he was able somehow to win the confidence of some of the exiles. The explanation for this is probably that such Old Bolsheviks as Grigory Petrovsky and Lev Kamenev were so pure of heart themselves that they could not suspect other comrades of treachery."

In March 1917, after the victory of the revolution in Petrograd, Dzhugashvili was sent with Boris Ivanov, another exiled Bolshevik, down the frozen Yenisei to Krasnoyarsk. Along the way Koba acted as though he were in charge of the guards escorting them. He decided when they would stop, how long they would travel, where they would spend the night. When they arrived the exiles were supposed to be turned over to the military authorities. But Dzhugashvili told the guards he was going to see some "good friends," and they let him go.

Boris Ivanov's memoirs have been locked up in the safes of Yaroslavsky, Pospelov, and company. But before that happened several other people had the opportunity to read them. The veteran St. Petersburg worker Boris Ivanov had no doubt that Koba was a police provocateur.

Stepan Shaumyan came to think so too. The address of his secret apartment in Baku, where he was arrested in 1905, was known only to Koba. Shaumyan was the undisputed leader of the Social Democratic workers in Baku. Stalin could not reconcile himself to that fact and hastened to betray his rival. It was only after the October revolution that Shaumyan finally realized the truth about Stalin, and he told his comrades in Baku about it not long before he died.

The Mensheviks who ran the Avlabar underground printing press were convinced that Stalin had betrayed its location to the police, and they boycotted him as a hoodlum and careerist. Many other activists in the movement were convinced that Koba had had a hand in the destruction of the printing press. The arrests of so many Social Democratic leaders in Transcaucasia, police raids on secret meetings, destruction of the secret printing shop—in all these events Koba was invariably present behind the scenes. Koba the ambitious adventurist, the provocateur.

Several authors have cited documents that expose Stalin as a police agent.[138] Unfortunately, other documents of this type have disappeared from the archives of the tsarist police. Not all historians are inclined, therefore, to place confidence in the two or three documents that have been preserved. That is unfortunate. For this was a man capable of anything. As early as 1908 in Bailov prison, he demonstrated an astonishing ability to provoke fights and confrontations, while keeping to the shadows himself.[139]

Dzhugashvili's fellow seminary students relate that in the fall of 1899, when he was expelled from the seminary, he betrayed all the members of the socialist study group to the rector. They were expelled as a result of this denunciation by the twenty-year-old Stalin.[140] Some may prefer to attribute this to the hotheadedness of youth. But what I see in it is a totally deliberate denunciation by an incipient agent provocateur. That's what he was by nature; that was his inner make-up. That's how he was in his years of underground work. That's how he remained in the revolutionary period. His treachery on the Polish Front in 1920 was of the same order.

The acts of provocation against the party that he used so lavishly in his struggle for power, and those in the years of his full-fledged despotism —how reminiscent they all were of the young Koba. Wasn't his road to supreme power really the road of political provocation?

SEXUAL PERVERT

While in exile in Turukhansk, Koba raped a thirteen-year-old girl. This happened in the hut where he was quartered. The gendarmes brought criminal charges against the future Father of the Peoples. Dzhugashvili had to sign a statement to the effect that he would marry the girl. She gave birth to a dead child. Later came another child, who lived.

On May 9, 1951, among the photographs that appeared in a local paper showing heroes of the Great Patriotic War was one of a major with slightly slanted Tungus eyes. But this detail hardly altered the resemblance between the major and the Generalissimo.[141] Many residents of the Turukhansk region knew of Stalin's criminal behavior in exile. Later on, this story became well known in the Yeniseisk region, to which many Turukhansk residents moved in the postwar years. Stalin's illegitimate son said that his mother sometimes received money from Moscow. Soon after the war the Master sought, through MVD agents, to persuade the mother and son to come to Moscow. But they wouldn't go. What they feared was not the long trip, but some short, swift blow in Moscow.

* * *

One summer day in 1926 the Gensek was at his dacha near Moscow talking with Kaganovich. He remarked: "Listen, Lazar, they say you have a good-looking daughter. Why don't you ever show her to me?" This was said in an offhand way as Kaganovich was leaving. Lazar promised to bring the sixteen-year-old Maya with him next time he came. And made good on his promise.

After an early supper, when Kaganovich, alert as ever, sensed that it was time to go and the Master, blunt as ever, said that he wanted to get back to important government business, Lazar and his daughter made ready to leave.

"What're you taking her for? Let her stay a few days. It would be good for her to get some sun and fresh air."

The father left the daughter with the Gensek.

And she became pregnant by the Great One.

Kaganovich and his wife, Maria, were living in Kharkov, at that time the capital of the Ukraine. An old friend of theirs, Boris Fengler, a worker from Kiev, used to visit them often. He spoke warmly of Maria, but never referred to Lazar as anything but a careerist. In the fall of 1926, Fengler returned from visiting the Kaganoviches completely depressed and upset. No one had ever seen him like that before.

"What happened, Boris?" his comrades asked him.

"Maria is in despair. Lazar took Maya to stay at the Gensek's dacha and now she's pregnant. What is one to do?"

* * *

At the very end of World War II, Soviet troops captured a great many pornographic films, among other things. The sixty-year-old Supreme Commander ordered the films delivered to his headquarters. Millions of soldiers died for his glory, while he, the Illustrious One, indulged himself in the pleasures of voyeurism. General Vasily Stalin, unknown to his father, made copies of the most breathtaking films and used to watch them with his friends at air force headquarters.

COWARD

In 1931, Molotov, Shkiryatov, Voroshilov, and Kuibyshev were all on vacation at Sochi, each in his own villa. Stalin's villa stood alone, farther up the hillside. A pipeline had been laid to his villa from Matsesta to deliver healthful mineral waters for his own personal bathing. The Gensek wanted to live a long life. For the good of the people, of course.

One evening the comrades gathered at Molotov's place. His wife, Polina Zhemchuzhina, acted as hostess. According to the Georgian custom, the guests came without their wives. Everyone had arrived, and they were waiting for Himself. They heard the outside door slam. Polina went into the hallway, but just then an odd thing happened. Sparks began flying in the fusebox by the door: a thunderstorm was coming up.

Stalin saw the sparks, bolted out the door, and shouted to his driver, "Datiko, let's go!"

The guests were waiting for the Gensek, along with Molotov. But Polina, who had witnessed the scene in the hallway, didn't know what to say about the Leader's sudden disappearance.

* * *

It was 1928. Boris Volin, editor in chief of *Rabochaya Moskva* (Workers' Moscow), reached into his pocket for a handerchief during a visit to the Gensek's office. Stalin instantly reacted, grabbed his visitor's hand, and only let go after he assured himself that Volin was unarmed. When he returned to his editorial offices Volin told the head of one of the departments what had happened. Volin couldn't understand it: "What happened to him? Why was Comrade Stalin so afraid?"

He was fear-ridden throughout his life. He never parted with his pistol. He forbade others to carry weapons and insisted that all visitors be thoroughly searched.

* * *

June 22, 1941. The German invasion. "This is the end," the Gensek concluded. "Everything that Lenin created has been lost forever." That was how Nikita Khrushchev remembered Stalin's remark.

In 1964 Ivan Maisky, former Soviet ambassador to Great Britain, wrote: "From the moment that Germany attacked, Stalin locked himself up in his apartment. He refused to see anyone and would not take part in any government decisions. . . . At that critical moment Soviet ambassadors outside the country received no orders whatsoever from headquarters."[142]

Yes, Stalin revealed to the world his total helplessness and cowardice. The Greatest Military Leader of All Times never led any troops into battle. He was afraid to appear at the front lines or anywhere near gunfire. He was afraid to travel abroad. In the fall of 1943 there were plans for Stalin to meet Churchill at Scapa Flow. The Gensek did not go, on the grounds that he was extremely busy. Supposedly, he was visiting the army in the field more frequently.

During the "election campaign" of 1946 Stalin gave a speech at the Bolshoi Theater. It went well; the "voters" paid rapt attention. But as it was drawing to a close, the speaker suddenly disappeared. One moment he was at the rostrum, the next he wasn't.

The Gensek had squatted down, and from that position, almost sitting on the floor, was staring in fright up at the gallery, shielding himself behind the speaker's stand. A man with a gun was standing in full view in the gallery, aiming directly at the Gensek. A horde of bodyguards rushed to the gallery. The terrorist turned out to be a newsreel reporter, and his weapon was a captured German movie camera with a telescopic lens.

The Leader resumed his place at the rostrum and finished his speech to thundering ovations. Later, when a report was given to Stalin, he ordered that the unfortunate reporter not be punished.

THE ACTOR

It was 1924, twenty years since Faro Knunyants had first met Koba. She was the deputy director of the statistical department of the Central Committee. Stalin frequently visited this department. She always tried to remain in the background and keep her head down. She now had the last name Riesel, her husband's name, and she feared the Gensek's yellow eyes as much as ever. Her brother, Bogdan Knunyants, had been one of the true leaders of the Transcaucasian Social Democrats in the underground years. (He died in 1911.) The vengeful Gensek never forgave anyone a crime like that—being related to a genuine leader.

Stalin would always show up last for meetings of the statistical department. He wouldn't walk in; he'd just slip in through a back door and take a seat far off to one side, just as he had in the Baku days. The Gensek behaved the same way at meetings of the Orgburo and secretariat. He didn't chair the meetings. That was left to Molotov, Kaganovich, or Kalinin. Even at the dinner table at home Stalin stuck to this tactic. Many years later, at his dacha in Kuntsevo, he invariably took the first chair to the left of the head of the table. At meetings the Gensek would always speak last. And his summarizing remarks had the ring of orders from on high.

Knunyants's recollections supplement those of Boris Bazhanov. As Stalin's secretary in 1923, Bazhanov attended Politburo meetings. Stalin liked to pace at the back of the room, with his hands behind his back, silent, never commenting on the proceedings. A bystander might think he was just an orderly. After the arguments and disputes, the Gensek always sided with the majority.

Maria Joffe, widow of the prominent Soviet diplomat and revolutionary Adolf Joffe, says this in her memoirs: "We used to see Stalin often. For example, we would run into him at Bolshoi Theater premiers, in box seats reserved by the theater management. Stalin would usually show up surrounded by his closest associates. Among them were Voroshilov and Kaganovich. . . . He would behave like such an ordinary pleasant fellow, extremely sociable, on friendly terms with everyone, but there wasn't a truthful gesture in any of this. . . . In general, Stalin was an actor of rare talent, capable of changing his mask to suit any circumstance. And one of his favorite masks was this one—the simple, ordinary, good fellow wearing his heart on his sleeve."[143]

With time, hypocrisy and dissembling became second nature to him, and his masks began to show features that were organically part of him. Whether he was playing the role of the straightforward, good-hearted fellow, or the strict and serious enforcer of the party's rules, or the omnipotent Leader, Stalin entered into each part so thoroughly that he sincerely began to believe it. Nature itself blessed him with this unusual capacity to assume many roles. When he lived with the Alliluyevs, in 1912 and again in 1917, he greatly amused those around him with his comic anecdotes. He gave very skillful imitations of prominent political figures. (Anna Alliluyeva tells about this in her memoirs, published in 1946.)

By his fiftieth year Stalin had accumulated vast experience as an actor. At any rate he was convinced that he had developed sufficiently to appear on the world stage. The debut came off well. Eugene Lyons, who visited the Kremlin at the end of November 1930, was quite favorably impressed by the Gensek. And this American journalist was fairly well informed about the dictatorial nature of Stalin's rule. With Rosita Forbes, Lady Astor, and several other influential ladies, Stalin achieved even greater success, performing scenes with children and dogs and putting his "worldly charms" to use.

With showmanship worthy of circus magicians and cardsharps, the Leader gave audiences to the German writer Emil Ludwig (in December 1931) and the British master of science fiction, H. G. Wells (in 1934). They did not withstand the Master's charms either. It's true that Wells commented that the Gensek never looked him in the eye, but that was just a detail. More importantly Wells wrote: "I have never met a man more candid, fair and honest, and to these qualities it is, and to nothing occult and sinister, that he owes his tremendous undisputed ascendancy. . . . I had thought before I saw him that he might be where he was because men were afraid of him, but I realized that he owes his position to the fact that no one is afraid of him and everybody trusts him."[144]

The list of writers he fooled—and perspicacity is supposed to be one of the traits of the true writer—includes Barbusse, Romain Rolland, André Gide, and Bernard Shaw. Yes, even Shaw.

Shaw first visited Moscow in December 1931. Impressed by the lavish reception arranged for him on the occasion of his seventieth birthday, the great satirist and lover of truth never noticed such an inconsequential trifle as the famine that was sweeping away Russia's grain producers by the millions. Nevertheless, Shaw did get to the heart of the Kremlin stage manager, writing that the dictator's manners would have been perfect "if only he had been able to conceal the fact that we amused him enormously." And with aphoristic exactness he described Stalin as a cross between a pope and a field marshal. On the whole, though, Shaw retained a favorable opinion of the Leader, and in 1941 he publicly attacked Stalin's critics—so thoroughly was the great Irishman taken in by the dictator's primitive posing.

During the war years the Gensek's talent as an actor reached its height. He struck just the right note in his discussions with other heads of state. He played with great care and restraint in the presence of the perceptive and distrustful Churchill. But with the good-hearted Roosevelt he used different make-up. In the end he upstaged them both, perhaps not at every point, but in general. Stalin tried to convince everyone that he was not a dictator at all but simply the first among equals, and that all important questions concerning the state and the party were decided collectively in the Leninist manner. It wasn't easy for him to practice polite respect or to mimic refined feelings and a noble bearing. But he overcame those technical difficulties.

Here's how he carried off a pose in dealing with Ilya Ehrenburg in March 1940. Ehrenburg had despaired of finding a publisher for his novel *The Fall of Paris,* so he sent the manuscript to Stalin. Within a month the Gensek called him on the phone.

"We have never met, but I am familiar with your writings."

"I know your work too," replied Ehrenburg.

"I read your manuscript and I'll try to get it through the censorship. Let's work on it together."

You can't say that he "assumed a pose." He was posing throughout his life. The brave revolutionary, the unyielding Bolshevik, the loyal Leninist, the hard-working simple man, the valiant military leader, the candid diplomat, the Lord and Master zealously concerned for his realm, the great thinker, the good-hearted fellow, the kind shepherd, the ascetic devoted to his principles. And, naturally, the man born to be Gensek. How many different masks he wore. But always the same costume—that of the simple soldier.

An actor performs on stage for only two or three hours. Stalin was always performing, everywhere—at party congresses, at Politburo meetings, at diplomatic receptions, and at private gatherings with his intimates. Stalin devoted himself entirely to his theater, but we cannot say he performed "with passion." Passion might carry a person too far. Stalin learned to restrain his fiery temperament quite early in life. Otherwise he wouldn't have won out in the struggle for power.

The revolution, the world Communist movement, the building of socialism—for him this was all the same stage production in which the chief role was assigned to him, the role of Leader. Too bad no one ever sent him the Oscar he so richly deserved.

THE LONER

The following story was told by Pyotr Mozhnov in 1949 to his comrades in exile in the Yeniseisk region. In the thirties, while working in Baku, he heard by chance from some old workers that a man who had rented rooms to Comrade Koba in 1908 lived nearby. Mozhnov had been a secretary of the Bailovo district committee of the Young Communist League. A typical YCL leader, ardent and enterprising, Mozhnov imagined himself calling the activists together, and maybe even inviting Young Communists from neighboring districts, to hear a gray-haired old worker tell his recollections of the Leader.

They found the house where the old man lived. Mozhnov brought along some others from the YCL district committee. But the old man and his wife were not at all responsive: "We don't know anything; we don't remember anything. Someone's been pulling your leg about us." In a word, they quickly showed the Young Communists the door.

Mozhnov suspected something wasn't quite right. Why would the old Baku workers have misled him? He waited a few days, bought a bottle of wine, and went back to that dilapidated house alone. The old people greeted him quite differently this time. The lady of the house found some snacks. She had a bit to drink too. Sitting around the table, they got to talking freely.

"What did you bring that crowd of people here for? Do you think such shameful things can be revealed in front of everyone? Yes, it's true that Koba and his wife, Keto, lived here in 1908. Listen, what kind of revolutionary is he? Scum, that's what he is. A creep. Keto was pregnant then, and he used to curse her in the most disgusting way. And kick her in the belly. We tried to look after her. She came down with TB afterwards. When Koba came home drunk, he always cursed her till he fell asleep."

The old man drained his glass in one gulp and said despondently: "Listen, don't you know what kind of Leader you've got yourself? Ay-ay-ay."

Mozhnov left, completely shaken. Should he believe what they told him? Things like that you don't make up. But what about the Leader? This God? Mozhnov didn't tell anyone about it. Not until that moment in exile in Yeniseisk.

* * *

Yakov, the son of Keto Svanidze, despised his father throughout his life and died a prisoner of war of the Germans, hated by Stalin, who would not intercede to save him. Vasily, Stalin's son by Nadezhda Alliluyeva, grew up to be a debaucher and hoodlum and died an alcoholic. Stalin's daughter, Svetlana, defected to America and did a strip-tease in the Leader's (posthumous) face. What a record. The details are no secret.

Yakov's wife was Jewish. Stalin ordered her arrested for allegedly plotting against his own sacred person. In general, things didn't go well for Stalin, a militant anti-Semite. When Svetlana fell in love with a Jewish screenwriter named Aleksei Kapler, the Leader gave orders to his minister of internal affairs. Beria called Kapler in.

"The Boss gives me no rest on account of you. What do you want *her* for?"

"I don't understand your question. I'm not forcing anybody."

"Ah, the man has no pity on himself. But I'll have pity on you. I'm not going to turn you over to my investigators. They'd break every bone in your body. And pin a spying charge on you. You'd be off to a labor camp for five years at least."

Kapler was taken directly from Beria's office to a transit prison, from which he was sent to a special camp with the very first convoy. It was called the Ministry Camp.

"Well, your Kapler's turned out to be an enemy of the people," said Svetlana's father.

It was 1949. Kapler had served his time and returned to Moscow. Svetlana found him immediately. The Master had managed to give his daughter's hand in marriage to Zhdanov's son Yuri, but she couldn't forget Aleksei. Another order came down from on high, and once more Beria had mercy on Kapler, ten years' worth this time.

He did not get out until 1953, after Stalin's death.

* * *

If we make a list of all the relatives of Stalin's first wife, Yekaterina Svanidze, and of his second wife, Nadezhda Alliluyeva, it might seem that they were victims of some relentless blood feud. But no, they were all felled by a single hand.

Stalin grew from a wolf cub into a hardened old wolf. But he never tried to join a pack. He became set in his solitary ways, a loner chosen by fate. Constantly surrounded by servile attendants, he himself did not realize how alone he was. He trusted no one. And he never blotted his reputation with friendship for any of the countless servants who were his associates.

Still, we should be able to find at least one person who had something good to say about the Gensek. And we can. Lezhava-Murat, who had known Comrade Koba in Turukhansk exile. In 1921 this is what he said to his fellow workers at the Bogatyr factory: "What a clever man, what a clever man. What a head he has on his shoulders. And such a conversationalist. A fantastic, big-hearted man."

Lezhava-Murat's rapturous remarks should be credited to Stalin's account—we shouldn't paint his portrait all in black. But there is one thing: Boris Ivanov reported that this Lezhava was known to the Turukhansk exiles as a police provocateur. In later life Lezhava had access to the Kremlin. And to the Lubyanka. What information we have about his career is very peculiar.

HIS APPEARANCE

In the police archives a description of Dzhugashvili has been preserved: "An ordinary man . . . of average height and build," with a dark-complexioned, pockmarked face.[145] This "ordinary man" was able to inspire an extraordinary sense of awe in his contemporaries.

In posters, paintings, and photographs he looks almost like a giant. But he was only 163 centimeters tall (about five feet, four inches). On top of the Lenin Mausoleum he was provided with a small bench to stand on. He didn't pose for pictures with tall people. But there was no hiding his forehead. When Panteleimon Lepeshinsky, an old associate of Lenin's, wanted to find out from his wife whether it was the Gensek on the phone, he wouldn't mention a rank or a name. He simply raised two slightly parted fingers to his forehead. The family of this legendary revolutionary knew immediately who he was talking about—the man with the pithecanthropoid brow.

One arm shorter than the other (crippled in childhood), a pitted face from a childhood case of smallpox, short stature—these physical defects, together with his psychological deformities, could produce great bitterness, which under appropriate circumstances could develop into extreme viciousness. And that is what happened.

HIS TEETH

Mikhail Metalikov, head of the medical services division of the Kremlin, complained to his comrades once in the spring of 1931: "What can I do about Comrade Stalin? His teeth are in terrible condition—black, rotten, ingrown. His mouth smells of decay. No matter how much we ask him, he won't agree to have a dental surgeon attend him. He refuses even to have the plaque removed."

Metalikov sought the advice of Abel Yenukidze, who oversaw the work of the medical services on behalf of the leadership. They discussed the problem with Ordzhonikidze and decided that as soon as the Gensek went to Sochi for a vacation, they would send to his villa in Zenzinovka a cook who had fantastic teeth. Whenever the Leader sat down to dinner, the cook could brag about his teeth and tell what a remarkable dentist he had in Moscow.

When the Gensek came back from Sochi, Metalikov called in the cook. The man swore that he had praised his dentist in front of Stalin every day. And so, before the Gensek could cool down, they sent the dental surgeon to his home. But it didn't work. Stalin absolutely refused to accept his services.

Several years later, in 1937, Abel Yenukidze was branded an enemy of the people and accused of all possible and impossible sins. And since he had been in charge of the medical services, Metalikov had to go too. On what grounds?

Stalin was not afraid of dirty work. He personally took a hand in all sorts of provocations. At the next Politburo session, after all the points on the agenda had been discussed, the Master declared: "I have learned that our respected comrade Rykov was forced to stand in line waiting for a doctor at the Kremlin polyclinic for a full hour. Why was this? Who is to blame? It isn't right to treat him this way. After all, he is a former member of the Politburo. I propose that a party commission look into this situation."

The commission was headed by Naum Rabichev, deputy head of the agitation and propaganda department of the Central Committee. The guilty party was of course found at once—Metalikov. He was removed from his post. And, naturally, that was followed by prison and all the rest.

The Gensek thus killed three birds with one stone. He demonstrated his sensitivity and concern for the disgraced Rykov, he got rid of Yenukidze's appointee, and he purged the medical services at the same time.

A fitting end to the story of the Leader's teeth.

HIS VULGARITY

In July 1917 Zhenya Yegorova was working at the office of the party's Vyborg district committee in Petrograd. There weren't enough people to do everything, and she spent almost all her time there. One day she closed the office and went to lunch as usual. When she came back she found someone she didn't know standing in the doorway. Those were troubled times, and Yegorova was on her guard: "Excuse me. Did you want to see someone?" The visitor didn't reply. She opened the office. The stranger followed her in and headed straight for the desk.

"Who are you? I didn't let you in."

Comrade Koba (it was him, of course) shoved her rudely out of the way. But she was a big, solidly built woman and she knew how to stand up for herself. A fight started.

It turned out that Central Committee member Stalin needed a quiet place to look over some materials for *Pravda*. And here some woman was getting in the way and demanding his name.

In the emerging years of Stalin's dictatorship, 1917–29, Yegorova spoke out against Zinoviev and the other oppositionists. And energetically supported the Gensek. She became a prominent party official in charge of the Central Committee's women's department. In 1937 Zhenya Yegorova was one of the first whom Stalin killed.

* * *

Early in June 1926 Stalin arrived in Tiflis along with Mikoyan. They stopped at Sergo Ordzhonikidze's apartment. Guests gathered; there was drinking, eating, singing, and the Gensek sang a very filthy ditty. Women were present, including Maria Orakhelashvili, who had been brought up in the best European tradition. Sergo's wife, Zinaida, asked that the words be repeated, but the man of the house said no. Finally he whispered something in his wife's ear. Her face turned scarlet.

* * *

Shortly after the war Stalin gathered twelve of his marshals at his home. Svetlana was at the table too, but now and then she stepped out to the kitchen for something. After a round of toasts, satiated with all the deference and servility of his marshals, the Generalissimo said: "Well, my friends, I bet you don't know who's fucking her now. . . ."

Svetlana leaped up and left the room, pursued by her father's obscene laughter.[146]

He was crude and vulgar by nature and by conviction, and remained that way to his very last day. Those who visited the Gensek's office in early 1953 remember the chamberpot he had on the floor by the wall. The Master would use it in front of visitors, his aides, or his female stenographer.[147]

HIS BOOTS

At one time in the late twenties, when Stalin was on vacation in Gagra, he had two party officials for dinner. The host went out into the garden with his guests and led them among his sweet-smelling roses. The villa was on a hillside above a canyon formed by a small river, the Tsikherva. At the gate, as they were taking their leave, one of the guests commented: "Joseph Vissarionovich, it's so hot, but you're still wearing boots. How can you stand it?"

In truth, his lightweight tussore suit was quite out of keeping with the black boots.

"What can I say?" the Gensek responded. "Boots are really comfortable things. And useful. You can kick someone in the head with them—so hard he'll never find all his teeth."

And he burst out laughing.

His boots were not just a passing costume fad or just a way of recalling the civil war years. His boots were a symbol of his life, a vital detail of his portrait.

In Baku in 1908, it was with his boots that Koba knocked his pregnant wife, Keto, around.

* * *

In 1918 the government moved from Petrograd to Moscow. When he moved into his Kremlin apartment Stalin found a large mirror in the entrance hall. "What's a mirror here for? We don't need these rich-folks' things." And he smashed the glass with his boot.[148]

* * *

The Master gave his son Vasily quite an unusual upbringing. Vaska used to goof off at school, but the teachers didn't dare give him bad marks. One day the Gensek came to school and asked that his son be treated more strictly. At home he would knock the boy down and let him have it with his boots—his boots. This happened before his daughter's very eyes.

* * *

On December 2, 1934, it was with a kick of his boot that the Gensek sent Leonid Nikolaev sprawling.

* * *

The Leader changed out of his boots only once. When he awarded himself the title of Generalissimo, he put on a military uniform with stars and other regalia and had himself photographed in the middle of a large group of military officials.

There he sits between Marshal Zhukov and Marshal Tolbukhin, with his legs wide apart, squinting picturesquely, with a diamond star just below his flabby double chin. Thus he remained, a *kinto* from the streets of Georgia, despite the fact that he was Generalissimo Stalin, the conqueror of half of Europe.

The laced shoes that he put on for the occasion didn't change a thing. Akhmatova's lines unavoidably come to mind:

> And innocent Russia grimaced
> Beneath the bloody boots
> And the wheels of the Black Marias.

CRIMINAL

The portrait of the tyrant is drawing near completion. Intriguer and provocateur, petty trader and demagogue, potentate and butcher, actor and hoodlum—his was a many-sided character. And at the same time quite primitive. For no matter in which aspect he appeared before the public, he remained a criminal. That was the essence. Everything else was stage props.

All of his accomplishments were those of a professional mobster. He was part and parcel of the criminal world. Both in prison and in exile he kept company with thieves and gangsters. In Turukhansk he was close friends with smugglers. At one moment he'd be with a crowd of thugs beating up an honest person; at another, with the criminals robbing the political prisoners. If it hadn't been for the revolution he would have become a petty thief. That's what he was, but he decided to play for bigger stakes.

Stalin had good reason to hide his past, especially in connection with the Turukhansk exile period. In 1923 the former exile S——v, an old working-class comrade, arrived in Moscow from the provinces. He looked up the Old Communist Aleksandr Ulanovsky and said he wanted to see the Gensek.

"Are you sure he'll see you?"

"No doubt about it. We were in exile together."

A few days later Ulanovsky ran into the worker again.

"Well, did Stalin see you?"

The newcomer waved his hand in disgust. "Ah, you've all become such big shots here. He didn't want to talk with me, your comrade Koba."

This happened back when Lenin was still alive. The Gensek was just getting started and he couldn't yet bump off his old comrades from exile. The hunting season on them didn't open until the mid-thirties. When it did open, they took Ulanovsky's wife, Nadezhda Markovna, first. The Ulanovsky couple were highly experienced in intelligence work, colleagues of the Soviet master spy Richard Sorge. Aleksandr Ulanovsky had known Comrade Koba personally in Turukhansk. Nevertheless, he took the risk of appealing directly to the Gensek in an effort to save his innocent wife. Ulanovsky was of course immediately invited to the Lubyanka himself.

After sitting out one ten-year term, plus a second ten years, he returned to Moscow. That was after the Twentieth Congress and the revelations about Stalin. He died in 1971, but managed to tell a great many things before that. Among them were the foul provocations Stalin cooked up against Sverdlov in Turukhansk to which we referred in the chapter "Out by the Roots!," an incident in which Central Committee member Koba accused Central Committee member Sverdlov of *treachery*. Against Sverdlov Koba also incited a gang of criminal prisoners who were ready to tear him apart simply because he had been born Jewish.

In the novel *The Gleam of the Campfire* published in Moscow in 1966, the popular Soviet writer Yuri Trifonov recounted an incident from the memoirs of Rosa Zakharova, an Old Bolshevik who, with her husband, Filipp Zakharov, was in exile in the Turukhansk region. In May 1913 the political exile Joseph Dubrovinsky died in the Yenisei region. His personal library became the common property of the exiles, a way of honoring the memory of that outstanding revolutionary. Stalin arrived in the village of Kostino in the Turukhansk region not long after (about August 1913). In early 1914 he was sent farther north to the settlement of Kureika. The political exiles soon learned that Comrade Koba had taken Dubrovinsky's books as his own. Filipp Zakharov went to Kureika about this. "Stalin 'received' him more or less as a tsarist general would receive an ordinary soldier who dared to appear before him with a demand."[149]

The Gensek began his thieving career as a youth in the town of Gori, where he burglarized a merchant's home. He got away with a lot of silver and was able to forget about the cares of poverty for a while. An old Menshevik by the name of Mibonia, virtually a life-long inmate of a camp in Kazakhstan, told other prisoners in 1943 that in the town where Soso was born the future Leader's acts of thievery were remembered by many.

And in every case—whether it was a trivial burglary or the sensational robbery of a post office or steamship line—Stalin skillfully dodged punishment, letting his partners, or entirely innocent people, take the blame. Even at a tender age, he wasn't bothered a bit by fraud, provocation, and treachery.

These truly Stalinist features are evident in his later robberies as well. The end of the Spanish Civil War in 1939 is growing dim in public memory, yet the brazen way in which the Kremlin usurper appropriated the gold of the Spanish Republic for his own use continues to amaze people.

Throughout his life Stalin broke laws—those of the party and state, and those of humanity. The only laws he abided by were the cruel ones of the criminal world.

Stalin's sly and lazy brain never produced a single beneficial idea. His corrupted soul was totally sterile. Honest or humane aspirations never disturbed him as long as he lived.

Some biographers are inclined to see him as a paranoiac. But that means attributing all of his crimes, which cost millions of lives, to mental illness. Would a sick or mentally unbalanced person have been able so masterfully to hamstring all his political rivals and build such a model apparatus of power? Could such a person have built a mighty empire, complete with substantial territorial acquisitions, despite the disastrous blunders he committed in both foreign and domestic policy?

No, Stalin was unquestionably of sound mind. Neither schizophrenia nor paranoia has any hold over such malicious natures. But his boundless ambition might seem maniacal to an outsider.

In December 1927 an international scientific convention was held in Moscow. Vladimir Bekhterev, the outstanding Pavlovian psychologist from Leningrad, enjoyed special respect among the foreign delegates. This aroused the jealous curiosity of the Great Genius of Mankind. No sooner had Bekhterev spoken at a gathering of neuropathologists and psychiatrists than he was invited to see Stalin. Bekhterev visited the Gensek accompanied by Samuil Mnukhin, his favorite pupil and assistant of long standing.

When Bekhterev left the Gensek's office, he spoke one word to Mnukhin, who was waiting for him in the reception room: "Paranoiac." At the hotel he told his assistant that Soso imagined himself to be a great leader. In fact a very dangerous man was now heading the Soviet state, with unforeseeable consequences for the country.

That evening the two scientists had dinner brought to their room. The waiter handed each a dish of soup, left the second course, and departed. Before Bekhterev could finish the first course he was doubled up by abdominal pain and fell to the floor. Mnukhin rushed to the phone but it was dead. He ran to the hotel switchboard and called a first-aid station. By the time he returned to the hotel room Bekhterev had succumbed.

Mnukhin lived until 1972. He told the story of Bekhterev's death to his closest friends and some of his graduate students.

* * *

Stalin was truly a phenomenon of the human species. A puny individual, ill-equipped in both body and mind. How was he able to accommodate such a vast, incinerating hatred for everything good and just? What a powerful character and what an abysmal one. And what an absolutely unique ability to discover the vilest and basest traits in others and patiently, lovingly, to nurture the darkest and most bestial instincts, breeding an entire new race of Oprichniks.

This misanthrope invested with a powerful will had a tremendous influence upon society. In fact he doomed it to deformity. We cannot speak of the development of Soviet society in the Stalin era as anything but pathological.

"Although you do not know him, he knows you and is thinking of you. Whoever you may be, you have need of this benefactor. Whoever you may be, the finest part of your destiny is in the hands of that other man, who also watches over you, and who works for you—the man with a scholar's mind, a workman's face, and the dress of a simple soldier."[150]

Those unbelievable lines at the end of Henri Barbusse's book on Stalin help us as much as any genuine archival document to re-create the true portrait of the tyrant. How could anyone have deceived and debased a man like Barbusse to such an extent, forced him to prostitute himself so vilely, a man who was rightly called "the conscience of Europe"? Only Joseph Stalin could have done that.

It seems he was competing with all the infamous despots of history. In the second decade of his rule he surpassed them all, and after that there was nothing with which to compare him.

If he is to be called a "mountain eagle," it is an eagle of the kind that tore at the liver of the chained Prometheus.

MEAN FOR EACH OTHER

3

Erich Mühsam, the German Communist poet, experienced Hitler's prisons. Fate placed his wife in Stalin's. She arrived in the Soviet Union at the invitation of Yelena Stasova. In no time she was invited farther, to the Lubyanka. Then to a prison camp. In Berlin in 1957, she met Anna Kipers, the wife of a Latvian poet. Anna had spent years in similar corrective camps. What the German ex-prisoner had to say to her Latvian ex-prisoner friend was this:

"*Weisst du—Stalin, das ist Hitler plus Asien.*" ("You know what Stalin is? Hitler plus Asia.")

They were meant for each other, the German Vozhd and the Soviet Fuehrer.* Their alliance was predestined, just as one criminal unerringly finds another in a crowd of thousands. And once they found each other, they "got down to it" together. The story of their alliance is reminiscent

*Vozhd, Fuehrer—the Russian and German words, respectively, for Leader.—TRANS.

of a provincial melodrama: love at first sight, boundless trust, perfidious betrayal, a sad ending.

In the years of Hitler's emergence, Stalin didn't miss an opportunity to lash out at German fascism. In 1936 he declared from the platform of the Eighth Congress of Soviets: "The new Constitution of the USSR will be an indictment of fascism." Those were his words. But in practice not one political figure strengthened the Hitler dictatorship as much as the general secretary of the Central Committee of the Bolshevik Party.

In the thirties Stalin promoted one of the most injurious doctrines imaginable: he *asserted* that all Social Democrats were allies of fascism. Yet if the German Social Democrats and Communists had joined together, they could have prevented Hitler's rise to power.[151] Trotsky argued against the split between the Social Democrats and Communists in Germany. He warned that the split might allow Hitler to come to power.[152] Nevertheless, Stalin insisted on the "relentless unmasking" of the Social Democrats as traitors.[153]

The responsibility for the split in the German working-class movement belongs to Stalin. That was his first invaluable service to fascism. His second, and no less important, service was to instruct the German Communists to refrain from active opposition to Hitler. In the summer of 1931 the German Communists voted against the Social Democratic state administration of Prussia, in a united front with the fascists and other rightwing groups. It was a suicidal tactic. As a result, hundreds of thousands of the best sons of the German people met their deaths.

On December 24, 1933, Hitler announced that Germany had to rearm, because it was the West's bulwark against the Soviets. Precisely at that time Stalin was laying the groundwork for rapprochement with the Führer. On August 17, four months before Hitler's memorable announcement, Abel Yenukidze met with the German ambassador, Dirksen. The secretary of the Central Executive Committee stated his government's view: "complete understanding of the developments in Germany." In explaining this attitude held by the Soviet Union's "leading figures" (read: the Gensek), Yenukidze expressed the notion that the Hitler dictatorship was akin to the Soviet system. And he saw in this the assurance that rapprochement was possible.[154]

If you think about it, you'll agree. The secretary of the CEC was expressing an entirely realistic point of view. Not only were Hitler's and Stalin's dictatorships similar; so were the two men's tactics in usurping party and government power.

Hitler declared his primary goal to be the creation of a *Neue Ordnung* in Germany. Stalin had begun to build his new order much earlier, but the head start he had stolen from history didn't do him much good. Utilizing the industriousness and organizational ability inherent in the German nation, Hitler managed—much to the envy of the Kremlin dictator—to establish a model barracks in a remarkably short time. On the other hand, Stalin achieved a remarkable submissiveness in his subjects—to the envy of the Fuehrer—the kind you find in patients on the operating table under general anesthesia.

Each man began a war against his own people by organizing a provocation: Hitler the Reichstag fire; Stalin the Kirov assassination. The Führer made skillful use of the assassination attempt of July 20, 1944, to get rid of undesirable generals. And why not? After all, his farsighted Moscow colleague had taken similar action six or seven years earlier.

They also complemented each other with respect to the eradication of heresy. The only difference lay in what each one called it. Hitler referred to his malcontents as *politisch verdächtig* (politically unreliable); Stalin called his "enemies of the people."

In the race between these two builders of a new order, first one and then the other took the lead. Hitler was the first to begin persecuting scholars and burning books. Stalin outdid him by organizing a massive famine. Hitler was the first to begin a campaign to exterminate all Communists. Stalin got back at him by establishing death camps. The grateful Führer made full use of Stalin's valuable experience in organizing such camps; he copied their structure, regime, and administrative system. But he introduced improvements in the killing methods.

In turn, the Lubyanka utilized the services of its sister agency, the Gestapo, at the very dawn of the alliance between Stalin and Hitler. In 1933 Lev Lebedev, an experienced party functionary, was sent to Germany on illegal business. He died in World War II, but his wife did not die until 1976, of tuberculosis. The time has come to make Lebedev's information public. It turns out that as early as 1933 and 1934 the NKVD sent agents to Germany to study the Gestapo's methods. Judging by the results, this on-the-job training proved extremely useful—*extremely*.

The contacts spread. The resemblance grew. Sometimes you get the impression that *Mein Kampf* had more than one author. While cursing German fascism from the party pulpits and even taking part in armed conflicts against it (let us recall the Spanish Civil War), Stalin consistently promoted his Asiatic version of National Socialism at home. At one point Benito Mussolini, observing the development of the Hitler-Stalin alliance, couldn't restrain himself. "Bolshevism is dead. In its place is a kind of Slavonic fascism."[155]

(Analyzing the peculiarities of the Italian Fascist system, a Soviet journal reported in 1923: "In the course of their activities the Fascists constantly look to the Bolsheviks. A whole series of tactical moves cannot be explained as anything but a politically conscious imitation of the Russian Communist Party."[156])

It's hardly fair, of course, to equate Stalin's "socialism" with Hitler's Reich. In Germany they enacted four-year plans for economic development; in the USSR we had *five*-year plans. As for the provisioning of the builders of paradise, flour was distributed to German citizens on holidays and on Hitler's birthday, while Soviet citizens received coupons for flour during "election" campaigns. There's a difference.

Nineteen thirty-nine came, the year of the turning point. At the Eighteenth Party Congress, General Secretary Stalin came down hard on England and France for attempting "to incense the Soviet Union against Germany." He described his former allies as warmongers "accustomed to having others pull their chestnuts out of the fire for them."[157] This was said on March 10. Three days later German forces entered Prague.

They already understood each other perfectly. All that remained was to codify the new relationship. Maxim Litvinov, the architect of the pro-British policy of previous years and a man who maintained some principles, proved to be an obstacle, though a trivial one. In the double game that Stalin began to play on the international stage, a diversionary role was assigned to the respectable Litvinov. With his left hand plainly visible to the audience, the Master directed Litvinov's diplomatic efforts. With his right, hidden from the world, he pulled the strings moving the "super-diplomat" Molotov in a totally different direction. While Litvinov was taking steps toward the creation of a European system of collective security, which would have included Germany, Molotov and his emissaries were directing their efforts toward rapprochement with Hitler.

According to Yevgeny Gnedin, former director of the press department of the Soviet Ministry of Foreign Affairs, one of the Gensek's secret agents was Karl Radek. Stalin personally assigned Radek to make contact with Hitler's agents long before the conclusion of the alliance with the Fuehrer.

Stalin's instructions calling for rapprochement with Hitler Germany were in effect as early as 1935. Vladimir Vasilenko, chairman of the Kiev provincial executive committee, spoke that year at a reception given by the German consul general in Kiev. Calling Litvinov's policy "unconvincing to the massess," Vasilenko urged friendship with Germany. As for the racial conceptions of the National Socialists—who could be worried about that?[158]

On May 3, 1939, Litvinov was relieved of his post as people's commissar of foreign affairs "at his own request." Two years later came the party decision to expel Litvinov from the Central Committee. Although he had been very close to Lenin and had one of the longest records in the party, he was "undeserving of the party's trust." After the February 1941 Central Committee plenum Litvinov approached the Gensek. "Why don't you arrest me? It would be simpler, and everyone would understand."

"No," answered the Master, "we're not going to arrest you."

After appointing Molotov to the vacant position, the Leader "purged" the last experienced personnel from the Commissariat of Foreign Affairs. (It is well known what the word "purge" signifies in a Stalin production.) On the day after the ouster of Litvinov, G. A. Astakhov, the chargé d'affaires in Berlin, suggested to the German Ministry of Foreign Affairs that they begin negotiations on amicable terms.[159]

Stalin hoped—no, he was certain—that Hitler would attack his Western neighbors. A war might weaken England and France. And Germany at the same time. Such a war would suit Stalin just fine. The Gensek was guided by one additional consideration: he was not morally prepared for a major war. Or, more simply, Stalin had cold feet.

Events developed swiftly. An agreement on trade and credit was signed in Berlin on August 20. Then Hitler sent Stalin a personal letter with the request that he receive Ribbentrop no later than August 23 (the day Hitler had wanted to invade Poland). On August 23 the official negotiations with Ribbentrop took place in Moscow, in Stalin's presence. They ended late in the night with the signing of the Nonaggression Pact. The historic event was celebrated with champagne.

"I know how much the German people love their Fuehrer. I should therefore like to drink to his health."

Let us remember Stalin's toast.

The Supreme Soviet ratified the Soviet-German treaty on August 31. Several hours later, German forces invaded Poland in full accordance with the secret protocol signed by Ribbentrop and the Soviet representative on the night of August 23. (German aircraft, for example, were guided by a radio tower set up in Minsk as they flew to bomb Warsaw.) This protocol was entirely in the spirit of the tsarist and imperialist secret diplomacy which the party had condemned and denounced for so many years.

Ten days later, Ribbentrop flew to Moscow again. Hitler's diplomat noted that when he was in the Kremlin, he felt as though he were among his old drinking buddies.[160] Forster, the Gauleiter of Danzig and a hardened Nazi, accompanied Ribbentrop. He reported that he had been so warmly received, it was as though he were "back with his old *Parteigenossen.*"

On September 23 the Frontier and Friendship Treaty between the USSR and Germany was signed. Once again—for the umpteenth time— Stalin justified his title of Supreme Master of Daring Revolutionary Decisions and Sharp About-Faces. But it was all quite logical: the policy of a great-power deal with Hitler flowed from Stalin's domestic policy of repressing and exterminating his own people, wiping out every last trace of the revolution—the slightest whiff of October 1917.

The Soviet leader was "a hell of a fellow," who had taken his entire country into his "iron grasp." This complimentary testimony belonged to Soso's new friend—Adolf. Among Hitler's enthusiastic judgments was that Stalin was a supreme blackmailer: "Look at the way he tried to extort things from us. . . ."[161]

Hitler had plenty of grounds for that opinion. During Ribbentrop's first visit to Moscow, the Gensek had bargained for the ports of Liepai (Libava) and Ventspils (Vindava). Instead Hitler offered Stalin freedom of movement in the Baltic region and Moldavia, which the Gensek did not fail to annex quickly to his crown. Thus he gained thirteen million new subjects. (Only two million of these "citizens" would have to be carted off to corrective-labor camps. Annexation is no obstacle to terror.) Maps of the USSR with its new borders were hastily printed. Historians were mobilized to show that the newly added territories had groaned for a long time under their yoke, that for centuries these peoples had longed for "reunification."

* * *

In criminal jargon there is a word *propul*. It means something like "share of the loot." Let's say a thief robbed an apartment or picked a pocket. If another thief happened to witness his good fortune, he would immediately demand: *Propul!* And receive a share.

Stalin demanded the Dardanelles from Hitler. The discussion about the Turkish straits began in connection with the possibility of the Soviet Union's joining the Anti-Comintern Pact, which Germany and Japan had signed in November 1936, Italy in the following year. When Ribbentrop commented at the first meeting in Moscow that "Stalin himself was now ready to join the Anti-Comintern Pact," it was taken as a joke.[162]

The joke turned out to be right on target. The ink hadn't dried on the friendship treaty when Molotov announced:

"It is possible to recognize or deny the ideology of Hitlerism, just as with every other ideological system. That is a matter of political viewpoint. However, an ideology cannot be destroyed by force. Therefore, it is not only senseless, but even criminal to wage a war for the 'destruction of Hitlerism.' "[163]

Included in the Nazi-Soviet Frontier and Friendship Treaty was a separate point, a mutual obligation to refrain from ideological propaganda against each other. It wasn't so long before, three years in fact, at the Eighth Congress of Soviets, that the Gensek had lambasted fascism, whose "turbid wave . . . spits on the socialist movement of the working class and mixes it with mud."[164] Not very grammatical, but sound. And now— friendly contacts between the fascist party and Stalin's.

Now it was the Soviet Union's turn to sign the Anti-Comintern Pact. Negotiations on this matter went on for a long time. By the fall of 1940 they were close to completion. Molotov, sent to Berlin, insisted on three points set by the Supreme Horse Trader himself:

Evacuation of German forces from Finland. (Stalin had his own plans for that country.)

Recognition of Soviet interests in Bulgaria.

Transfer of control over the Turkish straits to the USSR.

Stalin was prepared to make concessions on the first two points, but the Dardanelles, the age-old dream of Russian tsars, had become his dream as well.

"If you want to get this bank of the river, demand the opposite bank as well," says an old Georgian proverb. This kind of bartering with an "overbid" promised success. His German partners were bound to concede at least something. Then Lenin's loyal disciple and continuator would join the Anti-Comintern Pact. Why should He have to be tied down to that organization of ill repute anyhow? He had succeeded by then, incidentally, in executing the Executive Committee of the Comintern in its entirety and had rounded up many Comintern activists. Besides, everyone was sick to death of this dreary playing around with r-r-revolutionary slogans.

FORGET ABOUT OCTOBER. LET'S GET THE DARDANELLES!

What did the once holy temple of the revolution mean to Joseph Stalin? From the Bible we know what happens when the temple is filled with moneylenders.

Hitler was not attracted by Stalin's offer. He knew that the Gensek had put an end to October long before and that the Soviet counterrevolution was in good hands. The Dardanelles, on the other hand, could still be useful to the West.

The hint was made to Moscow, through Molotov: "Take India."

Stalin answered Berlin, also through Molotov: "We can manage that without your help."

Then Hitler suggested the Persian Gulf region. It turned out that Stalin already had his eye on that too, thank you. It wasn't very far at all from the USSR's southern border.

Adolf and Joseph, prospective joint owners of the globe, nearly came to terms. Just a bit more and the Rome-Berlin-Tokyo Axis would have acquired a fourth wheel. But the Dardanelles . . . Hitler could not agree to hand over the straits to the Soviets. That would mean giving Stalin the keys to the Mediterranean and the Black Sea.

Stalin backed down. But he couldn't give up his "dream" entirely, and so he didn't sign the Anti-Comintern Pact after all. Anyhow, it was possible to work hand in hand with Hitler, Mussolini, and the emperor Hirohito without the pact. For example, Stalin turned over to Hitler (read: the Gestapo) hundreds of antifascists—Germans and other Europeans—delivering them to certain death. Likewise a number of scholars who happened to be in the Soviet Union.

After the signing of the pact with Hitler's Germany, Stalin told Ribbentrop "that the Soviet Government took the new pact most seriously; he personally could guarantee, on his word of honor, that the Soviet Union would not betray its partner."[165] However, neither Ribbentrop nor Hitler was inclined to trust Stalin's word. Too bad. Because for once in his life Stalin meant what he said. He passed on to Hitler strictly confidential information concerning offers from the British government. He not only delivered Soviet provisions and strategic raw materials to Hitler's Germany—with truly German punctuality!—but even bought from other countries for the Fuehrer.[166]

When criminals—in prison cells or camp barracks—are playing cards, they will unceremoniously bet with the belongings of any "green-assed sucker" in the vicinity. But even the lowest criminal wouldn't dare to bet someone else's food ration without the owner's permission. The gambler will at least tell his cellmate, "Come on, let me put up your ration." Stalin didn't ask anyone when he gave Hitler Ukrainian and Russian grain, and meat thrown into the bargain.

The USSR's alliance with Hitler's Germany and Joseph Stalin's friendship with Adolf Hitler must be regarded in historical retrospect as one of the stages in the counterrevolutionary activity of the Soviet leadership.

Having secured his rear in the form of a reliable Stalinist ally, Hitler was able to occupy new territory without any difficulties. The leader of the Bolshevik Party outdid himself with his attentions and signs of encouragement to the aggressor. Stalin gave Hitler manganese. Hitler gave him a made-to-order, four-colored Mercedes Benz. A most heartwarming relationship developed between the Fuehrer and the Father of the Peoples. Knowing of Hitler's passion for Wagner, Stalin ordered the Bolshoi Theater to stage *Die Walküre*. The renowned film director Sergei Eisenstein saw to its production. Hitler congratulated Stalin on his birthday. Stalin congratulated Hitler on the day of the German army's invasion of Norway. He placed Soviet Arctic naval bases at the disposal of German warships for refueling.

However, the biggest surprise from the Soviet side was yet to come. World War II was in full swing. Hitler had already approved Plan Barbarossa, the design for the attack on Russia. But Stalin ruled out any active preparations for resisting Hitler's inevitable aggression.

"A hell of a fellow! Stalin is indispensable," exclaimed the rejoicing Fuehrer.

Mussolini echoed him: "Why, he's already become a secret fascist. He helps us and weakens the antifascist forces like no one else could."[167]

Stalin did everything possible to earn this rapturous praise from his Axis partners. He prepared the next surprise at the expense of the Polish people. After Molotov and Ribbentrop signed the Soviet-German friendship treaty and Stalin and Hitler had partitioned Poland—for the fourth time in the tragic history of that country—some of the Polish prisoners of war caught in the Soviet zone of occupation were handed over to the Germans. Among those Stalin kept for himself were fourteen thousand Polish officers. They were placed in special camps. Then suddenly the Poles disappeared; after April 1940 there was no more news of them. Soon, however, Hitler's divisions invaded Soviet territory, and Stalin began to make overtures to his Polish neighbor for an alliance. The first year of the war passed. Polish generals and diplomats began inquiring about the fate of their officer corps. One way or another, four hundred men were brought together from Stalin's prisons and camps.

"We, of course, made a great mistake in handing over your officers to the Germans. Besides that, some ran off, many ended up in other countries, and some died of illness on the way to prison. No one is guaranteed against illness. Please, draw up some lists of names. We'll check again."

That was how Molotov's chancery responded to the Polish inquiries. Beria's likewise.

The bodies of the Polish officers were found in the Katyn forest, without the "aid" of Soviet authorities and with an international commission looking on. A shocking scene of mass murder greeted the eyes of the world. Stalin rendered this service to Hitler in the spring of 1940. The perpetrators of this action were Beria and Merkulov.

Two years later it was time to think about the reputation of the Father of the Peoples. Stalin decided to lay the blame for the Katyn crime on his former ally. One frosty February night a column of covered trucks moved along the highway from Minsk to Moscow. In the backs of the trucks lay boxes of the most varied shapes—square, triangular, even round. These boxes didn't resemble coffins at all.

A blizzard whirled through the streets of Moscow. The trucks reached the appointed spot—the Institute of Forensic Medicine. The vehicles were unloaded in the yard of the institute, and the boxes with the bodies of the executed Poles were carried inside the building. The next day the column set out on the return trip. Now German bullets were found in the corpses. And in the pockets of their uniforms, the appropriate kind of newspapers and forged letters. Now the Master could send his *own* commission to investigate.

In the September 26, 1943, edition of *Pravda* there appeared a report from the Soviet commission: the Germans had organized the Katyn massacre. Metropolitan Nikolai, the writer Alexei Tolstoy, the academician Vladimir Potemkin, and two generals, along with several famous physicians, signed the commission's document to increase its power of persuasion. Among the last to sign was Viktor Prozorovsky, director of the Institute of Forensic Medicine (that very institute). The world didn't believe this forged document. Then *Pravda* published the report a second time, making a full two-page spread of it.

I happened to see that celebrated issue of *Pravda* at Vorkuta, where I was in confinement. There were many Poles in our camp. One day the head of our section of the camp came into the barracks, surrounded by his guards. He was a big, hefty colonel, always drunk. Colonels like him were transferred by the dozens from the occupied countries of Europe and the Far East to perform similar service in the Pechora and Vorkuta camps. As a rule, officers like him knew things that not even state security men were supposed to know. Apparently not all the perpetrators of Stalin's crimes were eliminated.

The colonel, tottering on his short legs, glared opaquely at the Poles. They stood before him with stoic calmness, these human skeletons in their shapeless gray jackets, but the chief cursed them foully, in the grand old Russian style:

"I didn't bag enough of you in the Katyn forest!"

I was in the barracks and heard it myself.

Forty years have passed since the Katyn massacre. The Soviet people do not know the truth to this day.

Those who suppose that Stalin was "deeper and more complex than Hitler" are mistaken.[168] Stalin's personality was pretty primitive. His intellectualism was only an outward appearance, a pretense at culture. However, Hitler considered him well read.

Stalin spoke less flatteringly of Hitler, in conversations during the war with Eden and Roosevelt. Hitler, in Stalin's opinion, though not lacking in raw talent, was uncultured and superstitious. Really, as far as "culture" goes, they deserved each other, Adolf and Joseph.

Stalin was more cunning than Hitler. More cunning and treacherous. His cruelty also knew no equal. "He is as cruel as a wild beast, but his baseness is human," Hitler said about him.[169] Stalin was ten years older than Hitler and surpassed him in his experience of political infighting. The opinion that Stalin was better versed in the military arts is wrong. As a strategist Stalin was exceedingly ungifted.

One shouldn't think that dictators are not of this world. Stalin planted birch trees with his own hands at his retreat on the shores of Lake Ritsa in mountainous Abkhazia. Hitler romped with his favorite German shepherd, and even took her to the front with him. Unlike Stalin, he often rode out to his army in the field, and didn't always impose his incompetent decisions on his generals.

You can't deny that Hitler had courage. Enough has been said of Stalin's cowardice. Hitler considered him to be "such a cautious man that if he had a pistol in his hands and all his opponent had was a knife, he would only attack when his opponent was sleeping."[170]

An amazing insight!

Not long before his attack on the Soviet Union, Hitler told his aides: "When I conquer Russia I will keep Stalin as ruler—under German control, of course—because no one knows how to handle the Russian people better than he does."[171]

A serious meaning lies at the bottom of this jest.

* * *

A famous scholar and professor of ecclesiastical law, Vladimir Nikolaevich Beneshevich, who was even honored by the Pope, lived in Russia during those years. Beneshevich, one of the few miraculously surviving "old-regime" scholars, kept up a correspondence with German colleagues. Then he received a letter from Berlin with the newly obligatory ending "Heil Hitler!" What should he do? He consulted with the proper authorities and in response sent a businesslike letter ending with "Long live Comrade Stalin!"

Yes, they found each other, Joseph Stalin and Adolf Hitler. And between them they could have divided the earth amicably.

But it wasn't fated to be.

AT THE HEAD OF THE FIFTH COLUMN

4

It was 1904. "Hurrah! We'll drown the enemy in a sea of our caps." That's how tsarist Russia's war with Japan began. It ended with the fall of Port Arthur and the destruction of a Russian fleet.

In 1939 they decided they could take Finland without any difficulty. "Don't boast before a fight; you'll end up without your head." Stalin could hardly have known that Finnish proverb. But even if he had, so what? It wouldn't have stopped him. More than half a million Red Army men laid down their lives on the Karelian Isthmus. Stalin never risked his.

"We will fight without shedding much of *our* blood!"

"The Red Army will smash the enemy on his own territory!"

"We will fly faster than anyone, higher than anyone, farther than anyone!"

These promissory slogans proved just as ephemeral as the rest of the slogans of the era of the Stalin blight. Hitler's Messerschmitts had the free run of the Soviet skies from the first days of the war.

In a speech to the graduating students of military and naval academies on May 5, 1941, the Gensek hinted that even if a war began, it wouldn't happen before 1942. He sincerely believed that he had fate by the coattails and could hold it still while unhurriedly completing preparations for war by the following spring.

Warnings of the imminent attack were pouring in from all sides— accurate and reliable. And not just from the Soviet masterspy Richard Sorge or the German ambassador to the USSR. Stalin knew that his army was not ready for war. That meant Hitler would wait. The Soviet people could relax. It was even promised:

"We do not want one foot of foreign soil, but as for our own soil, we will not surrender a single inch to anyone."

By showering Hitler generously with supplies, Stalin hoped to buy time. What else would mollify the Fuehrer? Stalin saw to it that Yugoslavia's diplomatic mission in Moscow was quickly closed, along with the embassies of Norway, Denmark, Belgium, and Greece, after the Germans had occupied those countries. This was followed by another measure violating party doctrine and damaging the interests of the state: Stalin recognized the pro-Nazi government of Rashid Ali in Iraq.

Then the head of the government put on a show at the Kazan Station in Moscow. Japanese Minister of Foreign Affairs Matsuoka was returning home on April 13. A treaty of friendship had just been concluded with the Japanese. Stalin appeared at the station (an extremely rare event) and in full view of everyone embraced the German ambassador, Count Von Schulenburg. "We must remain friends and you must do everything possible to that end," Stalin said for public consumption.

The ensuing *mise en scène* was in the spirit of provincial melodrama. Stalin spotted Colonel Krebs, the German military attaché, and declared, "We will remain friends with you under all circumstances!" And just before the curtain, at the end of the act—Matsuoka and Comrade Stalin embraced, and the Gensek said to the Japanese minister, "We too are Asiatics." Indeed so.

The thought of a German invasion struck fear in Stalin's heart. And when it came, he shut himself up in his Kremlin apartment. The Politburo delegated Molotov to summon him, but Molotov returned empty-handed. Then all the lesser leaders arrived at the Great Leader's place. The Master, pale and dismayed, finally opened the door and backed away. He thought the Politburo members had come to arrest him. The next day Stalin left Moscow and went into hiding at his suburban dacha.

He ran away without explaining to his stooges and without saying a word to his people. It fell to Molotov to speak to the country over the radio. He was terribly upset by Hitler's treachery: "The Soviet government has been absolutely conscientious in fulfilling the terms of the treaty." (Earlier Stalin's number-one flunky had complained, all gloomy and perplexed, to the German ambassador: "Did we really deserve this?") Molotov's radio talk ended with an appeal to the people to unite around "our Great Leader, Stalin."

In 1929, responding to greetings on his fiftieth birthday, Stalin had promised the people to give all his strength and even his blood—"drop by drop"—in the name of, etc. The war demanded neither his blood nor his life—just ordinary courage. But he didn't have it in him. The Great Leader was yellow.

It wasn't until two weeks after the war began that Stalin started to get hold of himself. On July 3 he spoke on the radio, and on July 12 he received foreign representatives. He appeared at a meeting of the High Command (Stavka) for the first time in the middle of July. Meanwhile, what had the Stavka been doing, led by the helpless "Marshal" Timoshenko? How had these people ever endeared themselves to the Master other than by their submissiveness and obsequiousness? In his absence what could they do? At whose feet could they grovel?

A perfect match for the lifeless Stavka was the pompously titled State Committee for Defense, established on July 30 under the chairmanship of the deserter in chief. Its members: Molotov, Voroshilov, Malenkov, Beria. These men were also members of that august body, the Politburo. But they were no more capable of organizing the defense of the state than of dancing the *pas de quatre* in *Swan Lake*.

A terrible war had begun, the most destructive war in the history of the planet. So what did the Master do? At the head of the defense effort he placed four men devoid of the slightest gleam of intelligence. Thick-headed Molotov represented the government on the State Committee of Defense. Voroshilov, the former locksmith from Lugansk, who had long since traded his worker's smock for the uniform of a court lackey, personified the armed forces. Behind Malenkov, the official scribe and palace intriguer, stood the Secretariat of the Central Committee. Secret Police Chief Beria rounded out the foursome. This man had mastered the murderer's trade without needing to study. He represented the organs of criminal detection and punishment.

Absolute incompetence and weak-willed leadership at the start of the war: history will enter this crime too against Stalin's personal account.

While the Leader hid himself from the people like a coward, Beria and Malenkov zealously sawed away at the chair holding Andrei Zhdanov, the first in line to succeed Stalin. They laid the groundwork for his transfer to the doomed city of Leningrad. No place was found for Andrei Zhdanov, Stalin's favorite, even when the structure of the State Committee of Defense was revamped.

And Leningrad really was doomed. After the first ten days of military activity, the entire seacoast up to Tallin was lost. The top command did everything, it seemed, to turn this defeat into a catastrophe.

Leningrad had no resources, no reserves, no communications. . . . But from Moscow they kept sending orders—one more absurd than another. If it hadn't been for the heroism of Leningrad's defenders, the city would have been lost in July. The Luga Line held for an entire month. Whole detachments of the home guard were destroyed. With what could they oppose the German tanks, guns, and airplanes—other than their lives?

Stalin kept a jealous watch over the observance of the party system of seniority and brutally crushed any initiative. How many practical plans and proposals were rejected by him simply because they came from "the wrong people"? Upon learning that a council of defense had been formed in Leningrad, Stalin fell upon Zhdanov and Voroshilov: "Why wasn't the Gensek informed? Why aren't you on the council yourselves?"

August was drawing to an end. The Germans had almost completely surrounded Leningrad, but the command did nothing about an evacuation. A government commission arrived in the city: Molotov, Malenkov, Kosygin, Marshals Zhigarev and Voronov, and Admiral Kuznetsov. Leningrad's fate was being decided—surrender, or hold on?

When their last hopes had fallen through and Stalin saw that even Georgy Zhukov was in no position to do anything, he decided to blow up the city—not just the fortifications and factories, but the whole city, with its priceless architecture. Hitler too intended to wipe St. Petersburg off the face of the earth.[172] A complete coincidence of aims.

Stalin didn't keep Zhukov on the Leningrad Front for long. As soon as the swift advance of German tank forces against Mozhaisk became known (October 5), Stalin recalled Zhukov to Moscow and assigned him the Western Front. But that front no longer existed. The Germans had surrounded four armies (the Nineteenth, Twentieth, Twenty-fourth, and Thirty-second) and were moving toward Moscow without meeting any serious resistance. There had been plenty of indication from field reconnaissance, but the Kremlin Strategist couldn't figure out the direction of the German offensive and take countermeasures. Later Stalin blamed the Stavka for this fatal error.

Moscow could fall any day. A panic began, and a spontaneous evacuation of the capital. And what about Stalin? The Leader, naturally, was one of the first to flee. Present "historians" conceal this deplorable fact.

In 1975 the Soviet journal *Problems of History* published the memoirs of Aleksei Shakhurin, former minister of the aeronautical industry. He described his visit to Stalin's Kremlin apartment on October 16, 1941. The empty bookcases "to the right along the wall" stuck in his memory. The Master asked of those present, "How are things in Moscow?" And when they outlined for him the unpleasant picture of the panic—the transit system at a standstill, stores and medical establishments closed, no money in the banks—Stalin remarked, "Well, that's nothing, really. I thought it would be worse."[173]

It's all authentic. But such a conversation could not have taken place on October 16, but only on the 19th, when Stalin decided for a time to return to the capital.

A home guard was established in Moscow too.

> Our step is firm, and the enemy never
> Through our republics will stroll.

Was it so long ago they sang this song almost everywhere? But now they were sending scholars, artists, musicians, pensioners, and sportsmen out into the fiercely cold winter—without any warm clothing—against tanks and mortars. Two million defenders laid down their lives in the December battles outside Moscow.

Stalin farmed out the power of command to several party functionaries—such as Zhdanov, Malenkov, Mekhlis, Shcherbakov—and several talentless old campaigners—such as Timoshenko, Voroshilov, and Budyonny. These men were unique in their incompetence. Hitler could have seized both capitals, old and new, in October without any real obstacles. However, the Fuehrer was unable to evaluate the situation accurately.

The very first weeks of the war showed how harmful one-man rule was, what disasters extreme concentration of power could lead to. Ironically, that fatal feature of Stalin's system permitted it to remain standing when scarcely any other government could have. The amazing dialectics of history. Meanwhile, thanks to Russia's expanses, the surviving armies had somewhere to retreat.

During the course of the war, the Gensek, known for his rock-solid orthodoxy, displayed rare political flexibility. His throne proved unexpectedly capable of collaborating with anyone—with yesterday's "enemies of the people" (if they could invent something useful), with the imperialists (if they donated money, provisions, technology, and troops), with the old rulers (if, in the past, they had repulsed foreign invaders), and even with the Lord God himself, in the person of the Orthodox Church. Since the

Germans were threatening to put an end to his private dictatorship, Stalin was ready to collaborate personally with Satan (if he would appear)—anything to hold on to power.

The eradicator of faith, the tireless persecutor of believers, the man who had sent a thousand priests to their deaths, began trying to ingratiate himself with the church. The Gensek not only brought a great many high-ranking clergymen back from the camps; he also permitted the theological seminaries and an academy to be opened and established a government Council for Russian Orthodox Church Affairs. Under the aegis of the NKVD, of course. The Criminal concluded a concordat with the church and set up an administrative body in which priests stood on an equal footing with agents of the secret police. This was the creative and original way in which the Gensek implemented Lenin's injunction on the separation of church and state.

Metropolitan Nikolai began referring to the general secretary of the Bolshevik Party as "the Father of us all, Joseph Vissarionovich."

When Stalin spoke to the people, he addressed them as "brothers and sisters." The old fraud really knew how to play it. Everyone rose to defend the motherland, even the children of the cruelly mistreated "kulaks," the emigrés abroad, and internal exiles. And he kept smiling in the stillness of the Kremlin: After all, wasn't he the personification of the motherland itself?

The propaganda apparatus efficiently reorganized itself in accordance with the impassioned tub-thumping of the heroic-patriotic theme. Things reached the point of outright pan-Slavist agitation. The Pan-Slavic Committee, created for the occasion, called for a holy war against the Germans. It was impossible to understand what was going on. If this was a class struggle, why were German workers killing Soviet workers? And if it was a race war, how did that fit in with the doctrines of Marx and Lenin?

During this period Stalin obviously didn't care about the strict observance of doctrine. He was using everyone and everything he could. That's how the unique political paradoxes of the war period arose.

Stalin's diplomacy didn't proceed without paradoxes either. When things were going poorly, the Gensek—the chief of government himself—begged the Allies for help. Having recovered from the first defeats, Marshal Stalin assumed a confident tone. Of course, after the fall of Berlin he behaved like the sovereign of half the world.

Three phases. Three roles. Three masks.

Negotiations with Churchill began in July 1941. The British government considered Hitler's earlier dealings with Stalin illegal and would not recognize the new Soviet borders. Meeting with British and American diplomats in September, Stalin tried to charm Lord Beaverbrook and Averell Harriman, but sometimes a crude remark slipped out. At the December talks with Anthony Eden, the Gensek was intractable (the Germans had been stopped!). Eden complained, "It is impossible to work with Stalin."

Stalin would reproach his allies—reproach them and ask for help. His September 4 letter to Churchill was filled with despair: half the Ukraine had been lost and Leningrad was blockaded. Stalin begged Churchill not to delay even an hour longer, but to establish a second front immediately, and send airplanes, tanks, nonferrous metals, etc.

Was it so long ago that the Gensek had assured the world that the Soviet Union wasn't about to pull anyone else's chestnuts out of the fire? Ah, he miscalculated, the Farsighted One.

The new year brought new defeats. At the end of March 1942, Zhukov offered to select a weak sector of the German Front and, by concentrating his forces, strike a crippling blow. The Supreme Commander, however, rejected this plan. He stuck to the strategy of "operations on a broad front." Three times during the summer of the first year of war, Stalin rejected Zhukov's strategically justified plan—to withdraw the army to the left bank of the Dnieper and surrender Kiev. Three times.[174] The stubbornness of the Supreme Commander cost the lives of more than a million soldiers. Georgy Zhukov later wrote that over time Stalin began to get the hang of military strategy. Most likely this "testimony" found its way into his memoirs against the author's will. Zhukov had plenty of opportunity to satisfy himself of the Gensek's unvarying incompetence. As did Marshal Voronov. Preparations for a large-scale operation on the Northwest Front in February-March 1943 were unbelievably poor. The Stavka had chosen highly unsuitable terrain—swamps and forests. And an unfortunate time. Voronov wrote to Stalin, but the Supreme Commander left everything as it was. Huge numbers were lost.[175]

The same with Marshal Vasilevsky, former chief of staff at Soviet general headquarters. It appears from his memoirs that Stalin "didn't always accept optimal decisions, but always displayed an understanding of our difficulties." Vasilevsky also says of the Generalissimo: "To some extent he was inclined to lead battle operations in too unilinear a manner."[176] Vasilevsky constantly qualifies his criticisms, suggesting objective reasons for Stalin's mistakes. The marshal asserts that by the time of the battle of Kursk, Stalin displayed an ability to direct military operations in fully up-to-date fashion. But if the marshal had written the truth—that the history of great wars had never known a less talented Supreme Commander in Chief—would his book have come out?

It was Stalin himself who took the greatest pains to fill the press with the legend of the Great Strategist Generalissimo. You take Lenin, now— he never considered himself an expert in military affairs. But he obliged us, young comrades on the Central Committee at the time, "to learn the business of war thoroughly."[177]

In 1968 Marshal Rokossovsky was dying of cancer at Kuntsevo Hospital. Before his death he had a few things to say about Stalin as a commander.

"That half-educated priest just interfered with everyone. We had to deceive him: whatever absurd order he gave, we said 'Yessir,' then went ahead on our own."

Marshals Tukhachevsky and Yegorov, not long before their arrests, used to tell their friends that the Gensek knew *nothing* about the art of war.[178]

It is 1967. Malinovsky is present at an evening ceremony at Moscow University to celebrate the anniversary of the battle of Stalingrad. The marshal declined to speak. After the official ceremonies, however, at the dinner table, he related the bitter truth about the battle to a small circle of military intimates. Two "leaders," two willful bastards, set up a mill at Stalingrad, said Malinovsky. They managed to grind up 600,000 soldiers to start with. But who really cared about the bare steppes beyond the Volga? As for Stalingrad, as a city it no longer existed; it had been smashed to bits, wiped off the face of the earth. Then a meeting was held with the commanders of five Soviet fronts. The mill—more accurately, the mincing machine—needed more victims. So how about cutting Paulus off from the main German forces and surrounding his army?

That's what they did, at a cost of 700,000 more killed. Altogether in the battle over the city that bore the Master's name, 1,300,000 soldiers fell.

Malinovsky's remarks cast a pall over the joyous celebration.

* * *

Stalin knew from his seminary days how to pick up bits of knowledge on the fly. However, not possessing a deep mind, alien to all work, he had no grasp of military theory, nor was he familiar with modern military technology. He had not fought at the front and had no idea what combat conditions were like. He steered clear of the life of a soldier. He managed only to master military terminology hastily, and he used other people's advice, which he passed off as his own. By the end of the war it wasn't at all difficult for this experienced pretender to play the part of military strategist in front of his generals.

Stalin obviously gravitated toward the obsolete doctrines of the civil war: frontal attack, fighting for each village and town in order. Unilinear operations. The new commanders were able to learn from the strategies and tactics of Hitler's Wehrmacht. But not Stalin. The stamp of his "military genius" lies on most of the catastrophic defeats during the first years of the war.

In the spring of 1942, Stalin, without taking the tactical situation into consideration, made a hasty attempt to break the Leningrad blockade. The new commander of the Leningrad Front, Mikhail Khozin, justifiably charged Moscow with failure to coordinate the operations of the inner (Leningrad) and the outer (Volkhov) fronts. Stalin didn't have to think long —he ordered the fronts to merge. (His old custom of reshuffling people's commissariats, enlarging them or subdividing them, influenced his thinking here.) The Leningrad reorganization brought swift results—the Germans destroyed the Second Shock Army.

Events unfolded along similar lines in the south. The Germans took Kharkov and seized the Crimea. Stalin ordered Kharkov retaken. The "offensive" launched by Stalin at Tsaritsyn in the summer of 1918 had cost the lives of several hundred Red Army men. In the Kharkov adventure he squandered 300,000 soldiers' lives. Different times, different dimensions. But the same old "strategy." And the same old attitude toward commanders. Stalin replaced four military commanders at Leningrad within a short time.

The losses during the first months were appalling. Every battalion was affected. Meanwhile, at the Bay of Nakhodka, in the notorious transit center there, seventy thousand prisoners sat idle. Idle? Every day entire divisions of "enemies of the people" were driven out under escort to dig holes in the frozen polar ground. The next day they filled the trenches they had dug at such cost. (Not quite the way it was for Dostoevsky. In his *House of the Dead* the convicts dragged stones from place to place.) How many armies, how many army corps, passed through the Nakhodka transit center? How many places like Nakhodka were functioning in the country —from Karakum to Novaya Zemlya?

But the front demanded more and more living forces. At that point the Merciful One decided at least to pardon the children of "enemies of the people." Then 100,000 criminals, straight from the prison camps, were admitted to the army. Anything would do as cannon fodder. No, not quite anything. They wouldn't let the politicals die for tsar and fatherland—that is, "For the motherland! For Stalin!" To this day I don't know whether this was for the better or the worse.

* * *

With time, better military equipment began to reach the front lines. Soviet factories were working at full capacity, and the powerful support from the Allies—the United States and England—was making itself felt. The iron necessity of war forced the more gifted and strong-willed generals to the fore. Unit commanders gained experience, and the soldiers themselves learned effective ways of defeating the invaders. A change came in people's consciousness. Hitler meant death; they *had to win*, to save their very lives.

After the battle on the Volga, the sun shone at a new angle, pointing toward victory. The Gensek sensed the change and let it be known immediately that the days of easygoing tolerance had passed. Draconian laws poured down on the heads of the "brothers and sisters." The time of the whip came for the battlefront and the home front alike. Stalin wanted to drive fresh armies to the slaughter. The soldiers, however, didn't express total rapture at the thought of the mincing machine. Their unskilled officers didn't fill them with confidence either. The whip cracked, and the Supreme Commander's henchmen devised an entire system for handling "unplanned retreats" (no one ever used the words "panic flight"). They worked out elaborate methods for stopping "deserters": "barrier" units behind the lines, penal battalions, and the security organs of SMERSH (an acronym from the Russian words "Death to Spies," *SMERt SHpionam*). A retired colonel, M., gives us this account.

Attached to our tank unit was a representative of SMERSH named Galenyi, a loathsome, evil man. Among ourselves we called him Govennyi (Shitty). He held the rank of lieutenant, but it was his habit to kick open the door of the regiment commander's dugout with his boot. And the battle-hardened colonel trembled before him.

Lieutenant Shit would summon a major or a captain and order: "Keep your eye on Major So-and-So. And report to me on him daily." He summoned me, also, but I refused to "report."

"How do you think I'm going to inform on a comrade who fights alongside me on the front lines?"

"What's wrong? You afraid of him? Listen, I can arrest him today, and send him out to be shot tomorrow. So don't be afraid."[179]

I haven't even mentioned the legions of political workers who were devoted to Stalin—an entire army that saw to the "maintenance of order" among the troops.

A steely, punishing sound began to be heard in the orders of the Supreme Commander in Chief. In the spring of 1943, headquarters at the Northern Front received a telegram:

"If so much as a single soldier retreats a single meter on the Valdai sector, the following will be shot: the commander of the front, the members of the military council, the commanders of the armies, and the chiefs of the political units. . . ."

A total of fifteen names were listed. Stalin's order was delivered to all fifteen.[180] They knew the Master wasn't kidding. It was on his orders, after all, that "the commander of the Western Front, General Dmitry Pavlov, and the chief of staff of that front, General Vasily Klimovskikh, were unjustly accused and shot. . . ."[181]

The old formula "We are free to put to death or . . . to have mercy" was revived. One of Stalin's old sidekicks from Tsaritsyn, Grigory Kulik, busied himself for a while as one of Beria's assistants, then became head of the artillery administration. When Kulik gave an order, he accompanied it with a thoughtful warning: "It's either a medal or prison." That was the Stalin style.

A new order went into effect at the front—anyone who retreats will be shot on the spot. Prisoners of war were placed in the same category as traitors: members of their families were sent to the camps.

Stalin didn't fail to provide new laws for his second kingdom too, the one behind barbed wire. The Criminal Code contained a certain Article 158: escape from confinement was punishable by two years in prison. This clause was replaced by Article 58, point 14—escape from Stalin's death camps was made tantamount to counterrevolutionary sabotage. For attempting to flee the forced labor and slow death of the camps, you could be shot. A certain humane logic might be seen in this, if one were so inclined.

In 1943, at a general conference for officials of the Organs, Vsevolod Merkulov, the minister of state security, issued a directive—create a massive network of agents that would "extend through Russia's entire population."[182]

* * *

Engels, in *Anti-Dühring,* cites a historical episode: "In the summer of 1873, [the Russian] General Kaufman ordered the Tatar tribe of the Yomuds [in Turkestan] to be attacked, their tents to be burned, and their women and children butchered 'in the good old Caucasian way.' "[183] Brought up on the touching traditions of blood feuds and intercommunal butchery and violence, Stalin adopted Kaufman's methods with unfailing success.

He commissioned Klim Voroshilov to supervise the deportation of the Tatars from the Crimea. The marshal's finest hour had come. On May 18, 1944, NKVD troops shipped all the Crimean Tatar women, children, and old people off to permanent exile. There was no one to intervene for them: their men were at the front defending the motherland.

After twenty-three years the charges of wholesale treason were finally lifted from the Crimean Tatar people. But the genocide of that people has not stopped. Even a letter with a million Crimean Tatar signatures did not shake the arrangements Stalin made.

People still talk and write about the deportation of the Volga Germans and the Chechens. But really it was extermination.

Merkulov and Beria's deputy Ivan Serov directed the eviction operations against the Chechens. In February 1944 the freedom-loving mountain tribesmen were tricked into participating in some "military maneuvers," whereupon they were surrounded by NKVD troops and loaded onto trains. Their families were sent along right behind them—without belongings, without clothing, without provisions, without water. They were sent in locked and barred railroad cars to the rigorous Kazakh steppes. At the destination the doors of the cars were opened. The corpses of the children were carried out first, then those of the adults. For those who resisted the forcible evacuation from the auls (mountain villages in the Caucasus), it was simpler: they were locked in sheds and burned. Cremated alive.

In 1956 a special government commission found the bones of women, children, and old people who had been burned alive in the *auls.* But no one made Merkulov and Serov answer for this. It would have been awkward. After all, Marshal Stalin had awarded the Order of Lenin to these emissaries of the Lubyanka for that combat operation.

The Father of the Peoples had had some prewar experience in that area. In the early thirties, whole villages were deported to Siberia for failure to meet grain delivery quotas to the state. In 1939, all the Koreans in Birobidzhan were relocated to Central Asia and Kazakhstan in two days. Not even those who had married Russians were left. Later the Koreans would be "resettled" again. How many of these hard-working, uncomplaining people would survive the cold, hunger, and violence? In 1939 also Galicians were deported from the Ukraine. And Greeks: How many of them perished in the camps? Not even the happy conclusion of the war stopped the Great Internationalist. In 1945–46, 3.5 million Germans were exiled from Czechoslovakia. They were natives of that country, and the overwhelming majority of them had not been involved in politics. This mass deportation went down in history as an outstanding case of inhuman cruelty. The people remember both the slaughter in the city of Usti and the death march from Brno. Hundreds of suicides, thousands killed—and then the camps.

It was all the Germans' fault. They could have disclaimed their national identity, but they didn't. And so they shared the fate of the millions of Crimean Tatars, Chechens, Greeks, and Koreans, the fate of their former countrymen—the Volga Germans.

This was unmistakably a Stalin operation.

* * *

The war with Hitler, no matter how badly it went at the start, couldn't be allowed to interrupt Stalin's internal war against his own people. Ulrikh and his team moved to a semibasement of Butyrka prison, to a room with the windows painted black. The prison supervisors explained to the curious inhabitants of death row that war maneuvers had started in Moscow.

A wave of preventive arrests swept the Baltic region. In the beginning of June 1941, thirty-five thousand were grabbed in Lithuania alone. Spy mania became the bread and butter of the Lubyanka, and the "spy" label became one of the Master's favorites. Not long before the German invasion, the Organs exposed 1,338 "spies" in the Baltic and Western regions of the Ukraine—out of a total of 1,596 persons arrested.[184] The year 1941 turned out to be a bloody one indeed in the prisons of the western and central regions. The watchword was: Don't abandon "enemies of the people" to the Germans!

At the start of the war there were about five thousand prisoners in the Oryol isolation prison for political offenders. Among them were Maria Spiridonova, a former leader of the Left Socialist Revolutionary Party (Left SRs), and Iosif Khodorovsky, former secretary of the Siberian Bureau of the Communist Party, a Bolshevik since 1907. When the Germans were about to take Oryol, the prisoners were herded into the basement, which was then flooded. They all died, all five thousand. (Khodorovsky's wife, who was shipped off to a camp, told about this atrocity.)

In the first months of the war, column after column of prisoners, starving, half-naked, were driven eastward over well-worn roads. The weak were finished off with bayonets. Those who survived the miles and miles of marching were shoved into railroad cars without water or food —and shipped east.

At Kirovograd prison in the Ukraine, as the Germans approached, trials were held in the yard. One or two questions, a verdict, and the victim was promptly dragged off to the death house. An appeal? A pardon? For heaven's sake! War means you dispense with everything.[185]

In 1941 the NKVD dug up the files of all previously arrested people, hastily concocted new cases, and again dispatched the "enemies" to the camps. The four-story building of Kirovograd prison, which could barely hold its thousand prisoners, was jammed with twelve thousand new ones.[186]

Any suspicious remark might be punishable under Article 58. Complaints about starvation, the unbearable workload, or the lousy streetcar system, or reference to the high level of German technology. Anything could bring arrest. And anyone could be arrested anywhere. Including in the camps.

In Section No. 11 of the Ust-Vym camp in 1942 there were four former district committee secretaries from Leningrad and an Old Bolshevik by the name of Vasily Yegorov, who at one time had been second secretary of the party's Moscow committee. They knew a lot. And they indulged in certain recollections dangerous for the state, about the death of Kirov. It was "up against the wall" for things like that. They were tried again and found guilty—in the camp. The charge this time was "defeatist conversations" about the war. They were among eleven persons shipped off to another camp, Vozhael, and never again seen alive.

The Master gave lavishly of his time to his favorite child, the Gulag. During the war the kingdom behind barbed wire was blessed with the revival of forced labor, given the name it had under the tsars, *katorga*. Life in the camps was further enriched by the use of leg irons. He had not invented them himself, the Father of the Peoples, but he knew they were the most important human invention after the wheel and had waited impatiently for the time when he could reintroduce them.

The war produced a new wave of emigration, the second since the revolution. Hundreds of thousands who had gained true insight left the country. But some who left had not lost faith in the Stalinist variety of "socialism," and when the time came they returned. The Organs grabbed them and saw to their further enlightenment.

Stalin took pains to enlarge the Lubyanka. It got a new department, for handling prisoners of war and other "returnees" from abroad. Its Russian initials were GUPVI and its operational department was headed by Bogdan Kobulov, Beria's deputy. Bogdan's younger brother, Amayak, headed another new government institution, the Chief Administration for Soviet Property Abroad, whose Russian initials gave it the acronym GUSIMZ. Murder and robbery are kindred crimes, and the Kobulov brothers were classic criminals. The lives of hundreds of thousands of loyal citizens who fought against Hitler's Reich must be credited to their bloody accounts. The country should know its heroes!

* * *

The last two years of the war were filled with diplomatic negotiations. Stalin met not only with Churchill and Roosevelt but also with their successors, Attlee and Truman. The Gensek hobnobbed with, among others, French President de Gaulle, Generals Anders and MacArthur, and the British foreign ministers Bevin and Eden.

Not all of them trusted him, by any means. But none of them saw through him completely. This was an outstanding achievement for Stalin the actor. He was accompanied by a worthy entourage. If a disagreement arose during negotiations, one of his underlings would take the foreign dignitary aside and ask him, please, not to contradict the will of the Leader.

His best part was the role of the respectable, considerate, and humane sovereign, as in the poem by Rustaveli:

> His just sword slew the guilty.
> >   (Only the guilty.)
> Law ruled supreme throughout the land.
> >   (Throughout the land and for all time!)
> The wolf and lamb lay down together,
> And never did he touch the lamb.
> >   (And never would! And the Terror was just an
> >   invention of the Trotskyites.)

Weary of Stalin's continual and obscene maneuvering, Anthony Eden once exclaimed, "The Russians always lie."

The Gensek's constant lying was not a "labor of love." His thirst for new territories was what prompted him to lie and deceive. In 1945 he resumed his bargaining for the Turkish straits, which had been interrupted by the war. Now he pressed the point in discussions with Churchill and Eden, and complained to Bevin: "England controls India and other countries. The United States is extending its influence to China. And we don't have anything." Again and again he insisted on the Dardanelles. His passionate desire ("his only one, but oh how ardent") found an echo in the soul of the émigré Pavel Milyukov, former tsarist minister and head of the bourgeois Constitutional Democratic ("Cadet") Party, who had been Russia's foreign minister briefly in 1917. Milyukov called upon his compatriots living outside of Russia to support Stalin's foreign policy, since its aim was to bring new lands into the Russian orbit. During World War I, Milyukov earned the nickname "the Dardanellesian" because of his constant preoccupation with the straits. But he's not the one who should have had that nickname; no, not he.

Having firmly decided to keep for himself a certain portion of Polish territory, what he called Western Byelorussia and Western Ukraine, Stalin assured Churchill that he had full respect for the Polish government in London and favored a "strong and free Poland."

Another matter for negotiation was Japan. In the Potsdam talks with Truman and Eden, Stalin bargained them into letting him have an occupation zone in Japan. He had his eye on the Chinese port of Dairen and the Chinese Eastern Railway as well. The Gensek was so carried away by his new acquisitions (remember the words, "We do not want one foot of foreign soil"?) that he forgot to sign a peace treaty with Japan. So today Japan's claims to the territories seized by Stalin are not devoid of legal foundation.[187]

Some details of Stalin's Far Eastern policy remain unknown to Soviet citizens to this day. Stalin was not merely aware of the Allies' intention to use the atomic bomb; he offered to provide an air base for the American bombers. He had no fear of the bomb; he had not yet understood its awesome powers of destruction. What he feared was something else— being late for the divvying up of the spoils. That's why he declared war against Japan two days after the American bomb was dropped. Three weeks later Japan surrendered. Stalin had time to seize a few small islands and return the southern half of the island of Sakhalin to the Russian crown. But at what a price: several hundred thousand more Soviet soldiers laid down their lives for no good reason, to take more foreign soil.

According to the proverb, the chicken says: "When they slaughter a ram they come for me too. When they slaughter a cow they come for me too. When they slaughter a hog they come for me too." The Russian peasants didn't know this Georgian proverb, although they died by the millions under the Master's knife—in the war as in the camps, in the camps as in the war.

A division was given the order to attack a railroad line. There was a high embankment open to crossfire from German artillery and machine guns. The entire division fell. Only a handful of staff officers were left. And the banner. That meant the division still existed. Reinforcements were brought in. There was a new attack, and once again they all fell.

In October 1943 a new shipment of prisoners arrived in Kolyma, fifteen hundred zeks. After two months only about seventy were still half alive. But a new load of prisoners arrived to reinforce them.

Is there a difference? No, just two types of slaughterhouses.

At Tehran Stalin insisted on the immediate opening of a second front. Churchill argued that this would result in the unjustified deaths of tens of thousands of Allied soldiers. Stalin replied: "When one man dies it's a tragedy. When thousands die it's statistics."[188]

A certain Swiss scholar has counted up the number of wars known to have occurred in the last five thousand years: approximately fifty-three hundred. The number that died were as follows:

In the seventeenth century, three million.

In the eighteenth century, three million.

In the nineteenth century, five million.

In the twentieth century, sixty million.

Germany's losses in World War I were 1,824,000 dead, 4,247,600 wounded.

Russia's losses were 1,664,800 dead, and 3,748,600 wounded.

On the Soviet Front in World War II, Germany lost 6.9 million soldiers.[189]

When Stalin was informed of the German losses he ordered the announced casualties of his army reduced by seven million. His subjects had no need to know the truth. They were overburdened with information already. Evidently, similar humane considerations guided the Gensek in reducing the number of officially announced casualties in the war with Finland by a factor of ten—to 249,000. Molotov gave that figure over the radio in 1940. How many times were the new losses reduced?

Specialists in demography have estimated that 27.5 million Soviet citizens died in battle against the German troops.[190] Not seven million, and not twenty million, as the official historians shamefacedly admit today, but 27.5 million.

This does not include the million and a half who died of hunger in Leningrad. And how many died throughout the country from war-related hunger and illness? How many died unknown to others? How many became cripples? Four, five, six million?

Statistics.

In the postwar period there was an old peasant woman in the camp in Pechora (sent there for "petty theft on the job": she had taken some corn for her starving grandchild). These were her data: "In my family seven people were killed in the war. Everyone is gone. No one but me is left."

How does statistics handle that?

At the Eighth Party Congress Lenin was indignant about the losses at Tsaritsyn, where sixty thousand Red Army men were lost because of Stalin and Voroshilov: "We would not have lost those sixty thousand if there had been military specialists and if there had been a regular army."[191]

To wipe out a military specialist was a matter of no importance at all to Stalin even in the civil war. At the closed session of the Eighth Congress on the military question, Aleksei Okulov commented:

"The absence of a command staff at the front means that soldiers don't march into battle, but to the slaughter."[192]

Stalin gave new force to these words in World War II.

The following testimony by Aleksei Yepishev, head of the army's political directorate, dates from 1963. At that time it was possible at least to write half the truth about Stalin's crimes:

"The mass repression against commanders . . . and Stalin's gross errors in evaluating the military and political situation on the eve . . . of the war, and his serious mistakes in directing the armed forces in 1941 and 1942 cost the Soviet people very dearly."[193] And what about the ruined factories, the mines that were flooded, the bridges that were blown up, entire towns and villages that were destroyed? They used to sing a ditty in the concert halls before the war about how every Soviet soldier would kill at least a dozen "Fritzes." In reality four Ivans died for every Fritz.

And to this day nobody calls Generalissimo Stalin to account for it, and no one dares pass judgment on him.

On one occasion at a Central Committee plenum—this was after the Twentieth Congress—a discussion began about the war. It was said that they too, the Politburo members, had helped to forge the victory. Georgy Zhukov rose and hurled this in their faces: "You people collaborated with Stalin in driving the troops like cattle to the slaughter."[194]

A truthful word had been spoken. But the party brass hid their rage. They put together a majority against Zhukov (they knew how to do that too) and forced Khrushchev to remove the overly conscientious commander.

It is hard to estimate or even to imagine the scale of the disasters Stalin organized. He had a worse fate in store for many of the soldiers who survived the front. The blame for their agonizing deaths is shared among Stalin, Churchill, and Eden. At the Yalta Conference Stalin won from his allies the agreement that they would repatriate all Soviet subjects. (I'll return twenty-five thousand British prisoners of war to you, and you give me the heads of all my traitors.) In 1944, during a visit to Moscow, Eden promised Stalin they would abide by this condition.

There turned out to be about two million displaced persons, including many soldiers and officers of Vlasov's army. Eden knew what was in store for them. Nevertheless he gave the order for all to be repatriated. And to use force, if necessary. In Austria fifty thousand Cossacks were handed over to the Soviet command along with their families. They were driven into railroad cars by rifle butt and sent off "home."[195] At the same time four thousand old émigrés who had left Russia at the time of the revolution were rounded up. They were not Soviet subjects. Many had fought side by side with British soldiers against the common enemy, Hitler's army.

The first batch of repatriates arrived in Murmansk in October 1944. They were loaded onto barges and into railroad cars and sent to the camps to their deaths. Thousands of them came to our camp in the Pechora region.

In March 1940 the Finns freed the Soviet prisoners of war they had captured. A triumphant welcome was organized for them in Leningrad. They marched under an arch bearing the banner "The Homeland Greets Its Heroes." Overjoyed, they marched the length of the city. Suddenly, before they had cooled off, they were ordered to march into railroad cars with barred windows.

Deception, a theatrical gesture, and as a finale, vengeance. How could one fail to recognize the hand of the Supreme Stage Director? When repatriates arrived by sea in Odessa they were led out behind the warehouses on the docks and shot on the spot. Not all of them, of course. Some were shipped off to the northern camps. Including women and children.[196]

The Leader would happily have killed everyone who fought in the war. Those who returned from campaigns abroad had been infected by alien moods, seen a different kind of life. Tens of millions of his subjects had lived under the German occupation. And imagine! They had lived through it. Who could vouch for their frame of mind now?

In 1814, after the Russian army had marched into Paris, the infection called the Decembrist movement resulted. But a similarity is not an exact repetition. The Red Army's campaign in Europe could not produce anything like the Decembrist movement. This time there was a *real* police machine.

Maybe, just in case, it would be better to put the entire adult population behind barbed wire. Introduce universal prison service. The people would understand. The people would support it. The Gensek's creative thinking began working in that direction, but he caught himself in time. There had to be someone at large, to work—and someone to stand guard over the arrested people. No, it wouldn't do to send everyone.

The Father of the Peoples did manage, however, to bring the population of the kingdom behind barbed wire back up to the high point of 1938 —sixteen million. Not great, but *some* consolation.

Many of the national minorities deported during the war also ended up in the camps—Crimean Tatars, Greeks, Chechens, Gypsies, and Volga Germans. I got to know some of the Volga German exiles at Vorkuta. They were in special zones, forced to work in the coal mines. After the war the barbed wire was taken down, but they still lived in barracks. Those who had belonged to the party were still considered members. Even they were not allowed to leave their place of exile, though, on pain of death. They held party meetings, gave reports to the district committee—in a word, did everything required by the party rules. My nonparty mind absolutely could not understand it.

The groans of the camp population did not reach Moscow's ears. The capital was booming with the celebrations of Victory Day in May 1945. "Where there is Stalin, there is victory," rang the slogan. Perhaps that was so. But the words should be reversed: "Where there is victory, there is Stalin." He invariably showed up after the enemy had been driven off, when the trumpets of victory were sounding.

The Generalissimo's chest bore two Orders of Victory and one gold Hero of the Soviet Union star. But he didn't win. Hitler lost. The strategic and political errors of the Nazi leadership are obvious to history. A verse of Pushkin's posed the following question about Alexander I's victory over Napoleon:

> Who helped most in this case—
> The aroused fury of the people,
> Winter, Barclay, or Russia's god?

The victory of 1945 was won not by Stalin but by the people under his domination—in spite of the tyrant. The people, emaciated and exhausted from hunger, lashed by the prison and exile system, bled white by terror, were left without commanding officers, equipment, food. Still they managed to defeat the vast power of Hitler's Reich.

The history of warfare has never known a Supreme Commander in Chief like this. He dealt the army a treacherous blow, laid waste the country, and opened the borders to foreign invasion. This doesn't quite jibe with Pospelov's statement about the vigilance of the Leader, who allegedly smashed the "fifth column" several years before the war. That fifth column existed in imagination only. There was a real one though— Molotov, Kaganovich, Malenkov, Zhdanov, Voroshilov, Mikoyan, Kalinin, Beria, and all the other Shkiryatovs, Mekhlises, and Kuliks.

At the beginning of the war Georgy Malenkov gained special favor in the eyes of the Master. It was no longer Zhdanov but Malenkov who seemed destined to become the aging Leader's successor. Molotov barely concealed his hostility toward Zhdanov. During the terrifying defeats of June and July 1941 Molotov and Malenkov took the place of the Master-turned-Coward. It was they who suggested to Stalin the idea of sending Zhdanov to Leningrad.

Malenkov is responsible, along with Stalin, for the disaster in Leningrad, when the Second Shock Army under General Vlasov was trapped and destroyed in an area of swamps and bogs. To advance his own career Malenkov was ready to betray the Leningrad front and have Zhdanov destroyed. Vlasov, who went over to the Germans, had been a protégé of Malenkov, but that didn't affect the Master's attitude toward his new favorite. For Zhdanov the fall of Leningrad would have meant the end of everything. If the city were surrendered, the triumvirate of Molotov, Malenkov, and Beria would totally supplant him in the Master's favor. For days on end Zhdanov didn't sleep, desperately putting together the remnants of ruined armies and demanding the impossible from the population.

In Beria's department, they had learned how to use poison quite skillfully long before the war—no worse than the doges of Venice or the Borgias. Lavrenty Pavlovich might have taken a hand in Zhdanov's premature death even without special orders from on high.

No, the fifth column led by Stalin was not monolithic. But to make up for it, the talents of some of those top party saboteurs flowered remarkably.

One of Stalin's favorites was of course Lev Mekhlis. Mekhlis was in charge of agitation and propaganda before the war, a highly profitable operation. In the words of one of his coworkers, he was "as energetic as he was obnoxious. The more decisive he became, the less competent he was. Knowledgeable in a general but superficial way, he was self-assured to the point of being rudely domineering."[197]

"General" Mekhlis became deputy people's commissar of defense and contributed more effectively than anyone, through his incompetent interference, to the fall of the Crimea in the spring of 1942. He brought charges against military leaders and insisted that commanders be replaced. Stalin himself made the cutting remark that "Mekhlis apparently wants to see Hindenburg at the head of the Soviet Army." But Lev Mekhlis wasn't easily embarrassed. He flew into a party administrator's rage and moved to have A. S. Frolov, commander of the Kerch naval base, shot. Mekhlis "worked" exactly the same way during the Finnish campaign. Stalin sent him to oversee the commanders at the Mannerheim Line. He removed many of the Ninth Army's top officers and insisted on having Gusev and Vinogradov shot, although they were guilty of nothing. They had commanded the 44th and 163d divisions, which had been smashed by the Finns. Admiral Kuznetsov unwittingly overheard Stalin talking to Mekhlis in April 1940, after the ill-starred Finnish war was over. The Master said to Mekhlis: "You've got into the habit, out there in the field, of carrying commanders around in your pocket and doing anything with them that crosses your mind."

But that was the Master's own style of "leadership."

In 1943 Mekhlis played commissar on the Bryansk Front. Things went just great for him there. One day, August 24, he got the idea that our pilots had attacked their own lines. He ordered the planes to land immediately and placed the pilots before a military tribunal. But for the brave intervention of an officer who had seen the results of their raids on the German lines, the men would have been shot.

In late 1943, Mekhlis was given a new assignment, on the Volkhov Front. How did he fight there? And against whom? Let Admiral Kuznetsov tell us: "Invested with broad powers, he sought to replace the military commanders everywhere, and to do everything his own way. He bore down unmercifully on everyone and at the same time took no responsibility for the outcome of military operations."[198]

A perfect match for Mekhlis was Grigory Kulik, Stalin's crony from Tsaritsyn. In the war he too was a deputy people's commissar of defense. Wherever Kulik appeared, defeat and death for entire armies and army corps were assured.[199]

Stalin appointed party luminaries to all the most responsible positions. To the extent of their vast incapacities they constantly sabotaged the orders given by individual commanders, resulting in millions of casualties. But the Leader could not do without the services of men like Mekhlis. They were devoted to him, with a piglike, squealing devotion to the Master. They held the officers' corps in a vise of constant terror, thus reducing the Gensek's fear of his powerful generals and marshals, like Zhukov.

As long as party mandarins like Mekhlis, Malenkov, Zhdanov, and Beria were at work on the front lines and in the Kremlin, Hitler could look to the future with confidence. No other conqueror has ever had such a reliable fifth column in the enemy's rear.

* * *

The subversive activity Stalin undertook in the late thirties did irreparable damage to Soviet military potential.

Korolev, Glushko, and Sevruk were talented rocket designers, engineers well known in their field. How Hitler would have loved to be able to recruit them, even one of them. Or to put them out of commission. But what could he do? The arm of German intelligence wasn't that long. Stalin's arm proved to be just the right length: he put all three of them in prison. He had two other important engineers killed—Georgy Langemak and Ivan Kleimenov, designers of self-propelled tactical rockets.[200] And thereby held up production for two years on the "Katyusha" rocket launchers, which struck terror into Hitler's armies.

When Stalin seized Libava in July 1940, he decided from the high seat of his unchallengeable incompetenence to base some warships there. An equally unsafe anchorage was found for some in the harbor of Tallin. The Gensek forced Admiral Kuznetsov to transfer several battleships from Kronstadt to Tallin.

The head of the fifth column provided Hitler with secret aid from outside the Soviet Union as well. When Soviet troops occupied Gdansk (Danzig), which had a base and an experimental yard for German submarines, Stalin refused to pass on to his allies any helpful information about the enemy's technical innovations.[201]

How many thousands of American sailors died on Stalin's account?

Stalin and Hitler fought shoulder to shoulder against the Soviet people. And against the American people.

* * *

On his chest the Generalissimo should have worn, not the Soviet Order of Victory, but Hitler's Iron Cross—the only medal Stalin truly earned in that war. He had the top generals shot, destroyed the officer corps, and undermined the army's fighting capacity. He sabotaged efforts to prepare for war and supplied the enemy with food and strategic war materials. He postponed mobilization of the land and naval forces, kept more than ten million men of draft age locked up in death camps, and had an army of "internal troops," three million strong, diverted to guard the camps and wage war against their own people. Once war began, he assisted the progress of Hitler's occupying forces in every possible way.

He seemed to be doing everything he could to make this the most shameful war in Russia's history. And if the Soviet people came to think of it as the *Great* Patriotic War, it was great—and this can't be emphasized too much—*in spite of Stalin.*

* * *

Tsarist Russia entered World War I unprepared. Nicholas I ordered Minister of War Vladimir Sukhomlinov, the man responsible for the catastrophe, to be tried. Stalin, who was to blame for the disastrous way the war began in 1941 and for the deaths of tens of millions, was proclaimed Savior of the Homeland.

The Nuremberg trials were held in a large hall; there was room enough for *all* the chief war criminals. But they weren't all tried. Some committed suicide. Others appeared in the role of accusers—Stalin, Molotov, Kaganovich, Malenkov, and the like. Why? There was rope enough to hang them all.

THE TYRANT WEARIES OF IT ALL

5

By 1946 Stalin took for granted the signs of devotion flooding in from all quarters. If you keep telling a man of limited intelligence he's a genius, in the end he'll believe it. Exceptional qualities are needed to resist constant flattery and servility—above all, intellect. That was not Stalin's strong suit. He actually came to believe in his kinship with Zeus. After all, his slightest wish or merest utterance took on the force of law.

Oddly enough, the peoples of the countries Stalin occupied after the war took a great liking to his model of socialism. Before long each new "socialist" state had its own personality cult. It's not hard to understand why. Some of Wladyslaw Gomulka's remarks at the eighth Central Committee plenum of the Polish United Workers Party in October 1956 shed light on the question.

"The cult of personality was a certain system which prevailed in the Soviet Union and was grafted onto probably all the Communist parties," particularly in "the countries of the socialist camp." The essence of this system, Gomulka explained, was "a hierarchic ladder of cults" at the top of which stood Stalin. "All those who stood on lower rungs of the ladder bowed their heads before him." Like Stalin, "the first secretaries of the Central Committees of the Communist parties [ruling the "socialist" countries] donned the robes of infallibility and wisdom in their turn." When power, and the right to a cult, were seized "by a mediocre man, one who blindly followed orders, or a rotten careerist," the result was that "socialism was buried—senselessly, but with absolute certainty."[202]

There's no denying Gomulka's powers of observation. But why refer so vaguely to the practice of deifying Stalinist leaders as a "personality cult"? It was a *power* cult, the cult of whoever held the seat of top party secretary.

Now, as Stalin towered over this system, having acquired more lands than Alexander the Great and more medals than a holy Indian elephant has ornaments, so that there was nowhere left to pin them on—as he came to feel that he had accomplished *everything*—the tyrant wearied of it all.

If it hadn't been for Tito, Stalin might have simply wasted away from boredom. Josip Broz Tito absolutely refused to submit to the Master. Not only that. He also had leanings toward that dangerous idea of Dimitrov's, a Balkan federation. Stalin succeeded in removing Dimitrov—the onetime heroic defendant in Hitler's frame-up trial over the Reichstag fire—without much trouble. But Tito, Tito, what a problem!

For starters, Stalin branded him an agent of fascism and imperialism. Then trials of "oppositionists," following the Soviet recipe, were held in Bulgaria, Romania, Hungary, and Czechoslovakia. "Confessions" ticking off Tito's crimes came thick and fast. Off the assembly lines poured books denouncing Tito, with titles like *The Tito Gang—Tool of the Anglo-American Warmongers.* In the workers' clubs ditties like this were sung:

> Tito, Tito, dear old Tito,
> You've gone so far, you've reached Wall Street—oh.
> There's nowhere further you can go,
> So now you'll have to fly, Tito. . . .

Stalin already had his eye on the Adriatic. As soon as this upstart was out of the way, we could start talking about reuniting with our distant brothers the Southern Slavs. But this time the Lubyanka proved powerless.

How many times the Master prodded Beria: "What are you waiting for? Why are you dragging things out like this?"

"Everything's set. This time we won't fail," Lavrenty would answer.

Coming out of the Gensek's office, Beria saw Kruglov, the minister of internal affairs.

"What were you talking about for so long?" Kruglov was curious.

"The Boss wants Tito taken care of faster. . . ."[203]

After the Gensek's death a letter from Tito was found in his apartment.

> Stalin,
>
> You've sent seven men after me—with pistols, grenades, and poison. If I send one, I won't have to send another.
>
> Josip Tito[204]

Hard as it was to liquidate Trotsky, the Chekist heroes had nevertheless coped with the task entrusted to them by the party. But Tito . . . Tito! In his hatred the Gensek went to absurd lengths. When the TsSKA soccer team lost to the Yugoslavs, Stalin ordered the team disbanded. Why didn't he order the members arrested, as he had the Starostin brothers from the Spartacus soccer team? He didn't want it thought that the war had eroded his magnanimity.

Hitler was no longer around. Whom could Stalin serve now? He volunteered as an agent of imperialism. Nothing helped the West consolidate its forces so much as Stalin's aggressive foreign policy. In that sense NATO was his direct offspring.

The tone of diplomatic negotiations changed abruptly. Uncle Joe dropped the mask of the good shepherd. He thundered against the enemy. The time had come to break with his former allies.

And now his postwar partners saw him in an aspect that was new for them—the hoodlum. This does not mean that the Gensek abandoned his tactics of intrigue and provocation. In May 1946 he tried to provoke a clash between Dimitrov and Tito. Whenever he could, he tried to set Communist leaders fighting among themselves, the same as with bourgeois politicians.

As ever, he bartered tirelessly. Litvinov described Koba as a petty merchant of the Asian-bazaar type. The kind who in buying a rug will go on bargaining long and stubbornly, down to the last penny, and end up making a profit, if only a tiny one.

However, on big political questions the merchant Dzhugashvili often enough lost out rather heavily. The negotiations at Potsdam ended up with the United States and Great Britain obtaining all German patents and technical documentation. The main victor in the war had his eyes on the machinery and equipment, the fixed capital in the German factories under his control; he also grabbed a certain amount of German gold. But the equipment he seized soon became obsolete, while in West Germany the construction of new plants began.

Balancing that, Stalin achieved impressive successes in the realm of social policy. After the war the party and the people became more monolithic than ever. Nothing solidifies the ranks like fear and suffering, and there was plenty of both under Stalin. Of course there were naïve fellows among the soldiers who returned from the war. They began talking about dissolving the collective farms and having something simply unheard of —"free elections" of some sort. Fortunately these types were far outnumbered by respectable and law-abiding citizens, taught since childhood to keep their mouths shut. And they treasured their muteness as their most precious possession.

Then there was discipline—the ironclad discipline of the party and the state, stronger than that at the battlefront. At least at the front you could rise from the ground when the time came to charge, to attack. In peacetime everyone had to crawl like a *plastun* (the special Cossack foot soldier skilled in the tactic of creeping up to enemy lines undetected). Under surveillance by millions of bosses on the job, teachers at school, party organizers, snoopy ladies on the staffs of the trade unions, ordinary informers, secret police, neighbors in apartments, and workmates, no one dared raise his head.

Postwar Stalinist society gave birth to another noteworthy paradox: the more educated people there were, armed with diplomas and academic titles, the less intelligence they exhibited. An apotheosis of careerism and philistinism. A philistine is not a very attractive figure to begin with. But when you add national chauvinism, he's frightening. Slaughtered by the millions in the years of collectivization and terror, thrust into the meat grinder of war by a totally uninspired strategist, the Soviet philistine was ready to bring all of Europe to its knees and, if the Leader ordered it, the whole world as well. Because the philistine himself knew no other way to exist than upon his knees.

Undoubtedly this consideration prevented Stalin from making public the Soviet government's endorsement of the United Nations Declaration of Human Rights in 1948. He signed it because it wouldn't have looked good to lag behind other countries. But there was no need to publish it. The Soviet people had been given enough rights under the Stalin Constitution. And there was no point in discussing phony bourgeois "liberties." The Soviet people had one great freedom, good enough for all. They had long since recognized freedom as the conscious necessity of serving him, the Leader of the Peoples.

It seemed that against all the laws of dialectics Stalin had succeeded in stopping the course of history. Society stagnated in his iron embrace. The last few reminders of the revolution of thirty years before were effaced as hateful birthmarks on the pure, clean body of Stalin's dictatorship.

After the victory over Hitler's Reich, cold and hunger reigned in the victorious country. More hunger than at the end of the civil war in 1920. In Moscow bread was rationed. In the breadbasket of the Ukraine the children of grain-growing peasants once again swelled up from malnutrition. Stalin had given the order to export "excess stocks" of grain. What else would you expect? He was the victor; he must be rich.

For three years in a row there was drought in the new Soviet Republic of Moldavia. Very little grain was harvested. But under the grain procurement plan a certain amount had to be delivered from every hectare of cultivated land. The entire meager harvest was exported to Russia. In 1951 real starvation began. As much as half the Moldavian population died.

But this had already happened before—in the Volga region, in the Kuban. . . . Everything had happened before; how could you help getting bored? There was a problem, though. Moldavia had only recently been incorporated into the state. So in the end, grain was sent back there. All the poets immediately began to sing the praises of the Leader's generosity. But this too had happened before. It was boring.

In Ethiopia in 1975, 100,000 people died of hunger. But the Ethiopians overthrew their emperor. Those backward, illiterate Africans did it. But in Stalin's Russia, no fewer than ten million died of hunger, and the Tyrant's rule only grew stronger.

* * *

A long line of official automobiles came driving out of the Kremlin gates and turned onto Gorky Street. They drove past the central telegraph building and the monument to Yuri Dolgoruky. At the corner of the next block a marble maiden raised her hand in greeting, reaching high above the roof of a building. They came alongside Pushkin's statue. Say, why was it on the left? Stalin touched the shoulder of his driver, who slowed down immediately.

"Why on the left?"

The Great One didn't even realize he had uttered those words. But the man with him, whose job it was to anticipate Stalin's slightest wish, heard them. The wish became a command, and in no time the bronze Pushkin was dragged to a new location. As if the poet hadn't had enough humiliations under the tsar.

Lord, what absurdities Stalin came up with, consumed with boredom as he was—he invented new ministries and official uniforms, had skyscrapers built and ancient monuments destroyed, introduced unheard-of holidays, and discovered new heresies.

There had been a time when Lenin sent Soviet officials abroad to borrow foreign experience for application to the Soviet economy. He urged that German and American literature be acquired. "In my opinion, the *most necessary* thing for us now is to learn from Europe and America," Lenin wrote to Varlaam Avanesov, deputy people's commissar of the Workers' and Peasants' Inspectorate. That was in September 1922.[205]

In the early fifties Stalin would have had both Lenin and Avanesov arrested for "adulating the West." Does that sound far-fetched? For remarks like "to learn from Europe" hundreds of thousands paid with their lives.

The campaign against "adulating the West" was headed by Andrei Zhdanov. The first victims were Anna Akhmatova and Mikhail Zoshchenko in August 1946. This war against the intelligentsia was opened up in Leningrad, the cradle of Russian culture. And it soon embraced the entire country. The greatest successes were achieved by the most blockheaded party bosses.

We can follow the clear, ascending line of steady qualitative growth among the leading cadres.

In the early Stalin era primitive fools predominated. The popular saying was "The fools have come to the fore." In the thirties Stalin gave preference to idiots. After the war, when he was really bored, clinically verified idiots only were promoted to top positions. It was easier to work with them and to wage campaigns against this or that. It was necessary not only to eliminate kowtowing to the West; rootless cosmopolitanism also had to be exposed. Poets and artists, actors and stage directors, inventors and teachers, and scientists too were rooted out. The man who headed the assault against any and all thinking persons was Georgy Aleksandrov, chief of a Central Committee department, a combination philosopher and criminal. Those were the kind of hybrids that grew in Stalin's garden.

Stalin personally took part in the persecution of the physicists Pyotr Kapitsa and Abram Joffe and the geologist I. Grigoryev. Some he removed from the institutes they had founded. Others he killed outright. The biologist Vasily Parin was appointed deputy minister of health. During an official visit to the United States he informed his foreign colleagues of some of the latest advances achieved by Soviet scientists in cancer research. His extremely meager information was imparted after receiving top-level permission, from Molotov. But it was enough for the Master to remark offhandedly, "I don't trust that man," for Parin to be hidden away where no one is ever found again.

Another campaign Stalin carried out in those years of boredom was telling the world all the things Russia had done first. One morning the world woke up and learned that the airplane and the locomotive, the radio and the rocket, potatoes and the game of chess—all had been discovered or invented in Russia. Neither paper nor human effort was spared to prove this. Anyone who dared to mention—only to mention—the name of a foreign inventor was unfailingly accused of heresy.

Party functionaries were mobilized to root out all heresies. They responded automatically to the order, "Sic 'em." Few of them could have pronounced correctly or in one breath a big word like *anti-Semitism*. The campaign was easier to carry out than to pronounce, but that good old tsarist tradition was still alive. (Ever since his youth, Stalin had hated people with long noses, and although he didn't succeed in wiping out all Georgians, Poles, Armenians, and Jews, he did try.)

In the anti-Jewish pogroms under the tsar the mobs were let loose on the shopkeepers. The Father of the Peoples didn't waste his time on such trifles. The pogrom he organized in late 1948 was directed squarely at the Jewish Anti-Fascist Committee of the war years. The war was over and there was no need to flirt any more with the Jews, or with the Slavs, or with the various Muslim peoples. How many thousands of Jews were repressed in those years? We know of 430 prominent figures in culture and the arts. Who will estimate the number of ordinary workers, teachers, engineers?

In early 1949 a group of Jewish wreckers was discovered at the Stalin auto plant. Its leader was the chief engineer Edinov. He and the other engineers, whose only crime was that they had been born Jewish, were sentenced to be shot. Life at the Lubyanka had also grown boring in those years. Someone decided to have a little fun.

The condemned men were taken outside the city and lined up in an empty pasture. Along with the convoy guards, some well-trained dogs were brought to the killing ground. "Run!" the chief of the guards ordered the Jews, and turned loose the dogs. The dogs tore the engineers to bits. Edinov was one of the first to die. Exhausted by his interrogators, he had no strength to run. A miracle happened: one of the engineers fell into a gully and escaped unharmed. After dark he managed to reach a nearby village.[206]

The anti-Semitic campaign picked up speed and strength. The year 1952 came. How long it had been since Stalin had taken part in meetings of the Politburo—that is, the Presidium of the Central Committee. Malenkov chaired the meetings in his absence. Suddenly, to everyone's surprise, the Gensek appeared at a meeting. Everyone stood up.

"I have come on a matter of special urgency," he began. "There is a danger of a pogrom against the Jews. Many cases of hoodlum attacks on prominent Jews have been reported. I think, comrades, we must save and protect our Jews. The best thing to do would be to relocate them, move them from Moscow and Leningrad to a safe place. I have here a list of people we are concerned about first of all."

Malenkov said: "Joseph Vissarionovich, we can't solve this problem immediately. We need to think it over, perhaps form a commission."

The Gensek turned pale and walked out of the room, snapping in two the pipe he was holding. A few minutes later Poskrebyshev came running in. "What happened? Comrade Stalin went home all upset. . . ."

The lists of Jews to be deported from the central cities were drawn up under the supervision of the Jew Lazar Kaganovich. The Master proposed that requests for deportation by prominent Jews themselves should be "organized." Among those who had already signed such appeals were Academician Isaak Mints and the violinist David Oistrakh. Those whom the Central Committee would allow to remain in Moscow would have yellow stars sewn on their sleeves.

In early 1953 the MVD publishing house issued a pamphlet by Dmitry Chesnokov, a highly placed police official. It bore a modest title: *Why Jews Must Be Resettled from the Industrial Regions of the Country*.

Such a nice, comforting little pamphlet. Actually it was an instruction booklet. Unfortunately, the entire run of a million copies remained in the warehouse. The untimely demise of the Great Internationalist prevented its distribution.

In tsarist Russia they didn't have to deport Jews from the cities. They had an institution called the Pale. As always Stalin decided to follow a new, untrodden path. Way back at the Fifteenth Congress, in 1927, he had noted sadly that "some little shoots of anti-Semitism" had sprouted.[207] In twenty years there was an entire brooding forest.

Olga Ivanovna Goloborodka had worked in the party underground in the Ukraine. The Petlyuraites shot her brothers and sisters, and it was thought that she too had perished. When an obelisk was erected at the site of the massacre, her name was chiseled into the stone as well. Later, she headed the pensions department of the Ministry of Social Security. In the fall of 1952 she accidentally overheard someone in the Council of Ministers building say that barracks were being built in Birobidzhan for the Jews who would be deported from the central cities.

"I sat there and thought I would go out of my mind. . . ."

Four years passed. At a government meeting a discussion was going on about where to store the harvest from the newly cultivated lands in Central Asia. There was no time to build granaries. Someone remembered there were empty buildings in Birobidzhan intended for the deported Jews. The special commission sent to investigate found only two barracks on the scene, each two kilometers long. The ramshackle walls were one board thick, with plenty of knotholes. Leaky roofs, knocked-out windows. Inside were rows and rows of double bunks. Everything was there that was needed for a Jewish ghetto. But as places for storing grain, the buildings were found unsuitable. Of which fact the commission informed Comrade Khrushchev.

On November 10, 1978, the fortieth anniversary of the *Kristallnacht*, when Hitler's Storm Troopers smashed the windows of Jewish homes and stores and broke every mirror and glass, the president of West Germany declared, "The German people have a debt to pay to the Jewish people." No president of the USSR has ever said a word about our Jewish fellow citizens who were the victims of the Stalinshchina. Life has taught Soviet Jews patience. They are still waiting for a kind word.

* * *

Generalissimo Stalin did not want to share with anyone the glory of being the Savior of the Motherland. Georgy Zhukov stood out among the Soviet marshals. The population honored him as the victor over Hitler. To begin with, Stalin sent the marshal to Odessa, to command the military district there. Two years went by. Zhukov was summoned by the Big Boss. The Gensek was pacing back and forth on the carpet, puffing on his pipe. He offered the marshal a seat but continued his measured pacing. Finally he went over to his desk, took a sheet of paper from a folder, and handed it to Zhukov. "Well, read it." In Zhukov's hands was a memorandum as follows: "We have established the fact that Marshal G. K. Zhukov has been an agent of British intelligence for more than fifteen years and has regularly revealed defense secrets of the Soviet Union to this hostile power." At the bottom were the signatures of Beria and Abakumov. Here is Zhukov's own account:

> As I read, the piece of paper trembled in my hands. I had been in battle more than once and had never flinched at incoming fire. . . . Stalin kept moving about the room. He stopped next to me and put his hand on my shoulder.
>
> "I don't believe this about you. But you can see for yourself—there are two signatures, and some typist did this copy. Two or three people on my staff have read it. You yourself can understand it would be awkward to let you stay in Moscow. You'll have to go away somewhere for a while. So go take command of the military district in the Urals."
>
> What surprised me wasn't being sent to the Urals, where there were no armed forces other than some three hundred militiamen. What surprised and offended me was something else. Did Stalin really think I was such a fool that I didn't realize Beria and Abakumov would never concoct a memorandum like that without a direct order from the boss?

After exiling Zhukov, Stalin circulated the rumor that the marshal had made a lot of money in Berlin selling captured treasures. A bureaucratic flunky who was assigned to the Yugoslav Communist Milovan Djilas explained to him, "You know, Comrade Stalin doesn't tolerate immorality." And Aleksei Antonov, the deputy chief of the Soviet general staff, told Djilas that Zhukov had turned out to be a Jew.[208] The Generalissimo didn't get around to killing this "thieving Jew."

After Stalin's death the marshal was able to publish his memoirs. When he wrote them he included the above account of the scene in the Gensek's office, but that passage, along with many others, ended up in the editor's wastebasket. "That book—it isn't mine," the marshal complained not long before his death.

The next to go was Nikolai Alekseyevich Voznesensky. At the age of thirty-five he took charge of the State Planning Commission and became a deputy premier; two years later he joined the Politburo. A devout believer in the party's glorious mission, he set to work on a book entitled *The Political Economy of Communism*. Everything fell apart suddenly on a day in March 1949. Voznesensky was removed from his high posts. He summoned his assistant, Vasily Kolotov, and dictated a note to Stalin. Voznesensky swore to the Gensek that he had always been true to the party and the Leader of the Peoples. Kolotov took the note to Stalin's secretary.

Months passed. The Master didn't answer the note. But if Stalin had turned his back on Voznesensky for good, he would have arrested him. Voznesensky believed in the fairness of the Central Committee—or so he told one of his old friends. The Leader's former comrade in arms had been working for more than half a year on his book. His wife and son could see how he suffered, expecting the worst.

A telephone call. Stalin invited Voznesensky to his dacha outside Moscow. There Stalin embraced the disgraced comrade and had him sit down with the beloved leaders of the people, the other Politburo members.

"I propose a toast to our dear comrade Voznesensky, our leading economist. He is a man capable of paving the way toward the bright future and planning our further victories. Such people are our most precious capital; men like Nikolai Alekseyevich are needed by our party. To Comrade Voznesensky's health!"

He was beaming with happiness when he came home. His wife embraced him and wept with joy. A phone call. No, it wasn't the phone. They had come for him. One agent sat down at the desk and efficiently began to dump out all the drawers. Papers, notebooks, honorary awards sailed to the floor. On the agent's face was a carefully practiced sneer. The manuscript of *The Political Economy of Communism* lay next to the typewriter. The agent took it by one sheet and slung it to the floor. As much as to say, "That's how they disguise themselves, the traitors. Writing about communism. Communism won't help you, buddy."

Voznesensky had good luck at the Lubyanka. They didn't torture him very long; the end came fairly quickly.

Why touch glasses over the dinner table in the evening with a man who would be dead the next day? There's a saying: "There's no need to water a bird you're going to slaughter." But Stalin did, and stroked its feathers playfully.

Toward the end, Stalin's tastes became extremely refined. He took more delight than ever in playing with his victims, and his greatest pleasure was to destroy his closest associates. The Leader gave himself over to other simple pleasures at his dacha in Kuntsevo, thirty-two kilometers from Moscow. There he had an enormous record player and his favorite record: a coloratura soprano singing against a background of howling and barking dogs. This "music" gave the Master immense gratification. He would laugh and laugh and laugh. It may be that that was the only time Stalin laughed sincerely.

The epicureans of Kuntsevo drank a great deal and ate a great deal, especially Himself. Through the hours of the night, surrounded by an abundance of gourmet food and drink, the Sovereign was lively and well disposed. Lavrenty Beria, with his innate oily cynicism, would regale the Master with obscene stories. Stalin would viciously mock the helplessly senile and fearful Mikhail Kalinin, then propose a toast to "our beloved president."

Milovan Djilas, who several times attended the saturnalias at Kuntsevo, recalled Stalin's talking openly and crudely at length in the spirit of traditional pan-Slavism, the ideological justification for Russian expansion into the Balkans under the tsar.

Once, during the war, Stalin came out with this remark: "This war will soon end. In fifteen or twenty years we'll have recovered. And then, on to the next!"

Praising the idea of unity among all Slavs and cursing the Jews—it was just like the good old tsarist days. Only cruder and more perverted.

Then there were toasts in honor of "our teacher Lenin."[209] And Sasha Poskrebyshev drunk out of his mind, and Anastas Mikoyan's trousers all wet where his comrades had slipped a ripe tomato onto the seat of his chair. And discussions of important matters of state, intrigues and plots against Dimitrov and Tito, and against the governments of France and Britain. Above all the presence of the Master.

Why did Stalin hold these nightly orgies? Wasn't it in order to assert his status as Master outside the Kremlin offices? Here in Kuntsevo, under the influence of drink (just try *not* to drink) the true face of each of his colleagues was revealed. Not all of the Gensek's henchmen received invitations, or not always. But they came when invited. Just try to ignore the invitation or plead illness.

Then the Master would get an urge to watch a movie—and his taste was no more refined than a street kid's. He would want to see it through a second and a third time, and all the rest would patiently endure this torture by movie. When the Gensek laughed, they would too. At the right places they would follow him in cursing the villain. This way Stalin demonstrated over and over again his absolute power over them and accustomed these mini-leaders over and over again to the habits of submission.

How could they hide their mutual hatred or their fear for their own lives? They underwent a severe schooling at Stalin's hands, years of painful drilling. Only the strongest survived, the hardiest and most thickskinned.

An army of bodyguards was on duty outside the dacha around the clock, three shifts with twelve hundred agents per shift. Who was he afraid of? In his last years Stalin lived like a lone wolf in a sheepfold after the slaughter. A sheep that had somehow survived would come wandering in and—zap!—he'd be gone. Could you call that living? You could almost howl from boredom. But it wouldn't do for the Gensek to howl. His was a businesslike nature. He went out in search of new sheep.

G. M. Zusmanovich, an intelligence agent with a long and distinguished career, has described how he was forced to testify about the alleged treachery of Marshal Malinovsky. Zusmanovich refused to slander the marshal. They told the stubborn man that Comrade Beria was waiting for his confession. They hinted that the Master was particularly interested. They also demanded "material" against Khrushchev from Zusmanovich. After Stalin's death Malinovsky searched out Zusmanovich in the remote labor camps and had him brought to Moscow. "You saved my life," said the marshal, and made arrangements for the old intelligence official to be well cared for, providing him with a three-room apartment in the attractive Sparrow Hills section of Moscow.

Concerned for the well-being of the top echelon, Stalin took into his own firm hands the command of the personal bodyguard of all members of the government. Toward the end, his suspiciousness greatly intensified. The Big Pope no longer trusted the Little Pope, Beria. Stalin promoted him in order to deprive him of direct control over the secret police. Stalin constantly shuffled the Lubyanka pack. He even grew sick of Abakumov, that charmingly dull-witted but dependable follower of orders. The Master hunted up a replacement for him in the Central Committee apparatus, and in 1951 the Organs got a new chief, Semyon Ignatyev.

After the war there was more and more work for the Organs. By 1947 they were in danger of being swamped. The prison terms of many "enemies of the people" from 1937 were coming to an end. For example, one of those who survived, the Old Bolshevik Ruben Katanyan, was given permission to settle near Moscow. He wrote a letter to the Gensek, his old party comrade, with whom he had shared a prison cell under the tsar. Katanyan wrote the Leader that he had completed his term although he was guilty of nothing, had remained true to the party, and was ready to serve it as before.

The Gensek called in Molotov. "What is this? Who allowed this to happen?" The chanceries prepared the appropriate decree. The Old Bolshevik Shvernik signed it in his capacity as "president." From now on all those who completed their prison terms could spare themselves the trouble of traveling to the capital. They were to remain in "eternal" exile in the vicinity of the camps.

Thus the Master saved the Lubyanka from superfluous labors. And he was right to do this. The Lubyanka should not be distracted from new enemies to pay attention to old ones.

It wasn't only the Leader who was getting bored. The same was true for the bone crushers in the Lubyanka. The war had been won. People were submissive. The party and the people were one. The old opposition groups had not existed for a long time, and no new ones had appeared. And so in 1944–1945 the YTO—Youth Terrorist Organization—was constructed by the men of the Lubyanka out of the children of Old Bolsheviks Stalin had slaughtered, along with the friends and acquaintances of these children. The YTO had fourteen members, among them Vladimir Sulimov; his wife, Yelena Bubnova, daughter of the former people's commissar Andrei Bubnov; and Yuri Mikhailov.

Vladimir Sulimov was the son of an Old Bolshevik who had been shot, a former chairman of the Council of People's Commissars of the Russian Republic. Vladimir returned from the front lines as a disabled veteran. Three of the other YTO members had submitted requests to be sent to the front lines. Some were studying (film, medicine, physics, mathematics) and some were working. Mikhailov too was a veteran. They were simply friends who got together once in a while to have a party or just to talk.

The Organs could not allow a group like this out of its sight. The investigation into the group was supervised by the investigative department for especially important cases of the People's Commissariat of State Security (the NKGB). But the Moscow regional bureau of the NKGB had direct responsibility for the case. The investigators in the Little House at the Lubyanka did the questioning, and the texts were reviewed "upstairs."

In 1944 everyone, even children, knew that it was better to "confess," that things were no worse in the camps than they were outside, and that not everyone in prison was shot.

In my case, in the fall of 1943, the charges were both terrorism and anti-Soviet agitation. After a few months it became clear to the investigators that they couldn't pin "terrorism" on someone who was half blind. So that charge was dropped and I was sent down the OSO conveyor belt with a "point 10" (anti-Soviet agitation).

The opposite happened with the Sulimov group. Caught in the vise of the investigation, the young people admitted to telling a few political anecdotes. The case was floating along in a fairly safe channel, with the relatively trivial charge of anti-Soviet agitation. Then at the last moment the authorities changed course and charged the young people with terrorism. One of the accused, Nina Yermakova, lived on Arbat Street, and the Master had the habit of allowing himself to be driven down this very street. Thus an attempt on the life of the Leader Himself, our dear Joseph Vissarionovich Stalin, was involved. Some hardened butchers from the Big House of the Lubyanka took over the case. It was overseen by the head of the investigative department, Lieutenant General Lev Vlodzimirsky. Colonel Rodos and Major Raitses did the questioning. The bone breakers' brigade was joined by Lieutenant Colonel Shvartsman and Majors Bukurov, Rassypinsky, and N. N. Makarov.

The names of the butchers should not be forgotten.

But I've already forgotten the name of my first investigator in 1943. His superiors I remember—Major Kasaev and Colonel Benenson. I remember the first interrogation, on the night of August 9, 1943, in the office of Commissar Solomon Milshtein. Can it be that they are still living comfortably today?

The investigators put together the scenario for the attempt on Stalin's life with speedy efficiency, not troubling themselves much about the details, such as evidence, witnesses, etc. Each member of the group was assigned a particular role: one to study the route taken by the Leader's car, another to manufacture a "bomb," another to calculate the trajectory it would follow when thrown, another to prepare ideological material.

The standard methods were used to obtain the "confessions"—insults and curses, rubber clubs, and threats of worse against the prisoners and their loved ones. The technique of personal confrontation with other victims was by now well rehearsed. One frightened defendant would testify in the presence of an investigator against another, who was even more frightened. Was there any need for evidence or facts? These confrontations were rehearsed as well as any professional theater group could do.

The investigator would tear up inappropriate records of the questioning before the prisoner's eyes. He would add entire sentences to the confession and force the "defendant" to learn the dictated words by heart. The Lubyanka was all-powerful, the defendant nothing. And between these two poles the thin thread of a human life could snap so easily.

"Since you're here, you're guilty, and the sooner you understand that, the easier it'll go for you," explained Vlodzimirsky. My investigator told me the same thing. Entire generations of "enemies of the people" heard those words in the Lubyanka.

The same words would echo in the ears of the torn and exhausted prisoners, whispered to them by "plants" in their cells, placed there by the prison authorities.

The investigation was moving toward the desired conclusion. Sulimov's son had already admitted that the attempt on Stalin was to have been made from the window of Yermakova's apartment. At one of the last interrogation sessions the investigator Raitses asked a prisoner named Levin where Yermakova's windows were located. It turned out they faced the courtyard, not the street. The investigator came across this inconsistency by accident. Facts were the last thing he was interested in.

The case was turned over to an OSO troika. Later, in 1956, the members of the YTO were rehabilitated, three of them posthumously. Among whose who died was Sulimov. Of course the case had been a frame-up, but the new authorities didn't have the nerve to announce that.

The YTO case served as a model. In 1948 the NKGB men fabricated a case against a similar group at Kharkov University. If it hadn't been for the quick thinking and courageous action of the rector, Ivan Bulankin, a dozen students who used to meet to share their love of poetry would not have escaped the prisoner's lot.

The Master didn't amuse himself just with young people, however. Veteran members of the YCL of the twenties were taken in hand. They had been enterprising youths. The biography of each could reveal, if one wished to hunt for it, some occasion when he or she had raised a hand in favor of the wrong resolution or had abstained. The old-timers were hastily sent down the conveyor belt.

* * *

After the war a struggle broke out around the Gensek's throne. The Malenkov-Beria group decided to put an end to Zhdanov's claims to the succession. He was a dangerous rival, who missed no chance to stir up Stalin's suspicions against Malenkov himself and who had succeeded once in having Malenkov sent out of Moscow. So, with the help of Beria and Khrushchev, Malenkov managed to discredit Zhdanov, accusing him of a plot against the party. Zhdanov fell ill and died suddenly on August 31, 1948.

Zhdanov's appointees in Leningrad held high positions in the party and state—men like Aleksei Kuznetsov, Pyotr Popkov, Mikhail Rodionov, and Aleksandr Voznesensky. They couldn't be left where they were.

The Leningrad affair cost the lives of thousands of party workers, military men, and industrial workers. They were accused of plotting to turn over the city to the British imperialists. The leaders of the plot were supposedly planning to destroy the fleet by planting explosives, surrendering the city, and at the same time proclaiming it the capital of the country once again, in place of Moscow. As usual, there wasn't a grain of logic or sense in the charges. But what was unusual was that this new Stalin provocation was not publicized in the press. In the Central Committee resolution of February 1949, Kuznetsov, Popkov, and the other Leningrad leaders were accused of violating state discipline. They were removed from their posts and reprimanded by the party. That was all.

Stalin remained true to himself. The rest supposedly happened without his knowledge—the arrests, the tortures, the killing. On Abakumov's direct orders, testimony against the late Andrei Zhdanov was extracted from these officials. Who gave the order to Abakumov? It's not hard to guess. Then came the trial, presided over by Ulrikh's traveling court, out on its judicial circuit.

Who were the men that died in the Leningrad meat grinder? Kuznetsov was the party's provincial secretary. Popkov was the chairman of the province's Soviet executive committee. All the secretaries of the party's district committees also went. Voznesensky was the rector of Leningrad University and brother of the former chairman of the State Planning Commission. Rodionov had been premier of the Russian Republic. In addition, two thousand military men were rounded up within a few days.

No sooner had Zhdanov been buried beneath the Kremlin wall than all traces of his days in Leningrad were destroyed, including material on the nine hundred days of Leningrad's resistance to the German blockade. Stalin ordered the Museum of the Defense of Leningrad closed and arrested its director, Major Rakov. (The museum was finally reopened in 1957, but the exhibits fail to mention certain matters. There is not a word about the cannibalism that occurred during the blockade, or about the destruction of the home guard, the popular militia mobilized to resist the Nazis, or about the crimes of Stalin's commissars.) Books dealing with achievements by Leningrad scientists and cultural figures were banned.

All of the late Zhdanov's close associates fell beneath the wheels of the

Beria-Malenkov juggernaut. The only exception was a man named Shty-kov. But he wasn't just a party official; he also worked for . . . a certain department.

Zhdanov's death belongs to a series of mysterious incidents.

Frunze 1925	Gorky 1936
Dzerzhinsky 1926	Raskolnikov 1939
Bekhterev 1927	Krupskaya 1939
Alliluyeva 1933	Trotsky 1940
Kuibyshev 1935	Zhdanov 1948
Barbusse 1935	Dimitrov 1949

This brief martyrology could be lengthened with the names of those who died in Stalin's prisons or committed suicide.

The Leningrad slaughter had a special meaning for Stalin. In December 1949 he would complete his seventieth year, so he decided to give himself a modest birthday gift. The anniversary celebrations were a great success. Politburo members outdid themselves in their panegyrics to the Great Genius. Writers, poets, artists depicted the divine image for the thousandth time. Ritual incantations were organized in kindergartens. Rallies, meetings, and parades overwhelmed the country. Much more and the mass hysteria would have got out of official control. But the valorous Organs of propaganda and the valorous Organs of state security, as always, stayed on top of things.

In the Bolshoi Theater gathered the flower of the people (or at least that's what they thought, in their good-natured simplicity). For four hours the pompous doxologies in honor of the celebrant droned on. For four hours they annointed his head with oil. When all the beautiful words had been said and the light-minded participants in these mysteries were spent from their heartfelt exclamations, they looked around and saw—the Leader was missing! He had risen from the huge table with its cloth of crimson velvet, gone out, and disappeared.

At first they assumed he'd come right back. After all, he had to reply to the greetings. As always he would give a historic speech, to which the entire planet would pay tremulous heed. But the Leader didn't come back. We may try to credit this to the natural disintegration of personality, but the process was only beginning in the Gensek's case, so we must seek the motive for this strange action somewhere else. The tyrant was sick of it all. Stalin was utterly bored.

No one dared argue with him any more. No one threatened him. Absolute power had one disadvantage: there was too much of it. The servility of those around him got on his nerves. And with age his vital fluids were wasting away, his appetite was starting to fail him, and wine didn't cheer him as before. There were fewer and fewer pleasures in life—there was no one to kill and no one to have mercy on. The debates had long been forgotten. Where were they, those Trotskys, Bukharins, Larins, Zinovievs?

All the political games had been played. All the rivals wiped out. It was bo-o-ring.

Time to hold a new party congress. There hadn't been one for thirteen years. No point to it. Again they would praise him and glorify him, but there wouldn't be any real work. (What about during the war, though? There'd been work *then*, all right.)

Even during the war Stalin had been too bored to bother with the party's leading body, the Central Committee. A plenum of that body, scheduled for October 1941, was simply never held. The members arrived in Moscow, waited around for two days, never came face to face with the Gensek, and finally went home. Again the Central Committee members gathered for a plenum in Moscow in January 1944. The Master presented them with a few trifling matters to discuss, then sent the party "leaders" on their way. He found the CC a burden, but he couldn't bring himself to abolish it, to remove the last trappings from the stage.

The Nineteenth Congress opened in October 1952. Stalin decided not to speak, reserving the right to make some concluding remarks. The main report was given by Malenkov. Khrushchev gave a speech on changes in the party rules. The unending ovations showered down on the Gensek's head.

An exhibit of the arts was timed to coincide with the historic congress. It was at the Tretyakovsky Gallery. The sculptor Sergei Merkurov presented the exhibition committee with two busts, one of Lenin and one of Stalin—grand representations forged of bronze. There were two rounds of voting, the first one open. All forty-seven members of the commission of course raised their hands. Some even raised both. The second round was a secret ballot. Only two voted for; the rest blackballed the statues.

Deplorable as this incident was, it had no effect on the monolithic unity of the people. Nor could it serve as an example, for it had taken place in secrecy. To the Gensek it was as though this handful of "rootless cosmopolitans" had given him the finger with their hand in their pocket. Could you really call that a protest?

Maybe the whole commission should be sent to the camps, along with its exhibit. However, in the Lubyanka all forty-seven of these scum confessed to dropping the blackball, so there was no way of finding out who the two were that really loved you.

The ordinary people—they were a different matter. His only satisfaction came from reading letters from workers. Here he found boundless love and selfless devotion. And all of it sincere, straight from the heart.

Anastas Mikoyan oversaw incoming letters in the postwar years. His office functioned around the clock. In two rooms a dozen young women sat at huge tables, sorting the mail for the Leader. The letters arrived in big sacks and were dumped out on multicolored trays. Complaints about cold and hunger and the arbitrariness of the authorities were thrown in the wastebasket. Good, loyal missives were piled on the tables.

Once, about three o'clock in the morning, Stalin came into the room.

He said hello to the young women, headed for a table, and took a tray. Someone jumped up. "Joseph Vissarionovich, what are you doing? We haven't gone through those yet." "That's all right. That's what I want," answered the Leader, who disappeared with the tray.

Later on the angry word came down: "Who dared to hide the letters of the workers from me? Every letter is the voice of the people. How could you not understand that? If I find this again, I'll have you all fired."

Mikoyan put out his own word. He let it be known that if a single seditious letter reached the Master's desk, he personally—he, Mikoyan—would see to the fate of the guilty party.

From that day on the canvas sacks full of letters were given a preliminary checking in a special cellar and only then sent up to the sorters.

The flood of letters never dried up. How could it? It came from the wellsprings of society. Ever more often, concern for the Leader's health was voiced in the letters. Millions of sons and daughters of the Father and Teacher feared they would be left orphans. They begged Comrade Stalin to live forever. His colleagues brought him such letters with pleasure. They too feared change. Stalin was convenient. There was no need to think or decide anything. He was a symbol of stability and calm. Who knew what a new boss would bring, Malenkov or someone else. And what if Comrade Beria suddenly got hold of the scepter?

Stalin had a premonition that the end was coming soon. The Genius's penetrating vision probably played its role here too. He became twice as irritable and three times as cruel. The case of the Kremlin doctors brings us back to the circumstances of Zhdanov's death. Zhdanov had suffered from hardening of the arteries, in the opinion of the Kremlin professors. To their misfortune, however, the X-ray technician Lydia Timashuk, after studying Zhdanov's electrocardiograms, had diagnosed his difficulty as coronary thrombosis. Meanwhile Zhdanov had not been alerted by anyone and had not taken proper care of himself.

When, some years later, the Organs heard about Timashuk's diagnosis, they had her write an official statement refuting the opinion of the Kremlin doctors. On the basis of this document the Lubyanka, following the Gensek's orders, fabricated the case.

Abakumov was the minister of state security at that time. When the head of the investigations division showed up with the materials for the doctors' case, Abakumov chased him out of his office. The Central Committee asked for the testimony of Dr. L. G. Etinger, who was in Taganka prison. It turned out he had died under torture. Stalin called in Abakumov. The minister returned from the Central Committee building to the Lubyanka as a prisoner. He was too primitive for such a high position.

Many of the Kremlin doctors were Jews, which meant that the case could be given a useful political coloration. Unlike the Leningrad affair, this campaign got a lot of press in early 1953. Anti-Semitism had long since become official policy. There was nothing to hide from the people. Let them know what the Yids were capable of, so they could participate fully in eliminating the danger.

Along with the others, the Master's personal physician, the cardiologist Professor Vladimir Vinogradov, was arrested. The son of a village deacon and a collector of old icons and paintings, he was known for his peaceable manner. At the Lubyanka an unexpected stubbornness took hold of him. He refused to endorse the works of the prison dramatists. The investigator turned to the new minister, but Ignatyev didn't know how to handle it.

At the first opportunity Ignatyev asked Stalin, "What shall we do with Vinogradov?"

"So you don't know what to do, huh? Link him up with Joint.* He's a weak character, good-hearted type. He'll sign anything for you."

Ignatyev dared to remind the Master that Vinogradov was a Russian.

"OK, then give him British espionage. Joint is sponsored by the British. It all fits."

"But he won't sign anything. He insists that we inform you that he's not guilty of anything."

"Not guilty, not guilty," Stalin repeated with annoyance. "We can't pardon people who've spied for foreign intelligence. Only you shouldn't beat him. Put heavier irons on his legs and he'll sign anything. I know him inside out."

Sure enough, Vinogradov signed everything they asked him to and, lying on his prison bunk, began to read Alexandre Dumas.

Those who bore themselves most bravely were Vladimir Vasilenko, an academician, and the neuropathologist A. M. Grinshtein.

Grinshtein, a powerful man, was tortured by electric shock and savagely beaten. His face was mutilated, and he was cruelly starved. The statistics are eloquent. His height had been 192 centimeters, his weight 100 kilograms. In prison he lost 63 kilograms. When he was released he could hardly get home. He had to crawl up the stairs. They took him by the arms, but he fell. At home he asked for a clean bathrobe, sat down in a chair, and told everything. His wife, the chief neuropathologist, also held firm and refused to sign anything.

The doctors were released after Stalin's death. All but two who had died in prison, Etinger and M. V. Kogan.

Stalin saw in the widely publicized "doctors' case" a sure way of whipping up anti-Semitic hysteria and thus distracting the rabble from other social concerns. The heirs of Stalin, bewitched by the stern simplicity of his conception and the total lack of investment needed to implement it, have shrewdly continued his brilliant anti-Semitic initiative. The dragon's teeth have produced a rich harvest.

*Joint: short for Joint Distribution Committee, an American organization involved in resettling European Jews after World War II. It was frequently mentioned in Soviet anti-Semitic propaganda in Stalin's last years.—TRANS.

At the Nineteenth Congress, the Presidium of the Central Committee was created to replace the Politburo and Orgburo. The Presidium consisted of thirty-six members (twenty-five full members and eleven candidate members). In such a large, loosely constructed supreme body the disappearance of one head or another wouldn't be noticed by the public. The Gensek had decided that the time had come to part with Molotov, Mikoyan, Voroshilov, and Beria. At the last Central Committee plenum Stalin called Molotov and Mikoyan agents of American imperialism. The Master had begun to gather "evidence" about the espionage activity of his right-hand men long before the war, testimony extracted from prominent intelligence agents and officials of the Commissariats of Foreign Trade and Foreign Affairs.

Not long before the Gensek's demise, Beria admitted to Mikoyan that he expected to be arrested any day: "He's going to wipe us all out."

At the first Central Committee plenum after Stalin's death, Khrushchev commented that the Gensek's evaluation of Molotov and Mikoyan had not been correct. Hardly anyone knew what evaluation Stalin had made of them, but they all knew that much more and their heads would all have rolled.

Some have said that the Teacher had had his fill of his disciples' blood. Come off it. Maybe Lady Macbeth and Pushkin's Boris Godunov saw bleeding infants in their dreams, but Stalin was never troubled by pangs of conscience.

The Sovereign was approaching eighty. By that age one should have had one's fill of the sufferings of others. Hadn't his lust for power been satisfied? No, he was the same as he had been twenty years before. His eager gaze surveyed his entourage. "Isn't someone going to step out of line? Isn't some brow going to gleam with intelligence?"

They should all go to the grave with me, he thought. Better yet, before me. According to the thieves' code: "You today, me tomorrow."

1953

6

That Hitler committed suicide, that his body was burned, that the remains were identified as his—these facts are fairly well established. But Stalin doubted the forensic evidence. He ordered the body delivered to Moscow, where it was carefully examined and an autopsy was performed. Only then could the Gensek experience the truth of the old adage, "The corpse of the enemy smells sweet."

Then something strange happened. Marshal Zhukov officially announced there was evidence that it was not Hitler's body that had been buried but the body of one of his doubles. The Fuehrer, it seemed, was alive and well somewhere in the British occupation zone in Germany.

What was Stalin's need for that kind of concoction?

Mussolini had been executed like a bandit, hanged by the side of the highway. The shameful end of his Italian partner weighed on Hitler's mind. This prompted his decision to kill himself. Hitler's body, wrapped like a baby doll in a blanket, was soaked in kerosene and burned in a pit. . . .

Stalin sincerely believed that every great dictator is entitled to a glorious death. A hangman's rope, a pit of flames—what would people think of next? True, the Gensek felt sure of his subjects, but who knows what they would have done to him in 1941, if defeat had come?

Stalin thought more and more about his approaching end. Once, chatting with Patriarch Aleksei, Stalin asked:

"What is the church's position on the immortality of the soul?"

"The soul is immortal," the pastor said.

"And what is the church's position on the immortality of the body?"

"The church does not recognize immortality of the body."

"That's very sad. . . ."

One thing consoled the Gensek: he was sure of a grandiose funeral, one worthy of his greatness. He had no fears about that. They would lay him next to Lenin. No, better, in his own mausoleum. He had earned a mausoleum through his unfailing service to the sacred cause of counter-revolution.

* * *

The fate of despots is instructive. One died in exile on a remote island. Another killed himself at the moment of defeat. Cyrus the Great was killed during one of his campaigns of conquest. His head was dumped in a skin bucket filled with blood. Cruel but just.

However, in the case of Stalin, the justice of history missed its mark. He managed to deceive even that. Stalin died at home.

After his death, various accounts were given. In Kuntsevo, Stalin had a housekeeper. She watched over his diet and his observance of the doctor's orders. In his last years, Stalin had difficulty sleeping. On the fateful day, the Gensek went to the city to see his son Vasily, "Vasya-the-General." There was a scene. The Master returned to his dacha and fell asleep in his chair. When the time came for him to take his medicine, the housekeeper touched him on the shoulder. Stalin leaped up, eyes wide, and fell to the floor. (This was the story told by the now deceased husband of the housekeeper.)

On the basis of indirect evidence, Abdurrakhman Avtorkhanov came to the conclusion that Stalin had fallen victim to a plot by Beria and

Malenkov.[210] But really, no one in Stalin's entourage had the backbone for something like that.

The Master was carried off by an illness. Otherwise he would have lived on and on. And ruled on and on, to the joy and happiness of humanity. The degenerate life he led—an unhealthy routine, gluttony, neglect of personal hygiene, and a sedentary existence—took its toll. He lived almost seventy-three years. Lived? In our human understanding of the word, he didn't live at all, because he had no love of life. Sowing terror and death around him, he himself, like a true coward, constantly trembled for his skin. But then, even a blind worm crawls away from death.

A March 4 government bulletin announced: "The results of the urinalysis are normal." Does a divinity also have urine? That announcement meant the end of the Stalin cult.

The newspapers continued to print false, comical bulletins about the "health" of the deceased Leader. In a way, his death recalled that of Ivan the Terrible in March 1584. At that time, the princes Mstislavsky and Shuisky and the boyars Romanov and Belsky—whom the tsar had appointed guardians of his eldest son Fyodor—spread stories that the monarch might recover. Likewise, the death of Nicholas I in February 1855 was concealed by a smokescreen of absurd bulletins.

Stalin was placed in a coffin in the Hall of Columns. (It was in this hall that the trials of Lenin's comrades had been held, the trials stage-managed by Stalin.) The mourners began to mourn, in the proper order, each according to his rank—Molotov, Kaganovich, Beria, Malenkov. . . . Vasya-the-General was there too. On the occasion of his sire's death, he was nearly sober.

It was a grandiose funeral. The embalmed body of the Gensek was laid out in the Generalissimo's uniform. Medals, medals everywhere. Wreaths upon wreaths. And thousands of the curious were crushed to death in the uncontrollable crowds at the approaches to the hall. All in the best traditions of the era.

Then came the funeral speeches on Red Square. The coffin containing the Gensek's body was taken up by Molotov, Kaganovich, Beria, Malenkov—each positioned according to rank, as always according to rank. And they bore the coffin into the mausoleum.

Who brought you? Who brought you here? Who brought you here, criminal? Who brought you here to Red Square, criminal, and laid you next to Lenin? Your associates, your criminal accomplices.

The Master—that was what they affectionately called him. It was a rare sort of master Russia got. No matter what task he undertook, he put the cart before the horse. That was what happened with collectivization. With industrialization. And his version of "socialism." No sooner was the country beginning to find its way out of the deep crisis into which his incompetent leadership had plunged it than Stalin proclaimed the victory of "socialism in one country."

In three decades, the Gensek didn't utter one intelligent word or carry out one good action. He gave an exemplary lesson for all present and future despots of how it is possible to rule over people without having either a heart or a brain.

But his stooges pronounced him a Genius. It was they who created the atmosphere of a people in mourning. The distraught faces, eyes wet with weeping, sobs . . . "How can we live without you, Father?"

A kindergarten—one of many Moscow kindergartens. The children were lined up were and ordered to cry.

"Uncle Stalin is dead. Cry, children, your own dear father is dead." They all cried, except one boy. He laughed, to the teacher's horror. The whole system of punishments was applied to this sacrilegious imp. His bottom was whipped, he was seated in a corner, and he was deprived of food for the entire day.

Vorkuta. At the mine there was a relatively small monument to Stalin. During the night, a dirty old jacket had been placed on the plaster-of-Paris shoulders, a greasy cap pulled down over the forehead. In the center of the city, near the Mining Administration building, another Stalin stood on a pedestal. Someone knocked off the head and rolled it into a ditch.

The death of the tyrant aroused the hopes of the prisoners for an improvement in their conditions, or even for release. In August, "disorders" started at the "main" pit. The pits in Mining Administration 2 went on strike, followed by the workers building the heating-and-power plant at Ayach-Yaga and the workers at Mine No. 18. Public Prosecutor Rudenko flew in from Moscow, along with General Maslennikov, deputy minister of internal affairs. They promised the prisoners that quick changes were on the way, even a reconsideration of their cases. In addition, to intimidate the prisoners, they staged a modest execution at Mine No. 18. The striking prisoners were inside the camp compound, behind three fences of barbed wire. They were cut down by fire from Tommy guns and mounted machine guns. (I had the opportunity to see this bloody funeral rite for the deceased Gensek.)

In Norilsk, twenty-five thousand prisoners took part in an "uprising." On May 25, 1953, the guards opened fire. Seven prisoners were killed; no tally was made of the wounded. The inmates responded by declaring a strike. They hung out a placard saying, "They are killing us and starving us." One of Beria's aides arrived and promised to start reviewing the prisoners' cases. In the meantime, experienced operatives "picked out" the "ringleaders" and liquidated them.

The security office at Vorkuta followed the same procedure.

Trujillo reigned for thirty-two years. He was buried in Paris. His family asked for sixty-four square meters in the cemetery. They were offered two. They settled for six. The imposing burial vault cost ninety million francs. A thirty-one-car train carrying the wealth stolen by the dictator went from Le Havre to Paris, and then across the Pyrenees.

In comparison with Trujillo, Stalin was a Spartan. He had an ordinary apartment, simple wooden dachas in the suburbs, and a modest grave. Two square meters of ground by the Kremlin wall was sufficient for him. If only he had gone there earlier, thirty years earlier.

On March 5, 1953, the great actor died in Moscow. Stalin's stooges had got so used to his constant playacting that some of them refused to believe the report of his death. They thought the news was just another one of his acts. Dmitry Manuilsky declared that the report of Stalin's death was a provocation.

Mark Twain's itinerant actors in *Huckleberry Finn* were only able to fool their country audience twice. On the third attempt, the people were ready to bombard them with rotten eggs and dead cats. The swindlers had to make a quick getaway.

Stalin dazzled his audience of simpletons every day. They were completely taken in by his performance. Dear, dumb Russia. The price that had to be paid for this amateur act was not small.

The dictator's "mistakes" were paid for with the lives of a hundred million people.

Let me repeat the figures and round them out: In the civil war, eighteen million people died as a result of the fighting, the 1921-22 famine, and the repression. The collectivization of agriculture, "dekulakization," and the repression and famine associated with those events cost the lives of twenty-two million people. In the period from 1935 to 1941, nineteen million were arrested. The war against Hitler Germany cost the victors thirty-two million lives. The repressive operations that were continued during the war and postwar periods (1941-53) took the lives of another nine million. This adds up to a hundred million.

Not all those arrested in the repressive campaigns perished, and not all those who perished were on Stalin's "conscience." But nearly all. Nearly all.

* * *

The scope of his crimes is staggering. It is hard to attribute them to one man alone, however godlike. There is no word to describe such crimes. Isn't that why some sociologists try to spread the blame to his associates, members of the government, local leaders (especially them!), even to the people as a whole? Nevertheless, Stalin is guilty of crimes against humanity. Nothing should be added to or detracted from those crimes.

After decades, why worry about it all? Some thinkers maintain that the victory of the counterrevolution was inevitable. They see Stalin as the product of the system, the unwitting instrument of social evil.

That does not make things any easier for history. Or for his victims.

"Terror implies mostly useless cruelties, perpetrated by frightened people in order to reassure themselves," Friedrich Engels wrote in 1870. "I am convinced that the blame for the Reign of Terror in 1793 lies almost exclusively with the bourgeois frightened out of their wits and demeaning themselves like patriots, with the small philistines quaking with fear, and with the mob of the underworld who know how to coin profit from terror."[211]

How sad that after a century, modern history has made Engels's words timely again. They stand as a condemnation of Stalin's rule. I would make only one qualification: the cruelties perpetrated by Stalin were not *useless*. This incomparable master of political utilitarianism extracted the maximum political advantage from the terror. Through the extermination of millions, he reduced the population to unquestioning obedience.

Those who survived could not escape the fate of having to work self-sacrificingly for the good of the Master (which was called "working for the good of the fatherland"). But the economic results of the work of a totally terrorized population could only be compared with those of slave labor. Nonetheless, Joseph the Builder was no more worried about the economic losses and failures of the epoch of "socialism" than the slavemaster was concerned about the productivity of labor in the silver mines of ancient Greece. What mattered for Stalin was the political effect.

The aftermath of the nuclear bombing of Hiroshima and Nagasaki is horrifying. Fifteen and twenty years later, many Japanese were still dying of radiation sickness. Children were born with incurable defects.

The aftermath of the Stalin terror is also tragic, and we must speak of it just as loudly and clearly. Through unrelenting work over many years, Stalin, this truly outstanding selective breeder, was able to produce a strain of splendid cretins. They formed a solid wall around the throne of the Leader through which no thinking or honest person could penetrate. But the Gensek endowed his dolts with power, with the right to rule, and with the ability to reproduce their own kind.

Who can foresee what the ultimate effects of this process may be?

In preaching aggressive immorality, Stalin infected his henchmen with this attitude. Immorality overwhelmed everything. It was even reflected in economic activity. There was total disregard for the interests of the state economy, as if Stalin were saying, "After me, the deluge."

Stalin left a legacy of gangsterism as a method of state policy. Thus far his successors have continued to employ this instrument within the country, no matter what. And in relations with other countries.

Without realizing it, Stalin created a deep crisis for Marxism. Thousands of books have been written against Marx. Stalin presented himself as a defender of Marx's doctrines. The result? No one has ever done Marxism such palpable harm. A substantial share of the blame goes to Him for the fact that the very idea of Marxism has been discredited in the West, actually opening the way for the extermination of Communists in some countries.

Lenin once correctly observed: "No deep-going and powerful popular movement in history has avoided becoming splattered with mud, has not been marked by adventurers and thugs attaching themselves to the inexperienced innovators."[212]

Wasn't there too much splattering of mud? And what should be said about thugs?

In ancient Russia, they used to say:

"Speak no ill of the dead."

But we *must* speak ill of this one.

IN OUR TIME
EPILOGUE

STALIN EXPOSED?

1

When news of the appointment of Georgy Malenkov as premier (chairman of the Council of Ministers) and Klim Voroshilov as president reached Vorkuta, the ordinary people rejoiced: "Our guys got in!"

They had no idea that "our guys" were worse than any "outsiders," that they were responsible for the death and suffering of millions. Nonetheless the Stalin yoke had lifted, and the people smiled, openly, without concealing their feelings. They smiled for the first time in long years.

The Kremlin doctors were soon released, at least those who had survived. Lydia Timashuk's Order of Lenin was withdrawn and a statement was made about it in the papers—probably the only time that has happened in the history of the state. They brought Marshal Zhukov back from his exile. And the peasants were relieved of some tax burdens. The premier was seeking popularity.

The Politburo was once again reduced to ten members. Stalin's henchmen were prepared to commit any crime to retain power. The most dangerous of them was Beria. If he got the chance, he would cut the throats of the other party Olympians to the last man, and his hand would not tremble. But even so, the henchmen didn't want to unite. By dint of great exertions and cleverness, and at the risk of his life, Khrushchev was able to weld together a majority and oust Beria.

In December 1953 Beria was executed—as an English spy. They also referred to him as an accomplice in crimes that had been committed. But the full truth was hidden from the population. "What would people say?"

Under the banner of half measures and indecisiveness, the rickety wagon of revelations about the Stalin era began its creaking journey. In February 1956 the Twentieth Congress was held under the same banner.

In the political report he gave for the Central Committee, Khrushchev referred to Stalin as bearing the main responsibility for organizing the illegal repressions. During the break, the Presidium members exploded: "Goddamn it. We agreed not to say anything about Stalin at the congress. . . ." At a Politburo session Khrushchev had appealed to the consciences of its members: "We cannot remain silent about Stalin's crimes at the very first congress we hold after his death." But Stalin's henchmen had defeated Khrushchev's proposal to tell the truth to the people.

Khrushchev decided to take another tack. He appealed to the Presidium of the congress:

"I think that the congress cannot pass over Stalin's crimes. We must expose the true face of Stalin. In the Politburo, Mikoyan was the only one who supported me. Now, since the Central Committee has been dissolved, the leading body is the Presidium of the congress. You decide."

The Presidium assigned Khrushchev to give a report. The material was hastily prepared while the congress was in session.

Molotov, Kaganovich, and company took countermeasures. They got the report shifted to the very end, after the official conclusion of the congress, after the election of the Central Committee. (They need not have worried. The delegates would have elected the same Central Committee anyway.) That's how the revelations were started.

So here's Nikita Khrushchev at the podium at last. He reads out information about the terror in the late thirties. But not a word about the decimation of the peasantry during so-called collectivization. The first secretary mentions the names of Lenin's comrades who fell as victims of the "personality cult," but says nothing about the destruction of the party as such. No statistics. Nothing about the extermination of tens of millions of people, about the limitless sufferings of the people. Not a word about the counterrevolutionary essence of Stalinism. He revealed a lot. But he concealed more.

When she heard about the suicide of Sergo Ordzhonikidze, Yelena Stasova, tough as nails and an old party fighter, burst into tears. But she didn't have the nerve to stand up and call for the accomplices in Sergo's murder to be brought to justice.

Stalin was no longer among the living, but the other members of his criminal gang, Molotov, Kaganovich, Voroshilov, and Malenkov, sat in splendor on the Presidium. They did not let "convicts" speak—that is what they called party comrades who had miraculously survived seventeen and more years in the camps.

Who would have dared stop Stasova from speaking?

When Khrushchev finished his report, the chair asked: "What resolution are we going to pass on Comrade Khrushchev's report?"

The answer was: "Make the whole report a resolution of the congress!"

This proposal was accepted unanimously, but the Stalinists managed to thwart the will of the congress. The text of Khrushchev's speech did not get into the minutes of the congress. "Rats recognize the trail of their own kind."

Later, in party bodies and in some public organizations, the Central Committee's secret letter on "the Stalin personality cult" was read. A party conference was held in the city of Maikop, capital of the Adygei Autonomous Region. Before beginning their discussion of the letter, the delegates checked one another's credentials. The report was given by the first secretary of the regional party committee, Chundokov.

"Doesn't anyone have any questions?" asked the chair.

No questions were forthcoming. Then a veteran party member made a proposal. He called for the posthumous expulsion of Joseph Stalin from the party, the removal of his name from institutions, factories, and streets, and the destruction of monuments to him. The man who did this was on the staff of the regional committee. I'll call him F.

"Maybe you would withdraw your proposal?" the chair asked. "After all, we don't have any directives about this. . . ."

"No. I'm accustomed to thinking first, then saying what I mean and acting on it."

The delegates to the conference didn't discuss Comrade F.'s proposal. When he returned to his seat, a void opened up around him. All those who had been sitting near him moved farther away from this tempter of fate.

After the meeting, the head of the local NKVD bureau came over to F.

"That was a daring speech you made. . . ."

The next day, a young woman came to F.'s office and asked him to put in writing the speech he had made the day before. That was the end of the "affair."

In Leningrad, at the I. E. Repin Institute, a crowd gathered in front of the door behind which a closed party meeting was being held. The people demanded they be allowed to hear the letter. When they were refused, the crowd began singing the Internationale, the party hymn. And these nonparty people were then allowed into the hall.

After Stalin's death, hope sprang up in the occupied countries for a revival of public discussion. In 1954, in Bulgaria, General Ivan Vylkov and his henchmen were publicly tried. In the twenties they had killed many intellectuals and slaughtered almost all the active Communists. Thousands of corpses, strangled with cables, belts, and barbed wire; broken bones and shattered skulls scattered about. A familiar picture. But in Sofia, the main criminals were *tried*. And the people were shown a documentary film about those events.

No such thing in the land of Stalin. Grigory Petrovsky tried to console Stasova at the Twentieth Congress: "Yelena Dmitrievna, if it was only Sergo they killed, the matter could be brought before a court and all. But they annihilated millions of innocent people. What kind of court could you bring a case like that before?"

What kind of court? An ordinary, honest one. They could all be put in the same dock—Molotov and Vyshinsky, Kaganovich and Ulrikh, Voroshilov and Shkiryatov, Mikoyan and Abakumov, Malenkov and Bagirov. And they could be judged together with the gang leader, Stalin. As for him, he could be judged posthumously; so could Zhdanov, Kalinin, Kuibyshev, Yezhov, and Beria. And no one should be frightened by the volume of evidence to be presented in support of the indictment. In Sofia it came to twelve volumes. In Moscow, it could be twenty. But get on with it!

Stalin's henchmen were not opposed to just retribution. With their agreement, Viktor Abakumov was tried in Moscow; in Baku, Beria's associate Dzhafar Bagirov; in Tbilisi, Nikolai Rukhadze; and lesser figures in other cities. But try the members of the immortal Stalin Politburo? What madman could think of such a thing?! There they are, the Teacher's comrades in arms, once again elected to the Central Committee and the Presidium. The party loves its leaders. That means the people love them. For the party and the people are one. Even children know that.

A year before the end of the war, showing signs of acute exhaustion, I landed in a prison infirmary. After my "recovery," I was shipped off to the territory of the Central Garment Trust in the Pechora regional camp complex. A lot of women prisoners worked there, but the porter in the bathroom was a husky youth who was deaf and dumb. If it had not been for these handicaps, Nikola, as the porter was called, would have been sent to chop down trees.

Nikola took care of the bathroom. He had plenty of problems to worry about. The women didn't feel shy in front of him. They told him everything that came into their heads. They teased him and harassed him. He only made a mooing noise by way of answer. What could he do? He was a deaf mute.

I was assigned to sewing mattresses. Some days I fulfilled the quota on the machine. And I started, like everyone in the filthy shop, to cut apart military greatcoats, which often had gray bloodstains on them. The coats were cut apart with razor blades and used to make cloth mittens for the prisoners chopping trees in the forest and breaking stones in the quarry.

Half a year went by. Then I witnessed something incredible. The porter talked. He had never been a deaf mute. He had only lost his voice in a game. When thieves sit down to a game of cards or some other game of chance, sometimes the stakes are lives—the lives of others, of course. Nikola had forfeited his voice and hearing for three years. For three years he had to remain silent. Violation of this agreement would be punished by death. No one can evade the law of thieves.

That summer the stipulated period had ended. The next day, they took Nikola out with the brigade of hard-working loggers to cut down trees. But he didn't mind! Now he could talk, like everybody else.

Stalin's henchmen forfeited their powers of speech and hearing to Stalin. But that was many years earlier. The death of the Gensek, the criminal in chief, freed them from their vows of silence. But they were in no hurry to talk. Only Khrushchev had enough nerve, and they grabbed him by the tail of his party coat and tried with all their might to pull him back.

The Stalinists tried to isolate the new leader from the rehabilitated Communists. They slandered them, had them followed. To Nikita Khrushchev's honor, when he was brought transcripts of "seditious" conversations by figures who had suffered from the repression under Stalin, he tore up the accusations and chased the accusers out of his office.

Every day the opposition to Khrushchev grew. The conspiracy of silence proved insurmountable. Maybe the party Olympians might want, once in a while, to express a personal opinion on some concrete question

—they could not, after all, have entirely lost all human qualities. But there was a powerful instinct for self-preservation at work, a carry-over from the era of Stalin's crimes.

At a Politburo meeting in October 1962, Khrushchev raised the question of publishing Aleksandr Solzhenitsyn's novella *One Day in the Life of Ivan Denisovich*.

"Should we print it or not?"

No one answered.

Khrushchev asked a second time, a third. Silence.

"OK," the Central Committee head concluded, "we'll assume, as the saying goes, that silence is consent."

The novel was published.

At the opening of the Twenty-second Congress, in October 1961, the opposition managed to block Khrushchev, even though he had already become dictator. In speeches at this congress, Khrushchev touched on the crimes of Stalin. He even hinted at the deceased Gensek's part in the murder of Kirov.

During the congress, Stalin's body was taken out of the mausoleum. But the followers of the criminal leader did not pull in their horns. Even Tvardovsky, a poet recognized as an immortal during his lifetime, was unable to break through the blockade against his *Tyorkin in the Other World* until Khrushchev personally arranged to have this anti-Stalinist poem published in *Izvestia*.

Yevtushenko had to run the same sort of gauntlet. During the night of October 21, 1962, when they were preparing the issue that contained his poem "Stalin's Heirs," some lackeys inserted the following lines:

> He believed in the great goal, not realizing
> That the means must be worthy of the great end.

This bit of bureaucratic poesy was a foreign body in the poem. But the author was so happy just to be published that he did not get very upset at the interference by the lord high censors.

Officials in the Central Committee apparatus, nurtured by Stalin, had an exact picture of the relationship of various forces. The apparatus pretended to support Khrushchev, while it was really looking back to the golden age. A copy of a letter written by the founder of the state to Grigory Shklovsky, one of Lenin's associates who was later executed, was preserved in the prosecutor's file. (The text of the letter appears in Part I of this book.) In it Lenin complained about the insurmountable opposition he faced from the Central Committee apparatus and drew the conclusion that it was necessary "to start over."

They brought the letter to Khrushchev. He read it through carefully and then asked a colleague to read it to him again, out loud.

"So, you see, Nikita Sergeyevich," the colleague said, "the apparatus was already putting pressure on Lenin back in the early twenties."

"Yes, it's very hard to fight a power like that," Khrushchev replied.

But the Central Committee apparatus was by no means a self-sustaining force; it rested on the mass of reactionary officialdom—party officials, military officials, state officials. At the least breath of democracy, all these officials buttoned up their uniforms as tightly as possible. Public discussion, freedom of speech—these bourgeois playthings are not for our people, the officials declared in the voice of command. They'll start by criticizing the deceased Leader and end—horrible thought!—by criticizing the system.

The veteran Communist Yevsei Shirvindt, the author of a book about Soviet "corrective labor" law, indignantly told of an argument he had had with M. Ya. Ginzburg, a rabid Stalin supporter and veteran member of the MVD academy.

Colonel Ginzburg's remarks are worth quoting:

"N. S. Khrushchev's report to the closed session of the Twentieth Congress of the CPSU does not prove anything. There is no serious evidence in it. Stalin never built up any personality cult around himself. Even Henri Barbusse wrote that 'Stalin is the Lenin of today.' And he was a great writer; no one forced him to say that. . . .

"People went to their deaths fighting for the fatherland, for Stalin. And some opportunists, too quickly rehabilitated, want to make a career out of running down Stalin.

"If Stalin was so bad, why did Molotov, the oldest member of the party and a comrade of Lenin's, cry at Stalin's funeral?

"Why seize on quotes taken out of context from Stalin's works? Everyone knows that Stalin was the greatest theoretician and that it is impossible to write or teach the history of the party without him.

"It wasn't Stalin who arrested these members of the Politburo (Kosior, Chubar, and others) but *all* members of the Politburo. They jointly made the decision and jointly acknowledged that these arrests were unavoidable. And the people who were arrested confessed, which means they were guilty.

"You can't carry out an investigation with white gloves on."

"It's disgraceful now to call workers in the Organs of security to account for the massacres of past years. The MGB and MVD workers were ordered to kill; they had to follow orders."

You read such things and you think, How does such a philistine, with all his thickheadedness and active hatred for human beings, manage to take the right, the safe, political position in every critical situation? The statements by Ginzburg, this "theoretician" of hangman politics, are typical of colonels trained in the Stalin school. Like the pilotfish that follow sharks, they were thrown into desperation by the death of the great predator they had served for so many years.

Who will take the place of the dead killer shark? The colonels sniff about, they listen, they seek to curry favor with the new powers.

"Sniff out, suck up, survive" (*ugadat, ugodit, utselet*).

Not so long ago, not so long ago at all, the colonels lived by this code known as the three *u*'s.

U-u-urrah! Everything has stayed the same—the well-paid jobs and choice sturgeon, the beautiful apartments, the villas and young mistresses, the profitable trips abroad, and the reserved seats at the theater.

Ginzburg served earlier in the Organs charged with investigation and punishment. Shirvindt, a victim of the terror, served eighteen years in prisons and camps. After his rehabilitation, he headed the research department of the Gulag. Was this a minor, local conflict, then, between the former prisoner and the former jailer?

No, of course not. Shirvindt's views were shared by millions. Millions of others have maintained the same position as Ginzburg. Statistics don't help here. There are no figures on the opinions of the inert millions, the vast swamp. There are no public-opinion polls in "the country of true democracy." In fact, could any real public opinion have existed in an era of social surrogates?

Learning of Stalin's crimes, the people stirred. For the first time since the revolution, a ferment of thinking began. This was noticeable especially in the big cities and among the intelligentsia. Attitude toward the Stalinshchina became a political barricade, dividing people into opposing sides.

Three of Stepan Shaumyan's sons survived him—Sergei, Lev, and Suren. The oldest, Suren, died in 1933 from leukemia. Lev Shaumyan, a historian, wrote an honest article about Stalin for the *Great Soviet Encyclopedia*. He studied Koba's past in detail and had no doubt that Stalin was a provocateur and the gravedigger of the revolution. The youngest son, Sergei, was left in Stalin's care during his childhood. He gained a position in the Academy of Sciences, where he earned a reputation as a diehard reactionary. Sergei hated his older brother, whom he called a "Trotskyist." Together with some other Stalinists like himself, he drew up accusations against Lev.

This was the sort of illogic characteristic of the party's "exposure" of Stalin, the illogic of the so-called struggle against the so-called personality cult.

How could one not be reminded of a line in one of Leskov's stories: "Half the truth is not a lie." They rode along on "half the truth," on an eighth of the truth, on crumbs. And later even the crumbs were swept from the table. And those who had a bad effect on others' appetite were withdrawn.

In the conflict between the two tendencies, only the party Areopagus functioned as a monolithic force. Khrushchev's endeavors were consistently supported by only one member of the Politburo, Mikoyan. And there was something unsavory about Mikoyan's position. How could the fawning Anastas be trusted to defend the surviving political prisoners, when he himself had taken part in the killings? (Nevertheless, for his active collaboration with Khrushchev, Mikoyan later paid with the loss of all his high positions, during his life, and with an ordinary burial in an ordinary graveyard after his death.)

For the multitude—pardon me, for the great Soviet people—Stalin had to remain a providential figure, the pride of the party, the honor of the party. On this "principle" the party heads hoped to maintain themselves in power and preserve their personal well-being.

History has given the twentieth century leaders in a hurry. Why have they been in such a hurry? Where were they rushing to? Hitler declared a blitzkrieg; Mao a Great Leap Forward; Stalin, blitz-socialism; Khrushchev, blitz-Communism.

Indeed, since Khrushchev, as first secretary of the Central Committee, promised this generation that it would see Communism, why stir up the past? Is there any point in exposing Stalin? After all, Christ taught the forgiveness of sins. And were they sins, really? Here we are, being overrun with embittered former political prisoners. The departed Leader was good enough to grant them their lives, and what have they given in return?

That's the way Stalin's followers argued. And they acted accordingly.

Ashot Ioanisyan, former secretary of the first legal Central Committee of the Communist Party of Armenia, endured eighteen years of suffering in prison, but he remained an optimist. On February 12, 1962, he wrote veteran party member Ruben Katanyan about the exposure of Stalin.

"Obviously, sooner or later the party will reject the view that the former acolytes of this idol are trying to impose.

"They are afraid that an unqualified exposure of Stalin would turn its cutting edge against them. These people are dancing cravenly around his image, sometimes playfully sticking their tongues out at it, sometimes, on the contrary, bowing and scraping before it, recalling his past 'services.'

"I think that this 'balancing act' on questions of the personality cult will end in political and ideological bankruptcy for these people."

Incurable optimism. I cannot remember a case when organized evil suffered bankruptcy. In fact, at that very time (at the end of 1962 and in 1963) the reactionary forces in the party were making Khrushchev execute a 180-degree turn. To one of his most energetic anti-Stalinist assistants, he issued the warning: "If you don't stop, you will place yourself outside the party. You are acting against the Central Committee!"

That was the natural course of events. The process of exposing Stalin and condemning the Stalinshchina was threatening to get out of the firm grip of the Central Committee. To be consistently honest, you had to admit that for a quarter of a century the party and the government had been run by a bandit. What would remain of socialism then? People would ask, Could it be that Stalin was building, not socialism, but something quite different? Irresponsible debunking of the reputation of the vanished genius was undermining the authority of the party ("Why didn't you say anything while he was alive?") The dethroning of the Leader of the World Proletariat was causing ferment in all the Communist parties of the world.

All these arguments were raised at a Politburo meeting. A resolution followed: "Stop it."

The alternative was to expose and condemn the Stalinshchina completely and disseminate to the entire world the truth about the crimes of Stalin and his henchmen, an act that would have required honesty and daring. Such qualities were not to be found in the top echelons of the party —as the result of the whole process of selection instituted under Stalin.

And so the exposure campaign, as is to be expected of all political campaigns, ended. It was time to drop the curtain. The personality cult had existed, that was true. But it wasn't worth recalling the rest; in fact it would have been harmful to remind people of it. Solzhenitsyn and the other zealots had to be banned. The tragic fate of the revolutionaries should not be mentioned any more, not in the press, not on the radio, not in the movies.

Under Khrushchev, Aleksandr Shelepin, the head of the Organs, went at midnight almost every night to the Party Control Commission offices. He was interested in the investigation of Stalin's crimes and the rehabilitation of those who had suffered and perished. Shelepin put the KGB files at the disposal of the Party Control Commission (on the orders of the Central Committee, of course) and pretended to be dedicated to restoring the truth.

But as soon as Khrushchev was removed, Shelepin revealed his true self. In the period leading up to the Twenty-third Congress (in 1966) he headed a brigade of Chekists who met outside the city to prepare a section of the political report. It contained a revision of the party's resolutions concerning the personality cult—reversing Khrushchev's policy. But the Stalinists did not dare come out openly at the congress. It was not the domestic protests that held them back, although they could have listened to the warnings raised by internationally famous Soviet scholars, poets, and writers. The leaders were embarrassed by a possible split in the international Communist camp. Such influential Communist parties as the French, Italian, and British spoke out sharply against the rehabilitation of Stalin which was in the works. Even the exemplary Bulgarian party showed signs of upset. A delegation of Communists from Bulgaria arrived early for the congress. Learning of the moves that were afoot, they at once informed Todor Zhivkov. The Bulgarian leader expressed categorical opposition. "This won't go down!" he warned the Moscow leaders.

At the congress, the Politburo decided to leave out that section of the report but to go ahead in practice to rehabilitate the Beloved Leader. They were going to do it, as they said, in a practical, working-class way. At a meeting of the active party membership of Leningrad (a restricted meeting, of course!), Shelepin announced: "We will restore the glorious name of Comrade Stalin in a practical, working-class way. Have no doubt about it! This Khrushchev was an outright Trotskyist! He followed an antiparty policy, rehabilitating them all indiscriminately one after another. We have already drawn up a list of twenty-five thousand people who were wrongly rehabilitated. And we will continue this work."

What "a practical, working-class way" means is all too obvious. A new directive followed immediately: Cover it up! Hush up the crimes of Stalin, hush up even the campaign to combat the notorious personality cult. They had toyed around with some revelations, and that was enough. Now the public was to be offered a new game, but it strangely resembled the old one—the glorification of Stalin. This new-old game was supposed to commence in December 1969. It was decided to commemorate the ninetieth anniversary of the Father of the Peoples in a manner befitting his illustrious memory. *Pravda* was preparing a big anniversary article.

But the Communist parties in the Western countries did not comprehend this brilliant design, and for some reason were in no hurry to take part in the re-Stalinization. The anniversary article did not get into print.

Gomulka, Kadar, and Husak also protested against publicly praising the tyrant. Moscow retreated. But the order from the Central Committee of the Soviet Communist Party did not reach Ulan Bator in time, and the Mongolian Communist newspaper *Unen* published the ill-starred article, giving *Pravda* as its source! The theses of the Institute of Marxism-Leninism, which had been prepared by the obliging "academician" Pospelov, likewise did not make it into print. They remained in a red folder wrapped in gray ribbon.

Who will unwrap that package?

WHO IS REHABILITATED?

2

The very first weeks after the Gensek's death showed that there was no quiet way of overcoming the consequences of his misrule. One example of this was the dropping of "the doctors' case," which attracted a lot of attention. But that wasn't the only problem. There were tens of millions of people illegally victimized for so-called political offenses. How could you clear all their records in a short time?

In 1954 a government commission was set up to deal with rehabilitations. All city and district courts, all military tribunals, and all departments of the procuracy got orders to begin reviewing the cases. The Supreme Court was given the responsibility of reviewing the material on the illegal activities of the illegal Special Boards (the OSOs).

The tried and true Comrade Ivan Serov was put in charge of the government commission. He was also appointed chairman of the newly formed KGB. General Serov had functioned for *fifteen years* as Beria's deputy. On his record belonged the responsibility for the Katyn massacre, the extermination of the Chechens and other non-Russian "outlanders," and much more.

General Serov understood, his acute instincts told him, that haste in carrying out the rehabilitations was quite uncalled for.

When they came to the cases of the internal exiles, they discovered that the Criminal Code had no provision for condemning "enemies of the people" to eternal banishment. Children had shared the fate of their parents, living with them in the localities to which they had been banished. Even when they reached sixteen years of age, they were left without passports, entrusted to the supervision of the local MVD commander. The exiles suffered terrible deprivations. They were left hungry and without rights, unable to obtain jobs. General Serov was against any "indulgence" toward them. However, the Politburo adopted a resolution calling for freedom for all deportees, starting with those who had been given five-year terms. The Ministry of Internal Affairs was given the responsibility for drawing up directives based on this decree.

A week went by, then two, then a month. But the decree was not published. Some Old Communists came to Mikoyan.

"Such things don't happen!" Mikoyan burst out. "The Politburo sends each resolution to the Supreme Soviet, along with a draft decree. What's the matter, don't you know what the procedure is?"

But the comrades had already called the Supreme Soviet. No draft decree had been received.

Then Mikoyan called Khrushchev.

"That can't be! Come off it!" the first secretary interrupted him. But even Khrushchev had to face it. For the first time in history, a resolution of the Politburo of the Central Committee had not been implemented.

The decree was published the next day. The secretary of the Supreme Soviet, Nikolai Pegov, was removed from his post and sent off to an ambassadorship in Iran.

Pegov had followed Malenkov's orders. Malenkov did not act alone either. But those are details.

It wasn't only the police apparatus under Serov that was holding one of the wheels of the rickety cart of rehabilitation. The Central Committee apparatus had grabbed one too. They did their sabotage in unison, with style and taste and a first-rate knowledge of their work—two organisms with a single circulatory system.

The campaign for judicial review required the mobilization of an enormous staff of prosecutors and assistants, and thousands of reliable legal personnel. In the Lubyanka, a surprise awaited them. Many of the file folders turned out to be *empty*. There were no transcripts of interrogations, no copies of denunciations, not even the names of the investigators. In two years, they succeeded in reviewing barely 10 percent of the cases. All the others that had been sentenced (nine-tenths!) remained behind barbed wire.

The infernal conveyor belt had carried as many people to the camps as live in a country like France; it resisted a reversal of gears. Why create unnecessary problems? In five or six years, all the "enemies" who had not yet been finished off would die. Then, if Number One hadn't dropped this notion, we could consider the question of posthumous rehabilitation. But the surviving Communists from the party's Old Guard would not accept this "approach" to the problem by Stalin's henchmen. One of those rehabilitated, a former coworker of Sergo Ordzhonikidze (let's just call him "Coworker"), urged General Prosecutor Rudenko to send special commissions endowed with full powers by the Presidium of the Supreme Soviet to all places where prisoners were being held. The prosecutor rejected the plan. "This is unacceptable from both the political and the judicial point of view."

Coworker proved to be a stubborn individual. A few months before the Twentieth Congress, he turned up on Khrushchev's doorstep. The comrades prepared a memorandum, and at the next session of the Politburo it was decided to send commissions with full powers to the prisons and camps. The Central Committee secretary Averky Aristov was given the task of briefing the members of the commissions. General responsibility for directing the work was given to Politburo member Anastas Mikoyan.

During the Twentieth Congress, Mikoyan called a meeting of those who held responsible positions in the project (this was like a session of the central commission, although such a body did not officially exist). Opening the session, he apologized to these people trained in the law: "Unfortunately, we cannot always observe the formalities. This work is too pressing."

"What are you talking about, Anastas Ivanovich?" Rudenko interrupted. "Everything was always done on a sound legal basis. . . ."

Mikoyan asked Serov, "How many people are in prison for criticizing Stalin without having violated any provision of the Criminal Code?"

Serov: An insignificant number.

Coworker: Insignificant? I've got a number that runs into five figures.

Mikoyan: I propose that the MVD be given instructions right now to release those prisoners.

The resolution was adopted. The task of implementing it was given to the MVD head, Nikolai Dudorov. On the eve of the Twentieth Congress he had replaced Kruglov as minister of internal affairs. Within a few days, eighty commissions were set up—one for each of the big camps. Three additional commissions took up the task of looking into the isolation prisons for political offenders. The staff of each commission included one representative of the procuracy, one representative of the KGB, and one veteran party member chosen from among those who had been rehabilitated. A fourth member was designated by the local authorities. Usually the provincial committee of the party assigned an official from the procuracy of the province.

Lists including the names of one hundred rehabilitated Communists to serve on the commissions were submitted to the Central Committee for confirmation. Twenty extra names were included, in case some of those designated could not serve because of illness or other circumstances. The Central Committee might also strike out some of the names.

And the Central Committee did. When the lists reached the secretariat they didn't include *a single* rehabilitated Communist. People rushed to demand an explanation from the director of the Bureau of Administrative Bodies, Mironov. The latter declared that the Old Communists had refused to participate in this campaign.

"Did you see them? Did you talk with them?" they asked Mironov.

"No."

Behind Mironov stood the same Malenkov and the Stalinist majority of the Politburo.

They went to Aristov. The Central Committee secretary threw up his hands. Mironov had managed to turn over the lists to the highest level, and the members of the Politburo had efficiently, one after another, approved the documents—"in a practical, working-class way."

They had to call in Khrushchev. Only after his intervention was it possible to restore the lists.

What should have been done then was to clarify the role played in this diversion by every apparatchik, and to make an example of those responsible. But we won't demand too much of party policy. Consistency has always been foreign to it.

April 1917. Grigory Fyodorov was the only worker elected to the Central Committee. The St. Petersburg Bolshevik organization issued him party card No. 1. Fyodorov took an active part in the October armed uprising and in the civil war.

Why did Stalin need to include him in the list of those who organized the assassination of Kirov? The "terrorist" Fyodorov perished. His wife, Beti Mikhailovna, spent eighteen years in the camps. His five daughters suffered everything that could fall to the lot of the children of victims of the repression.

Back to 1956. Molotov, Kaganovich, and Malenkov, who had put together a Stalinist majority on the Presidium, opposed the rehabilitation of Fyodorov. Only on his second attempt was Khrushchev able to get the necessary resolution through. It appeared that even posthumous vindication did not come as a gift from heaven.

The start of rehabilitations threw the serried ranks of informers into disarray. When the Central Committee withdrew the false charges against the Young Communist League leaders headed by Kosarev, the star of the provocateur Olga Mishakova fell. In 1937 she had denounced Kosarev. Now the slanderer was asked to leave the YCL Central Committee. But Mishakova couldn't give up her important position just like that. For a whole year after she was dropped from the Central Committee, she continued to come to the YCL offices. Throughout the working day, she sat in an empty office, even taking a break for lunch. One day they confiscated her pass, and the watchman would not let her into the building. Mishakova kept coming anyway, every day. Now she would stand by the entrance during the designated hours. It proved necessary to transfer her husband to Ryazan, but Mishakova still would not give up her post. Every morning, at four o'clock, she got on a train and went to Moscow. She remained at the entrance throughout the hours of the working day. This went on until they took her to a mental institution.

In the case of another veteran provocateur, Serafima Gopner, things didn't go as far as a mental institution. But she did take the rehabilitation of "enemies of the people" as a personal tragedy, for herself. After the arrest of her husband, Emmanuil Ionovich Kviring, a comrade of Lenin's, Gopner, though an Old Bolshevik herself, presented a letter to the party committee: "I am ashamed that for more than twenty years I was linked with this reptile. There were signs of his enemy activity." (Gopner had strong reasons for her hatred. Shortly before his arrest, Kviring had left her and established a new family.)

After Kviring's rehabilitation, an evening to commemorate him was scheduled at the Institute of Marxism-Leninism (IML). The widow was worried. Would the slanderous letter suddenly turn up? And other things in the same vein? She asked the veteran party member Aleksei Rudenko, who had spent seventeen years in the camps, "Do you know where the denunciations of former enemies are kept?"

Rudenko reassured Gopner: "These papers could be in a lot of different places."

Gopner called the IML and asked them to postpone the anniversary meeting because she was ill. Then she did so again. Kviring's son had come to Moscow from the Urals especially for the occasion but was unable to wait long enough to attend the meeting in honor of his father.

Gopner soon relaxed—no one had impugned the honor of Stalin's *provocateurs*—and once again she began putting herself forward in the press and in meetings. At the meeting in honor of Andrei Bubnov held in the Museum of the Revolution in 1963, Gopner accused this revolutionary, who had died in Stalin's terror, of having held a negative view of the Brest-Litovsk treaty. During the Brest-Litovsk negotiations Gopner herself had been working in Yekaterinoslav, and at the plenum of the provincial committee she had had a resolution passed condemning Lenin's line: "Brest is a betrayal of the revolution. . . ."

A vast collection could be made of such cases, and a prominent place in it should go to Galina Serebryakova.

Both Leonid Serebryakov, her second husband, and Grigory Sokolnikov, her first, had died in prison. Galina herself spent twenty years in prison. She became an informer, denouncing her fellow prisoners to the security officer.[213] Galina Serebryakova had three daughters: one by Sokolnikov, one by Serebryakov, and one by a camp guard. She outlived Stalin, but she refused to make a statement to the Central Committee calling for the rehabilitation of her liquidated husbands. At the Moscow trial in 1937

Leonid Serebryakov had been accused of plotting to assassinate Yezhov and Beria. Stalin's prosecutor Vyshinsky gave special importance to those charges.

An appeal for Serebryakov's rehabilitation was sent by Yelena Stasova. She tried to make a joke. "If Serebryakov really did what he was accused of, he should be posthumously decorated as a Hero of the Soviet Union. . . ."

Here is how Serebryakova introduced her trilogy on Marx, published after she was released from the camps:

"Thirty years ago, my first novel about Karl Marx—*The Young Marx* —was published, and I began gathering material for subsequent volumes. But my life took a sudden and tragic turn in 1936. Release came in 1956. In 1960, I finished *Stolen Flame*, and, filled with gratitude for the Twentieth Congress, I dedicated the first part of this novel to it. The second part I dedicated to the man who headed the Leninist Central Committee in the hard days of struggle against the devotees of the personality cult, dear Nikita Sergeyevich Khrushchev.

"With the novel *The Pinnacles of Life*, I completed my trilogy on Marx and Engels, which I have entitled *Prometheus*. Thus, despite all the unkind twists and turns of fate, I accomplished my dream of putting the life and works of these two geniuses in artistic form."[214]

No sooner was a shift noted in the policy of de-Stalinization, with the "devotees of the personality cult" getting the upper hand, than Serebryakova, following the Central Committee, made a dazzling right face. At party meetings, her generous heart poured forth denunciations of the opponents of the new hard line. Galina Serebryakova adjusted effortlessly to all the unkind twists and turns of fate.

* * *

No, there's no doubt about it. Since the revolution a grave change must have taken place in people's psyches. This had to have happened if a son of the revolutionary Yakov Sverdlov could serve under Beria. If Galina Serebryakova, widow of two of Lenin's colleagues, could become a prison-camp agent provocateur and, after her release, continue to betray those who had lost their lives. And if, on top of this, she could publish a novel about Marx and Engels.

In the 1930s, when Nikita Khrushchev directed the organizational section of the Ukrainian party's Central Committee, the propaganda bureau was headed by Maria Shmayenok. Khrushchev had a high opinion of her and often asked her advice. Stalin liquidated Shmayenok's husband, Nikolai Demchenko, who was a secretary of the Central Committee. He sent Maria and her sons Nikolai and Feliks to a camp. In 1948, Shmayenok returned to the Ukraine. Nikita Khrushchev—at that time secretary of the Ukrainian party's Central Committee—turned her away and sent her to the NKVD. From there Shmayenok was sent to Zaprozhstal to work as an economist. The party members in this industrial complex started out, with comradely affection and eagerness, in pursuit of this "masked enemy of the people." They hounded her in the planning department, in the party committee, at meetings, before meetings, after meetings, and when there were no meetings. . . .

In 1955, Maria Shmayenok came to Moscow and dropped a note in the mailbox addressed to the first secretary of the Central Committee. Khrushchev received her immediately.

"You must have felt hurt back in 1948, didn't you? I refused to see you. But what could I do *then?*"

And what could he do now that he was first secretary?

For example, could he declare a general amnesty for political prisoners?

He could not, even though he wanted to.

None of the other party brass wanted that. The limited amnesty proclaimed in 1953 affected only Stalin's cohorts, the hardened criminals, plus the minor offenders, for whom ten days' detention would have been more than enough.

However, the camp regime was moderated: there was a thin stream of rehabilitations, and the prison guards stopped shooting inmates out of hand.

By the spring of 1958, however, the wind shifted. The police system was given a new impetus. Special barracks started being built in the camps. The return to the hard line came down first of all on the political prisoners, although the trickle of rehabilitations continued.

In Pechora in 1944, I met Professor G. M. Danishevsky, an outstanding therapist. They arrested him in 1937 in connection with the murder of Gorky, and threw in the charge of spying for England, Germany, and four other countries while they were at it. The professor had represented the Soviet medical profession at six international congresses.

A Central Committee commission came to Pechora in 1955. Danishevsky was asked to make a statement regarding review of his case. He came up with one that was thirty-six pages long. A commission member, an old acquaintance of the professor's, accepted the statement, but just in case, he asked the prisoner to sign a blank sheet of paper as well.

Nikita Khrushchev had a hard time getting into the long statement by Danishevsky. Then the well-meaning friend handed Khrushchev the blank sheet with the professor's signature.

"Perhaps this could be used."

Khrushchev agreed and dictated the following text:

"To the First Secretary of the Central Committee of the CPSU, N. S. Khrushchev, from the former chairman of the scientific council of the People's Commissariat of Health and former director of the Institute for Upgrading Physicians' Skills, G. M. Danishevsky.

"Statement: I am not guilty of anything. Please release me."

Khrushchev stamped an authorization to that effect. "As for this," he said, holding out the first statement, "keep it as a memento."

After his release, Danishevsky worked at the Myasnikov Institute of

Cardiology. In 1955, his book *The Acclimatization of Human Beings in the Northern Regions* came out. This fundamental work contained a study of health problems related to geography. On the title page were the words: "To the memory of a never forgotten friend and comrade, Anna Davydovna Danishevska-Rozovskaya. September 21, 1955."

A statement from the illegally imprisoned Rozovskaya also reached Khrushchev. A party member from 1904 on, she had worked closely with Lenin. A photograph still exists showing Rozovskaya standing next to Lenin and Sverdlov on Red Square.

She was lying in a hospital bed following a heart attack. Shvernik's deputy came to see her, bringing her a party card. Two hours later she died.

Rozovskaya lived no more than two months after her release from a prison camp.

The very principle on which the rehabilitations were based, if you can call it that, had a fishy look to it. All political prisoners had to appeal on their own behalf (if they were alive), or their relatives could appeal for them. Even in such a humane operation as the rehabilitations, there was no logic, no respect for the rights of the individual.

The appeal for the rehabilitation of Aleksandr Bekzadyan, former people's commissar of foreign affairs for the Transcaucasian Federation, who perished in 1937, came from some of his former comrades.

By dint of some unknown circumstances, the record of the Bekzadyan case survived. Inside the thick green folder was a report with the Gensek's decision—"Shoot him." And there were pictures of the executed man. The prosecutor called the Old Communist Faro Knunyants and showed her the pictures.

"Do you recognize this man?"

"How could I not recognize him? That's Comrade 'Yuri.' . . . We worked together for the party in the underground."

The picture showed a mutilated face, swollen eyes. . . .

Knunyants read Bekzadyan's testimony. "My father, who came from an aristocratic background, was a justice of the peace. We had a large family and we were poor. I paid for my own education. I joined the party only to seek retribution for my hard life. But my main objective was to hurt the party."

"What's your opinion of Bekzadyan?" the prosecutor asked.

"He was a very honest and upright person, an excellent Communist."

And what if no one had asked about him? What if his comrades had abandoned him?

Looking back at the short years of the thaw, you see that rehabilitation was a kind of lottery. Considering the principle on which the rehabilitations were based, Vladimir Antonov-Ovseyenko was lucky. At the Twentieth Congress, Anastas Mikoyan mentioned my father as a man whose memory had been blackened.[215] (It turned out that the slanderer he had in mind was the historian A. V. Likholat.) That is, the Central Committee recognized that the revolutionary was innocent, I thought. Shortly afterwards I received an official statement of my father's posthumous rehabilitation. Of course, they didn't send it without my asking; no one sought me out. I had to write for it on my own initiative.

But what's this? Hardly any time had passed when, in 1963, a scholar working for the Academy of Sciences' Institute of History, D. I. Oznobishin, publicly accused Antonov-Ovseyenko, who was supposed to have had "Trotskyist inclinations," of carrying out an antiparty strategy on the Ukrainian Front in 1919. Two years later, *Izvestia* published an item by A. Sovokin, a researcher at the Institute of Marxism-Leninism. This "historian" claimed that Antonov-Ovseyenko and his fellow plotter Dybenko had altered the text of a coded telegram of October 1917 that had served as the signal for a naval unit to proceed from Helsingfors to St. Petersburg. In attributing this telegram to themselves, Antonov and Dybenko were alleged to have "falsified a historic document" out of careerist motives.[216]

This journalistic concoction was put together by Sovokin, who had a "candidate's" degree in historical science, and by another candidate, Andrei Sverdlov. (This was the son of Yakov Sverdlov who had worked productively for a number of years under Beria; so there is no reason to go looking for Andrei Sverdlov's motive.) But what led Yuri Sharapov, another candidate in historical science and member of *Izvestia*'s staff, to take part in this slander operation?

When I met with a person of authority at the editorial offices to discuss the problem, I commented: "Three people with candidates' degrees. Isn't that a lot for one vulgar slander?"

The journalist laughed. For me it was no laughing matter. I decided to file suit against Sovokin and the editors. I could do this only because, in the post-Stalin era, the right of citizens to demand satisfaction was added to the Criminal and Civil Codes, after a slight delay of forty years. I brought suit in a People's Court. Of course, it refused to accept my statement. In the municipal court, the result was the same. It was only thanks to the intervention of some Old Bolsheviks and a personal order from the public prosecutor that the municipal court agreed to hear my complaint—and then immediately closed the case. *Izvestia* published a letter from Sovokin. Did the slanderer apologize to the readers and to the editors? No, he cited "new evidence"—do you see?—and therefore felt obliged to state that he had "made an error."[217] That was all.

From the editors of *Izvestia*, not a word.

There is an article in the Criminal Code stating that the right to defend someone's honor and good name exists. You can file a complaint.

Around the same time, the Institute of Marxism-Leninism (IML), the Social Sciences Academy (AON), and the Higher Party School (VPSh) began publishing a series of new books on party history. Now Stalin was no longer Leader of the Revolution, not even Leader Number Two. The authors took the discreet approach of not mentioning his name at all. To make up for that omission, they redoubled the anathemas against Trotsky and the "Trotskyists." Without a turgid mass of such denunciations, coming sincerely from the heart, you could not have a dissertation approved or a book or article published. Among the "Trotskyists" thus denounced was Antonov-Ovseyenko, on any and every pretext. Or with none at all.

During the years of World War I, Antonov-Ovseyenko directed an internationalist journal in Paris. He expressed his solidarity with Lenin's journal *Sotsial-Demokrat* and publicly differentiated himself from Trotsky and Martov. And Lenin hailed Antonov-Ovseyenko's position. However, who could be expected to comprehend such subtleties? It was easier to cling to the old reliable labels. And the Central Committee's three leading bands, the IML, the AON, and the VPSh, beat all the drums of anti-Trotskyism.

There was another handy pretext for accusing Antonov—the discussion that had taken place in 1923–24. This provocation by Stalin subsequently cost the lives of thousands of honest revolutionaries.

But beat the drums! Everyone who did not support Stalin was a "Trotskyist."

And all the documents opposing the Gensek were "Trotskyist."

This absurd campaign was not as absurd as it seems. Without it, how could you explain the destruction of the backbone of Lenin's party?

And don't say that the left hand doesn't know what the right is doing. It knows very well.

As a consolation for the rehabilitated, commemoration dates were scheduled. On the eightieth anniversary of Antonov-Ovseyenko's birth (1963) and the ninetieth (1973), one or two newspapers printed items about him, invariably referring to his "Trotskyist" past. The revolutionary's old comrades tried to organize commemorative evenings for him at the Museum of the Revolution and in the Soviet Army building. But in Moscow, in Leningrad, and in Kiev, the officials were unable to "understand" this request. In the central writers' hall, the proposal to hold a commemoration for the writer, critic, and poet Antonov-Ovseyenko was also turned down flat.

"He's one of the 'exes,' isn't he?"

"Antonov-Ovseyenko was rehabilitated by a resolution of the Central Committee."

"And who can guarantee me that tomorrow he won't be unrehabilitated, like Fyodor Raskolnikov?" one official replied.

There ensued another series of slanderous articles in the press.

I am a member of the Association of the Blind. For several years I gave lectures to the Association on my father's revolutionary career. Subsequently a slanderous denunciation was lodged against me, and I was forbidden to "popularize a Trotskyist" any longer.

But you can file a complaint! I tried. I wrote a lengthy statement to the chairman of the Party Control Commission. I asked the chairman, Arvid Yanovich Pelshe, to look into the way that the Central Committee resolution was being implemented, and, unless this resolution had been rescinded, to stop this campaign against my father. Two weeks later, an aide of Pelshe's gave me the telephone number of an official on the Control Commission, the party "instructor" Petrova. I waited another two weeks (the question was being studied). Then, I called and heard:

"Ye-e-es."

It was such an arch, lordly "ye-e-es." You felt the power oozing from every pore, and the best caviar.

"I am studying your statement." There was such condescension in Petrova's voice. "Your father's file is on my desk. I can't understand what you want. He joined the party in 1917, but before that . . ."

"Pardon me, I would like to put in a word to set the record straight. My father joined the party in 1903. That is shown in the minutes of the congresses that were published in Lenin's time. I can supply all this material for you. After all, I am a historian by profession. If you will see me in person . . ."

"There's no need of that. I have your file here too. What kind of historian are you? In 1938 you were expelled from the institute. . . ."

"But I was reinstated right away. And got my diploma within a year."

"That cannot be," Petrova concluded in a haughty tone.

"Please hang on a minute and I'll give you the number of the diploma."

"Don't trouble yourself. I already told you that I have your file on my desk."

"So, what do you think, that I'm a swindler and that my diploma is a forgery?"

"I think that we have discussed this question sufficiently." Petrova hung up.

I called Pelshe's assistant.

"I asked you to protect my father's name from defamation. But this colleague of yours, Petrova, is ready to slander me too."

The assistant laughed heartily.

It was an eloquent answer. I was grateful to them, to Pelshe and his assistant, and to Petrova, who was herself a former assistant of the unforgettable butcher Matvei Shkiryatov. They helped me understand, in the sixth decade of my life, what had long been clear to others—that the good name of a revolutionary means nothing to the party bosses.

At that precise time, the VPSh started publishing a series of books entitled "Party Publicists." Initially there was a proposal to include Antonov-Ovseyenko, who had written a number of books and many hundreds of articles and essays and who had founded and directed several newspapers and magazines. This suggestion was received favorably, but there turned out to have been a misunderstanding. The higher-ups refused to have anything to do with such "exes.'

Vladimir Nevsky wrote more than a thousand articles, among them the important work "Party History as a Science." A close associate of Lenin, Nevsky never "deviated," never joined an opposition. But they would not recognize Nevsky as a party publicist either. The same for Mikhail Kedrov. How much easier just to reprint the articles of Kuibyshev, Voroshilov, and Ordzhonikidze, articles that were the work of ghost writers.

Then, lo and behold, a collection of Aleksandra Kollontai's articles appeared. The whole frame-up logic that they used raised the question: "Why? After all, Aleksandra Mikhailovna was involved in more than one deviation. . . ." I thought I was beginning to see a certain thread of consistency. Kollontai had escaped the purges! The same was true of Olminsky, Lunacharsky, and Yaroslavsky. They all got into the "series."

So, now there are two histories of the party—one for those who died in their beds and another for Stalin's victims. Clearly, Marxism-Leninism cannot stand still but must progress as a science. But we can't blame Marx and Lenin for this. They died long before the age of belated rehabilitations.

This age has obviously become prolonged. To this day, not one book has been published about the "rehabilitated" Vladimir Nevsky. The IML and the Moscow and Leningrad Museums of the Revolution have stubbornly refused to observe his anniversary.

In 1933, Lenin's comrade in arms, the courageous revolutionary Nikolai Skrypnik, chose to end his life by suicide. Skrypnik was rehabilitated, but the press keeps on repeating Stalin's insinuations about him. And who contributed especially to this campaign of persecution? Likholat—the very same Likholat who was called a slanderer by Mikoyan at the Twentieth Congress. Now he is slandering Kosior again, and Antonov-Ovseyenko, and Skrypnik . . . whoever they sic him onto.

A year after the Twentieth Congress, Khrushchev was given material on Bukharin's trial. The following morning, he called one of the researchers.

"I spent the whole night reading your report and weeping. You know, I had to lend a hand in that bloody business too. . . ."

The trials of the thirties were reviewed by a special commission of the Presidium of the Central Committee. Honest comrades were appointed to head the teams of party investigators. The Central Committee commission collected *sixty-four volumes* of documents, the testimony of the victims and witnesses of Stalin's tyranny.

In 1960, Maurice Thorez, general secretary of the Central Committee of the French Communist Party, came to Moscow. A folder containing the conclusions of the Central Committee commission lay on Khrushchev's desk. One of those who had directed the work was present.

Thorez: Nikita Sergeyevich, please do not overturn all the trials at once. After your party's Twentieth Congress, when Stalin's crimes were revealed, the French CP lost forty-eight thousand members.
Khrushchev: And there's nothing to regret about their leaving if they were in the CP only out of love of "Generalissimo" Stalin.

Thorez: Nevertheless, I ask you not to overturn all the trials at once. At least keep it to one a month.

Khrushchev: But why? Everybody has known for a long time that those trials were frame-ups. This question has to be got out of the way once and for all. We will only gain from this in the eyes of public opinion.

Thorez: The Socialist Party leaders knew back in the twenties and thirties that the trials were frame-ups. The Western press had no difficulty in debunking all those so-called secret meetings between Soviet party leaders and Trotsky. It exploded those stories the very day after they were published in the Moscow papers. Everyone knew that Bukharin wasn't a Japanese spy and that Zinoviev didn't kill Kirov.

Khrushchev: Well, on that point, there is evidence here in the commission's files that Kirov was murdered on Stalin's orders. Now, we are going to overturn all those frame-up trials. And we are going to do it all at once and without unnecessary delays.

But Khrushchev underestimated the power of the Stalinist opposition. They pressured him relentlessly. Every weapon was brought into play, slander of the Old Communists, intimidation, and arguments like this:

"If the trials are overturned the people may misunderstand us. . . . Just think, Nikita Sergeyevich, what the effect would be on the international Communist movement. . . . Remember what Lenin bequeathed to us. God forbid, dear Nikita Sergeyevich! . . ."

And Khrushchev retreated.

After the Twenty-second Congress, the Old Communists reproached the first secretary: "You promised to overturn all the trials and publish the evidence exposing the real murderer of Kirov. . . ."

"No, it's out of the question *now*. We'll do it, of course, but fifteen years from now."

All the evidence collected in the investigation of Stalin's crimes was consigned to the archives.

An absurd situation developed. Of the twenty-two people condemned in Bukharin's trial in 1938, more than half were rehabilitated. But the trial itself was not overturned. Leading party figures—Stasova, Karpinsky, and Katanyan—appealed to the Twenty-second Congress to restore Bukharin's good name. Their voices were not heeded. The leaders of a number of Communist parties who appealed for Bukharin's rehabilitation didn't even get the courtesy of an answer.

To this day there has been no posthumous rehabilitation of Rykov, Tomsky, and Bukharin. And now, from all party platforms, there is a loud outpouring of slander against "the enemies of the people" and the "hired agents of the bourgeoisie."

* * *

The widow of Aleksandr Shlyapnikov, one of Lenin's closest comrades, spent eighteen years in the camps. But she found herself completely unable to win rehabilitation. Some Old Bolsheviks appealed to Central Committee Presidium member Podgorny. "What's going on? In regard to her civil status—that is, in accordance with the penal code—Shlyapnikova has been cleared. But her party membership hasn't been restored. The Control Commission ruled: 'Rejected because of age!' "

Podgorny promised to help get a personal pension authorized for Shlyapnikova. As for her party status, he advised her to reapply to the Control Commission.

"The time is not yet ripe for your reinstatement in the party," Shlyapnikova was told.

Two months later she died. Her daughter called the Control Commission and said: "The time is quite ripe now. Mother was buried yesterday."

But why seek restoration of party credentials if rehabilitation provides no guarantee against the systematic blackening of your name after you are dead? If those who survived the camps are to be subjected to a campaign of degradation?

At the insistence of Molotov and Kaganovich, the rehabilitated Communists were given party cards with a note that membership had been interrupted from 1937 to 1954. Those who protested about this were told sanctimoniously: "What kind of party work did you do in prison?" (Incidentally, Molotov did not fail to provide his wife, Polina Zhemchuzhina, with a "regular" party card that had no notation about an interruption in membership.)

No one should think that a genuine rehabilitation policy was opposed only by the henchmen of the dead Gensek. A broad Stalinist current in public life participated in the battle for this unjust cause. The poet Pavel Vasilyev was liquidated at the age of twenty-six. It is not known who denounced him. Several prominent literary figures used to write regularly to the Organs—Yermilov, Stavsky, Fadeyev, Bezymensky. It took a fight to win Vasilyev's rehabilitation. A number of opponents appeared. The fiercest of them was the poet Bezymensky.

* * *

Mikhail Yakubovich, a great-grandson of the Decembrist Aleksandr Yakubovich, was an active participant in the revolution. From 1930 to 1941 he was imprisoned. Then, after a few months of "freedom," he was imprisoned again. When he was rehabilitated in 1956, only his second conviction was overturned. His first conviction, in the so-called Union Bureau case,* was not annulled.

They all knew he was innocent—including Mikoyan, for whom Yakubovich had worked in the apparatus. In 1967, after thirty-seven years, Mikoyan and Yakubovich met in Moscow. Mikoyan transmitted Yakubo-

*Union Bureau case: one of the series of frame-up trials against imaginary "wrecker" organizations staged in the 1928–31 period.—TRANS.

vich's statement to the public prosecutor. But Rudenko needed the approval of the Politburo. They refused. .

"In the Central Committee, they think," Mikoyan told Yakubovich, "that now is not an appropriate time for reviews of the political trials, or for new rehabilitations either." The Central Committee refused to grant a pension to the former labor-camp prisoner. At that point Mikoyan made an agreement with Kunayev, the first secretary of the Kazakhstan Central Committee, enabling Yakubovich to get a pension.

The rehabilitation process, like the process of "exposing" Stalin, had its ebbs and flows. "It's not the right time." "It will embarrass us in the West." "What will people say?" Convenient formulas. They were well suited to the official desks where they were hatched.

One formula sticks in my memory particularly: "Moscow is not made of rubber." That was the answer I got from the secretary of the Moscow Soviet executive committee, Pegov, after I had been rehabilitated, when I was pleading with him to give me a pass for residence in Moscow. Getting to see him was almost impossible. It was even harder than getting scarce goods without waiting in line.

"I was born in Moscow. I graduated from an institute here. They arrested me in Moscow. So according to the resolution of the Council of Ministers, I have the right to reside in the capital."

I explained all this to Pegov. And got the answer about "rubber."

Memories of life in the camps came back to me. There is a list. Your name is on it. There is a check next to your name. But there is no sugar.

I didn't want to appeal to the Central Committee. After the Arctic camps, I was tempted by southern climes and settled in Gagra on the Black Sea in Georgia. I wrote to the Central Committee from there. I asked them at least to let me know where my father was buried. After all, the remains of a notorious hangman like Vyshinsky repose in the Kremlin wall.

I was told that establishing the circumstances of my father's death "does not seem feasible."

Yet another formula for refusal.

During this period, I began to be troubled by dreams. One dream was inspired by medieval history.

. . . In ancient Saxony, it was the custom that, to make amends for a wrong committed, the criminal paid "atonement money" to the relatives of the murder or robbery victim. In addition, the guilty party put a stone by the side of the road. These "atonement stones," engraved with crosses or coats of arms, have survived to this day.

In my dream I saw a dreary, deserted gray road with heaps of rubbish along the side. I walked down it a long time, so long that I started to get tired. But I had to keep walking; some obscure goal pulled me on. The road was endless, and I was losing hope when a big gray house loomed before me. The people in it were also gray. Silently they led me up to the very top, to the grayest person of all. They told me that this person could grant you anything, but you could ask for it only once.

I asked him to have the rubbish cleared from the roadside and trees planted in memory of those whose lives had unjustly been taken from them.

"This isn't the Middle Ages," the gray creature responded. It was said with imposing finality. I shuddered, and awoke.

* * *

The posthumous rehabilitations were carried out in an impromptu way. This was particularly true at the beginning. Random impulses of good will produced random lists of the dead and the survivors. The murderer had acted in quite a different way. Stalin had a plan; he kept things in their proper order. And he did not fear publicity. In his day, the drums were beaten as loudly as possible against certain "enemies of the people."

The rehabilitation of Stalin's victims was carried out very quietly. Probably this reflected a natural feeling of embarrassment on the part of leaders who had themselves had a part in the liquidation campaigns. They have not overcome their embarrassment to this day. The dates of the murders of Lenin's comrades, the military commanders, the scholars, and the writers are being kept secret. When they print material about those who perished—which still happens—the publishing houses and editorial boards accept the MVD reports at face value. The trustworthiness of this institution is well known. It was ordered to spread out the dates of the deaths of Stalin's victims over the period 1935–45. Even so, a grim picture emerges for the years 1937–39.

The leaders did not oppose publicity in principle, as long as proportion and tact were observed. About Rosa Luxemburg, Karl Liebknecht, and Ernst Thaelmann, they wrote: "brutally murdered." About Lenin's comrades they wrote: "victims of repression." Fine and simple. And not so alarming. The party, faithful to the Leninist truth (another enduring formula), rehabilitated those it considered convenient to rehabilitate. So what if a lot of people weren't satisfied? Rehabilitation isn't made of rubber.

Many Old Communists wanted to work for the good of the party, as they had before. They were not understood. One of those rehabilitated, A. A. Medvedev, while at the Central Committee offices, had the gall to cite the story of Radishchev. After Alexander I came to the throne, he invited this archenemy of serfdom, who had spent six years in prison and internal exile, to draw up new laws. Medvedev's hint was not understood either.

A few years later, Medvedev died. Many people came to pay their last respects to this revolutionary. Party leaders came to Moscow from Udmurtia (where the famous division commander had fought during the civil war). The German Democratic Republic posthumously decorated Medvedev for his services to the revolution. But the secretary of the district committee where Medvedev was registered as a party member threatened the Old Bolsheviks: "What's this? You want to stage a fancy funeral for your rehabilitated buddy? Well, you're not going to get away with it."

The district committee sent a dependable personage to the funeral, a party secretary who was one of the most solid Stalinist worthies.

The first graveside speech was short and unceremonious.

"Close the lid!" the dependable personage ordered. But the lid of the coffin was in the hands of an honest man.

Then the first secretary of the Udmurt Republic spoke. "Close the lid!"

He was followed by the secretary of the Votkinsk municipal committee.

"Close the lid!" the personage commanded.

Finally, a car pulled up from the embassy of the German Democratic Republic, bearing an enormous wreath of fresh roses. The chairman of the German-Soviet Friendship Society got up to speak. Then the ambassador came to the coffin and pinned a medal onto the suit of the deceased. They had not had time to warn the ambassador, and he mentioned the victims of Stalin's terror.

"Now close the lid!" the personage ordered for the last time.

* * *

The funeral bells fell silent. The 1970s arrived. One High Unnamed Personage felt it was time to say, "We're sick of these commemorations!"

From that very day, all the anniversary articles about Lenin's ill-fated comrades have concluded with a thick goo of commendations for their loyalty to the party. But no dates are given for their deaths, or any descriptions of the circumstances. Such words as "repression," "execution," "slander," "victim," and "abuses" have become strictly taboo. This is the kind of immortality on paper earned by those Stalin murdered.

But, so that their shades would not disturb new generations, the names of the revolutionaries were taken out of the history books. The revolt of the Left SRs was put down in 1918 by units commanded by Vatsetis, Muralov, and Nevsky. However, in his play *The Sixth of July*, the dramatist Mikhail Shatrov was obliged to put a man named Podvoisky in their place. The novelist Gennady Fish described the revolutionary events in Finland. Heading the Bolsheviks in Helsinki and the Baltic Fleet was Antonov-Ovseyenko. The order came down: "Delete that." And so the writer deleted it from his book *June 1917*.

Tourists are shown the stairway up which Antonov-Ovseyenko led the insurrectionary forces into the inner rooms of the Winter Palace. Only today, instead of mentioning him, they attribute this to someone else, a man who died in his bed. This is the sort of thing they do today with the names of many revolutionaries.

Khrushchev's coming to power and his attempt to expose Stalin and exonerate his victims were historical accidents. As was the failure of Beria. The Stalin terror need not have ended with the death of Stalin. If circumstances had worked out differently, Beria might have seized power and carried out a new bloodbath. There was a power struggle within the tiny circle of Stalin's stooges, and the outcome of such palace intrigues is hard to predict. The laws of history do not extend to wrangles among thieves. (After his death, they could find no space by the Kremlin wall, where the hangmen are laid to rest beside their chief, to bury a man so accidentally thrown into leadership as Nikita Khrushchev.)

The exposure of Stalin and the rehabilitation of his victims is, in essence, a single process. Its parts are dialectically interconnected and, as practice has shown, interchangeable. It has turned into a rehabilitation of Stalin and an exposure of the "enemies of the people," of those so thoughtlessly rehabilitated by "that damn Khrushchev!"

That's how the age of belated rehabilitations ended. The age? Isn't that too highfaluting a term for the few years in which mercies were doled out with an eyedropper?

I would like to tell another story about . . .

"Enough! Close the lid!"

IN OUR TIME

3

In December 1926 Stalin wrote to Filipp Ksenofontov: "I do not have any disciples."[218] Today there is a superabundance of them.

What holds them together, these admirers of Stalin and apologists for his rule? Almost all of them belong to the Soviet Writers' Union. Another thing they have in common is a glaringly obvious lack of talent. You can't say they're bad writers; they aren't writers at all. What they publish can't be classified as literature.

All kinds of sects abound in the world today, Seventh-Day Adventists, Children of God, the People's Temple, Aquarians. Maybe in our country pro-Stalin writers like Aleksandr Chakovsky, Ivan Stadnyuk, Sergei Semanov, and Feliks Chuyev, along with bureaucrats from various government offices, have formed a secret sect of tyrannophiles. The decisions of the Twentieth and Twenty-second congresses have not been publicly retracted; they remain in force. Yet the campaign for the rehabilitation of Stalin keeps gaining strength. Everything suggests that an antiparty conspiracy is at work in our country aimed at restoring the age of idol worship. The conspiratorial members of this secret sect—writers, poets, artists, historians, officials—are not afraid of dissenting from the official line of party congresses and of the Central Committee.

However, unlike certain leaders, I do not insist on the arrest of dissidents. It's not even necessary to lock them up in psychiatric hospitals. But
since work in the ideological arena seems to have a negative effect on their
psychological health and since the responsibilities they have assumed in
the creative and scientific spheres are clearly beyond the capacities of the
people we have mentioned (and many we haven't), it would seem appropriate to relieve them of the burdens of mental labor. If this is not done,
these dissidents may gain the upper hand, and idol worship once again
become the norm, the substance of our lives.

The conspirators don't miss a single occasion. In 1967, at the celebration of the fiftieth anniversary of the revolution, on Pushkin Square in
Moscow, alongside the portraits of the heroes of October was placed the
portrait of the man who put them to death. In 1969, around his ninetieth
birthday, a marble bust of the Gensek appeared at the Kremlin wall.
Without a resolution to that effect by the Central Committee. Does this
mean the dissidents have wormed their way into the higher bodies of the
party?

In 1974 a book honoring the 350th anniversary of the Academy of
Sciences was published. Among the photographs of distinguished members of the academy appeared the face of Stalin. The next year a collection
of orders of the day issued during the Great Patriotic War came out. At
the last moment someone had slipped a portrait of the Generalissimo onto
its title page.

Visitors to the All-Union Arts Exhibit at the Manezh in 1975 stopped
in front of a huge canvas bearing the caption "Delegates to the First
All-Russia Congress of Soviets." There was Grigory Kotovsky in his soldier's greatcoat, giving one of his eloquent Red speeches. Next to him
were Tukhachevsky, Yegorov, and Ordzhonikidze. There was a smiling
Chubar, and, a little farther back, Antonov-Ovseyenko. In the left corner,
in profile, was the familiar face of the Gensek.

A group portrait of the chief executioner and his victims.

The editors of the mass-circulation weekly *Ogonyok* were quick to
publish a reproduction of the painting. Time for the mass readership to
become accustomed once again to that visage. Certain influential figures
in radio, television, and film hold similar antiparty views. More and more
often they present their audiences with a spruced-up image of the Good
Shepherd. The dissidents have infiltrated all the mass media. In December
1979, for example, they were able to celebrate the hundredth anniversary
of Stalin's birth with articles in *Pravda* and *Kommunist*, official publications of the party's Central Committee.

A year earlier, on December 21, 1978, Stalin's ninety-ninth birthday,
a literary discussion on "Classicism and Modernity" was held at the Central House of Writers in Moscow, attended by nearly a thousand young
people, many wearing Stalin buttons. Pyotr Paliyevsky, deputy director of
the Gorky Institute of World Literature, spoke with praise of the Stalin era
as a period of the greatest flourishing of Soviet literature. He was seconded

by Stanislav Kunyaev, secretary of the Moscow branch of the Soviet Writers' Union, who had won notoriety not long before with his verses on the "Jews in the Pentagon."

The supporters of Hitler, Mussolini, and Franco also celebrate important dates in the lives of their idols. Honest people, however, consider the worship of dictators and idolization of bloody terror an insult to humanity. In 1886 Russia was preparing to honor General Mikhail Muravyov, who had drowned Poland and Byelorussia in blood. Aleksandr Suvorov, governor general of St. Petersburg, refused to sign a letter of greetings. "I don't pay compliments to cannibals," declared the grandson of the famous field marshal Suvorov. Have we run out of Suvorovs in Russia?

These days the countenance of the deceased Gensek pursues Soviet citizens everywhere—on the streets, on trains, in movie houses, in people's homes. Perhaps Soviet citizens do not wish to behold the visage of the tyrant. Perhaps they do not need a superintendent of police with a brass plate on his leather shoulder strap and a medal on his chest. But the conspirators aren't interested in the opinion of the people. They smuggle Stalin in through every crack, despite the party's decisions. They trust in the philistines who can't imagine life without a tsar, a little father, around their necks.

The poet who wrote the following lines (which were removed from his song before it could be published) was right:

> And yet it's a shame that our dreams fill with idols again,
> And sometimes we count ourselves lackeys and slaves as before.

The new Stalin blight has proved to be highly infectious. Even among party members who suffered from Stalin's repression, the air has not been cleansed of stale idolatry.

The snows were heavy in Moscow last winter and the streets weren't easily cleared. As I was going down Kirov Street, I slipped and fell. Coming toward me was an Old Bolshevik, one of those who returned from the camps. As he gave me a hand he remarked: "Now, if Comrade Stalin was alive, he'd take a walk through Moscow *himself*, then he'd go see Vladimir Promyslov, our mayor, and put him in jail for three days. They'd clear the streets of snow and ice in no time."

Nowadays you often hear it: "Under Stalin there was *order.*" Ah, what age-old longing for the whip I hear in that persistent refrain. But why did they bother to have that campaign of anti-Stalin revelations?

Khrushchev was called a loyal Leninist. So why do highly placed people recall him with such hatred? He wasn't able to carry things to completion. He held his tongue about many of the crimes of the Gensek's henchmen. Fifteen years have passed. Isn't it time to forgive Khrushchev for his sins?

Questions, questions, so many that lately they give me no rest.

Prowar propaganda and praise of militarism are punishable under Soviet law. But pro-Stalin propaganda is encouraged. Why?

Pytor Pospelov, a professional falsifier of history, one of Stalin's henchmen and official biographers, was made an academician and a member of the presidium of the Soviet Academy of Sciences. The first Karl Marx medal, a recent innovation, was awarded to him. For what services? After his death this appointed academician was declared an "outstanding Marxist." Why?

Why hasn't a biography of the real Stalin yet been published? Is it that the dissidents, once they knew the truth, would stop praising the Criminal?

An interesting and bold experiment was made recently by a person leaving the Soviet Union. He took two portraits with him—one of Stalin, one of Khrushchev. The second portrait was confiscated at the border. Stalin they let through. What is this? Just the local initiative of customs officials?

Throughout the country unknown people are distributing privately produced objects—calendars, scarfs, pins, and buttons bearing the portrait of Stalin. I have some questions for those in charge of the KGB: If portraits of Hitler were circulated this way, would you also disregard it? And why, at the same time, are other forms of private production and sale, such as *samizdat,* punished? I have a question for the Party Control Commission: Why are people who now try to expose the truth about Stalin expelled from the party?

There is silence in our day about many of Lenin's associates. But Stalin's henchmen are praised. Why? If the Kremlin wall must be adorned with the names of such cannibals as Shkiryatov, Mekhlis, and Vyshinsky, perhaps room could be found for others too—Malenkov, Yezhov, and Abakumov, for example. And don't forget Beria. There was a time when the Big Pope and the Little Pope worked together so fruitfully. So why not put Beria's grave next to Stalin's?

Disabled war veterans are surrounded with universal care and attention. Why not the disabled veterans of Stalin's prisons too? Why are they regarded as second-class citizens?

Why aren't any public-opinion polls taken or referendums held in our country? I make bold to suggest that not all citizens, not even all party members, would answer the questions I have asked in the same way. Why not hold a referendum?

Everyone knows that a veritable paradise is flourishing in every part of our country. So why not explain this to the Volga Germans, the Crimean Tatars, or the Greeks who were deported from their homes under Stalin and wish to return to the lands of their forefathers? Why not explain to them that there's no point to it?

The heirs of Stalin call for harsh measures against those who wish to emigrate from the Soviet Union. Why? There's no doubt most of them would return. In the West you have to *work.* And, what's even more humiliating, if you don't do good work, the boss fires you.

An international organization concerned with human rights, the so-called Russell Tribunal, is not allowed to come to the USSR. Why not? Every day when I walk down Komsomol Prospekt I see a huge poster three meters high, "The USSR Is the Land of True Democracy." Let the gentlemen of the Russell Tribunal come here. Why hide our democratic achievements from world public opinion? Especially the achievements of our socialist agriculture. Aren't they obvious to everyone?

Less than fifteen years after the death of Lenin, Stalin proclaimed that socialism had been built. More than a quarter of a century has passed since the death of Joseph the Builder, and in the intervening time our country has only arrived at "developed socialism." But I suspect we're already living under developed *communism*. Not because Nikita Khrushchev promised twenty years ago that the blessed era would arrive in two decades, and not because our country has achieved unheard-of abundance.

The main proof of communism is that we have stopped shooting troublemakers. Now they are carefully placed in jails and provided for. Even members of the Central Committee are no longer shot. My fellow historians, when they publish the minutes of party congresses and the decrees of top party bodies, no longer have to include lists of Central Committee members who were almost all massacred by Stalin. This means there have been major shifts in our sense of shame—another vivid and irrefutable indication of the coming of the new communist era.

At the Twenty-fifth Congress, Leonid Brezhnev stated: "We have created a new society, a society such as humanity has never known. It is a society without crises, with a steadily growing economy, mature socialist relations, and true freedom. It is a society with firm confidence in the future and the bright perspective of communism before it."

This was a wise observation, as are all the utterances of general secretaries. Firm as the rock of Gibraltar. It deserves no discussion. Yet there should be a limit to our modesty. Why speak of the perspective of communism when, visibly and tangibly, it has already been achieved?

On this point I differ with the party. But since I am not a party member and never have been, I grant that the party may overlook this disagreement. Nevertheless I console myself with the knowledge that I am doing my duty. Article 49 of the new Constitution grants citizens the right "to suggest improvements in the work of government bodies and public organizations and to criticize shortcomings in their work." And so I am suggesting we not belittle the greatest achievement of our age.

I am extraordinarily happy to have lived to see the era of communism. My one regret is that it has a defect: its past has been amputated. It's as though the Stalin blight had never existed, and we never went through decades of bloody counterrevolution.

Chekhov was right when he said that in order to live in the present we must first atone for the past. The antiparty conspirators want to prevent people from knowing their past.

Aleksandr Blok didn't live to see the Stalin era, but the early terror was enough to shake the poet deeply.

Those born in faraway times,
Did not know what paths they had taken.
We children of these troubled times,
We haven't the strength to forget.

I hear the insidious voice of one of the conspirators: "So you haven't the strength? Here, let us help you."

Here's how they help: BAM! BAM! BAM!

Those aren't church bells banging. That's the radio, the television, the movies, the newspapers praising the builders of the Baikal-Amur Mainline, the BAM. They aren't praising the prisoners shod in *chuni* (those boots made of pieces of tire held together by string, remember?), not those who under convoy guard built a second rail line to the Far East in the thirties. That was the Bamlag (the Baikal-Amur camp complex), eternal memory to its victims.

What do I mean, "eternal memory"? I am asked. Why does a young builder of the BAM today want to know that beneath the area his bulldozer is clearing lie the bones of his grandfather?

* * *

Ignorance can be criminal, but unpunished crime is doubly criminal. There is no adequate punishment for the fanatical bigotry and cruelty of the Stalinschina, but at least Stalin's thugs should not be left in comfort, prosperity, and obscurity. The butchers of Ravensburg, Auschwitz, and Dachau have been punished. Almost all of them. Why haven't the butchers of Solovki, Kolyma, and Bamlag even been named? I'm not asking for punishment. Simply that their names be published.

At the beginning of World War II, when German troops were threatening our northern borders, evacuation of the political prisoners from Kandalakshi was begun. They were moved out of the camp, but no one worried about where to transport them.

The slaughter of this column of many thousands of prisoners was directed by an experienced operative of the Leningrad branch of the Lubyanka, a certain Vasilyev (his full name isn't known). He began by ordering the smithy to make a number of heavy clubs with iron plating at one end. The first batch of prisoners were lined up in front of Vasilyev's team. Then the order was given: "Turn around." Vasilyev and his assistants came up from behind and smashed them over the head. They got so carried away that they laid bets on who could smash a skull with one blow, who needed more than one.

After two days it was all over. But some of the perpetrators blabbed over a bottle of wine. Someone informed on them. Vasilyev was taken to court for "overstepping his authority." They gave him three years. He hadn't served half his time when he was paroled and given a new assignment. He went on to become a colonel of state security.

Nowadays you can see Vasilyev at markets in Leningrad. He sells flowers that he grows at his own dacha. The venerable colonel has turned out to be a great hand at flower growing. (Joseph Stalin also loved flowers. At his dacha in Kuntsevo he planted roses with his own hands, tended the flowers, and showed guests around his rose garden with pride.)

There is a statute of limitations. But in regard to war criminals and crimes against humanity, many governments have adopted a convention waiving this statute. The convention was signed by, among others, a representative of the Soviet Union.

Who made the exception for our flower growers? Evidently the conspirators have infiltrated our judicial agencies as well. They have reached the point where they denounce all critics of the government as criminals. That's how things were under Yezhov and Beria. So I don't advise anyone nowadays to enlist as a dissident. What decent person would want to become a criminal? Let me take this opportunity to state clearly that I am personally opposed in principle to any violation of the Criminal Code.

Chichiko Kekelidze joined the political struggle long before the 1917 revolution. He fought in World War I. Under the Menshevik government established in Georgia in 1918, he became commander of the garrison in the town of Poti. In 1921, when Bolshevik troops marched into Georgia, repression began. Among the first to be seized was a member of the Central Committee of the Menshevik Party of Georgia by the name of Khomeriko. He was one of the leaders of the armed resistance against Bolshevik power. His comrades decided to free him from prison, but they had to let the arrested man know in advance. Chichiko undertook the task. He kidnapped the investigator's eight-year-old daughter and notified the father that they would be waiting for him in a certain café. The meeting took place over the inevitable cup of tea.

"We have your daughter," said Chichiko. "She's in good health and we'll let her go. All you have to do is carry out a small request: deliver this note to Khomeriko."

The investigator delivered the note and the Mensheviks sent his daughter home.

Kekelidze was of course risking his life, but he didn't think about that. Cruelty and vindictiveness were alien to him and his comrades. During the fighting Filipp Makharadze fell into their hands. But they let him go. Makharadze was to become chairman of the Central Executive Committee of the Soviets of Georgia.

But the new government had mercy on no one. All the active Mensheviks were arrested, including Chichiko. He fell into the category of perpetual prisoner. Formally the category of hard labor for an indefinite term did not exist, not even in the thirties or after. But people like Chichiko were simply never released.

In 1937 Kekelidze was in Pezmlag (the Pezmog camps) in the Komi Autonomous Republic. That year trainloads of arrested party officials began arriving at Pezmlag's transfer station No. 11. Among the new arrivals Chichiko recognized an Old Bolshevik with whom he had clashed many times at revolutionary meetings. Chichiko called out, "It gives me pleasure to welcome you to *this* territory."

And it was true. The territory of the Soviet state was divided in two: the Lesser Zone, of the barbed-wire prison camps, and the Greater Zone, the rest of the country. Social classes were disappearing. In their place arose two categories of citizens—those in confinement and those still waiting to be arrested.

At last Chichiko Kekelidze came to the end of his endless term, after his second ten years at corrective labor. But the experience had not reformed him. For some reason he would not believe that while he had been in prison Stalin had succeeded in building socialism.

The Pezmog River flows into the Pechora. Pezmlag was the younger brother of Pechorlag (the Pechora camp complex). When Kekelidze was freed—at the end of the war—he decided to stay and work as a base-level supervisor in the supply system at Pezmlag. There was no use going home. They would just bring him back from the Caucasus in the next prisoner transport.

For four whole months Chichiko was "free."

In the courtroom several frightened stool pigeons unenthusiastically repeated the testimony they had been coached on in the district security office. Chichiko couldn't stand it and said to the presiding officer of the court: "Katso, why are you torturing these people? Why are you making them lie through their teeth? I'll tell you myself. Ever since this system came to power I've been against it. And I'll die that way. Go ahead, sign the verdict, please." What a shame Chichiko didn't live to see the humane phase the system has entered now.

* * *

On a walk outside the city last spring, I came across a stone quarry. The stone was going to be used for the Olympic Games in Moscow.

During the thirties, you know, they set up stone crushers in some prison cellars. The hoppers were filled with prisoners' corpses. After half an hour the bloody mess was flushed into the sewers.

I stood at the edge of the quarry and listened to the machines rumbling. What a humane era we live in, I thought. This year the Olympics will be held in Moscow. And the stone crushers are only crushing stone.

Stalin's incomparable era ended a quarter of a century ago. Some people are bored; some want to try to repeat it. The one they are conjuring will come. And he'll come with a vengeance. Still, insistently, they keep calling him.

NOTES

Titles of Russian books and periodicals and some other bibliographic information in the author's notes are given in the Library of Congress system of transliteration. Material in parentheses is by the translator, not the author.

References to the stenographic records of congresses of the Soviet Communist Party are given with the Roman numeral followed by *s"ezd*, the Russian for "congress." Thus, *XII s"ezd*, rather than *Dvenadtsatyi s"ezd*, for the Twelfth Congress. The date and place of publication are sometimes given to indicate which edition of such a stenographic record was cited.

References to the works of Lenin are given as *PSS*, for *Polnoe sobranie sochinenii*, the fifth Russian edition of his "Complete Collected Works." (This edition is not actually "complete," as several citations in the present work show.) I have sometimes listed the corresponding reference in the official English-language version of Lenin's *Collected Works (CW)*, published in the 1960s by Moscow's Progress Publishers. However, I have usually not followed the Progress Publishers translation, either because it is inadequate and misleading or for stylistic consistency within the present translation.

References to the Russian edition of Stalin's *Sochineniia* (Works) are given simply as "Stalin, Vol. —, p. —." The wording of the English edition (*Works*, 13 vols., Moscow, 1952–55) has not always been followed, for the same reasons as in the case of Lenin's *CW*.—TRANS.

1. A relative of Gukovsky, whom I shall identify only as Z——a, confirms that he presided at the party court that investigated the attempt on the life of Zharinov, one of the first who dared make known the criminal behavior of "Comrade Koba."

2. *Vperyod*, April 13, 1918.

3. See the collection of articles by Krupskaya on Lenin, *N. K. Krupskaya o Lenine*, Moscow, 1965, p. 24. In her memoirs of Lenin (*Vospominaniia o Lenine*, Moscow, 1972, p. 462) Krupskaya recalls, along the same lines, that after Martov's death (on April 4, 1923) she hid the news from Lenin, but he, though no longer able to speak, found an obituary in a Paris émigré newspaper and "reproachfully showed it to me."

4. *V. I. Lenin. Biograficheskaia khronika* (Lenin: A Biographical Chronology), Vol. 5, Moscow, 1974, pp. 436, 477, 500.

5. *J. V. Stalin. Kratkaia biografiia* (Joseph Stalin: A Short Biography), Moscow, 1948, pp. 72–73. (An English version was published in 1949 under the title *A Political Biography*, with authorship attributed to "the Marx-Engels-Lenin Insti-

tute." That English version differs somewhat from the Russian original. This quotation, therefore, is translated directly from the Russian.)

6. *Geroicheskaia oborona Tsaritsyna v 1918 godu* (The Heroic Defense of Tsaritsyn in 1918; a collection of documents), Moscow, 1942. See also *Voenno-istoricheskii zhurnal* (Military-Historical Journal), 1965, No. 2, p. 49.

7. V. I. Lenin, *Polnoe sobranie sochinenii* (Complete Collected Works), 5th ed. (hereafter cited as Lenin, *PSS*), Vol. 50, p. 108. (Cf. the English edition, Lenin's *Collected Works*, Vol. 27, p. 533.) See also *Lenin. Biograficheskaia khronika,* Vol. 5, pp. 584, 612.

8. *Direktivy komandovaniia frontov Krasnoi armii (1917–1922)* (Directives Issued by the Commanding Bodies of the Red Army Fronts, 1917–1922), Vol. 1, Moscow, 1971, pp. 343–45.

9. *Geroicheskaia oborona.* . . .

10. Ia. M. Sverdlov, *Izbrannye proizvedeniia* (Selected Works), Vol. 3, 1960, p. 28.

11. *J. V. Stalin. Kratkaia biografiia,* p. 73.

12. L. D. Trotsky, *Kak vooruzhalas' revoliutsiia* (How the Revolution Armed Itself), Vol. 1, Moscow, 1924, pp. 350–51.

13. Klimenty Voroshilov, *Lenin, Stalin, i Krasnaia armiia* (Lenin, Stalin, and the Red Army), Moscow, 1934.

14. *Voenno-istoricheskii zhurnal* (Military-Historical Journal), No. 5, December 1939, p. 11.

15. *Leninskii sbornik* (The Lenin Miscellany), No. 37 (1970), p. 107.

16. Lenin, *PSS,* Vol. 54, p. 86.

17. Part of this letter was quoted by Zinoviev, without naming the addressee, in the Moscow magazine *Iunyi kommunist* (Young Communist), 1924, No. 3, p. 8. An archive copy of the letter is in the Central Party Archives at the Institute of Marxism-Leninism, *fond* (collection) 2, *opis* (list) 1, *delo* (folder) 24562. See also *Lenin. Biograficheskaia khronika.*

18. Reported by Grigory Petrovsky.

19. Reported by N——v, former secretary of a provincial committee. A copy of the letter, sent to Khabarovsk, is preserved in the party archives.

20. Lenin, *PSS,* Vol. 45, p. 388. (Compare *CW,* Vol. 36, p. 485.)

21. K. G. Sverdlova, *Yakov Mikhailovich Sverdlov,* Moscow, 1957, p. 266.

22. *Stalin. Kratkaia biografiia,* p. 88.

23. *XIV s"ezd,* Moscow, 1926, pp. 455, 456.

24. *Kontinent,* 1976, No. 8, pp. 396–400.

25. *XIV s"ezd,* p. 506.

26. From the unpublished memoirs of the daughter of Bobrov, who was a political deputy to Otto Shmidt, the Arctic explorer who headed the *Chelyuskin* expedition.

27. Lenin, *PSS,* Vol. 7, p. 430.

28. *XII s"ezd,* Moscow, 1968, pp. 94–95, 170–72, 176.

29. Feliks Dzerzhinsky, *Izbrannye proizvedeniia* (Selected Works), Vol. 2, p. 233.

30. Central Party Archives.

31. *KPSS v rezoliutsiiakh* . . . (The Communist Party of the Soviet Union in Resolutions, etc.), Vol. 4, p. 418.

32. From the unpublished memoirs of Mikhail Polyak, p. 5.

33. (The circular, issued by Antonov, dealt with the subject of party democracy

and went out to party cells in all military units, according to E. H. Carr, *The Interregnum,* London, 1954, p. 332.)

34. Stalin, Vol. 6, p. 43.

35. Central Party Archives of the Institute of Marxism-Leninism, *fond* 124, *opis* 2, *edinitsa khraneniia* 665, sheet 12.

36. *XII s"ezd,* p. 46.

37. J. V. Stalin and K. E. Voroshilov, *M. V. Frunze,* Moscow, 1938, p. 4.

38. *XIV s"ezd,* pp. 165, 166.

39. *XIV s"ezd,* p. 244. See also pp. 245, 248, 255, 259, 274, 275.

40. *XIV s"ezd,* pp. 274, 275.

41. Stalin, Vol. 10, pp. 34, 47, 48, 53, 54, 55, 59, 60, 81, 83, 87.

42. From the still unpublished stenographic text of the plenum, p. 27.

43. Stalin, Vol. 11, pp. 288, 289.

44. Reported by Chagin, who outlived the camps and the organizer of the camps.

45. Stalin, Vol. 10, p. 87.

46. Stalin, Vol. 11, p. 278.

47. Stalin, Vol. 10, pp. 221, 225.

48. Stalin, Vol. 12, p. 149.

49. Stalin, Vol. 10, p. 311.

50. *Selskoe khoziaistvo SSSR. Yezhegodnik* (Soviet Agriculture Yearbook), Moscow, 1936, p. 222.

51. *Voprosy istorii KPSS,* 1975, No. 5, p. 140.

52. From the unpublished memoirs of D. V. Romanovsky.

53. Stalin, Vol. 13, pp. 236–47.

54. *Istoriia VKP(b). Kratkii kurs* (History of the All-Union Communist Party [Bolshevik]: Short Course), Moscow, 1945, pp. 304, 314–15. (The *Short Course,* first published in 1939, rewrote Soviet history in the light of the purge trials of 1936–38. It was personally edited and partly written by Stalin himself and became the bible of party orthodoxy for the rest of the Stalin era.)

55. *Istoriia KPSS* (History of the CPSU), Moscow, 1962, pp. 444–45.

56. (The text of Stalin's remarks, which he later suppressed, were published by Trotsky in exile in his *Biulleten Oppozitsii* [Bulletin of the Opposition], No. 29–30, September 1932, p. 34.)

57. Stalin, *Problems of Leninism,* Moscow, 1953, p. 456.

58. *Pravda,* July 15, 1928.

59. *Pravda,* April 9, 1964.

60. Sergei Kirov, *Stat'i i rechi* (Articles and Speeches), Moscow, 1934, p. 170.

61. Alexander Orlov, *The Secret History of Stalin's Crimes,* New York, 1953, pp. 29–30.

62. *Pravda,* December 4, 1934.

63. According to I. M. Kulagin's account.

64. See Khrushchev's concluding remarks at the Twenty-second Congress, in *XXII s"ezd,* Moscow, 1962, Vol. 2, pp. 583–84.

65. *Pravda,* December 2, 1934.

66. *Pravda,* December 20, 1934.

67. *Pravda,* December 27, 1934.

68. *Pravda,* December 30, 1934.

69. *Pravda,* December 22, 1934.

70. *Pravda,* December 21, 1934.

71. *Sudebnyi otchet po delu antisovetskogo pravo-trotskistskogo bloka* (Report of Court Proceedings in the Case of the Anti-Soviet "Bloc of Rights and Trotskyists"), Moscow, 1938, p. 494.

72. *Pravda,* December 24, 1934.

73. St. John Ervine, *Bernard Shaw,* London, 1956, p. 518, cited in Ronald Hingley, *Joseph Stalin: Man and Legend,* New York, 1974, p. 224. (The author cites the Russian edition of Hingley, apparently, here and subsequently.)

74. Lenin, *PSS,* Vol. 54, pp. 130–31, 539. (Compare the inadequate translation in *CW,* Vol. 45, pp. 443–44.) Details on this incident are in the unpublished manuscript of T. I. Til.

75. First Corinthians, 11:19.

76. From memoirs by Maria Joffe, *Vremia i my* (Time and Us, Russian-language periodical published in Israel), 1977, No. 20, p. 186.

77. Abel Yenukidze, *Bolshevistskie nelegalnye tipografii* (Illegal Bolshevik Printing Presses), Moscow, 1930, pp. 11, 25, 31, 56, 82–83.

78. (*Biulleten Oppozitsii,* No. 73, January 1939, pp. 2–15. An English translation is in Leon Trotsky, *Portraits, Political and Personal,* New York, 1975.)

79. The magazine *Bolshevik,* 1937, No. 10, p. 19.

80. The magazine *Russkoe proshloe* (The Russian Past), 1923, No. 3, pp. 147–48.

81. *Pravda,* January 30, 1937, p. 2.

82. *Izvestia,* June 30, 1936.

83. *Sudebnyi otchet,* 1938, p. 688.

84. Stalin, Vol. 10, p. 311.

85. Lenin, *PSS,* Vol. 45, p. 20. (The translation in *CW,* Vol. 33, p. 257, is inadequate.)

86. *XVII s"ezd,* Moscow, 1934, p. 505.

87. From the unpublished manuscript of Raskolnikov's memoirs.

88. See *Vsesoiuznaia kommunisticheskaia partiia (Bolshevikov)* (All-Union Communist Party [Bolshevik]), published as a separate volume of the first edition of *Bolshaia sovetskaia entsiklopediia* (Great Soviet Encyclopedia), Moscow, 1930, p. 541.

89. Raskolnikov's letter to Stalin. (It was published in a Russian émigré newspaper in France in October 1939. The original was brought to Moscow by Raskolnikov's widow in 1964. See Roy Medvedev, *Let History Judge,* New York, 1971, p. 257.)

90. From the preface to M. Sayers and A. Kahn, *The Great Conspiracy.* (The author cites the Russian edition published in Moscow in 1947: *Tainaia voina protiv Sovetskoi Rossii* [The Secret War Against Soviet Russia], p. xvi.)

91. From oral accounts by Anastas Mikoyan.

92. Orlov, *Secret History of Stalin's Crimes,* p. 244.

93. *Iz istorii VChK* (From the History of the Cheka), Moscow, 1958.

94. *Pravda,* December 21, 1937.

95. Lev Nikulin, *Mertvaia zyb* (A Swell of Waves During a Calm at Sea), Moscow, 1965, pp. 356–57.

96. *Novosti dnia* (News of the Day, a newspaper), No. 67, June 24, 1918.

97. *Partiia shagaet v revoliutsiiu* (The Party Strides into Revolution), Moscow, 1964, p. 236.

98. From recollections by Aleksandr Milchakov.

99. Aleksandr Milchakov, *Pervoe desiatiletie,* Moscow. 1965, p. 6.

100. (Aleksandr V. Gorbatov, *Gody i voiny*, Moscow, 1965; English translation, *Years off My Life*, New York, 1965.)

101. *Chudak* (an official satirical magazine whose title means "crank; eccentric"), 1929, No. 6.

102. *Leningradskaia Pravda*, February 12, 1929.

103. *Istorik-marksist* (Marxist Historian), 1933, No. 2, p. 78.

104. *Istorik-marksist*, 1933, No. 2, p. 79.

105. Central State Archives of the October Revolution and Soviet Union, *fond* 130.2, *delo* 1104, sheet 50.

106. Lenin, *PSS*, Vol. 50, pp. 121, 308, 320, 327, 488.

107. *Dvadtsatyi vek* (Twentieth Century, the *samizdat* journal that was edited by Roy Medvedev in Moscow in 1975–76 and published in London), No. 2, 1977, p. 75.

108. "F. Mezhlauk i A. Kraval," *Vestnik statistiki* (Bulletin of Statistics), 1975, No. 3, pp. 60–61.

109. The number of prisoners in South Africa was 279 per 100,000 inhabitants, according to an article by Heinrich Jenicke in the Hamburg magazine *Der Stern*. See *Za rubezhom* (Abroad, a Soviet foreign-affairs publication that specializes in reprinting selections from the world press), 1977, No. 8.

110. The source of the table is the article by B. Ts. Urlanis, "Dinamika urovnia rozhdaemosti v SSSR za gody sovetskoi vlasti" (Birthrate Levels in the USSR in the Soviet Period), in *Brachnost, rozhdaemost, smertnost v Rossii i v SSSR* (Vital Statistics—Marriage, Birth, and Mortality Rates in Russia and the USSR), a collection of articles edited by A. G. Vishnevsky, Moscow, 1977, p. 12.

111. Nikolai Cherkasov, *Zapiski sovetskogo aktera* (Notes of a Soviet Actor), Moscow, 1953.

112. Henri Barbusse, *Stalin. Chelovek, cherez kotorogo raskryvaetsia novyi mir*, Moscow, 1936, pp. 117, 119. (English version, *Stalin: A New World Seen Through One Man*, New York and London, 1935.)

113. Astolphe, Marquis de Custine, *Nikolaevskaia Rossiia*, n. p., 1930, p. 57. (The author cites a Russian edition of the French conservative's famous account of his travels in the Russia of Nicholas I, *La Russie en 1839.*)

114. *XIV s"ezd*, pp. 8, 55, 508.

115. *XIV s"ezd*, pp. 65, 80, 311–13, 358, 367.

116. *XVI s"ezd*, Moscow, 1950, pp. 7, 17, 707.

117. *XVII s"ezd*, Moscow, 1934, pp. 505, 665.

118. *Pravda*, September 28, 1934.

119. *XVIII s"ezd*, Moscow, 1939, p. 3.

120. As told by Maria Ulyanova to Grigory Petrovsky.

121. As reported in the newspaper *Kommunisticheskii trud* (Communist Labor), No. 29, April 25, 1920.

122. *X s"ezd*, p. 191.

123. *Izvestia*, June 30, 1936.

124. Nadezhda Mandelstam, *Kniga vtoraia*, Paris, 1972, p. 26. (See English version, *Hope Abandoned*, New York, 1974, p. 20.)

125. *IX s"ezd*, Moscow, 1960, p. 52.

126. *Chastotnyi slovar russkogo iazyka*, Moscow, 1968. For every million words in context, the adjective *velikii* (great) appears 692 times, the noun *liudoyed* (cannibal) three times, and the noun *ugolovnik* (criminal) only once.

127. Vladimir Nabokov, *Vesna v Fialte* (Spring in Fialto), New York, 1956.

128. *J. V. Stalin. Kratkaia biografiia,* p. 5.

129. Stalin, Vol. 13, p. 113.

130. Joseph Iremashvili, *Stalin und die Tragödie Georgiens* (Stalin and the Tragedy of Georgia), Berlin, 1932.

131. Noi Zhordania, *Moia zhizn* (My Life), Stanford, 1968. The activities of Dzhugashvili in Transcaucasia have been examined in careful detail in the basic work by Robert C. Tucker, *Stalin as Revolutionary, 1879–1929,* New York, 1973.

132. S. T. Arkomed, *Rabochee dvizhenie i sotsial-demokratiia na Kavkaze* (The Workers' Movement and Social Democracy in the Caucasus), Moscow, 1923 (an essentially unchanged reprint of the 1910 edition, which was published in Geneva). Three biographers of Stalin—Trotsky, Robert Payne, and Edward Ellis Smith—assume that the unnamed "young comrade" was Dzhugashvili. So does Tucker. Hingley finds it highly plausible.

133. Yenukidze, *Bolshevistskie nelegalnye tipografii,* p. 11.

134. Arsenidze, "Iz vospominanii o Staline," *Novy Zhurnal,* No. 72, June 1963, pp. 218–36.

135. Faronzem ("Faro") Knunyants, unpublished memoirs, p. 5.

136. Faro Knunyants, p. 8.

137. Arsenidze, p. 221.

138. Isaac Don Levine, *Stalin's Great Secret,* New York, 1956; Alexander Orlov, "The Sensational Secret Behind the Damnation of Stalin," *Life,* April 23, 1956.

139. Semyon Vereshchak, "Stalin v tiurme" (Stalin in Prison), *Dni* (Days, Russian émigré paper published in Paris), January 22, 24, 1928.

140. Vereshchak, "Stalin v tiurme."

141. Svetlana Alliluyeva confirms that a child was born to Stalin during the Turukhansk exile period. See *Only One Year,* New York, 1969, pp. 381–82. Stalin's rape of the thirteen-year-old girl during his exile was recounted in 1927 by Vladimir Khutulashvili to members of the Bailovo-Bibi'eibat district committee of the party in Baku.

142. Ivan Maisky, "Vospominaniia sovetskogo posla" (Memoirs of a Soviet Ambassador), *Novy mir,* 1964, No. 12, pp. 162, 163. This passage was removed from the book version of Maisky's memoirs (Moscow, 1965).

143. *Vremia i my,* 1977, No. 20, pp. 183–84.

144. H. G. Wells, *Experiment in Autobiography,* New York and London, 1934, pp. 799–807; cited by Hingley, p. 225.

145. Central State Archive of the October Revolution, *fond* DO—Departamenta politsii, osobyi otdel (the tsarist Department of Police, Special Section; more commonly known as the Okhrana), *opis* 167/1905, sheets 4–36.

146. Oral recollections of Marshal Vasily Chuikov.

147. Reported by the poet Aleksandr Tvardovsky.

148. One of the stories told by Stalin's elder son, Yakov.

149. Yuri Trifonov, *Otblesk kostra,* Moscow, 1966, pp. 47–48.

150. Barbusse, *Stalin* (Russian edition), p. 360. (English edition, pp. 282–83.)

151. The vote for Hindenburg, who appointed Hitler chancellor, was 10 million; the vote for the Communist candidate, Thaelmann, was 5.5 million, and for the Social Democratic candidate, Ebert, 8 million.

152. That didn't prevent Pyotr Pospelov from following the lead of other paid falsifiers and charging that "Judas Trotsky established direct, secret ties with the Hitlerite chiefs Rosenberg and Hess." See Sayers and Kahn, Russian edition, p. xv.

153. See the resolution adopted by the enlarged Presidium of the Comintern

Executive Committee in February 1930, entitled "Tasks of the Communist Party of Germany," in *Kommunisticheskii Internatsional v dokumentakh, 1919–1932* (The Communist International in Documents), Moscow, 1933, p. 946.

154. Yevgeny Gnedin, *Iz istorii otnoshenii mezhdu SSSR i fashistskoi Germanii: dokumenty i sovremennye kommentarii* (From the History of Relations Between the USSR and Fascist Germany: Documents and Commentary), New York, 1977.

155. *Hitler's Table Talk, 1941–1944,* London, 1953.

156. Ye. Nikolaev, "Fascism," in *Kommunist,* magazine of the Nizhny Novgorod provincial committee of the Soviet Communist Party, 1923, No. 6, pp. 16–29.

157. Stalin, "Report to the Eighteenth Congress . . . ," *Problems of Leninism,* pp. 755, 760.

158. Gustav Hilger and Alfred G. Meyer, *The Incompatible Allies: A Memoir-History of German-Soviet Relations, 1918–1941,* New York, 1953, p. 269.

159. Gnedin, p. 49.

160. Hilger and Meyer, pp. 302–03, cited in Hingley, p. 296.

161. Hingley, p. 300.

162. Hingley, p. 295.

163. *Izvestia,* November 1, 1939.

164. Stalin, *Doklad o proekte Konstitutsii SSSR* (Report on the Draft Constitution of the USSR), Moscow, 1937, p. 70.

165. Hingley, p. 295.

166. Hingley, p. 299.

167. Boris Souvarine, *Stalin,* New York, 1939; or *Staline,* Paris, 1935. (The author's references to Souvarine are incomplete.)

168. Robert Conquest, *The Great Terror,* New York, 1973, p. 116.

169. Souvarine.

170. Souvarine.

171. Souvarine.

172. Secret instruction of October 7 and order of the supreme command No. 44-1965/41.

173. *Voprosy istorii,* 1975, No. 3, p. 352.

174. Georgy Zhukov, *Vospominaniia i razmyshleniia* (Recollections and Reflections), Moscow, 1970, pp. 318, 327, 337. (Translated into English as *The Memoirs of Marshal Zhukov,* New York and London, 1971.)

175. Nikolai Voronov, *Na sluzhbe voennoi* (In Military Service), Moscow, 1963, p. 352.

176. Aleksandr Vasilevsky, *Delo vsei zhizni* (The Work of a Lifetime), Moscow, 1974, pp. 126, 127.

177. *Bolshevik,* 1947, No. 3, p. 6.

178. Reported by G——o.

179. From the manuscript of M.'s unpublished memoirs, p. 19.

180. In 1957, V. M. Bochkov, a former member of the military council of that front (and at one time public prosecutor), showed the text of that order around.

181. *Velikaia Otechestvennaia voina Sovetskogo Soiuza, 1941–45. Kratkaia istoriia* (The Great Patriotic War of the Soviet Union, 1941–45: A Brief History), Moscow, 1965, p. 68.

182. From a report by Public Prosecutor Rudenko in Leningrad, May 6, 1954.

183. Frederick Engels, *Anti-Dühring,* Moscow, 1959, p. 140.

184. V. V. Platonov, *Eto bylo na Buge* (It Happened on the Bug River), Moscow, 1966, p. 24.

185. From the manuscript of the unpublished memoirs of G. D. Zalmanovskaya, p. 12.

186. Zalmanovskaya manuscript, p. 2.

187. Byrnes, p. 263. (The author is apparently referring to James F. Byrnes, *Speaking Frankly*, London and New York, 1947.)

188. Churchill. (Author's incomplete reference, apparently to a Russian edition of Winston Churchill's *The Second World War*.)

189. In official Soviet publications today, the figure ten million is given.

190. Information provided by I. Yu. Pisarev, former deputy chief of the Central Statistical Agency of the RSFSR.

191. *Leninskii sbornik* (Lenin Miscellany), XXXVII, p. 139.

192. Central Party Archives, *fond* 41, *opis* 2, *edinitsa khraneniia* 3.

193. *Voenno-istoricheskii zhurnal*, 1963, No. 1, pp. 4–5.

194. From a letter to the Politburo by the Old Bolshevik A. A. Medvedev.

195. Nicholas Bethel, *Posledniaia taina* (Russian version of *The Last Secret*, London, 1974).

196. Nicholas Tolstoy, *Zhertvy Yalty*, 1978 (Russian version of *The Victims of Yalta*, London, 1977).

197. Lev Kopelev, in the collection *Literaturnoe nasledie sovetskikh pisatelei na frontakh Velikoi otechestvennoi voiny* (The Literary Heritage of Soviet Writers at the Front Lines in the Great Patriotic War), No. 78, Moscow, 1966, Vol. 1, p. 535.

198. Nikolai Gerasimovich Kuznetsov, *Nakanune* (On the Eve), Moscow, 1969, p. 265.

199. Voronov, *Na sluzhbe voennoi*, pp. 125, 132, 136, 165, 166, 167.

200. M. Novikov, "Ognennye trassy" (Lines of Fire), in *Ogonyok* (Light; a large-circulation Soviet weekly magazine), 1964, No. 13, pp. 28–29.

201. According to General Deane, head of the American military mission in Moscow. (Cited in Hingley, p. 351.)

202. Polonia, Warsaw, 1956, pp. 38–40. (The author is apparently citing a Russian version of Gomulka's speech put out by Polonia Publishing House. Compare the English version published by Polonia, Warsaw, 1956, pp. 34–48; see also the version of the speech in *National Communism and Popular Revolt in Eastern Europe: A Selection of Documents on Events in Poland and Hungary, February–November, 1956*, edited by Paul E. Zinner, Program on East Central Europe, New York, Columbia University, 1956.)

203. According to the personal testimony of Kruglov in 1957.

204. The letter was discovered by V———v. I cannot vouch for the exact wording.

205. Lenin, *PSS*, Vol. 54, pp. 277–78.

206. It happened that he outlived Stalin and told his cousin, an air-force general (now deceased), about the fate of Edinov and the others. Our thanks to him for not taking the secret to his grave.

207. Stalin, Vol. 10, p. 324.

208. Milovan Djilas, *Razgovory so Stalinym*, pp. 160–61. (The author cites the Russian edition; see the English edition, *Conversations with Stalin*, New York, 1970, p. 170.)

209. Djilas, *Razgovory*, pp. 98, 100, 109, 140, 152.

210. Abdurrakhman Avtorkhanov, *Zagadka smerti Stalina* (The Riddle of Stalin's Death), Frankfurt am Main, 1976.

211. Engels's letter to Marx of September 4, 1870 (see Karl Marx and Friedrich Engels, *Selected Correspondence*, pp. 302–03).

212. Lenin, *PSS*, Vol. 36, 193.

213. Testimony of Aleksei Isidorovich Rudenko, which is confirmed by other former inmates of the camps.

214. Galina Serebryakova, *Prometei*, Vol. 1: *Iunost Marksa* (The Young Marx), Moscow, 1963, p. 5.

215. *XX s"ezd*, Moscow, 1956, pp. 35–36.

216. *Izvestia*, July 10, 1965.

217. *Izvestia*, August 31, 1965.

218. Stalin, Vol. 9, p. 152.

INDEX

357

About the Author

Anton Antonov-Ovseyenko was born in Moscow on February 23, 1920, the son of the famous Bolshevik revolutionary Vladimir Antonov-Ovseyenko. His father, who led the seizure of the Winter Palace in October 1917, served as a Red commander in the Russian civil war of 1918–21, political head of the Soviet Army in 1922–24, and later as Soviet ambassador to Czechoslovakia, Lithuania, Poland, and Republican Spain. In 1937, while serving as commissar of justice of the Russian Republic, he was arrested during Stalin's great purges and killed in prison the following year. The author's mother, Rosa, also died in Stalin's prisons, a suicide in 1936. Anton himself managed to complete his high school studies in Moscow in 1939. But he, too, was arrested in 1940, released, and rearrested on June 23, 1941. He spent the next twelve years, except for a brief period in 1943, in Stalin's prisons and forced labor camps. After his release in 1953, he settled in the southern region of the Soviet Union. Legally blind as a result of his years of imprisonment, he received a small disability pension. In 1960, Anton Antonov-Ovseyenko returned to Moscow, where he has worked as a historian.